Gilded Age Cato

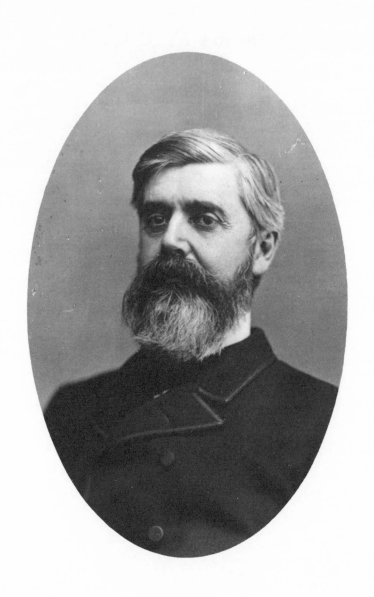

Gilded Age Cato

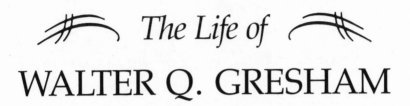 *The Life of*

WALTER Q. GRESHAM

Charles W. Calhoun

THE UNIVERSITY PRESS OF KENTUCKY

Frontispiece: Walter Quintin Gresham. *Library of Congress*

Copyright © 1988 by The University Press of Kentucky

Scholarly publisher for the Commonwealth
serving Bellarmine College, Berea College, Centre
College of Kentucky, Eastern Kentucky University,
The Filson Club, Georgetown College, Kentucky
Historical Society, Kentucky State University,
Morehead State University, Murray State University,
Northern Kentucky University, Transylvania University,
University of Kentucky, University of Louisville,
and Western Kentucky University.

Editorial and Sales Offices: Lexington, Kentucky 40506-0024

Library of Congress Cataloging-in-Publication Data

Calhoun, Charles W. (Charles William), 1948-
  Gilded Age Cato: the life of Walter Q. Gresham / Charles W.
Calhoun.
      p.   cm.
  Bibliography: p.
  Includes index.
  ISBN 0-8131-1615-5
  1. Gresham, Walter Quintin, 1832-1895.   2. Statesmen—United
States—Biography.   3. United States—Foreign relations—1865-1898.
I. Title.
E664.G82C34   1987
973.8'092'4—dc19
[B]   87-24171
                                                                CIP

190568

CONTENTS

To My Father
Robert C. Calhoun
and
To the Memory of
My Mother
Juanita M. Calhoun
(1923-1985)

ACKNOWLEDGMENTS

In the course of writing this book I have incurred countless debts to individuals who have accorded me assistance, advice, and encouragement.

I owe my greatest intellectual obligation to two mentors in my academic training. At Yale University I first began to learn something of the intricacies and significance of Gilded Age political history in a seminar conducted by R. Hal Williams, now dean of Dedman College in Southern Methodist University. A demanding teacher and a model scholar, Williams displayed a zest for his work that largely influenced my own determination to become a professional historian and to specialize in the late nineteenth century. At Columbia University I enjoyed the privilege of studying with John A. Garraty, one of this country's outstanding practitioners of the historian's craft. Garraty's vast knowledge and expertise, his gentle guiding hand and unerring editorial touch, as well as his great personal warmth made my graduate studies truly rewarding and enjoyable. Without the help of these two teachers and friends, I could not and would not have written this book.

I also thank the many other scholars who have read versions or portions of this study: Robert G. Barrows, Vincent P. De Santis, Sigmund Diamond, Roger Hilsman, Michael F. Holt, John T. Hubbell, Shirley S. McCord, James McLachlan, H. Wayne Morgan, David Pletcher, James P. Shenton, John G. Sproat, and Lorna Lutes Sylvester. I am grateful to them for generously giving me the benefit of their advice and criticism, but of course the responsibility for the flaws that remain is mine alone.

Historians' chief coadjutors are librarians and archivists. While researching this study, I received the assistance of many who were both able and interested. Especially helpful were those in the Manuscripts Division of the Library of Congress and at the Indiana Historical Society Library. I also appreciate the help given me by the staffs of the National Archives, the Rutherford B. Hayes Library, the Indiana State Library, the Lilly Library of Indiana University, the Illinois State Historical Library, the Newberry Library, the Filson Club Library, the University of Louisville Law School Library, the Columbia University Library, and the Yale University Library. I am particularly indebted to Don Carlin and the other inter-library loan librarians of the Woodward Library of Austin Peay State University.

Parts of this book have appeared in somewhat different form in several previous publications. For permission to use this material here, I am grateful to the publishers of the following: "American Policy toward the Brazilian Naval Revolt of 1893-94: A Reexamination," *Diplomatic History* 4 (Winter, 1980): 39-56; " 'Incessant Noise and Tumult': Walter Q. Gresham and the Indiana Legislature during the Secession Crisis," *Indiana Magazine of History* 74 (September, 1978): 223-51; "Morality and Spite: Walter Q. Gresham and U.S. Relations with Hawaii," *Pacific Historical Review* 52 (August, 1983): 292-311; "Rehearsal for Anti-Imperialism: The Second Cleveland Administration's Attempt to Withdraw from Samoa," *The Historian* 48 (February, 1986): 209-24; "Republican Jeremiah: Walter Q. Gresham and the Third American Party System," in *Their Infinite Variety: Essays on Indiana Politicians* (Indianapolis: Indiana Historical Bureau, 1981), 223-63.

In the final stages of preparing this work for publication, I have been fortunate to have the assistance of the capable and efficient staff of the University Press of Kentucky; I am especially grateful to Trudie Calvert.

In addition to all these professional debts, I have incurred a number of personal obligations. Throughout the years I have spent preparing this book, I have had the unfailing support of my families—Calhouns, Blakelys, Foords, and Kneens. But greatest of all is the thanks I give to my dear wife, Bonnie. She accompanied me on numerous trips to libraries where she served as a skillful and discerning research assistant. In addition, she aided me in countless ways as editorial adviser, counselor, and friend. Her encouragement and devotion have sustained me.

INTRODUCTION

Walter Quintin Gresham has been described as "one of the Gilded Age's most complex and enigmatic public figures." Despite a record of substantial achievement, his career exhibited a blend of success and frustration. That he was ambitious there can be no question. His aspirations soared as high as the presidency. From the time of his youth men of prominence urged him forward in politics, in the words of one friend, to take command of "the generality of people [who] yield naturally to you." His official career covered service in a broad range of positions, including a Union army generalship, two federal judge-ships, and three separate cabinet posts. From the time he entered the Indiana legislature in 1861 at the age of twenty-eight until he died at sixty-three as secretary of state, he was out of public office for little more than five years. In the 1880s he was a serious contender for the Republican presidential nomination, and in 1892 he came close to being nominated by the Populists.[1]

Yet throughout his life Gresham's ambition seemed constantly in conflict with a nagging pessimism and self-doubt, a fear of failure, and a longing for tranquillity. He yearned for power and responsibility and felt, he once admitted, "fearfully moved by something within to come to the front." But he often hesitated to put his ambition to the test and feared rejection and humiliation. Significantly, all but one of his public offices were appointive. Once tapped to bear a responsibility, whether commanding a Union army division or conducting foreign policy, he did so vigorously and with little doubt about his own judgment and capacity. But he hesitated to submit himself to the rigors of politics, doubting his ability to excite the popular imagination. "I haven't the cheek," he once declared, "to stand up and contend for a seat in the U.S. Senate."[2]

Gilded Age politicians have long borne an unsavory reputation among historians influenced by the writings of contemporaries such as Henry Adams and E. L. Godkin and by Progressive School writers such as Vernon L. Parrington, Matthew Josephson, and Charles and Mary Beard, all of whom dismissed the period's politics as an issueless scramble for spoils between Tweedledum and Tweedledee.[3] More recently, however, historians who challenge the traditional view argue that important policy differences did divide the parties, and several scholars have employed quantitative methods to explore the ethnocultural roots of party affiliation.[4]

At the same time historians are reevaluating the nature of political motivation and leadership. A recent biography of Chester A. Arthur, for instance, contends that Arthur had no real desire to remain in the presidency and ran only halfheartedly for nomination in 1884 to achieve vindication and to quiet suspicions about his failing health. James A. Garfield, whom Josephson portrayed as one of the self-seeking "politicos" who fashioned his views to further "his climb of the political ladder," is described by Allan Peskin as "painfully lacking in self-confidence," harboring a "superstition against office-seeking," and preferring "to drift with the tide of fortune rather than take the initiative." These and other studies challenge the stereotype of brazen, grasping ambition as the central impulse in late nineteenth-century American politics.[5] It now seems clear that alongside such spoils bosses as Thomas Platt and Matthew Quay stood other politicians who were frequently bewildered and sometimes affronted by the new organizational imperatives of the post–Civil War party system—men who found it difficult to reconcile themselves to what Morton Keller has called the "triumph of organizational politics." Gresham clearly belonged to this latter class. Profoundly uncomfortable with his times, he charged that politics had degenerated into "an art and a mystery intelligible only to the adept and initiated." In many ways he was not unlike the Mugwumps, described by Geoffrey Blodgett as men who "remained in the two-party system yet not of it," "temperamental outsiders" with a tendency toward "nervous depression." "There is nothing so unsatisfactory as political life," Gresham once wrote. "The most successful politicians are constantly on the ragged edge of anxiety."[6]

If appearance counted for anything in politics, Gresham possessed an imposing physical presence. Six feet tall and firmly built, he was once described by General William T. Sherman as "the finest speciman of a man I ever saw."[7] Beginning with the war years he wore a beard, which along with his shock of thick, dark hair rapidly turned gray after his thirtieth birthday. His most remarkable feature, however, was his eyes, which stare out sadly from photographs, revealing a soul that knew little peace. Reared in circumstances not much removed from the frontier, Gresham never completely threw off a frontier demeanor. He displayed an air of nonchalance that frequently masked the seriousness with which he took business at hand. As a judge, he often sat at the front of his courtroom with one foot propped up on the bench while he toyed with his pocket knife, but in a flash he could lash out at a lawyer with whom he disagreed. As secretary of state, he greeted foreign diplomats in his shirt sleeves. To him, the artificial trappings of diplomacy were meaningless in taking the measure of a man.

Gresham possessed strong emotions, but he was not always fully comfortable with them. Although he was devoted to his wife and children, his expressions of affection showed no gushing hyperbole, and they seemed more genuine therefor. Similarly, he did not much like public speaking. Unlike many of his contemporaries, he shunned bombastic rhetoric and instead addressed audiences in quiet, measured tones. He was most at ease in small groups of people, where he mixed well and gave vent to a playful sense of humor. Because his personality betrayed little artifice or pretense, he easily made friendships that proved deep and lasting. Twice he entered the cabinets of presidents who were virtual strangers to him, and each time he quickly established strong emotional ties with his chief. After his death while serving as secretary of state, President Grover Cleveland was overcome with grief, and cabinet colleagues discovered him hugging Gresham's coffin with tears in his eyes.

But though Gresham loved many men and enjoyed their love in return, he was also a good hater who could hold a grudge for years. He did not accept criticism easily. In matters of judgment regarding policy, he rarely admitted making a mistake and often attributed his failures to other men or to circumstances. He spent most of his political career in bitter antagonism with the leaders of the Indiana Republican party, first Oliver P. Morton and later Benjamin Harrison. He tended to view disagreement as a personal affront and usually responded in kind. In Harrison's words, few other politicians were "so given to aspersing the motives of other people."[8]

Indeed, Gresham was inclined to regard political opposition as a species of moral turpitude. He viewed the success of his enemies with suspicion and often masked his own failure with self-righteousness. He was never very religious in a formal sense, was not much of a churchgoer, and at periods in his life flirted with agnosticism. Nonetheless, he was highly moralistic. The mentors who superintended his education implanted in him a strong sense of duty and justice. He cherished a deep faith that certain moral precepts governed men's lives and was convinced of his own ability to apply those precepts to all manner of questions. Thus the lack of self-confidence that sometimes inhibited his political success was in no sense matched by a diffidence in the realm of principles. Indeed, this confidence that he knew what was right and that, therefore, public responsibility ought naturally to be his made his political alienation all the more distressing.

Perhaps most striking about Gresham is the degree to which he expressed his discomfort in the language of republican ideology. Born during the age of Andrew Jackson, reared in the political turmoil of the antebellum middle border, matured by the War for the Union, he arrived at political manhood with a set of ideals deeply rooted in the nation's republican tradition. He truly believed in the notion of civic virtue, was contemptuous of corruption and venality, and conceived of politics as essentially a moral enterprise. Yet he soon concluded that the postwar political world had little use for such ideals, and he spent the remainder of his public life generally at odds with the political culture he encountered. The Lorelei of political prominence continued to call to him, but he believed that to seek office was somehow unbecoming or morally suspect. If he were to receive preferment, it must come as the people's unsolicited recognition of his talents. If success eluded him, he decried the era as one in which there was "little or nothing at stake which appeals to the judgment and conscience of the people." Moreover, in addition to his personal disappointment, he grew disenchanted with the Republican party, first because it seemed a haven for charlatans and thieves and later because it seemed a stooge for trusts and monopolies. The Democrats seemed no better, representing, he believed, the most dangerous classes in society and lacking sufficient vigor in defense of law and order. He flirted momentarily with the Populists but finally cast his lot with Grover Cleveland, whose rugged honesty and courage seemed to promise a return to right principles.[9]

To be sure, Gresham's professions of political propriety served as camouflage for his self-doubt and as refuge from an unmanageable political reality, but nonetheless throughout his life he sensed a declension from what he perceived as the ideal, almost arcadian early Republic. What the country needed, he urged, was a return to leaders "with strong and resolute character, unspoiled by luxury, clear-minded and level-headed, able to see men and things as they really are, undeceived by outward show and conventionality." That he saw himself as such a leader there is little reason to doubt, but he sometimes lacked the will and the fortitude to push himself forward to take command. Yet neither did he willingly accept the leadership of those around him. Profoundly dismayed by the drift of his country, he was more inclined to criticize than to conform.[10]

Gresham carried this sense of a need to restore the nation's lost virtue into the State Department, where he sought to stay the rising tide of hypernationalism and imperialism which he believed threatened to destroy the Founders' republican experiment. His two-year term as secretary of state in Cleveland's second administration is the portion of his career that has attracted most scholarly attention. For years historians tended to view him almost as a do-nothing secretary who was, in the words of Harry Thurston Peck, "over fond of lounging about the corridors of Willard's Hotel."[11] In fact, however, a great many problems confronted the State Department during his tenure, and he gave his personal attention to most of them. Most recent writers recognize the painstaking direction Gresham gave to foreign policy.[12]

The interpretation of his diplomacy that has in the last few decades gained widest currency is that set forth by historians who posit an overriding economic motive for American expansionism at the end of the nineteenth century. Led by William Appleman Williams and Walter LaFeber, these writers have portrayed a quest for foreign markets and investment opportunities as the driving force behind American foreign policy in this period. As a "commercial expansionist" who opposed the annexation of noncontinental territory, Gresham, in LaFeber's words, "provides the purest example of the economic expansionist, anti-colonial attitude of the new empire." According to this view, Gresham based his policies on the belief that the expansion of American economic interests abroad, especially foreign markets for the fruits of America's overproduction, would cure the depression of the 1890s and dispel the specter of revolution among unemployed labor.[13]

The present work takes issue with this interpretation. In truth, when Gresham formulated his foreign policy, he followed no such design as that imputed to him by the "new empire" school. He rarely drew a connection between overseas economic expansion and the nation's labor troubles. He did on occasion express apprehension about "symptoms of revolution," but he recognized that the labor problem antedated the depression and that it was rooted not simply in overproduction but more fundamentally in a general maldistribution of wealth. Rather than looking to economic imperialism, he saw that the solution to class difficulties must come through some change, as yet undefined, in the domestic economic system. What the country needed, he argued vaguely, was "a more equitable division of the joint product of capital and labor."[14]

Instead of charting a course of either political or economic expansionism in foreign affairs, Gresham sought to reverse what he saw as the unwarranted and dangerous outward thrust launched by the previous administration of Benjamin Harrison. At a time when many people in both parties called for an aggressive foreign policy, Gresham, in the spirit of the Founders' warnings, worked to limit the country's overseas entanglements, with the result that nearly all his acts and policies encountered bitter denunciation. Inexperienced in foreign affairs, overworked, and often ailing, he tended to treat problems on an ad hoc basis. He was not indifferent to what he perceived to be America's traditional foreign policy interests, including overseas economic interests, but his defense of them was conservative and legalistic. As a federal judge for twenty years, he had acted as an impartial arbiter adjusting questions brought before him; as secretary of state he recreated that juridical role to a remarkable degree, guided in his opinions by standing policy and practice, precedent and tradition, international law, and his own sense of justice and equity.

But despite his traditionalism, the accelerated pace of diplomatic activity and interest made Gresham's term as secretary one of the most important in the late nineteenth century. Many of his policies foreshadowed the anti-imperialist movement that opposed the acquisition of island possessions at the end of the century. While many people in the 1890s clamored for empire, Gresham was a leader among those who warned against the "tendency . . . to get away from the conservative teachings of the founders of our government." "Popular government," he argued, "will not long survive under such a policy." This high moralism and anxiety for the future of democratic institutions echoed Gresham's earlier career, when he had denounced the "practical politics" of his day as a threat to republican government. Much of his foreign policy was unpopular, and the frustrations and furor that marked his two years as secretary of state constituted a predictable last chapter in a lifetime of political alienation. Nonetheless, he continued to voice what he believed to be the country's true republican ideals. The high purposes of the Revolutionary generation, he believed, had been subverted in later days by politicians who displayed neither conscience nor sense of public duty and by expansionists and jingoes who failed to see the immorality in stealing foreign territory or the dangers of meddling in other nations' affairs. In the end, not unlike the Cato of the ancient Roman republic, Gresham spent a lifetime in both politics and diplomacy, as he once put it, trying to call "the people back to proper views of things."[15]

Two decades ago the historian Robert Wiebe published a seminal work describing post–Civil War American society as beset by a crisis of values. The central fact of nineteenth-century American life was the transformation of the nation from a largely agricultural, rural, isolated, localized, and traditional society to one that was industrial, urban, integrated, national, and modern. In the midst of profound flux, Americans engaged in what Wiebe called a "search for order." Most turned away from old conventional beliefs that no longer seemed relevant and reached for new organizing principles that offered them a way to comprehend and manage the vast changes overtaking their society. But the rejection of inherited values was neither total nor universal. Indeed, for some the search for order in the Gilded Age led directly back to a reassertion of those earlier values—to a conviction that the ills besetting American society could best be conquered by a return to first principles. Especially in the realm of politics and diplomacy, no one exemplified this faith in civic regeneration more than Walter Q. Gresham. In Gresham's mind, the best hope for preserving all that was good in the republic lay in "the sound, honest and patriotic teachings of its founders."[16]

ONE

APPRENTICE
Mission of Great Responsibility

When Walter Quintin Gresham was born on a farmstead near Lanesville, Harrison County, on March 17, 1832, Indiana was still emerging from the frontier period. The state had entered the Union only sixteen years before, and Indians still inhabited much of the northern half, although the southern portion, especially the counties along the Ohio River, by this time exhibited a well-established, growing white settlement. Harrison County, nestled in a broad bend of the river just west of Louisville, was the fourth oldest county in the state and in 1830, with over ten thousand people, the sixth most populous. Most of its settlers had come westward from states of the upper South, especially Virginia, North Carolina, Tennessee, and Kentucky. Corydon, the county seat, and other small towns supported the usual quota of merchants, lawyers, and artisans, but the great majority of people made their living through farming.[1]

The first of Walter Q. Gresham's paternal ancestors to settle in America was his great-grandfather Lawrence Gresham, who went from England to Virginia as an indentured servant in 1759. Lawrence served in the Continental Army during the Revolution and later moved with his son George to Kentucky. In 1809 George moved the family across the Ohio River into Harrison County, where he staked out a large farm near Lanesville. George's son William, Walter's father, was born in Kentucky in 1802 and grew to manhood in Harrison County, where he practiced the trade of cabinetmaking to supplement his living as a farmer. On his mother's side, Gresham's forebears were of Scotch-Irish descent, and they, like the Greshams, went to Indiana by way of Virginia and Kentucky. In 1815 his grandfather John Davis settled in Harrison County with his sixteen children, including daughter Sarah who had been born in Kentucky in 1807.[2]

William Gresham and Sarah Davis were married on November 3, 1825, and moved into a log cabin on the Gresham farm. Within eight years the couple had five children, including a boy and two girls older than Walter and a boy younger. Although financial success eluded William Gresham, his neighbors respected him enough to make him

colonel of the local militia unit. In 1833 he won election as sheriff of
Harrison County, but within a year he was killed by an outlaw he had
set out to arrest.[3]

Sheriff Gresham's death left his widow and children destitute, and
the Lanesville farm provided only a bare subsistence. Years later
Gresham remembered the "poor—very poor" days of his early childhood with shame and was annoyed by his political friends' attempts to
publicize his Lincolnesque beginnings. "The question is not what a
man has been," he insisted, "but what he is now."[4]

The psychological impact of the loss of his father is more difficult to
assess. The infant Walter knew little of this heroic episode firsthand,
but no doubt there was some truth to the claim, later made by a friend,
that its periodic retelling over the years instilled in the boy a "high
sense of duty." He was not long without a male figure with whom to
identify, for Mrs. Gresham soon married again, to Noah Rumley, by
whom she had three more children. But Gresham left no reference to
his stepfather in his correspondence, nor is there any other evidence
about their relationship, although he did get on well with his step-
siblings, even naming his own daughter after a half-sister. In any case,
Gresham later wrote that he had "never had any childhood" and that he
knew "from experience that the dark and melancholy days of childhood hang to one in riper years like a nightmare."[5]

But the death of William Gresham was not without its compensa-
tions in young Walter's development, for prominent men of Harrison
County took an interest in the welfare of the dead sheriff's family. A
local politician, Samuel J. Wright, acted as legal guardian for the
Gresham children. Dennis Pennington, uncle of William Gresham,
administered the estate, and he more than any other man became the
children's surrogate father. A leader of the Whig party, Pennington had
wielded great influence in Indiana public affairs since territorial days.
He designed the first state capitol at Corydon and served in the legislature for nearly twenty years. Pennington succeeded William
Gresham as sheriff and gave Walter his first lessons in politics.

Pennington took great care in the moral training of the children,
mesmerizing them with tales of frontier struggle and affairs of state.
Both he and their mother made opposition to slavery an object lesson
in their moral instruction. Pennington's brother Walter, an itinerant
Methodist minister, reinforced these lessons through sermons pep-
pered with abolitionist rhetoric. Young Walter, the preacher's name-
sake, was raised in the Methodist church, although in adult life he gave
little concern to formal religion and became something of a skeptic.[6]

As he grew up, Gresham joined his brothers in working the farm and attending school as well as hunting, roaming through the hills and woods, and swimming in the Ohio River. It soon became apparent that Walter's intelligence and curiosity exceeded those of his siblings. Starved for stimulation, the boy sat intoxicated listening to Pennington's anecdotes and reminiscences, which gave him an early notion of the heroic side of public service. His mother later recalled: "Wat would ask questions until midnight, tumble and toss the balance of the night, and then pester the life out of us for books about France, Spain, George Rogers Clark, and the Northwest Territory." Still, his intellectual frustration ran deep. He later expressed deep regret that he had not been "brought up in such an atmosphere" that stressed a "love of books."[7]

But Pennington recognized the boy's talents, and thanks to his intercession Gresham's youth was filled with study and hard work. By the time he was sixteen he was teaching in the little school he had attended on the Lanesville farm. His older brother Benjamin's absence to fight in the Mexican War left him the chief hand on the farm, but when Ben returned Pennington and guardian Samuel Wright, then serving as Harrison County auditor, secured the seventeen-year-old "Wat" a job as minute clerk to the county board of commissioners. Here Gresham received his first taste of the law. Later, after moving over to the county court clerk's office, where he entered orders and recorded decisions, he began to acquire a knowledge of legal rules and precedents as well as a general "feeling" for the way the law worked. Among his new acquaintances at Corydon was William T. Otto, who was then serving as judge of Indiana's second judicial circuit and later became reporter of the United States Supreme Court. Otto set up a reading program for the young man and joined Pennington in encouraging him to study law.[8]

In 1849 Gresham entered May's Academy in Corydon, holding on to his clerkship by doing his work at night. After completing two years at May's he returned to teaching in the winter of 1850-51. Spring found him back in the clerk's office until September, when he set off for Indiana University in Bloomington, where Judge Otto was a professor in the Law Department. Gresham enrolled in the Preparatory Department, a program designed to give students with inadequate preparation a background sufficient for college-level work. The department offered a crash course in English grammar and composition, mathematics, geography, and Latin grammar and readings. At Bloomington Gresham acquired new friends from around the state, among them John W. Foster of Evansville, whom he later succeeded as secretary of state.[9]

After a year, unable to afford further study at the university, Gresham returned to Corydon and began to read law in September 1852 in the office of William A. Porter, one of the most accomplished lawyers of the area and a leader of the Whig party. Porter had been probate judge for five years and had served three terms in the lower house of the legislature, the last as speaker. When Gresham entered his office, he was completing a term as state senator. An exacting preceptor and rigid Calvinist, Porter taught the uses of the law as a moral instrument and gave Gresham a thorough grounding in the legal background of the slavery question. From Porter, Otto, and others who took a hand in his legal training Gresham acquired an enduring commitment to order in society. On Porter's motion he was admitted to the bar on April 1, 1854.[10]

The young student did not devote all his time to his books. Gresham enjoyed socializing with the townsfolk of Corydon and joined the local Masonic lodge. He did not lack invitations to parties, and at one such affair in the winter of 1853 he met a fourteen-year-old Corydon schoolgirl named Matilda McGrain. Born in Kentucky, "Tillie" was the daughter of a Louisville businessman who in 1849 had moved his family into an elegant brick farmhouse just north of Corydon. At this first encounter, the handsome law student saw her merely as the "little girl in the red dress," but clearly she had caught his eye. By the time she left for boarding school at Bardstown, Kentucky, in the fall of 1855, Tillie and Wat were sweethearts.[11]

That Gresham would pursue a political career was a natural result of the attention of men such as Pennington, Otto, and Porter. Years later he confessed that since boyhood he had believed "I had a mission, that some great responsibility was going to be cast upon me." Led by the hand into the company of the local elite, he acquired a sense that power and prominence were naturally his due, but he had less appreciation that one had to fight to attain them. To an impressionable youth, pioneer politicians such as Pennington were great, self-sacrificing heroes, natural leaders whom the people had tapped to carry on the high, honorable work of government. Pennington's career strikingly illustrated the deference politics that had characterized an earlier period in American history; from such models Gresham acquired idealistic notions of politics and a sense of destiny about his own career. Unfortunately, he did not fully understand that the age of deference was largely over by his own time and that power and responsibility went to men not "naturally" but as the result of self-interested struggle. The moral instruction of Pennington and others bred in him a tendency to perceive controversies in simple terms of right and wrong. In later life

Gresham possessed an almost complete confidence that he knew what was right, but he came to believe that "practical politics" had little use for moral convictions. It was in large measure this belief that made his later political defeats so frustrating and embittering.[12]

During much of Gresham's youth and early manhood Indiana was in a state of political flux. The state did not exhibit a fully developed two-party system until the late 1830s. The Whigs capitalized on the popular presidential candidacies of former territorial governor William Henry Harrison and enjoyed momentary success, but in the early 1840s the Democrats emerged as the state's majority party and remained so for nearly twenty years. Under the leadership of Pennington and Porter, however, the Whigs had predominated in Harrison County. Gresham naturally inclined toward following them into that party, but the disastrous loss in the election of 1852 had dealt the organization a fatal blow in Harrison County no less than in the state and nation. Hence Gresham came of age the following year at a time of great political uncertainty.[13]

The question of slavery was particularly salient to residents of Harrison County and others in Indiana who lived just a few miles from the institution's domain. Many of the farmers who continued to pour into the state had abandoned their southern homes, in part at least to escape the competition of slave labor and political and social domination by the planter class. But they had little sympathy for blacks, free or slave, and the seeds of abolitionism fell on infertile soil in southern Indiana. Complementing their antiabolitionism was a fervent Unionism. They looked upon the Ohio River less as a barrier than as an avenue of commerce and comity; ties of family and friendship made Kentucky truly a sister state. Thus Hoosiers saw sectional agitation as a threat not only to a united republic but to their way of life as well.[14]

Gresham largely shared these sentiments. His early training had taught him a repugnance for slavery, and before he was old enough to vote he expressed approval of the views of the Free Soil party. But, Uncle Walter Pennington's sermons notwithstanding, he did not favor the immediate abolition of slavery in the southern states. He believed that as the country grew and developed, public opinion would change and abolition could be achieved without endangering the Union. Of paramount concern was the lesson he had learned from Dennis Pennington: "Always stand by the Union."[15]

In the aftermath of the Whig defeat in 1852 Hoosier politics for a time became a matter of the Democrats versus the "isms"—the antislavery forces, the temperance movement, which had steadily gained strength in the last few decades, and the nativist movement, which had arisen in reaction to the influx of foreign immigrants—mostly Germans and Irish—in the 1840s. Standing alone, no one of these groups could hope for statewide victory against the Democrats. But in the spring of 1854 they drew together into a united front against Stephen A. Douglas's Kansas-Nebraska Act, whose popular sovereignty provision allowed settlers to vote in slavery in areas where the Missouri Compromise of 1820 had banned it. Fusionism, as the new anti-Democratic coalition was known in Indiana, caught fire, and a state convention on July 13 fielded a state ticket and pledged the "freemen of Indiana" to "waive all former party predilections" to oppose the extension of slavery.[16]

In the conservative Unionist southern border counties of the state, where many equated any opposition to slavery with abolitionism, Fusion leaders laid less stress on the anti-Nebraska aspect of the movement. Here the new coalition was dominated by the anti-immi-grant secret order known as the Know-Nothings, whose nativist pro-gram sought to divert attention away from the vexing sectional controversy. Gresham's antipathy for the spread of slavery led him to enlist in the anti-Nebraska effort, but he also recognized the Know-Nothings' greater popular strength locally and joined the order in mid-1854.[17]

Gresham's motive for joining the Know-Nothings derived not solely from political expediency. The training in moral stewardship he had received at home and in his legal studies contributed to his decision. Moreover, German immigrants constituted a majority in his township, and he felt for them a dislike that found confirmation in the order's xenophobia.[18] But perhaps most important was his entry into part-nership with a prominent Know-Nothing, Thomas C. Slaughter, soon after his admission to the bar. Twelve years Gresham's senior, Slaugh-ter had long been a leader in local anti-Democratic politics. He joined Porter and Otto in sponsoring the young man's promising political career, and the new partners formed a lasting friendship. Like many other conservatives, Gresham and Slaughter found Know-Nothingism useful as a means to avoid the sectional question and to oppose the Democrats on a national basis.[19]

In the summer of 1854 the Know-Nothings and Fusionists nomi-nated Gresham, then only twenty-two years old, to run for prosecuting attorney for the court of common pleas in a four-county district. They also nominated Slaughter for Congress. Although the state Know-Nothing organization dispatched speakers to aid their campaign against heavy Democratic odds, both men lost. Gresham did carry Harrison County by about fifty votes out of twenty-five hundred. In the rest of the state the anti-Nebraska forces won a significant victory, capturing nine of eleven congressional seats and all the statewide offices.[20]

Throughout their brief history the Know-Nothings in Indiana, as in the nation, were bedeviled by the slavery question. Members from the central and northern portions of the state believed the organization should oppose the extension of slavery, but southern Indiana Know-Nothings thought sectionally divisive questions should be kept out of politics. Although in 1855 the organization was beginning to crumble in many parts of the North, in southeastern Indiana its members continued to regard it as a more powerful vehicle for opposing the Democrats than the incipient Republican party. "If we form a party exclusively on the Anti-Slavery issue," Slaughter maintained, "we can have no hope of peace." Hence Gresham retained his membership, and in the summer of 1855 the Know-Nothings and other anti-Democratic elements nominated him to run for county clerk in a special election. His opponent had served for years as deputy clerk and seemed a likely victor, but Gresham campaigned vigorously, challenging Democrats to debates at several points in the county.[21] In one such encounter in a township with a large German population, Gresham spoke (according to a later unfriendly account) to the effect that the "Know-Nothing party did not have to persuade him to become a member of their order, for he always had an American heart; that he was brought up in Lanesville, where Americans could hardly get to the polls for the LAZY, LOUSY, FILTHY, LOP-EARED, GREASY DUTCH. That he was in favor of stopping immigration from the Old Country to ours." Gresham later denied having used such language, but a contemporary newspaper account of another speech said that he "demolished every person that was not born in this country and did not worship God as his party dictated."[22]

Alongside the politics of ethnicity and despite Slaughter's misgivings, Gresham invoked the slavery question in his campaign for clerk. Concluding that the battle in Kansas between proslavery and free-soil forces had made discussion of the issue permissible, he denounced the subversion of the March territorial elections by proslavery "ruffians" from Missouri. But he straddled the question of fugitive slaves. He condemned the Fugitive Slave Act's provision that awarded United States commissioners a higher fee for upholding than for denying a master's claim to an alleged fugitive, as well as the requirement that private citizens assist in capturing fugitives. But he also defended the slaveowners' right to the return of their property and assailed as unconstitutional the "personal liberty laws" whereby some northern states sought to block the capture of runaways.[23]

Gresham lost the clerkship race by about 150 votes out of nearly 3,000.[24] His defeat marked the end of his association with the Know-Nothings. The order had failed to achieve a wide enough appeal to constitute an effective challenge to the Democrats. Both he and Slaughter had always cooperated with other anti-Democratic forces, and when the Know-Nothings took on a public character in the American party, they abandoned the organization and allied themselves with the nascent Republican party. Slaughter attended the party's first national convention in Philadelphia, and Gresham stumped Harrison County for its presidential nominee, John C. Frémont. Although the Democrats carried the county by a clear majority in 1856, Frémont outpolled the American candidate, Millard Fillmore, by 150 votes.[25]

The continuing struggle for Kansas, the brutal caning of Massachusetts antislavery senator Charles Sumner by a South Carolina congressman, the *Dred Scott* decision, and other national events, along with the collapse of nativism and temperance as separate movements, nourished the Republican party. Gresham's prominence grew with the organization. In 1858 the party selected him to represent the second district on the state central committee. In March the state convention denounced as "notoriously obnoxious" the so-called Lecompton constitution whereby the proslavery forces sought to defy majority opinion and bring Kansas into the Union as a slave state. The Lecompton issue dominated the 1858 campaign, especially in the second district, where national attention focused on the the reelection bid of Congressman William English, who had sponsored a recent act setting a new referendum under conditions designed to induce the Kansans to accept the proslavery constitution. Gresham and other Republican speakers described English's bill as a "bribe" and a perversion of popular sovereignty. But the district's Republicans eschewed what they considered the state party's radicalism and once again ran no candidate of their own but instead united behind an anti-Lecompton Democrat against English. In organizing the local campaign Gresham invited the more conservative of state Republican leaders, including former Congressman Henry S. Lane, to speak in Harrison County. English won again, but the Republicans took seven of the state's eleven congressional seats, and an eighth went to an anti-Lecompton Democrat.[26]

The professional standing of the law firm of Slaughter and Gresham was enhanced by its proprietors' political prominence. Like most small-town lawyers, they were general practitioners, handling all manner of legal business, both civil and criminal. But in 1859 the partners dissolved their association amicably when Slaughter's service as an administrator of estates prevented him from carrying his share of the firm's business. Gresham continued to prosper and occasionally lent his services to the local Democratic prosecutors in criminal cases.[27]

Gresham also found time for affairs of the heart and continued his courtship of Matilda McGrain. The suit succeeded well enough with Tillie but met with less favor from her father, Thomas McGrain, who disliked the young man's political views. McGrain was a Dublin-born Irish-American who had come to the United States as a boy. He had been raised in the Roman Catholic faith, and even though he had converted to Methodism and later to Presbyterianism, he maintained an abiding reverence for his original church and sent Tillie and her sisters to a boarding school at a Catholic convent. Originally a Whig, he had gone over to the Democrats in reaction to Know-Nothingism. Moreover, McGrain owned a few slaves in Kentucky and equated Gresham's opposition to the expansion of slavery with abolitionism. Nonetheless, he found the young man's personal character acceptable and allowed the courtship to go forward. On February 11, 1858, Tillie's nineteenth birthday, she and Gresham were married.[28]

After a brief wedding trip to Louisville the couple settled in Corydon. There on January 30, 1859, Tillie bore a son whom they named William Otto after Gresham's friend and counselor. In April they purchased a house in the center of town. Here the young family settled into a routine, Gresham walking to his law office and the courthouse nearby and Tillie tending the vegetable garden and caring for baby Otto. McGrain's attitude toward his son-in-law softened, and the two men enjoyed frequent discussions of the issues of the day.[29]

By 1860 Republicans in Indiana, especially in the southern portion of the state, recognized a need for a stance more conservative than that represented by the Philadelphia platform of 1856 or the state platform of 1858. Party meetings in the Ohio River counties denounced the "fanaticism of Abolitionism" and declared that Republicans were "ready to stand and abide by" Stephen A. Douglas's principle of popular sovereignty. In southern Indiana William T. Otto enjoyed considerable backing for the gubernatorial nomination, but several weeks before the Indianapolis convention he threw his support to Henry S. Lane, who was more conservative than his chief rival, Oliver P. Morton. Gresham joined Otto in backing Lane.[30]

Otto's withdrawal opened the way for other men in southern Indiana to contend for berths on the state ticket, and Gresham became a candidate for clerk of the state supreme court. Otto urged Lane to back Gresham, while Slaughter drummed up state convention votes portraying his former partner as "a staunch Republican and a true man."

Gresham himself sought to influence the selection of delegates as he made the rounds addressing county conventions in the second district.[31]

The February state convention averted a party-rending fight when Morton agreed to run for lieutenant governor on the condition that should Republicans win the legislature Lane would become United States senator and Morton would succeed to the governorship. The seven other nominees were chosen with an eye to balance geography, national origin, and former party affiliation. In the race for supreme court clerk, in a field of seven candidates, Gresham, with 76 votes, ranked third behind James Burgess of Hendricks County with 181 and John P. Jones of LaGrange with 151. Geography clearly favored Jones, whose home county lay on the Michigan border. None of the convention's other seven nominees hailed from the northern third of the state. Gresham's Know-Nothing antecedents may also have counted against him because the ticket already had a former American party member in its candidate for attorney general. In addition, Jones had served eight years as a county court clerk, whereas neither Gresham nor Burgess had ever won election to office. Jones prevailed on the third ballot with 251 votes to 160 for Burgess and 48 for Gresham.[32]

The clues are scanty as to why Gresham entered the apparently hopeless clerkship race at a relatively late point in the campaign. Perhaps Republican leaders in the southeastern "pocket" believed that his growing popularity and proven ability on the stump could cut into Democratic majorities in the river counties. Otto had promised that Gresham was "able & willing to stand any amount of labor in the canvass." Perhaps Otto and other second district leaders viewed his candidacy as a trade-off in bargaining for nominees for the more important offices who would be acceptable to southern Indiana. In either case Gresham could have no objection to the use of his name, for it brought him the attention of Republicans from all over the state and placed him in a position to command an important local nomination.[33]

At the national level, Hoosier Republicans welcomed the nomination of Abraham Lincoln over William H. Seward and Salmon P. Chase, both of whom they regarded as too radical on the slavery issue. So encouraged was Gresham that he believed the second district party should discard the strategy of 1858 and put a congressional nominee of its own into the field. Perhaps with a candidacy of his own in mind, he told the district convention at New Albany that it must nominate a man who was "square on the Republican platform." But other delegates feared a purely Republican nominee would have no chance against the regular Democrat. In an effort to "harmonize all factions" Gresham backed a move to adjourn for two weeks during which time county organizations would hold primaries to select delegates who would then convene to make a nomination. He made clear, however, that he still favored "a straight-out nomination."[34]

By the time the second convention met, Gresham had come round to the view that a separate Republican nominee would have little hope against the regular Democrat and an independent already in the race. In the spirit of conciliation he secured passage of a resolution endorsing the independent, John S. Davis, an ardent Unionist who had begun his political career as a Whig but since 1852 had refused to affiliate with any party. In his resolution Gresham avoided the word "Republican" but simply commended Davis to "the Opposition of the district."[35]

In assembling a legislative ticket the Republicans of Harrison County likewise strove for a broad appeal. In conjunction with the Republicans of Washington County they nominated for state senator the incumbent Democratic representative, who had failed to win renomination by his own party. For state representative they nominated Gresham. In the campaign Gresham reiterated his commitment to the Union, acknowledged the immorality of slavery, but pledged to uphold the Constitution and the laws, which in the code of the day meant leaving slavery alone where it was and enforcing the Fugitive Slave Act.[36]

In general, the Republicans waged a campaign of reassurance, promising not the abolition of slavery but its containment. Conservative appeals to Unionism and protection of the white race from black competition proved successful in the state at large, and the Republicans elected the Lincoln electors, the state ticket, and a majority in the legislature. But in Harrison County, where Gresham confronted a large Democratic majority, he and his campaign workers adopted the tactic of urging Democrats to split their tickets. With little regard for the fate of the Republican state and national tickets locally, on election day they distributed Democratic ballots with Gresham's name pasted over that of the Democratic nominee for representative. The tactic worked. As expected, both the national and state Democratic tickets prevailed in Harrison County, but Gresham squeaked past his Democratic rival by sixty votes.[37]

Gresham had at last won his first and, as it would turn out, his only popular election to public office. The path from Uncle Dennis Pennington's lessons in Whiggery to election to the legislature as a Republican had been relatively short but nonetheless tortuous. For six years Gresham had engaged in political work. He had achieved recognition and success. But by 1860 his sense of party affiliation was far from intense. The timing and locale of his political apprenticeship—south-ern Indiana in the 1850s—inspired little confidence in the effectiveness of political parties. The dissolution of the Whigs, the futility of Know-Nothingism, and the cat-and-mouse partisanship of middle-border Republicanism all conspired to make the value of party regularity the least of the lessons Gresham learned. The politics of "opposition," with its fuzzy ideology and ephemeral organizations, did little to instill in him an appreciation of partisanship for its own sake. He was a Republi-can; he ran for office as a Republican and held offices within the party. But he was not a Republican above all else. Indeed, one of the defining principles of the "opposition" had decried blind adherence to party as a vice of the "corrupt Democracy." Unlike many other Republicans, Gresham could not easily transform that Democratic vice into a Repub-lican virtue.

TWO

PRESERVING THE UNION
Something for Myself

Republican victory in the 1860 election aroused anxiety for the Union on both sides of the Ohio River. A week later Gresham spoke to a gathering of Unionists at Brandenburg, Kentucky, to assure them that their state's future was safer in the Union than out. He appealed to the Kentuckians' state pride by quoting extensively from Henry Clay's defense of the Union in 1850, reminding them that Clay had prescribed the "fate of a traitor" for anyone who raised the "standard of disunion." But he also asserted that the Republican party was "pledged not to attempt to interfere with slavery in any of the States" and would enforce the Fugitive Slave Act, "however harsh some of its provisions seem to me." Southerners might have legitimate grievances, but, he warned, "secession is no remedy for any evil. The Union dismembered, all will be lost. Within the Union all differences can be settled, all rights adjusted."[1]

In this spirit Gresham set off for Indianapolis in early January 1861 and arrived a few days before the General Assembly was scheduled to convene. He immediately penned a letter to his wife, saying, "I have some little more hope for the Union than I had when I left home, but the prospect is anything else than cheering now." For the moment, he felt greater concern for Tillie, who was enduring a difficult pregnancy with their second child. He had left his mother to care for her but still felt uneasy. "Be of good cheer," he wrote, "and don't despond & get gloomy." Rather austerely, he encouraged her to "show that you have got the nerve to meet any emergency. Nothing looks better in a woman than fortitude and firmness." In less than two weeks Tillie gave birth to a girl, whom they named Katherine. From Indianapolis the proud father sent his "most earnest thanks" and assured his wife he would now rest easier.[2]

While his domestic concerns grew less worrisome, Gresham's labors in the legislature began in earnest. The General Assembly convened on January 10 and for the next two months addressed the usual concerns over taxation, education, incorporation, state banks, and crime. The records show that Gresham played an active but not a dominant role in the House, speaking occasionally and introducing four bills. Only one, a bill to change the court terms in southern Indiana, became law.[3] What distinguished this session from previous ones was the attention given to national affairs. By February 1 seven states had announced their secession from the Union. Although the General Assembly could do little to resolve the crisis, Republicans and Democrats alike were convinced that the image Indiana projected to the South would serve as an index of northern intentions. But there agreement ended, for Democrats tended to favor conciliation with the South, while Republicans, unwilling to back down from their platform's strictures against the expansion of slavery, were less fearful of "coercing" the South to maintain the Union.

Over fierce Democratic opposition, the Republican majority in the House created a Committee of Thirteen on Federal Relations to control the sectional debate. As the session wore on and the secession crisis worsened, Gresham became more willing than most Republicans to see Indiana take the side of compromise. Like many others in both North and South, he saw a possible solution in the application of Stephen A. Douglas's popular sovereignty to a reinstatement of the Missouri Compromise. He believed that the territories, all of which were "now free," should be divided by a line north of which "shall be free—south slave, subject to the popular will, without question or restraint." He considered such a scheme more equitable than the so-called Crittenden Compromise then being debated in Congress, which would have recognized and protected slavery below the line.[4]

Gresham's ideas were hardly original, but few other Republicans in the legislature shared them. Instead, they took their cue from Governor Oliver P. Morton, who denounced any compromise with the "wickedness and folly" of secession. Following Morton's lead, the assembly endorsed a resolution that said nothing of compromise and instead focused on the suppression of secession as the nation's main task. Although Gresham voted for this resolution, he still favored "any reasonable compromise" that was not "an ignominious one." He took heart from Virginia's proposal for a peace conference to meet at Washington and introduced a resolution accepting the invitation. But Morton insisted on naming the delegates and demanded from each a commitment to oppose any compromise involving amending the Constitution, recognizing slavery in any territory, or granting any further guarantees to slavery in the states. Still hopeful the conference could accomplish some good, Gresham persuaded Morton to pick his friend Thomas C. Slaughter as a delegate—an office Gresham considered "more honorable than U.S. Senator."[5]

Like many other Americans, Gresham found that his mood fluctuated with every bit of news brought by the telegraph. In mid-February the crisis in the South worsened. Texas voted to abandon the Union, the seceding states organized the Confederacy, and Jefferson Davis assumed its presidency. With the administration of Democrat James Buchanan apparently standing idle, Gresham for one brief moment thought the unthinkable—peace before Union. He wrote his wife:

My opinion is that the sooner the North & South have a peaceable separation the better—that is, if the Border slave states are not willing to remain in the Union. There are thousands of good & true Union men in KY. Tennessee Mo. Md. & Va. but I fear they will be overpowered. The Democrats have made the southern masses believe the Republicans are all Abolitionists and Negro thieves. Their retribution will be awful. The party is now broken into fragments, but it has done more mischief than it can atone for in centuries. The Republicans never proposed to meddle with slavery where it exists, but only to keep it out of free territories.[6]

But by the first of March Gresham thought the "prospect for the Union grows brighter every day," especially with the imminent assumption of the presidency by the "great and good" Lincoln. The Washington Peace Conference had completed its work and sent to Congress a set of resolutions calling for a restoration of the Missouri Compromise substantially as Gresham had advocated. Although Congress failed to act on these recommendations, on the final day of the assembly's session Gresham made one last attempt to have the House endorse the peace conference's proposal. The Republican majority refused.[7]

Gresham's support for compromise reflected the concerns of his constituents, who feared disunion because of their strong ties with the South. But he was not blind to the possibility of conflict and worked just as hard to ensure Indiana's military preparedness. At the beginning of the session he was appointed chairman of the House Committee on Military Affairs, which was responsibile for revamping the state's militia. Why so important an assignment went to a first-term legislator is difficult to say. Gresham had become fairly well known in statewide Republican circles; the party organ, the *Indianapolis Journal*, called him "one of the most promising and able young men in the state." No doubt his residence in Harrison County influenced the choice because concern for the state's defense focused on the border. In addition, he had served as a captain in a local militia company in Corydon. Perhaps most important, he brought to the position a deep conviction that should compromise fail, Indiana must be on a secure footing to defend itself, and the North at large must be prepared to crush the seceders' treason.[8]

Indiana's militia in January 1861 consisted of only a half dozen active units totaling fewer than five hundred men. The whereabouts of the state's arms, uniforms, and equipment were unknown. Nonetheless, efforts to strengthen the militia encountered serious Democratic opposition. For the past decade a succession of Democratic governors had filled offices with members of their own party, some now serving in the legislature, who feared that new legislation would destroy their control of the militia. Moreover, Democrats opposed reorganization because of their reluctance to approve anything that might lead to "coercing" the South.[9]

On January 25 Gresham introduced Bill No. 105—"A bill for the organization of the Indiana militia." Settling upon obstructionist tactics, the Democrats offered amendments to strike out over fifty sections, and the bill was soon referred to the Committee on Military Affairs. When the committee returned the bill, Democrats tried unsuccessfully to substitute one of their own. At last, when a vote was imminent, the Democrats bolted the chamber to break the quorum, but the Republican speaker counted enough of them as present to carry the measure. In the end, however, the Democrats had the final say. On the night Gresham's bill passed the House, Democrats from both houses caucussed and agreed to stay away from the statehouse if necessary to prevent passage of the military bill and a reapportionment measure they regarded as a Republican gerrymander. The legislature had yet to pass a money bill, and the Republicans, as the party in power, were unwilling to accept the blame for the failure to provide appropriations. They relented on both bills, and the assembly resumed business with no further action on either.[10]

Gresham's service in the legislature marked the beginning of an antagonism with Morton that lasted until Morton's death in 1877. As well as disagreeing with the governor and the Republican majority on the compromise issue, Gresham occasionally flouted party discipline even in matters of patronage. He opposed the partisan election of the directors of the state's benevolent institutions by the legislature, refused to attend the Republican caucus to select nominees, and voted for a Democrat for one position. He also spearheaded an attempt, joined by several Democrats, to take the selection of the state printer—chosen by the legislature—out of partisan politics and let the printing to the lowest bidder. Gresham argued that the "printing business is purely mechanical, and there is no reason why we should make a state officer to do the printing." The "sentiment that to the victors belongs the spoils," he told the House, "is preposterous. When it comes to that, sir, your government will be rottenness, and there will be no more hope for the patriot." Gresham saw more than mere symbolism in the

Republican party's name; the party must honestly strive to restore the
sense of public virtue that he believed had animated the leaders of the
early Republic. Nonetheless, the Republican majority defeated the
reform measure and elected the *Indianapolis Journal's* editor, who was a
close associate of Morton, to be printer. Gresham did not vote.[11]

For a young man with high ideals in regard to public service, two
months in the legislature brought profound disillusionment. Nor did it
raise the low opinion of party regularity Gresham had acquired in
southern Indiana politics. He concluded that both symbolic sectional
compromise and military preparedness had been sacrificed to partisan
selfishness. In the House he found that "the majority of those who
consume our time in discussion are great dolts with no influence"
whose only aim was "getting their names in the reports." Tillie had
been unenthusiastic about his political career to begin with; at the end
of the session he told her, "I think you may congratulate yourself upon
my election to the Legislature, for it has pretty effectually disgusted me
with public life." This sense of futility was compounded by the melancholy he felt at being separated from his family, an early indication of
the ambivalence that marked his entire career. "I often feel lost," he
confessed to Tillie. He found it incomprehensible that many of his
colleagues seemed to prefer the "noise and tumult" of the legislature to
the tranquillity and security of "home and family [which] are dearer
than all earth besides." At the end of the session in early March, he
promised Tillie that he would "straight way come home and *try and stay
there.*"[12]

But events soon forced Gresham to break his promise, for the fall of
Fort Sumter compelled Morton to call the legislature back into special
session. Three days after the fort's surrender Gresham wrote Morton
from Corydon to tender the services of a local militia company, ready
to "stand by the Government & fight her battles." Back in Indianapolis,
he noted that in the regular session some had called him "a sort of
submissionist," but with the opening of hostilities, "submission would
not answer." The rebels must either "come to terms or meet the vengeance of an outraged people. There can be no doubt about the final
result. God is with the just." Before Sumter he had hoped for compromise to maintain Union, law, and order; now he looked to war to restore them.[13]

Within a week Gresham introduced a new militia bill. Because Indianapolis was full of hastily organized military companies, his Committee on Military Affairs was able to profit from the advice of the
state's best military men, some of whom had seen action in the Mexican
War. Although Democrats objected to appointment of officers by the

governor and secured an amendment for the election of majors, the House took only three days to pass the bill by a vote of seventy-four to five, and the Senate soon followed suit. In addition, the legislature provided for the enrolling of federal troops and appropriated money to purchase arms.[14]

The anxiety that Gresham and other Hoosiers felt for the safety of their state derived largely from the uncertain status of Kentucky, which professed neutrality when the war began. Gresham called that position a *"quasi* partnership with the Jeff Davis concern."·He and other Republicans defeated a Democratic move to send a committee to persuade the Kentucky legislature to remain in the Union and to prohibit Tennessee troops from passing through Kentucky to attack the North. Such a mission, Gresham declared, "would be credited only to our fears." Yet he also showed concern for the large number of his constituents who traded with Kentuckians. Early in the session he blocked a measure prohibiting commercial intercourse with Kentucky, loyal and disloyal alike, and instead favored a bill that forbade trade with "enemies in open war or persons in rebellion" but which set no geographical limits on commerce. Before long, state action became moot when the Treasury Department banned shipments of provisions to states actually in rebellion.[15]

The special session brought renewed animosity between Gresham and Morton. Gresham and a few other Republicans thought that the governor's attention to political considerations in handling the crisis jeopardized the state's defenses and the well-being of its soldiers. They sought to impose more legislative control over the executive. Law called for the enrolling of military companies in the order they first offered their services and for a maximum of twelve months, but evidence surfaced that Morton was promising quick enrollment to men who would agree to sign up for three years. Charging "gross injustice or gross ignorance," Gresham demanded an investigation, which revealed that irregularities had occurred in the enrollment of troops. Gresham and others objected to the actions of Morton's commissary general, Isaiah Mansur, who had been the governor's roommate in college and who now owned a meatpacking firm in Indianapolis. When an investigation revealed that Mansur had supplied troops with meat of "inferior quality" from his own packinghouse, the legislature demanded his dismissal, forced Morton to replace him with a Republican state senator, and established an oversight committee that had to approve all purchases. Finally, Gresham and a few other Republican critics charged Morton with using military appointments to create a personal political machine. In a resolution designed to "censure the

Governor," they condemned the appointment of officers with no military knowledge or experience and charged the administration with "inefficiency and utter confusion" in handling the state's military affairs. Only Gresham and five other Republicans voted for this resolution, but they succeeded in airing their criticisms. When the special session ended on June 2, Gresham's wife later recalled, so ended also "all the friendly relations that had ever existed between Walter Q. Gresham and the Governor."[16]

Despite his growing influence, Gresham left the legislature with the same distaste for politics he had felt after the regular session. "I have found out a little more of the insincerity of men during my stay here," he wrote home when the House adjourned. Moreover, prolonged absence had begun to strain his relationship with Tillie, who was upset when he remained in Indianapolis to tend to legal cases and feared he might enlist in the army before coming home. Despite his declarations that he "would make any sacrifice for you, even to that of laying down my life," she mistook his attention to other matters as a sign of diminishing affection. He found it difficult to reassure her. "I have frequently thought you have never comprehended my nature. I *can't* act as some do. Some show all & even more than they feel. I am just the opposite of that. I know I *seem* stern & indifferent, but I hope you will never attribute that to a want of affection for you." Once again he promised her that "politics shall not call me away from you in the future unless it be in a time of very great public necessity."[17]

If Gresham's struggles in the legislature had signified anything, it was his belief that the country faced just such a necessity. It was only a matter of time before he would be in the army. "My country called me," he said. "I couldn't do otherwise than go." At the end of the special session he hoped for appointment as colonel of a regiment and enjoyed the support of powerful Republicans, including Lincoln's interior secretary, Hoosier Caleb B. Smith. But Governor Morton welcomed the opportunity to punish the upstart freshman legislator and denied him a commission even as a lower-grade officer. For Tillie this was good news, but Gresham was outraged. He returned to Corydon and soon enlisted in the Thirty-eighth Indiana Volunteer Infantry being organized at New Albany. Eventually Morton yielded to pressure from citizens of Harrison County and appointed him lieutenant colonel, or second in command of the regiment.[18]

As Gresham set off for Kentucky with his regiment in late September, he reported to Tillie that he "never was in better spirits in my life." She, however, sank into depression. Influenced by her father, who sympathized with the rebel cause, Mrs. Gresham saw little justification for the war and even less for the absence of her husband to fight and perhaps die in it. In letter after letter he tried to reassure her with details about the comforts of camp life, the abundance of provisions, and his "presentiments" that he would be neither killed nor injured. "Don't despond," he wrote, "but cheer up and look forward to the time when this wicked rebellion shall be conquered and our little family again brought together with peace and quiet restored to our now convulsed and distracted country. Without our government what becomes of our liberty, our prosperity, our family enjoyment, or anything else? When the government is gone all is gone."[19]

The rebel army had invaded Kentucky in early September, breaking that state's professed neutrality. The Thirty-eighth Indiana was among the troops hastily assembled there to prevent a Confederate advance to the Ohio River, although the unit saw no serious action. The men and officers busied themselves drilling eight hours every day, and Gresham soon earned the respect and enjoyed the friendship of his brother officers and subordinates. "I verily believe there are men in this regiment who would deny themselves almost everything to accommodate and please me," he wrote Tillie. With an eye to promotion, he used the lull in activity to study military science, for he was "determined to be up with the best of them."[20]

In early December 1861, William T. Otto urged President Lincoln to make Gresham a brigadier general. Gresham considered such a promotion "climbing a little too fast," and Governor Morton agreed. Perhaps to forestall such an appointment, Morton offered Gresham the colonelcy of the Fifty-third Indiana, then being organized. Gresham was reluctant to relinquish his secure place in the Thirty-eighth to train a regiment of raw recruits. When he reached Indianapolis in late December, he discovered that recruitment for the Fifty-third was stalled. Worse, Morton told him that a new regulation required the colonel of a new regiment to put up $2,500 to help defray recruitment expenses. Gresham bitterly accused Morton of devising this scheme to drive him from the service. Nonetheless, he returned to Corydon, and with the help of his former law partner Thomas C. Slaughter and others he raised the money within a week.[21]

Morton next tried to undermine the Fifty-third's enlistment by allowing another regiment to recruit in the Corydon and New Albany area. After Gresham protested this "act of injustice to me," the other unit was limited to its own congressional district. Even then, Gresham and his aides found it difficult to convince the suspicious Hoosiers that the war's sole purpose was the restoration of the Union and not the abolition of slavery. Not until late February 1862 was the regiment filled

and mustered into service, but again Morton delayed Gresham's return to the field by assigning the Fifty-third to guard Confederate
prisoners at Indianapolis. Finally, in mid-March, after Gresham had
"kept up such a *fuss* with the Gov that he was anxious to get rid of us,"
the Fifty-third left Indianapolis to join General Ulysses S. Grant's army
in Tennessee. A few days later Colonel Gresham celebrated his thirtieth
birthday in Dixie.[22]

Thus far, Gresham had spent more time fighting with Morton than
with rebels. Moreover, because of his legal training, it was his "misfor-
tune to be caught up on court martials wherever I go." The Fifty-third
was part of Grant's army during the battle of Shiloh in early April 1862,
but again Gresham took no part in the fighting. As commander of the
Union post at Savannah, Tennessee, six miles away, he forwarded
reinforcements and organized hospitals. Although he won high praise
for his administrative skills, he fairly begged Grant to let him take his
regiment into the fray, but the general refused to alter existing arrange-
ments. "I feel miserable beyond description," Gresham wrote Tillie. "It
seems like bad luck attends me."[23]

After Shiloh the Fifty-third joined General Henry W. Halleck's army
in the siege of the railroad center at Corinth, Mississippi. Impatient
with the cautious Halleck, Gresham believed that a timely attack on the
rebel garrison would have yielded "a big haul" instead of the bloodless
capture of the abandoned city in late May. In the aftermath, Halleck's
grand army was scattered, and for the remainder of 1862 the Fifty-third
operated in southwestern Tennessee and northern Mississippi, where
Gresham chafed under the restraints of defensive warfare. "Our army
needs someone to lead it against the enemy," he complained. "The
men are more than willing to fight, but they can't get a chance to
fight."[24]

Meanwhile, Gresham's military service gave new life to his political
prospects in southern Indiana. While he was home on leave in the fall
of 1862, second district Republicans nominated him for Congress. He
declined to make the race, however, pleading that he could "do quite as ·
much good with my regiment as any where else at this time." Even so,
his timely trip home, his nomination, and his spirited adherence to
duty in the field left his political reserves intact for the future.[25]

While Gresham was home, the battle he had been hoping for came at
Davis Bridge on the Hatchie River, in connection with the battle of
Corinth. Under Lieutenant Colonel William Jones, the Fifty-third
made three unsuccessful charges against rebel lines and finally fell
back, sustaining heavy losses. At Corydon the news sent Gresham
"topsy turvy," and he rushed back to the front. The incident was a

turning point in his military career. His men were dissatisfied with Jones, and Gresham reported that he "never saw men so much gratified as the boys were when I arrived." Under his leadership, they said, they were "ready to go in every day." He now reaped the reward of his patient labors in molding the regiment into a disciplined and loyal organization. "I love them because they have such confidence in me," he exulted. Although eager to fight before the Hatchie battle, he had often expressed a longing for the tranquil life at home; now he grew less tolerant of Tillie's complaints about his absence: "How can I content myself to be at home when I have got a regiment of men that I know rely on me to be with them in the hour of danger? Thus, my honor, *that* which ought to be as dear to you as it is to myself, will not suffer me to enjoy such inglorious ease at a time like this."[26]

Gresham's concern for his regiment helped rekindle his fight with Morton. In January 1863, Gresham's old guardian, Samuel Wright, told him that he had been enrolling several men in Harrison County to restore the strength of the Fifty-third. When Gresham received none of the recruits, he complained to Morton, who said none had expressed a desire to join the regiment. Meanwhile, the Hoosier delegation in Congress again suggested Gresham for brigadier. When wind of this recommendation reached Morton, he dashed off a telegram to Lincoln declaring that Gresham had "done nothing to deserve [promotion] & in my opinion is incompetent & unworthy." Finally, when Gresham continued to insist on receiving new recruits, Morton demanded his resignation. To compound his problems, Gresham contracted typhoid fever. Fortunately, Tillie was visiting him in camp and nursed him. His brother officers rallied to his defense, preparing testimonials which William T. Otto, now serving as assistant secretary of the interior, forwarded to Lincoln, along with an endorsement by Hoosier congressmen. In the words of General Stephen A. Hurlbut, Gresham was "a capable, brave, energetic officer," in "no wise deserving" Morton's condemnation. In Washington General in Chief Henry W. Halleck agreed. Gresham retained his colonelcy, but Lincoln could not entirely ignore the powerful governor, and Gresham received no promotion.[27]

Like many other Union soldiers, Gresham found that "the further south I go the more I am satisfied that slavery destroys the life, energy, and enterprise of the people." He was shocked to hear that his four-year-old son Otto had expressed a desire for a slave and shot back a request to Tillie to "instill in him a disgust for the 'Institution.' " As he saw it, the system raised a fraction of the whites to a "bastard aristocracy" while keeping the remainder "in a state of ignorance and stupidity that is shameful." Most appalling was the sale block, which violated all familial relations and set a premium on pregnant women. "It looks to me," he wrote Tillie, "like a God of justice would yet punish a nation that permits such abominations." Although before Lincoln's preliminary Emancipation Proclamation Gresham maintained he was "no abolitionist," the exigencies of war helped change his convictions. Influenced by the arguments of reformer Robert Dale Owen, he came to accept emancipation as a military necessity. But more important, Lincoln's September 1862 preliminary proclamation offered a way out of the long-standing dilemma Gresham and others had faced of trying to oppose yet coexist with a recognized evil. "The truth is," he concluded, "slavery is wrong, and the moral & Christian sentiment of the civilized world condemns it. . . . We can already clearly see one thing as the result of this war and that is the doom of slavery."[28]

Not all northerners found their moral convictions reinforced by the president's act. Gresham's brother-in-law Thomas McGrain resigned as major in the Fifty-third to protest the proclamation. Gresham condemned McGrain's action, but as the war dragged on it seemed to him symptomatic of a flaccid northern will. He welcomed Confederate General Robert E. Lee's invasion of Pennsylvania as a way to stiffen northern determination. In southern Indiana and other border areas it appeared that not only apathy and fatigue but treason menaced the cause. Men in Gresham's regiment received letters from their own fathers urging them to desert. He complained to Morton that action had to be taken to stop this "vile practice" and called for "every possible exertion" to arrest and punish deserters in Indiana. In his own regiment he ordered "the extreme penalty of the law meted out to every man who disgracefully and cowardly" abandoned his duty.[29]

In the spring and summer of 1863 the Fifty-third participated in the siege of Vicksburg. Gresham was at last involved in significant fighting. In one daring incident he led a work party in the dead of night to redig rifle pits which other northern units had abandoned. Although six of his men were wounded within the first ten minutes, he forbade them to return the fire. The Confederates concluded that the party had withdrawn, as others had done on previous nights, and ceased firing. Gresham's men continued their work and not only reopened the pits but extended them two hundred yards. Gresham won high praise from his superiors. He interpreted the episode as further evidence of his men's willingness to follow his lead.[30]

In retrospect, Gresham's eagerness to fight makes him appear almost bloodthirsty or cavalier about losses, but in fact he showed great concern for his troops. "I watch my men closely when they are skirmishing & keep them covered as well as I can," he wrote from Vicksburg. When men fell under wounds or ill health, he visited the hospitals daily to "cheer the sick up." He begged the adjutant general's office for more supplies to relieve those who lacked shoes and clothing, and when their pay was six months in arrears, he complained bitterly to Washington officials that "their families are suffering for want of what the government has agreed to give them." If it appeared to Tillie that he was being "weaned of home," in reply he could only urge her to "be of good cheer & look forward to the day when I can come home without leaving my *men* behind."[31]

As Gresham found himself seeing more action, he hungered for greater recognition and responsibility. In late July 1863, Grant recommended him for promotion to brigadier general. Gresham greeted the news with a characteristic amalgam of humility and pride. In one moment he was humbled by Grant's approbation; in another he looked on his elevation as long overdue. He wrote Tillie: "I could have been advanced long ago if I had surrendered my own manhood & been a sycophant, but that I will never do. I fought my way up in spite of some unscrupulous scoundrels at home who have exerted themselves to keep me down. I have served my country long and faithfully under men whom I knew to be my inferiors, but light is at last dawning. I will not be indebted to governors, congressmen or any other civil magistrates for my promotion, as more than half our genls are." The promotion raised Gresham's ambition. In the early years of the war, when his "inferiors" had seemed easily to surpass him in honors and recognition, he had said it was "foolish for a man to struggle all the time for a little distinction." A brigadiership changed that attitude. "It is my intention to win a name for myself," he wrote Tillie, "I admit I am ambitious. I want you to feel that you have a husband that you are not ashamed of. How would you feel after the war is over to see me in the condition that many spiritless men will be in whose names will in no way be connected with their country's history in putting down this infamous rebellion?"[32]

Gresham's promotion again subjected him to the caprice of politicians because it required confirmation by the Senate. Fearing that Morton and other Hoosier politicians "may think that now is the time to strike me," he asked General William T. Sherman to explain his case to his brother John, senator from Ohio. He told Sherman, "Inasmuch as I was promoted on the recommendation of my commanding officers, unsolicited on my part, I think it would be hard to be rejected and disgraced. I would infinitely prefer being killed in action." Sherman did champion Gresham's case, portraying the young colonel as "a fine gentleman" who showed promise of becoming "an elegant soldier."

Even so, it was not until April 1864, nine months after Grant's original recommendation, that the Senate confirmed the nomination.[33]

Despite this delay, Gresham served as brigadier general from the date of his commission in August 1863, when he took command of the Third Brigade, Fourth Division, Seventeenth Army Corps. The brigade saw little action in the fall and winter of 1863-64, and Gresham was assigned as commander of the federal post at Natchez, Mississippi. There he established comfortable quarters in a plantation mansion, and Tillie was with him from September to early November. As post commander, he was as much concerned with civilian as with military affairs, his responsibilities ranging from maintaining law and order to providing rations for the city's orphans' home. The Natchez area had given a strong vote against secession, and Gresham tried to give little cause for ill-will from the conquered Mississippians and to foster Unionist sentiment. He halted the forcible enlistment of recruits among southern refugees and Confederate deserters in his district on the grounds that men who had voluntarily left the rebel lines in search of protection by the Union forces could not be detained against their will. He issued strict orders against soldiers' stealing or other molestation of civilians and forbade the sale of liquor in the district. In addition, he furnished guards to protect Unionists' homes and property and secured permission to levy a tax to support Unionists driven from their homes.[34]

Gresham's approach to the problem of the freed slaves followed a conservative pattern set by other Union commanders of occupation forces. He limited military recruitment of freedmen in his district to one regiment, and he allowed no enlistment of former slaves who were employed as laborers by the Union army. Nor did he permit the recruitment of those occupied in working on plantations. Moreover, he sanctioned the return of former slaves to their old plantations, "provided it be their wish to do so." Like other Union commanders, Gresham considered this approach necessary for the peace and order of his district.[35]

The conditions of war did, of course, require certain disruptions in civilian life. He allowed the conduct of business only by permit and instructed his provost marshal to seize the goods of any enterprise operated without permission. But such policies did not seriously diminish the goodwill Gresham won among the citizens of Natchez. One Confederate colonel later wrote that Gresham had shown a "broad humanity which earned for him the respect, the esteem, and even the affection of our people here over whom for a time he was virtually the ruler." In late January 1864, when Gresham was ordered back to Vicksburg, he noted that "the people of Natchez all seemed to have the blues because I was leaving." For the rest of his life he received letters from men and women with whom he had formed warm friendships during his stay. Although the petty details of administration often annoyed him, command of the Natchez district was in some ways ideally suited to Gresham's temperament. Elevated by fiat into a position of nearly absolute power, he administered the district fairly and firmly and came away with a heightened sense of his ability to govern. Moreover, the approval of Natchez's citizens must have renewed his belief that he could excite the popular imagination to succeed in politics. So pleased was Gresham with his Natchez experience that he concluded to settle there when the war was over.[36]

But for the moment he was eager to return to more active warfare. His brigade left Natchez in late January as part of Sherman's grand plan for a march into Georgia in the spring. But the approaching expiration of the three-year enlistments of most of his men delayed Sherman's plan, and Gresham kept busy in March addressing soldiers, appealing to their patriotism, and urging them to reenlist and see the fight to the end. After Lincoln's Emancipation Proclamation and with Congress just beginning to consider the Thirteenth Amendment, reenlistment speakers were hard-pressed to persuade some soldiers to continue to fight for the Union, which, even should the North be victorious, promised to be radically altered at war's end. Gresham gave particular attention to Indiana units and took pride that his old regiment, the Fifty-third, boasted 383 reenlisted veterans.[37]

The reenlisted men received thirty-day leaves, after which Gresham's brigade moved slowly through Tennessee and northern Alabama waiting for the Seventeenth Army Corps to reassemble. With most of Sherman's army already pushing into Georgia, Gresham grew "restless almost beyond endurance." Battles raged in Virginia and the Wilderness, but Grant's "brilliant success" gave Gresham only "a kind of melancholy pleasure." "I would like to have my name identified with the campaign," he wrote Tillie. "I have more confidence in myself than I used to have."[38]

Shortly after the corps finally got under way, division commander Marcellus M. Crocker fell ill and relinquished his command to Gresham. On May 27, 1864, Gresham took charge of the Seventeenth Army Corps' Fourth Division, which, with seven thousand men, was one of the largest in the Army of the Tennessee. Although the trek across northern Alabama was arduous, Gresham declared, "I can stand anything when I have got responsibility enough on my shoulders." After months of waiting, he told Tillie, "I am now going where I will have an opportunity to do something for myself."[39]

Meanwhile, his reputation at home continued to grow. Once again in 1864 Republicans wanted to nominate him for Congress, but he refused to abandon the "good position" he now held in the army. By the middle of June his division had joined Sherman in the march toward Atlanta. "We used to think it was something to fight or skirmish for a whole day," he wrote Tillie, "but now we have been fighting continually for over a month, and our loss attests the character of our work." Determined to make a name for himself, he wrote home from Atlanta, "I have now got a good chance & am improving it."[40]

In the end, fate denied Gresham his "good chance." On July 20 the Army of the Tennessee was steadily pushing the Confederates southward until they halted behind fortifications at Leggett's Hill, a mile and a half from Atlanta. Here, while supervising his skirmish line on foot, Gresham was hit in the left leg by a Confederate sharpshooter. The minié ball shattered the tibia. Army doctors operated that night, but there was never any chance that he would return to duty. Although it had perhaps been unwise militarily for a general to expose himself in the danger of the skirmish line, Gresham's superiors withheld criticism. Corps commander Francis P. Blair reported that he had "displayed the greatest courage and skill in the management of his troops on that day," and Sherman much regretted the loss of his services.[41]

Gresham had once condemned the army surgeons' "mania for cutting off arms & legs," and he now rejected their proposals to amputate his own leg. Facing the prospect of a long convalescence, he headed for home. At New Albany, because of the danger of gangrene in the local army hospitals, his bed was set up in a tent outside a friend's house. After about a month he and Tillie moved into a house, where army orderlies aided Tillie in the nursing chores. After ten months the wound showed so little improvement that doctors again suggested amputation, which Gresham again vetoed. After fifteen months he could walk with crutches, but the healing continued to be slow. There was never a complete restoration of the bone in the injured left leg, which remained weaker and smaller in circumference than the right. For the rest of his life he suffered occasional severe lameness that required the use of a cane.[42]

Gresham remained on the army's rolls with an extended medical leave that allowed him to collect his salary until he could resume the practice of law. In late 1865 he attended a reunion of the Fourth Division at which William W. Belknap, who had served under him as a colonel and later became Grant's secretary of war, noted that Gresham "feels somewhat" his not receiving a complimentary promotion to major general. Belknap initiated a movement to secure his former commander a second star, endorsed by Blair, Sherman, Grant, and prominent Indiana Republicans. On April 26, 1866, the Senate confirmed him as brevet major general of volunteers. Four days later he was mustered out of the army.[43]

Temporarily incapacitated by his wound, Gresham seemed to depart the war on a down note. The opposite was true. For the three years before July 20, 1864, his career had shown a steady rise from lieutenant colonel to brigadier general, from second in command of a regiment to first in command of a division. The affection of his men and the endorsement of his superiors had given him a new self-confidence. Triumph in the army, his success at Natchez, and his popularity at home combined to obscure the crisis of will wrought by his frustrations in the legislature. The sharpshooter's bullet that halted his quest for glory in the field left unscathed his determination to "do something for myself."[44]

The first order of business was to assure himself and his family a living. Since his pension amounted to only $30 per month, he would have to resume the practice of law. During his convalescence in New Albany, he and Tillie decided to remain in that city. Located in Floyd County, adjacent to Harrison and just across the Ohio River from Louisville, New Albany was the second largest city in Indiana, with a population in excess of twelve thousand. Long a commercial and boat-building center, it boasted a growing manufacturing establishment in the 1860s. On November 1, 1865, shortly after he was able to walk with crutches, Gresham opened a law office. Before long he went into partnership with John H. Butler, a prominent lawyer from the small town of Salem, about thirty miles away. Butler's son Noble read law in the office and joined the firm after his admission to the bar. The two younger men soon formed a close friendship that lasted the rest of Gresham's life.[45]

Once more earning a living, Gresham resumed political activity, serving on party committees and attending conventions. In the immediate postwar years politics in Indiana, as in most of the nation, focused on war-related issues: how to get the rebellious states back into proper relation with the federal government and the rest of the Union and how to deal with the former Confederates and slaves. Led by Oliver P. Morton, Hoosier Republicans maintained that the Democrats, the coadjutors of rebellion, could not be trusted to handle these questions. Gresham warmly endorsed this approach, for besides rekindling his ambition, the war had given him a greater sense of partisanship. It was time, he argued, for Republicans to "be aggressive" against the Democrats and "force them to the wall on the Grand Indictment of Treason."[46]

Most Indiana Republicans initially rallied behind the new president, Andrew Johnson, and hoped that his "restoration" policy in the South would soon bring a return to loyal government there. Even after the beginning of the quarrel between the president and congressional Republicans, most Hoosier party members clung to the hope that they would be able to reconcile their differences and pursue a harmonious policy. Three days after Johnson's veto of a bill to renew the Freedmen's Bureau, Gresham labored at the Republican state convention for a balanced set of resolutions commending Johnson for "all his constitutional efforts to restore National authority [and] law and order" in the South but also contending it was "the province of the legislative branch of the General Government to determine the question of reconstruction." As the antagonism between the two branches deepened in the spring of 1866, Morton and most other Indiana Republicans abandoned Johnson. But Gresham had doubts about this new drift in party opinion. He withheld public criticism of Johnson and told Senator Henry S. Lane that Congress ought to "adopt some definite plan of reconstruction" to allay "a fear in the minds of some Republicans that the South is to be kept out indefinitely without any defined policy on the part of Congress." He continued to defend Congress publicly but argued that the coming election campaign should focus on the "treasonable record of the Democracy."[47]

In the second congressional district the Democrats maintained a commanding majority, and the Republicans, clinging to the wartime "Unionist" label, reverted to their time-honored strategy of seeking a disaffected Democrat to run against incumbent Michael C. Kerr. In the district convention Gresham made the nominating speech for William T. Spicely, a former Democrat who had served as a colonel in the Union army. Although nominated, Spicely declined for business reasons, and the district committee turned to Gresham as the "uniform, earnest, and spontaneous" choice of Union party members. Gresham had hoped to give more time to building his law practice, but he accepted, promising that "no effort shall be wanting on my part" to carry the district.[48]

Gresham's opening speech set the tone for the campaign: "There is but one issue before the American people. We stand today as we did during the war. It is union or disunion. We are either on the side of our country or we are enemies to it. . . . We charge here today that the Democratic party, as a party, was, and still is, the disloyal party." Arguing that former rebels should be barred from Congress "until the nation had some evidence of their loyalty," he defended the Fourteenth Amendment, recently submitted to the states, as the ideal way of returning southerners to citizenship while providing "security for the future."[49]

The race question pervaded the campaign. Although Gresham praised the Emancipation Proclamation as "the greatest instrument ever conceived by man," he matched the Democrats' virulence in appealing to the antiblack prejudices of his southern Indiana listeners. Denying that Republicans favored black suffrage, he labeled whites the "superior race" and said the Union party had "no disposition to make the negro equal to the white man." He ridiculed Democrats for their apparent belief that "now [that] the negro was free he would improve so rapidly that the good Democrats would soon be equalled or surpassed by him, unless his advancement was checked by law."[50]

Gresham and Kerr made several joint appearances and spent much time exchanging personal accusations. Gresham charged Kerr with having been a member of the Sons of Liberty, an allegedly traitorous secret society during the war. Kerr dredged up Gresham's Know-Nothing past, including the anti-German speeches he was purported to have made during the campaign of 1855. It was a rough campaign. In one town, after Gresham's enemies locked him out of the hall, he climbed in through a window, "laid a revolver on the table, and made the bitterest campaign speech ever heard on the banks of the Ohio." Indianapolis lawyer Benjamin Harrison, Morton, and Kentucky Unionists Benjamin Bristow and John Marshall Harlan all made speeches for Gresham, but he nonetheless lost by 1,750 votes out of 25,000. In the state at large, the Republican ticket was elected, with eight of eleven congressmen and a majority in the legislature.[51]

After Gresham's "brilliant and gallant fight" against impossible odds, some local Republican groups proposed him as a likely candidate for governor or United States senator in 1868. In January 1867, the General Assembly elected him agent of state, a position in which his chief responsibility was to manage the state's indebtedness and particularly to pay the interest and principal on debt certificates. Several times a year he traveled to New York City to redeem internal improvements bonds from the 1840s, war bonds, and other certificates. The office gave him experience in finance and left him ample time to practice law.[52]

Difficulties involving reconstruction heightened during 1867 and so did Gresham's concern over the direction of the Republican party. Morton had become one of Johnson's most caustic critics. Although Gresham had joined in protests against Johnson's patronage policies, he could still claim in the fall of 1867, "I have never allowed myself to speak of the President disrespectfully." He warned the Republican state chairman to "stop talking about impeachment & try and make the best terms you can with the President." He considered the "Negro question" a heavy burden to the party and a substantial cause of the "disastrous" reverses in the off-year elections in Ohio and Pennsylvania. Moreover, he was dismayed by the inflationist greenback agitation, which, he believed, had wielded "ten times more influence" in the election of Democratic legislatures in both those states. Gresham had recognized the need to issue greenbacks during the war, but as a hard money advocate he now warmly favored Treasury Secretary Hugh McCulloch's efforts to contract the volume of paper currency. Again he disagreed with Morton, whose ardent inflationism more nearly reflected the views of the majority in both parties in Indiana.[53]

The start of 1868 brought mention of Gresham for the gubernatorial nomination, but he gave his backing to his friend Conrad Baker, the incumbent, who had succeeded to the office upon Morton's election to the Senate. Gresham served on the state central committee and in May went as a delegate-at-large to the national convention, but he vowed he would *"not be a candidate for anything"* and discouraged efforts to renominate him for Congress. When the district convention could not agree on another candidate, however, the "earnest solicitation of his Republican friends," especially Baker, moved him to accept the nomination.[54]

If his 1866 congressional campaign had been trying, his bid two years later was hopeless. In 1867 Morton and the Republican legislature had passed a reapportionment that sacrificed the second district by isolating Democratic counties in it and subtracting its Republican counties to make other districts more solidly Republican. In addition, Gresham and his former law partner Thomas Slaughter had had a falling-out with *New Albany Commercial* editor James P. Luse, and the paper gave Gresham no aid in the campaign. Again the race issue dominated, with Democrats charging that Republicans in Congress would use the newly ratified Fourteenth Amendment to pass legislation enfranchising blacks in the North as well as the South. Although Gresham again had the help of outside speakers, he lost the October election by over six thousand votes. For the next month he toured the state campaigning for the national ticket.[55]

Gresham's "honorable scars and arduous party services" again prompted some Republican newspapers to mention his name for the Senate seat to be filled by the legislature in 1869. Even Morton spoke of him in a "manner very flattering," which "surprised" Gresham more than it persuaded him to run. Citing his age, thirty-six, and "inexperience in public affairs," he protested to Slaughter that "a man soon disgusts people, even his friends, when he aspires to something to which he is not clearly entitled." His two defeats for the House had obviously dampened the self-confident ambition with which he had returned to politics after the war. "I haven't the cheek to stand up and contend for a seat in the U.S. Senate," he told Slaughter. With a wistful sigh for the deference politics he had witnessed as a boy, he noted, "I should not think of the office unless it was tendered me and such things as that are not tendered to men these later days." For the rest of his life a yearning for political power but a reluctance to fight for it—a desire to reach but a disdain to grasp—was a defining characteristic of Gresham's personality, with a stultifying effect on his political career. When the legislature convened in January 1869, it chose him not for the Senate but for a second term as state agent.[56]

Like other Republicans, Gresham welcomed the election of Grant to the presidency. The general was "modest, sensible," and "his good, honest, old fashioned sense" made him fully "equal to the emergency" wrought by Johnson and Congress. No one could control him, Gresham noted with unwitting prescience, "except by conning his judgment."[57]

As one of Grant's wartime associates, Gresham wielded considerable influence in Indiana patronage, although he hesitated to procure an office for himself. Five weeks before the inauguration, Grant surprised him by offering him a choice of lucrative plums at New Orleans— collector of customs or collector or assessor of internal revenue—so that the new administration might have an "unquestionably honest and efficient man" on the scene to distribute patronage in Louisiana. In early February, after some hesitation, Gresham accepted the post of collector of internal revenue, but in less than two weeks he withdrew. "I am disgusted with politics," he wrote Slaughter. "I will accept no office—I care not what it is." In the interim the Senate had passed a version of a constitutional amendment for black suffrage that had already passed the House, thereby giving the lie to the promises made by Gresham and other moderate Republicans during the congressional campaign. The Republican party seemed to be turning its back on the true republican principles of civic virtue in public servants and enlightened responsibility in the electorate. On the day Congress completed passage of the final version of the Fifteenth Amendment, Gresham unburdened himself to Slaughter: "I know that you will laugh when I say that I have no political aspirations and that I would not today go to the U.S. Senate, if I could. I am disgusted with the whole thing and I think the Republican party is an infernally corrupt concern, & I don't care how soon it is broken up, if the Democracy do[es]n't survive it."[58]

But neither did Gresham find satisfaction as state agent or in private life and the practice of law. "I don't feel that I am doing anything in comparison with what I could & might do." In long conversations with Grant at West Point he discussed his future but "couldn't tell him much." "It is not ambition," he wrote Slaughter, "so much as a natural craving for some kind of a load to carry. You will no doubt think it is a very foolish craving, and I guess it is; still I can't help it."[59]

In September 1869, the president offered Gresham what seemed the ideal solution—appointment as district judge for Indiana, a post that became available after the unexpected death of Judge David McDonald in late August. In nominating the young and relatively inexperienced lawyer, Grant passed over several obviously more qualified men, but Gresham maintained that the appointment was "both unsought and unexpected." The state party organ, the *Indianapolis Journal*, pronounced the choice "a good one," and the Democratic *Indianapolis Sentinel* conceded that Gresham would make "an acceptable judge."[60]

Gresham had seen a good deal of judicial duty on courts-martial in the army, but his own sense of his inexperience gave him pause before accepting this "undeserved honor" from "my too partial friend, the President." McDonald had been a lawyer of wide learning, the first professor of law at Indiana University, and president of Indiana Asbury College. But when members of the Indiana bar urged Gresham to accept, he overcame his doubts. Senator Morton, who had backed another candidate, acquiesced in Grant's determination. The senator was not entirely self-sacrificing, for the proprieties incumbent in a federal judgeship might preclude any future overt challenge by Gresham to Morton's control of the Indiana Republican party.[61]

It was no doubt this political—or, rather, nonpolitical—dimension of the office as much as any belief in his fitness or any desire to exercise its functions that persuaded Gresham to accept. Twice defeated for Congress and at odds with the acknowledged leader of the state party, he saw the district judgeship as a haven from the torments and frustrations of party politics. He would now have an important "load to carry." It had come effortlessly and could be his for life. He would never again be required to "stand up and contend."

But how long the judgeship would satisfy Gresham's "natural craving" remained to be seen.

THREE

DISTRICT JUDGE
Cultivate Contentment

Gresham took up his responsibilities as district judge in September 1869, nearly three months before his confirmation by the Senate. He felt some trepidation but found encouragement from Supreme Court Justice David Davis, the circuit justice with responsibility for Indiana. "If I fail it shall not be because I don't *try* to do right," he told Davis. The two men had not met before but soon became close friends. Gresham also received assistance from his experienced clerk, John D. Howland. Learned and highly capable, Howland had been considered a possibility for the judgeship, but he now cheerfully helped Gresham master his new duties. In a short time he reported to Davis that "Gresham does well and will make a good judge."[1]

With jurisdiction over the entire state, Judge Gresham followed an arduous routine, riding circuit to hold court in each of the large towns. Ill health marred much of his first five years on the bench. A half year after assuming office, he fell while fishing and broke the hip of the same leg that had been wounded in the war. The prospect of a long convalescence convinced him that he ought to resign, but friends and lawyers who practiced in his court dissuaded him. Although after three months he could walk with crutches, his general physical condition remained less than satisfactory. Over the years he made extended visits to various spas, during which times Gresham's brother judges of the circuit assumed much of his business.[2]

Gresham's first reported opinion did not appear until nearly three years after he had taken office. A wide variety of cases came before his court, many of them linked to the country's burgeoning industrialization and economic change. The Panic of 1873 and the subsequent depression required him to devote a large portion of his time to bankruptcy work. He also handled a good deal of railroad litigation, which multiplied after the panic because of the increase in the number of lines going into federal receivership. For railroads that had trouble meeting their debts, Gresham believed that revenue should be paid first to labor and other creditors involved in the operation of the railroads rather than to bondholders. He also became expert in the mechanical intricacies of patent law. "Many a time," his wife later wrote, "was our library cluttered up with briefs, records, and models of machinery in patent cases."[3]

During his first few years as judge, Gresham followed the dictates of judicial decorum and avoided participation in politics. But he still held strong opinions on the issues of the day, and his views sometimes clashed with those of Senator Morton and other party leaders. Morton and other Radical Republicans continued to argue for vigorous federal support for Republican regimes in the South, but by 1872 with four of the region's states already "redeemed" by conservative Democrats, the shape of the future was clear. Gresham saw little reason for alarm at this trend, especially after witnessing southern Republican rule firsthand while taking the waters at Hot Springs, Arkansas. "The more I see and hear of the South," he wrote home to Thomas Slaughter, "the less I think of Carpetbaggers."[4]

The Panic of 1873 diverted public concern from Reconstruction issues and brought renewed agitation for currency expansion, particularly through issuing of greenbacks, as a way to alleviate economic distress. In response, inflationists in Congress led by Morton and other midwestern Republicans passed the so-called Inflation Bill in April 1874 to raise the level of greenbacks to $400 million. A veto by Grant blocked the bill but also laid bare the serious division within the Republican party on the currency issue. Gresham applauded Grant's stand and resisted Morton's efforts to commit the state party to currency expansion. When the senator initiated a movement to pack the upcoming state convention with inflationists, Gresham warned his friend Benjamin Bristow, who had just become secretary of the treasury, that certain treasury officials in Indiana were using their influence against the administration's position. Such activity, Gresham claimed, did not reflect the sentiment of the "solid sensible men of the party." Nonetheless, the convention platform did call for additional currency, and Morton waged the subsequent election campaign squarely in favor of inflation.[5]

The split in both major parties on the money issue and the rise of an independent Greenback party indicated to Gresham that the major parties were "evidently breaking up." He thus had little hesitancy about using his influence behind the scenes to help his old foe Michael Kerr secure renomination to Congress. Kerr agreed with Gresham on the currency question, but many Democrats in the New Albany district favored inflation. As a lawyer Gresham had met and represented Democrats throughout the district, and he now urged many of these friends and former clients to rally to Kerr's support. Kerr won renomination and went on to win a narrow victory in the fall.[6]

After nearly five years on the bench Gresham began to feel a certain restlessness, and the year 1874 witnessed a mild revival of his political ambition. In the spring he told Thomas Slaughter that he was going to run for the United States Senate, although he made no public announcement of his intention at that time. Still plagued by illness, he now suffered from "bleeding at the lungs." Doctors assured him that it was not consumption but recommended an extended break from work, and he moved his family to California in June. He yearned to return to Indiana near the end of the election campaign, but his health was not fully recovered, and he yielded to the objections of his wife and family. As it turned out, the Democrats won a majority in the state legislature and elected one of their own to the Senate.[7]

The Greshams remained in California for nearly a year, making San José their headquarters. On doctor's orders, Gresham began to eat more to increase his weight—145 pounds distributed over his six-foot frame—back to its average of 175 in earlier days. In late summer he and fifteen-year-old Otto took a four-week camping trip through the Yosemite valley, hiking during the day and sleeping on the ground every night. The trip gave Gresham a rare opportunity to get to know his son better. He found the boy to be "quite manly and companionable," but he also wrote home to a friend, "It almost scares me some times to see how old and ambitious he is in some ways." When fall arrived, Gresham enrolled Otto in Santa Clara College, a nearby Jesuit school, which suggests that he had overcome some of the prejudices of his Know-Nothing days in the 1850s. He soon regretted the choice of school, however, not so much because of its specifically Catholic character as because he believed the teachers spent too much time on religious instruction and too little on intellectual training. This view reflected his growing disenchantment with organized religion in general. "I have but little faith in dogmas, creeds, and systems," he noted. "I don't believe that in order to keep the Creator on good terms with us, we must spend a good part of our time in mumbling Masses and prayers. Christianity is a *life*, not a belief, and it follows that we are answerable for the uprightness of our belief and not for its rightness." Although he welcomed the social control exercised by the organized sects, for himself he believed in "taking care of the mind & body and letting the soul take care of itself."[8]

In the fall of 1874 Republicans lost heavily in the congressional elections, and for the first time since before the Civil War the Democrats won a majority in the House of Representatives. "No doubt," Gresham wrote to Thomas Slaughter, "the tight times and the late panics have had their effect, for the multitude are shallow and absurd in their reasoning under such influences, but we must not in our blind devotion to party overlook other causes. . . . The Republican party has grown arrogant, extravagant, and corrupt, and the President has either lacked the sense to understand the interests of the party that elected him, or he has been indifferent about its further ascendancy." Grant's cabinets had been "incomparably the weakest the country has ever known." Since becoming president, Grant had developed "low vulgar traits of character" and had "run after and with rich men, simply because they were rich, whether they had any sense or not." Despite Gresham's friendship with Grant and his initial hope that the hero of Union victory would restore a sense of civic virtue to public affairs, he could not escape the conclusion that "the President's conduct must be numbered amongst the multifarious causes of the late defeats." But the Republican party was no better, he told Slaughter, for its members cared only "for mere party ascendancy, for the spoils, and not for principle." Hopelessly divided on such issues as the tariff and the currency, the party could do nothing "but talk about its glorious record and the sins of the Democracy and we are getting too far removed from the war for that." Forgetting the true republican significance of its founding, the party had stagnated. Gresham had no intention of joining the Democrats; nor did he welcome the various independent movements springing up around the country. But in the future his action within the Republican party would be aimed toward reform and a return to first principles.[9]

The only hope, he believed, lay with leaders such as the reforming secretary of the treasury, Benjamin Bristow, with whom he had been friends since the Civil War. The Kentuckian had made speeches for Gresham during his congressional campaigns, and in 1874, when Grant offered Bristow the Treasury Department, Gresham had encouraged him to accept and "make for yourself a great name." Prosecution of the Whiskey Ring offered him that opportunity. A far-flung conspiracy among distillers and internal revenue agents who defrauded the government of millions of dollars in excise taxes, the ring operated with the connivance of revenue officials in Washington and reached as high as Grant's personal secretary, Orville Babcock. In the spring of 1875 Bristow seized many of the country's largest distilleries and launched a year-long legal battle to convict the ring's members and recover evaded taxes.[10]

The first convictions in the scandal came in Gresham's court at Evansville in June 1875. The charge against distillers Gordon and John Bingham was relatively minor—operating a distillery in the absence of a government "storekeeper"—but the case was significant as the pioneer prosecution. After a pointed charge from Judge Gresham, the jury returned a guilty verdict that gave treasury officials their "first blood." In later proceedings Gresham ordered the Binghams to produce evidence that led to further prosecutions. In December indictments were returned against more than twenty-five men, several of whom were tried in Gresham's court at Indianapolis in January 1876. Nearly all were convicted, the notable exception being Hiram Brownlee, an internal revenue agent accused of accepting a bribe. Despite Gresham's heavy-handed charge to the jury, Benjamin Harrison's skillful defense won Brownlee's acquittal. In sentencing others, Gresham made clear that he considered public officials such as Brownlee, who had "betrayed their sacred trusts," far more blameworthy than the distillers. All told, Bristow's investigation netted scores of convictions and the recovery of over $3 million in evaded taxes.[11]

In the fall of 1875 Gresham and his family moved to Indianapolis, where court business had always required him to spend much time. The capital city's population of sixty-five thousand was four times that of New Albany. Although he missed friends like Slaughter and Noble Butler, Gresham found that Indianapolis, as the social and political center of the state, offered a more stimulating atmosphere. Before long he became a charter member of the Indianapolis Literary Club, whose membership included the leaders of the city's social, intellectual, and political life. Tillie soon began to "mix a little with the ladies," and fourteen-year-old Kate quickly made friends in school. At age seventeen, Otto set his heart on attending West Point. "The boy is developing very satisfactorily," Gresham wrote to Slaughter. "He is not brilliant, but, I think, his understanding and his moral perceptions are good, perhaps even strong." The boy's hopes were dashed when he failed the grammar section of the military academy's entrance examination. After further preparation he attended Wabash College in Crawfordsville, Indiana.[12]

In Gresham's mind the Whiskey Ring prosecutions represented a welcome resurgence in civic morality that offered the Republican party an opportunity to refurbish its tarnished image. "Vice seems to be abroad," he told Kentucky Republican John Marshall Harlan, "but it is everywhere confronted by virtue." He argued that the party must reject politicians who had "steadily given their influence to scoundrels" and find leaders who were above suspicion. Perhaps with the aim of easing his own return to politics, he accepted an invitation to address a large reunion of Civil War veterans in Indianapolis in October 1875. In his speech he dispensed the standard encomiums to the soldiers' bravery and devotion to duty, denounced "the pernicious doctrine of States Rights," and hailed the war's outcome as the "final repudiation by the nation of the wicked heresy that the Union is a simple compact between sovereign states." But he avoided the more rabid "bloody shirt" oratory practiced by many other Republicans and looked forward to the time when the South would be prosperous again and the past forgotten. On the money question he offered an unequivocal defense of specie payments and the payment of all national obligations "to the uttermost farthing." Echoing the concerns many Americans felt over reckless business methods accompanying the country's industrial development, he lashed out against the "different forms of gambling which have done so much to demoralize and degrade society and which seek to hide their real character under the more respectable names of speculation and trade."[13]

Morton, who planned to run for president the following year, delivered one of the uninhibited bloody-shirt harangues for which he was noted. Gresham believed the senator and his friends "acted indecently . . . to turn the whole thing into a demonstration for Morton personally." Gresham had hesitated to speak in the first place because of his supposedly nonpolitical position. Afterward, he promised Justice Davis that "you shall never hear of me figuring in another meeting of the same kind."[14]

But Gresham's speech did attract attention, and it set off speculation that he might run for governor in 1876. He received many tempting assurances of support but saw "so many reasons both for and against" going into politics that he was "forced into a state of indecision." His stay in California had left him deeply in debt, and he still felt "somewhat broken" in health. Moreover, he had begun "to experience a real pleasure in the examination of legal questions" that made him reluctant to relinquish the comfortable security of the bench. He also held back because of the possible candidacy of Benjamin Harrison, who, as a Civil War brigadier, one of Indiana's most successful lawyers, and a party leader second only to Morton in the esteem of many Republicans, would be a formidable opponent. But in early December Harrison decided not to make the race and confidentially offered his support to Gresham. Morton also intimated that he would have no objection to the judge's heading the state ticket. Ironically, Morton hoped to exploit Gresham's reputation for independence. Like other national party leaders, the senator recognized the need to appeal to reform-minded Republicans, many of whom had deserted the party and backed Horace Greeley against Grant in 1872. If Morton were to succeed in his quest for the presidential nomination, he would need a united state party at his back; Gresham's nomination for governor could help bring Liberal Republicans and other disaffected party members back into the fold. Still, Gresham hesitated, suspecting "some scheme that I don't understand."[15]

At bottom, self-doubt and fear of putting his ambition to the test held him back. "I am satisfied that you overrate my abilities," he wrote Slaughter. He conceded that he "might succeed somewhat as a leader" and that "my experience, my association with men, which has been considerable, has given me some confidence in my own powers." But, he argued, "I do think you give me credit for more than I am entitled to." His final decision against running was less important than the way he had reached it; his two months' vacillation contrasted sharply with the self-assurance of both Morton and Harrison. In the end, he concluded he should "take no risk."[16]

Gresham nevertheless labored behind the scenes to assist the nomination of national Republican candidates identified with reform. For the first time since 1860 there would be an open contest for the presidential nomination, and there was no dearth of candidates. The front-runner was former Speaker of the House James G. Blaine, who enjoyed the loyalty of legions of regular Republicans but found little favor among reformers in the party. Blaine's bitter foe, Senator Roscoe Conkling, head of the spoils-based New York Republican machine, challenged Morton for support among Grant Republicans, especially in the rotten boroughs of the South, where the party fed almost exclusively on federal patronage. Several states offered favorite sons, including Ohio's Rutherford B. Hayes, whose prospects rested chiefly on his recent election to a third term as governor after a hard-fought campaign.[17]

None of these men, Gresham believed, was suited to redeem the party after eight years of Grant. Politics in the centennial year had come down to a struggle between the "influences of *right*" and the forces of "error and wrong." Rank-and-file Republicans were still far superior to the Democratic masses, but the party machinery had fallen into "the hands of leaders, who as a class are corrupt." To nominate Morton, for example, whom Gresham considered "low in his instincts," would "encourage and even embolden the thieves" in the Republican party. Instead, the party must choose "a man who has shown that he is honestly in favor of good old-fashioned honest administration—a man of pluck and sense, who will put the public service on a higher plane." Like many other reform-minded Republicans, Gresham believed that man was Bristow. Indeed, he said, the choice was "Bristow or ruin."[18]

Throughout the winter and spring Gresham remained in close contact with Bristow's chief strategist, John Marshall Harlan. As early as January he warned the Kentucky leader that he must "counteract

Morton's schemes" to win southern delegates. Bristow, however, was reluctant to become an open candidate, particularly because of his delicate relations with Grant. In February, during the Whiskey Ring trial of Grant's secretary Orville Babcock, Gresham answered an urgent request from Justice David Davis and hurried to Washington to discuss the possibility of Bristow's resigning from the cabinet. Gresham had little desire to *"fight* Grant after receiving so many evidences of his friendship," but still he believed the president was wrong. Secretary of State Hamilton Fish eventually persuaded Bristow to stay on for the sake of party unity. Even so, Bristow emerged from the incident determined to step up his presidential campaign, and Gresham returned from Washington even more determined to "bid defiance to political despotism." He began to work openly to convert Indiana delegates to Bristow.[19]

Bristow enjoyed support among the old Liberal Republicans, some of whom, under the leadership of Carl Schurz, planned a conference that would issue an address threatening to field an independent ticket if the Republicans should nominate anyone of "less moral & intellectual stature" than Bristow. Gresham at first considered Schurz a "great fool" for pushing a scheme that party regulars would resent as "insolent dictation." But after meeting with Schurz, Gresham was satisfied that the resolutions would not mention Bristow by name but instead would speak in broad terms "of the absolute importance of reform, of the imminent danger which now threatens our institutions, [and] of the danger of allowing the claims of party to override the demands of patriotism." He dropped his objections to the conference and later congratulated Bristow on having the support of "the good honest people in the party."[20]

Despite entertaining such elevated sentiments, Gresham was not above engaging in less lofty tactics. Although he concentrated much of his effort against Morton, he recognized that Blaine was a greater threat. As much as any other man, Gresham set in motion the chain of events leading to the discovery of the famous Mulligan letters, which contributed largely to Blaine's failure to win the nomination and dogged his subsequent career. In early March Gresham learned from John C.S. Harrison, a director of the Union Pacific Railroad residing in Indianapolis, that in 1871 Blaine had received $64,000 from the Union Pacific in exchange for worthless bonds of the Little Rock and Fort Smith Railroad. The implication was that railroad officials had made the transaction as a reward for favorable treatment by Blaine in Congress. By April Gresham had devised a plan to have "Morton & Blaine take each other by the ears." He knew that Morton was aware of Blaine's deals, and he also knew that Blaine knew Morton possessed the information. If the material were to become public, Blaine would infer that Morton had revealed the secret. "I don't see that in this I am guilty of wrong doing," Gresham wrote Slaughter. "Bristow's friends will not be responsible for Blaine's *inferences*." The tactic was justified because it would eliminate the two unacceptable candidates and have a great "moral effect" on Bristow's candidacy.[21]

Gresham moved circumspectly, believing that as a judge he "must not be known in the affair." On April 11 the Democratic *Indianapolis Sentinel* printed the Union Pacific story without revealing the source. John Harrison denied giving the information to the paper and expressed "great surprise" when it appeared. Indeed, the publication baffled many who had been privy to the story beforehand. When the pro-Blaine *Chicago Tribune* drew the intended inference and blamed Morton's men, the senator's brother-in-law, Indianapolis postmaster William R. Holloway, could only reply that the facts "were sent here from another quarter and given to the *Sentinel* for the purpose of injuring Morton." Gresham gave no hint of his agency in the paper's report.[22]

The revelations jolted but did not stop Blaine's campaign. Gresham hoped that the incriminating Mulligan letters discovered during a congressional inquiry would persuade Republicans not to "put a lame nag on the track," but on June 5 Blaine rose in the House to give a masterful self-defense that included selected readings from the letters themselves. He continued to amass convention delegates.[23]

As the convention drew near, Gresham feared that "the politicians' wirepulling" would defeat Bristow and "cheat the people out of their choice." After some hesitation because of his position as a judge, he decided to attend the Cincinnati convention, where he quietly canvassed for Bristow. One newspaper claimed that Gresham was on hand to "repay Morton for his unjustifiable and treacherous conduct toward him during the war." As it happened, court business called him back to Indianapolis before the convention was fully under way. Blaine led at the outset of balloting, but when neither Bristow nor Morton attracted enough strength to defeat him, his opponents united behind Hayes. Gresham accepted Hayes's nomination as a "narrow escape" for reform, although Bristow's defeat left him "blue as indigo." He had no doubt of Hayes's honesty but feared he might not possess "sufficient strength of character to resist the evil elements in the party." In any case, Gresham was satisfied that Morton's "cock can never be brought into the ring for another fight."[24]

Gresham took no part in the fall canvass. Hayes's letter of acceptance called for civil service reform and a restoration of sectional harmony, but in Indiana Morton set the tone, scoffing at reformers as "sorehead Republicans" and waging a bloody-shirt campaign as virulent as any in the past. In early August scandal rocked the Republican camp when gubernatorial nominee Godlove Orth, a Morton man, withdrew in the face of conflict-of-interest charges. The Morton-dominated state committee replaced Orth with Benjamin Harrison, who had probably dreaded Morton's nomination for president as much as Gresham had but had kept quiet and avoided the "spoiler" label Gresham had earned. Hoosier Republicans welcomed Harrison almost as a savior. By assuming the hopeless race and waging an enthusiastic though losing campaign, he took an enormous step toward placing himself behind Morton in the line of succession for leadership of the Indiana Republican party.[25]

Republican loss of the October state elections boded ill for the national ticket in November, but Gresham saw little cause for alarm. Indeed, he considered Democrat Samuel J. Tilden a leader of "uncommon capacity," who was sincerely trying to get his party "out of its old Bourbon rut." "The government is not necessarily gone if the Democrats succeed," he assured Slaughter on the eve of the election. "Democrats are not all scoundrels or traitors."[26]

This attitude permitted Gresham to adopt a tempered approach to the months-long controversy that followed the November elections. With neither Hayes nor Tilden receiving a clear majority in the electoral college, both sides claimed twenty disputed votes, nineteen of which came from Louisiana, South Carolina, and Florida, the only southern states still under Republican Reconstruction governments.[27] In Congress Morton took the lead among those who argued that the Constitution empowered the president of the Senate (who was a Republican) to count the electoral votes and declare the winner. But in January 1877, Republican Senator George F. Edmunds, with Democratic backing, offered a bill to create an ad hoc commission to examine the votes and determine the outcome. Gresham welcomed this bill. "I am a decided Republican as you know," he wrote Slaughter, "but I can't go to the extent of claiming that we should manage to hold power simply for the spoils, and by methods both fair and foul." While debate raged in the Senate, he organized support for the bill in Indiana, gathering signers for a telegram to Edmunds, which New York's Roscoe Conkling used against Morton. The Hoosier senator and his lieutenants tried to dismiss Gresham and the other signers as a "host of dead beat dishwater politicians" who had no influence, but the judge confidently reported to Slaughter that his telegram had dealt "a staggering blow to Morton, and strong as he is he felt it." In the end the bill passed, and the electoral commission awarded the disputed votes to Hayes.[28]

This peaceful outcome strengthened Gresham's "faith in popular institutions" and in the American people's "infinite amount of good common sense." But the nature of Hayes's election placed a special burden on the new president. Unless he continued to elevate "the tone of things generally," Gresham said, the Republican party would be "swept out of existence" in succeeding elections. In Indiana Morton's recent setbacks offered a propitious opportunity to challenge his hold on the party. Many Hoosier Republicans, like Gresham, had long accused the senator of "having bad men appointed to office" to maintain his political machine. Taking heart from Hayes's pronouncements on the civil service, the senator's enemies decided, in the words of the independent *Indianapolis News*, that they would no longer "accept Mortonism as Republicanism." Less than two weeks after the inauguration Gresham was in Washington discussing patronage with cabinet secretaries and with the president himself.[29]

Morton did not remain idle in the face of this threat. He and his allies saw differences of opinion such as that reflected by Gresham's telegram to Edmunds as violations of party discipline for which the patronage whip was the most effective punishment. "The party is all right," an organization man wrote Morton in early 1877, "but like an old sore before the cure is perfect, the dead flesh must be cut off and we Republicans who do the work and stand the brunt of the fight now demand that all such Republicans as [Gresham's court clerk] John D. Howland, Judge G. . . . and many others must go over to the Democratic Party where they have belonged for over a year."[30]

Although several offices were at stake, the patronage struggle centered on the post of pension agent at Indianapolis. Morton backed the incumbent, W.H.H. Terrell, while Gresham and others favored Frederick Knefler. Dragged out over many weeks, the fight grew bitter. When the administration finally decided upon Knefler, Morton was incensed, certain that Terrell would have encountered no trouble "if Gresham had kept his hands to himself." Although the position was relatively unimportant, Gresham was satisfied that the fight had signaled "quite a revolt" against Morton's leadership.[31]

Nonetheless, Gresham did not take the triumph as a signal to make a more overt challenge for party leadership. Once again he greeted suggestions that he assume a more public part in politics with his customary hesitation and resignation. "I have less ambition as I grow older, for I realize how very vain and empty such things are," he wrote Slaughter. "What does a little reputation amount to? Absolutely noth-

ing. Perhaps there is not a man now in any official station in this
country whose name will be known to the public 50 or 100 years after
he is gone. We should cultivate contentment. That is the true philosophy."[32]

Gresham had little time for repose in the summer of 1877, for he and
others in Indianapolis grew increasingly apprehensive that a strike
against many of the nation's railroads would soon tie up traffic in that
important rail hub. Triggered by cuts on several lines, the strike began
at Martinsburg, West Virginia, in mid-July and spread steadily across
the country. Its unprecedented scope, coupled with violence and loss
of life in Pittsburgh and other cities, caused many to see the walkout as
the beginning of a working-class revolution in response to the four-
year-old depression. In Gresham's mind, the strikers were influenced
by the "doctrines of the Commune." When the strike reached Indianapolis a week after it began, he responded vigorously as a leader
against it both on and off the bench.[33]

Railroad workers struck at Indianapolis on Monday, July 23, "with
no crowd, no excitement," and "in a quiet and peaceable manner," as
one newspaper put it. Warren Sayre, secretary of the Brotherhood of
Locomotive Engineers and unofficial leader of the local strike, promised there would be no violence, and local officials responded cautiously. Hoping to avoid a confrontation, Republican Mayor John
Caven swore in more than two hundred strikers as special deputies to
keep the peace. Similarly, Democratic Governor James D. Williams
vowed he would call out the state militia only in the event of actual
violence. In the evening a meeting of two thousand of the city's
laborers expressed sympathy with the strikers but went on record as
strongly opposing violence. The railroad men at Indianapolis remained peaceful; over the next several days the U.S. Army Signal
Corps officers stationed at the local federal arsenal reported no violence in the city.[34]

Yet the strikers did interrupt the movement of trains. They generally
left mail operations alone, but they stopped trains carrying freight and
disrupted some passenger service as well. As the strike moved into its
second day, the *Indianapolis Journal* editorialized that even though it
entertained "no fear that the public peace will be disturbed," the
"unlawful interference with public business cannot be permitted."
Gresham agreed. Believing that the governor and mayor were "determined to do nothing to protect or defend the railroads," he worked in
concert with his immediate superior, Seventh Circuit Judge Thomas
Drummond at Chicago, to aid those roads managed by court-appoint-
ed receivers. Acting upon a plea from the receiver of the Indianapolis,

Bloomington, and Western, he issued a writ for the arrest of persons interfering with the receiver's operations and ordered U.S. Marshal Benjamin Spooner to "aid, assist, and protect" the receiver "in the discharge of his duties as prescribed in the orders of this court for the management and operation" of the road. He warned "all persons" against "interfering with or interrupting said receiver in the discharge of his duties, under the penalty of the law." After some hesitation, United States Attorney General Charles Devens approved this approach, although he stipulated that the marshal must "act only on processes issued" by the court. For Gresham to hear and pass on pleas from each of the receivers in his district would have entailed serious delay. Hence he and Judge Drummond issued a blanket writ ordering the marshal to prohibit "any unlawful interference" with "any property in the custody of any receiver in this court."[35]

Gresham's original writ recognized the need for an "adequate force" to enable the marshal to sustain the orders of the court and protect the receivers' property. On the same day he asked Devens for federal troops, but the attorney general replied that none were available. Marshal Spooner and Gresham next asked for authority to appoint up to a thousand deputies—one for every striker. But the strikers were abiding by Gresham's writ regarding receivers' roads, and Devens ordered Spooner to wait before enrolling so many deputies. At this juncture Gresham and Spooner described the situation as "critical and dangerous." The marshal claimed that "a large majority of the Laborers are in strong sympathy with the strikers and there is an element which is anxious to rob & murder." Gresham sent a plea for help directly to Hayes, arguing that "the mob is the only supreme authority in the state at present. They commit no other violence but to interrupt railroads, but they sheep together, stop all business, & by the suspension of business large numbers of men will soon be out of employment, upon the streets, and swelling the mob. . . . There may be an outbreak at any moment and the consequences will be most disastrous." The next day Devens promised to send troops and authorized Spooner to swear in "a sufficient force of special deputies." All that remained was to raise and organize volunteers. Gresham led in the creation of a Committee of Public Safety which set about enlisting a local militia. The judge himself headed a company that used his courtroom as its barracks. Here, one reporter noted, Colonel Gresham and his men spent the night "scattered about over the floor, with arms stacked and sentries at every turn, reminding one forcibly of the stirring scenes of 1861."[36]

The next day Gresham appeared before the city council to secure ex post facto approval of the Committee of Public Safety. "We hope," he

told the councilmen, "that as the result of this consolidated public
sentiment and of the active and determined expression which it has
given in the instant organization of a large force already armed and
ready for duty, that the law may be promptly and thoroughly re-
established in our streets." Two hundred federal troops arrived later,
but they had nothing to do. By Friday afternoon, July 27, the strike had
been broken.[37]

The Indianapolis strikers were arrested over the weekend, and on
Monday Gresham was prepared to undertake contempt proceedings.
He asked Judge Drummond's advice as to "adequate punishment,"
and the senior judge replied that he intended to "punish them by
imprisonment so that there will not be likely to be any interference
soon again." Perhaps for political reasons, Gresham apparently shrank
from sending the men to jail, for he insisted that Drummond come to
Indianapolis to take his place in the Indiana cases. Drummond convened the proceedings on August 1. Gresham sat with the senior
judge, although Drummond noted that the "legal responsibility" for
their acts would be solely his own. In the course of the hearing, which
as a contempt proceeding was not a jury trial, Gresham occasionally
participated in the examination of witnesses, even challenging the
veracity of those whose recollection of events differed from his own.
After two days Drummond sentenced all but two of the defendants to
three months in prison and required the other two to post bond for a
year's good conduct.[38]

Drummond and Gresham's use of the writ of assistance and contempt proceedings had the effect of outlawing strikes on railroads in
receivership. Although their actions were less sweeping than the processes judges later used, they constituted an important step in the
evolution of the labor injunction. For the most part Gresham and
Drummond won high praise for restoring peace and business to the
public highways. An important exception came from the noted jurist
Thomas McIntyre Cooley, who objected that such proceedings could
threaten the right to trial by jury. Gresham himself later came to see the
justice of that objection, and by 1894 he considered the blanket injunction such as was used against the Pullman strike as an abuse of
executive and judicial power. But in 1877, as one legal scholar later
noted, the contempt proceedings "were responsive less to legal principles than to emotions" inspired by the strike, which as the first widespread tie-up of its kind easily seemed more revolutionary than it
was.[39]

For Gresham, who had brooded over the threat to American institutions posed by a corrupt political system, the strike aroused further

anxieties. "I fear that the disturbances of the last few weeks are but the beginning of a conflict which will shake the very foundations of society itself," he wrote Slaughter. "The doctrines of the Commune have been very successfully propagated in the cities and manufacturing & mining districts during the last four or five years. . . . An overwhelming majority of the mechanics and laboring men of this city hate those who have managed to accumulate a little property." The whole episode seemed to deny the vitality of the American experiment in republicanism. "Our institutions are now on trial. All honest thoughtful men know that the ballot must be restricted, and, I suppose, that can be done only through blood. It is by no means clear that our revolutionary fathers did a good thing for us when they severed the ties that bound the colonies to the Mother Country. Certainly they went too far with their notions of popular Government. Popular Government as we have it now is simply the government of the mob." Just a few months earlier, when the electoral commission bill had triumphed in Congress, he had praised Americans' "good common sense," but now he confessed, "the future looks bloody to me. I am fearful we are trusting too much to the seeming common sense of our Anglo-Saxon people." Gresham's ideas about labor mellowed, and he later earned a reputation as a friend of the workingman, but his anxiety over popular government persisted— not the momentary doubt he felt in 1877 about the wisdom of the Founders' handiwork, but rather his fear that the sound republican institutions they had created were being subverted by unscrupulous and venal politicians.[40]

As the echoes of the strike faded away, citizens of Indiana received another shock when in early November Oliver P. Morton died. To fill his Senate seat, Governor James D. Williams chose former Democratic congressman Daniel W. Voorhees, an ardent advocate of currency expansion. The appointment alarmed Gresham, for he saw it as another sign of the strength of the dangerous soft-money heresy in the Democratic party. To be sure, Congress had in 1875 passed legislation mandating the payment of specie for the greenbacks beginning in 1879, but, as Gresham warned Ohio's James A. Garfield, "many in Congress [who] pander to the ignorance and prejudice of the times" advocated repeal of the Resumption Act. Moreover, many inflationists had turned to silver as a way to expand the currency. In early 1878 Congress bowed to the pressure by passing the Bland-Allison Act, which restored limited coinage of the white metal. But the new law did not satisfy expansionists like Voorhees, under whose leadership the 1878 Democratic state convention called for the repeal of the Resumption Act and the unlimited coinage of silver. Such sentiments, coupled with the

Democratic press's defense of the 1877 strikers, led conservative Republicans to label the Democrats the party of radicalism. In Gresham's mind, that party was growing "more and more dangerous." Though willing to accept Tilden's election in 1876, he now saw the Democracy as "the almost open and undisguised enemy of law, order, and society itself."[41]

With Morton's death the attractions of Republican politics brightened for Gresham and like-minded men. Slaughter saw it as a perfect opportunity for his friend to return to active politics and assume the leadership of the state party. Gresham was less certain. "I don't know what to say," he wrote Slaughter. "Others have talked to me in the same vein. I confess that I have, at times, an intense desire to be in political life. I even sometimes feel conscious of a power to lead (to anyone else I would not say this) and I will admit that I am not always without ambition. Occasionally I am fearfully moved by something within to come to the front. But"—here the doubts crept in—"that may not prove that I could get there. And again, if I should get to the front, I would be mortified beyond measure not to be able [to] do the work of a leader." He would promise only to "think of the matter."[42]

As 1878 opened, Gresham was soon receiving reports of a revitalized party throughout the state. More insistently, Slaughter argued that with Morton gone the party needed "some strong-willed, courageous, able, and organizing mind, to consolidate its forces." He wrote Gresham, "You have the faculty—power—whatever you choose to term it—of impressing, dominating men. The generality of people yield naturally to you." He urged Gresham to run for Morton's, now Voorhees's Senate seat. Scolding his friend for his timidity, Slaughter caught the essence of Gresham's personality: "While I have great respect for your judgment on all other subjects, I do believe where you are yourself concerned you have made great mistakes. Ordinarily you have sufficient faith in yourself, and where responsibilities are devolved upon you of a public character, or affecting others, you have the courage to act promptly upon the suggestions of your own mind, but when it comes to your own personal affairs, you are always disposed to underrate yourself. . . . You are not wholly unconscious of your power and influence over men, yet I don't believe you realize your own strength." As for the Senate race, Slaughter promised that he and other friends would "work it up" through correspondence "without involving you" and with no "public demonstration or display" to soil the judicial ermine.[43]

But neither a Senate seat nor Morton's mantle of leadership would fall to one who shied away from the political fray. Republicans of

Indiana were looking for a leader to challenge the Democrats on the stump and fight the party's battles unhesitatingly. No one understood that more than Benjamin Harrison, who jumped headlong into the 1878 campaign. Gresham as usual did not campaign but instead expressed satisfaction that Harrison was sound on the currency and "meeting the issues squarely." Although the Hoosier Republicans went down to defeat in a general Democratic sweep, Harrison had marched to the head of the state party.[44]

Charges of fraud in the election brought a case into Gresham's court, and his nonpartisan handling of it irritated many Republicans. Thirteen Democrats were accused of conspiring to import over a hundred voters into one of Indiana's congressional districts to swing its vote to their candidate. Gresham was not entirely certain that the men could be indicted under federal law, but he rejected a defense motion to quash. When the case moved to jury selection, Harrison, who was serving as special prosecution counsel, and the Republican United States marshal, William W. Dudley, proceeded to reject Democratic jurymen and to replace them with Republicans from the courtroom audience. The Democrats' lawyers, led by former Democratic Senator and Governor Thomas A. Hendricks, objected, whereupon Gresham dismissed the jury, ordered a new venire, and chose a jury of six Republicans and six Democrats. The Democratic *Sentinel* praised him as "a fearless judge," but Harrison's partner fumed that it was "impossible to convict a Democrat in Judge Gresham's court." All but one of the defendants won acquittal. In passing sentence, Gresham defended the trial as fair and added, "If the principle of governing by a majority, under proper limitations, is to be maintained, the elective franchise must be sacredly guarded; unscrupulous tricksters who conspire to prevent a fair and honest expression of the popular will through the ballot box should be punished with a severity that will deter others from committing similar offenses."[45]

While Gresham strove for political impartiality in his court, he played an active role in the national Union veterans' organizations, which sometimes appeared to be little more than adjuncts to the Republican party. He was a member of the Grand Army of the Republic and the Loyal Legion, but he took greatest interest in the Society of the Army of the Tennessee and served several times as its vice-president. In 1879 he was the principal speaker at the society's annual reunion in Chicago. Such gatherings carried considerable political impact; press coverage was extensive so an invitation to deliver the annual oration offered an opportunity to make a national reputation. In preparing his address, Gresham turned to his newly appointed clerk Noble C.

Butler, who, since Slaughter's death in January 1879, had become his
most valued counselor. Together they produced one of the few elaborate public statements of Gresham's political philosophy.[46]

Gresham devoted much of his address to commending the "sentiment of nationality" as "a source of vitality to the Government and an
element of its strength and capacity." Under the Articles of Con-
federation, he said, national weakness permitted outbursts like Shays'
Rebellion, and "socialistic notions that were quite as radical and subversive of existing institutions as those of France found a lodgment
here." The Constitution, embodying the spirit of nationalism, was
designed to redress the disadvantages of a powerless center and to
create a supreme national authority. The "most subtle and dangerous
foe" to American nationalism was the heretical states'-rights theory
that the Constitution had created a compact of states rather than a
unitary nation. The proponents of that theory had gone to war in 1861
to assert its validity, and by their defeat "the National sovereignty was
plainly and conclusively demonstrated." Moreover, the outcome had a
moral dimension, for "the soldiers of the Union fought to maintain the
principles of popular government and the great natural rights of
man,—while their enemies fought to fasten the fetters of slavery."[47]

Yet Gresham was willing to concede that the rebellion had not been
"wholly the act of conscious and deliberate wrong-doers." And it was
"time for passion to give way to interest and duty." A return to military
occupation of the South in peacetime, as some Republicans advocated,
would threaten American institutions as much as the rebellion itself
had. "We must stand for the purpose for which we fought, and that was
the maintenance of the Government of our fathers." Under the Constitution, all states, North and South, were entitled to equal rights and
equal treatment. "The war legislated; it established the supremacy of
the nation in every power conferred on it by the Constitution, but it did
not destroy the states or the right of local self-government."

Gresham did call for a larger military establishment, ready to respond to the continuing threat to order in society that had burst forth in
the railroad strikes. "Instead of personal liberty, the rights of property
are now threatened. Doctrines subversive of the right to acquire and
hold property, and, therefore, subversive of society, are boldly proclaimed in Chicago and elsewhere. With our large cities full of these
dangerous agitators—the dread of all civilized communities—it might
be better if the Federal power were more accessible, if it were not so
remote from those who need and are entitled to its protection."

Gresham closed with a condemnation of the country's debased
politics—the main message he hoped to convey. "The decay of public

virtue is almost always the sure precursor of national ruin," he told his listeners, his words reminiscent of the warnings of James Madison and Thomas Jefferson. "Vices are readily initiated under any circumstances, but they are more alluring when tricked out with the insignia of authority." Election fraud cases in his court had made him particularly attuned to the need to restore the sanctity of the ballot box. Presidential elections had come to "resemble revolutions." Unless steps were taken to protect the franchise from fraud, "the horrors of anarchy" would result.

The root of the problem lay in the "moral convulsion" of the Civil War, which tore many men from the "sober and methodical pursuits of peace" and thrust them into "an adventurous and irregular mode of life, while the necessary inflation of our currency served to stimulate all forms of speculation and gambling. At such times and under such circumstances the popular conscience naturally becomes more or less depraved." As a result, "Mere tricksters, with no proper notions of social or political duty, aspire to office, expecting, if successful, to get rich in the shortest possible time by plundering the public." The leadership of parties had passed to "those politicians who believe that conscience is out of place in politics."

The solution must come from a return to first principles. "Much that is discreditable in our history," he observed, "might have been avoided by a closer adherence to the wise precepts and virtuous methods of our ancestors." The "honest and intelligent men of the country" must rise to combat these evils "not by merely writing and declaiming about them, but by their votes, their active personal efforts, and the exertion of their legitimate influence upon others." Perhaps with pangs of conscience at his own reluctance to return to active politics, he declared that "too many of those who are the most interested in good government refuse to actively participate or interest themselves in public affairs." But he ended his review optimistically: the people had only momentarily surrendered "their judgment and conscience" to bad party leaders. Under new leadership they would reject the "demagogues" who had abused their confidence, and they would "surely assert themselves as they did in 1861."

Gresham's speech appeared in newspapers throughout the country and inevitably aroused political speculation. Noble Butler's father, Gresham's old law partner, reported that some southern Indiana friends were even suggesting that Gresham "would be a good person to place at the head of affairs for the next four years." Such talk about a man who had just begun to build a national reputation was idle, but it reflected the anxiety many Republicans felt over the choices they faced in the coming presidential election. Gresham himself was perplexed. By the middle of Hayes's term he had concluded that the Ohioan was "a small man in a high position" and that his reform measures were "not in good faith." Blaine would be in the field again, but Gresham had not changed his low opinion of the Maine senator. John Sherman of Ohio was able but unpopular. Except for a few minor candidates, the only one left was former President Grant. As early as the 1877 strike Gresham had expressed regret that Grant was no longer president. As the scandals of the general's second term faded from memory, he seemed to Gresham and many others the ideal person to restore vigorous leadership after a period of drift under Hayes.[48]

After leaving office, Grant had gone on a two-year tour of the world, returning to a triumphal welcome in the fall of 1879. In November he attended the reunion of the Army of the Tennessee in Chicago, where he heard orator Gresham praise his "extraordinary courage and firmness united with a cool and unerring judgment." Few men, Gresham said, had "done so much for popular liberty or contributed so much to the happiness of the human race." With no mention of his two terms in the White House, Gresham told the assembled veterans that Grant had returned from his travels "with a love for his country and a confidence in its institutions which have been strengthened and confirmed by his observations and experience in foreign lands."[49]

In short, Gresham, like many other Republicans, believed that Grant was now ready to be president as he had not been before. When the Republican convention opened in Chicago in early June 1880, the judge was on hand working in the general's behalf. He returned to Indianapolis before the start of balloting, which became a prolonged struggle culminating in the defeat of Grant and his principal rivals and the selection of dark horse James A. Garfield. Some of Gresham's Indiana friends sought to boom his name for vice-president, but he wired delegation chairman Benjamin Harrison that he would not accept the nomination even if it were offered.[50]

The Republican state convention followed soon after the national gathering. Although for months friends had been urging Gresham to "disrobe" and run for governor, he forbade the consideration of his name. He planned to return to politics but in the safest way. If he aimed for the United States Senate, he could retain his judgeship until after the election, read the complexion of the legislature, and gauge his chances of winning the Republican caucus nomination. This strategy had no chance of success, for as usual Gresham took no active part in the campaign. Privately he encouraged Republican candidates around the state but pleaded that his judicial position precluded a public role.

Moreover, he angered many Republicans when he refused to use his office for partisan purposes. As the campaign heated up, charges of contemplated fraud by both parties abounded, and in response Gresham appointed several special deputy marshals and election supervisors, but over the objection of U.S. Marshal William W. Dudley and other Republican leaders, he did not assign these positions solely to Republicans as other Republican judges had done but instead divided them equally between the two parties. To state party leaders, this act seemed to indicate that he was "more for the other fellows than for us."[51]

On the eve of the October state elections Republicans charged that a Democratic organization known as Hancock Veterans, named after presidential nominee Winfield S. Hancock, was going to receive arms from the Democratic state administration to act as a special militia to ensure Democratic victory. The charge achieved credence even among some Democrats, but at a bipartisan citizens' meeting at Indianapolis Gresham accused the Republicans of "magnifying the danger" and said there was no "necessity for doing anything." He secured passage of a resolution expressing the citizens' confidence that "those charged with the duty of enforcing the law and maintaining order will do their duty." He feared and thus thwarted Republican intimidation of voters in the guise of opposing Democratic frauds. The next morning, however, the *Indianapolis Journal* denounced "the bare cowardice of men who will allow the ballot-box to be debauched rather than defend it." Significantly, the paper noted that "the absence of Governor Morton from Republican councils was never more noticeable than at the citizens' meeting yesterday. There was no one to take his place, else the smooth and gracious assurances of the men he had met, opposed, and defeated so often would not have availed to defeat the very object of the meeting."[52]

While Gresham thus antagonized the state party organ and many state leaders, Harrison was busy waging the party's battle on the stump. The Republicans won a majority in the legislature, and the contest for the United States Senate seat was spirited. Although Harrison was the clear front-runner in a crowded field, Gresham decided to become a candidate. Actively seeking public office for the first time in over a decade, he was almost apologetic. "If your judgment is against me," he told one potential supporter, "I will think none the less of you." His clerk Noble Butler managed his correspondence campaign, but the response was mixed. Even those who were favorable recognized that "the average member of the Legislature is looking to the array of active leading politicians" rather than to Gresham.[53]

   The Gresham men acknowledged Harrison's preeminence and for a time adopted the strategy of pushing him for a place in President-elect Garfield's cabinet as fitting recognition not only of Harrison's abilities and party services but also of Indiana's important role in Garfield's nomination and election. Unflattered and preferring the Senate, Harrison assiduously gathered support for himself. Both he and Gresham needed the backing of Fort Wayne's Robert S. Taylor, who had senatorial ambitions of his own and controlled several votes in the legislature. The methods the two men used to seek Taylor's support epitomized their contrasting political styles. Harrison wrote the Allen County leader immediately after the October election, consoled him on his defeat for Congress, and promised to back him for appointment to his own seat on the federal Mississippi River Commission (with a salary of $3,000), which Harrison would vacate upon entering the Senate. Gresham, on the other hand, made no contact with Taylor until prompted to do so by one of Taylor's lieutenants, and then he wrote simply, "You have doubtless heard that I will be a candidate before the Legislature for the Senatorship. . . . I shall make no combinations." Neither did he make any headway. A full month before the Republican legislative caucus he withdrew. Obviously bitter, he fiercely denied that Harrison's superior strength had forced him to give up. "My hands and feet were tied so to speak by the restraints of my position," he claimed. He excused his defeat by his own conscientious determination to do "nothing that was unbecoming a judge."[54]

   The Senate race went Harrison's way, but Indiana's representation in Garfield's cabinet remained an open question. Gresham felt that "having retired from the senatorial race it would not do for my name to be used for a Cabinet appointment and fail." But in response to promptings from political friends he "seemed to favor the proposition," although, as one put it, "with his usual manner of protesting against the probable success of the effort."[55]

   The prospect of his receiving a cabinet place was hardly less chimerical than that of his election to the Senate. Even his friends were at a loss as to how to demonstrate to Garfield that tapping Gresham would satisfy Indiana's cabinet claims. Organization men such as Assistant Postmaster General James N. Tyner, Republican state chairman John C. New, and United States Marshal William W. Dudley let it be known that they could live with the appointment of any Indianan except Gresham. Their opposition focused on the judge's past record of independence, his unwillingness to work openly for the party, and especially his conduct during the 1880 election. Dudley reported to Garfield that out of twenty-seven Hoosier Republican leaders who visited the president-elect in late January to press the state's cabinet claims, not one had expressed a preference for Gresham.[56]

Harrison took a more subtle stance. He told Garfield that Gresham did not really want a cabinet job but preferred instead to succeed Thomas Drummond as judge of the Seventh Circuit. In fact, Drummond told Harrison he endorsed Gresham for the cabinet, but Harrison failed to pass this information on to Garfield. Harrison warned the president-elect that state chairman New and others "would fight the nomination of Judge Gresham for any Cabinet place." "Should your mind incline in that direction *at all*," he pleaded, "please do nothing until I can see you." Harrison suggested that there were plenty of lesser offices through which the president could show "a generous appreciation" of Indiana's support.[57]

Gresham did have at least one powerful friend at court, Secretary of State–designate James G. Blaine. Blaine apparently had no inkling of Gresham's effort to have him "scotched" in 1876, for in the winter of 1881 he told Garfield that he thought *"very highly"* of the judge and consistently advocated his appointment as a representative of the Union veterans in the Republican party. Garfield was still "discussing Judge Gresham" when he arrived in Washington, but he soon received further evidence of Gresham's unacceptability. Republican national secretary Stephen W. Dorsey, who had played an important part in carrying Indiana in 1880 and had seen the judge's performance first-hand, denounced Gresham as "a democrat and a trimmer." "I have no words to express my abhorrence for the man," Dorsey wrote Garfield. "He is not fit for anything."[58]

But Blaine was persistent. On the morning of the inauguration he urged Garfield to select Gresham rather than Minnesota's William Windom for the Treasury Department, and Robert Ingersoll telegraphed Gresham to ascertain his attitude. Just at this time Tillie Gresham was gravely ill with uterine hemorrhaging, and Gresham feared for her life. He replied that at the moment he could think of nothing but his wife, but he gave no indication that he would refuse an appointment. Blaine informed Garfield that "Gresham will accept," but the president offered Windom the treasury post. On March 5 Gresham was still under consideration for secretary of the interior. That morning Garfield dispatched Blaine and Windom to survey feelings of Republicans in Washington toward Gresham and Iowa's Samuel J. Kirkwood. A few hours later the two returned and confirmed Garfield's judgment that Kirkwood was the "safest suggestion." In Indianapolis, meanwhile, Gresham had concluded that if Garfield should tender him an appointment he would decline. The offer never came.[59]

Aside from Mrs. Gresham's illness, Gresham felt there were "other good & sufficient reasons" for deciding against reentering political life in Garfield's administration. His nonpartisan course during the election had greatly offended those politicians who, in Gresham's words, "had an idea that the Federal Courts belonged to the Republican Party." "The plain truth," he confided to former Justice, now Senator David Davis, "is that many of the Republican politicians in this state think I am unsound on some questions, and they fear that I would not be a good party man in the Cabinet or in any other political position. They may not be far from right." A month after Garfield's inauguration he used the occasion of responding to a toast at the national reunion of the Army of the Tennessee to charge once again that "popular government" as practiced by American political parties had "degenerated" into a "petty and pitiful quarrel" over patronage. "Little can be accomplished in our politics without the aid of parties, but we need always to have in mind that they are instruments and not ends," he told the veterans. "In order to be wholesome," parties must aim "for the attainment of ends that concern the entire people." They "lose their value as well as their dignity when they are devoted solely to the acquisition and distribution of the offices of the Government."[60]

Such expressions reflected not only lofty ideals but personal disappointment and bitterness as well. Gresham knew that the opposition to his appointment in the new administration extended beyond such blatant spoilsmen as John C. New. He had no doubt that "in some way Harrison gave the President to understand that he didn't want me in the Cabinet." Harrison's rise to leadership among Hoosier Republicans had served to retard Gresham's political career. By the spring of 1881 it appeared to Gresham that Harrison's domination of the state party differed little from the control Morton had exercised. Just as he had complained of Morton's policy of proscription, he now charged that Harrison represented "the narrow and intolerant element in his party." And just as his opposition to Morton had been the central feature of his political career in the postwar years, his rivalry with Harrison would be a defining feature in the years to come.[61]

FOUR

POSTMASTER GENERAL
No Tranquillity or Happiness

By the early 1880s Gresham had grown uneasy in the district judgeship
and considered returning to the private practice of law. His failure to
reach either the Senate or the cabinet showed that it would be difficult
to fulfill such ambitions unless he resigned from the bench. Moreover,
the judicial workload had increased steadily since his appointment in
1869, but the $3,500 salary had remained the same. During 1881 he
held court for 253 days in addition to work done in chambers. At
Indianapolis alone he disposed of 423 cases and presided over 30 jury
trials. In early 1882 the Hoosier delegation in Congress sought to raise
his compensation but without success. Hence, at age fifty, having done
little to provide for his old age or the security of his family, Gresham
was attracted by the offer of a partnership from Joseph E. McDonald, a
Democrat whom Benjamin Harrison had succeeded in the Senate.[1]

Balancing these considerations were the comfort and lifetime security of a seat on the federal bench, where he was free to give full rein
to his independence of mind without fear of political reprisal. The
decision whether to stay on or resign was therefore difficult, but
fortunately circumstances suggested a way out: promotion to circuit
judge. Seventh Circuit Judge Thomas Drummond was over seventy,
and his retirement had been predicted for years. If Gresham could
move into the position, he would receive almost double his current
salary. By the spring of 1883 he had decided that if he could not be
reasonably certain of succeeding Drummond, he would resign and join
McDonald. In March John W. Foster, who had just been appointed
minister to Spain and had been a friend of Gresham since their days
together at Indiana University, laid the judge's case before President
Chester A. Arthur. When Arthur appeared amenable, Foster advised
Gresham not to accept McDonald's offer.[2]

Just at that moment, Arthur confronted a more immediate problem:
finding a new postmaster general to succeed Timothy O. Howe, who
had died on March 25. Since succeeding the assassinated James A.
Garfield in September 1881, Arthur had replaced all but one of the
cabinet secretaries; now he was forced to fill the politically sensitive

Post Office slot a second time. Recommendations flooded in, but his conference with Foster led the president to thoughts of Gresham. Foster observed that Gresham was qualified, but his appointment might be "impolitic" because Senator Harrison would probably oppose it. Nonetheless, Arthur and his advisers could agree on no other choice. On April 3 Foster wired the judge to ascertain his reaction. Gresham was surprised but indicated that he would take the position. Arthur immediately decided to appoint him, selecting Harrison to convey the news to Gresham, a task the senator no doubt executed with distaste. Gresham accepted the next day. Here, indeed, was an office that had sought the man. Unexpectedly and effortlessly Gresham walked onto the national stage.[3]

The appointment met with wide approval. The *New York Times* hailed Gresham as a "discovery." Speaking for reformers, the *Nation* expressed satisfaction that Gresham had never belonged to "the class of narrow-minded, hide-bound politicians." Even the *Indianapolis Journal*, whose proprietor, John C. New, disdained Gresham as a lukewarm partisan, obliquely commended his selection as a "recognition of the services and importance of the Republican party of Indiana in the person of one of its native and distinguished sons."[4]

Gresham lost no time in setting off for Washington. He refused the offer of a private railroad car and won plaudits from the crowd at the depot when he remarked that he would rather walk to the capital than accept such a favor. He arrived on April 10. Since Foster was about to take up his duties in Madrid, the two men arranged for the Greshams to rent the minister's Washington residence.[5]

Tillie and the two children, both in their early twenties, joined Gresham in May. Otto enrolled in the law department of Columbian (later George Washington) University. He was graduated in the spring of 1884 and joined the Indianapolis law firm of railroad attorney Charles W. Fairbanks. Kate assisted her mother in entertaining and took responsibility for managing the household's financial affairs. The full social season that went with cabinet life was a new but not uncongenial experience for the family. One old friend soon observed that "Mrs. Gresham and Kate are rather elevated by the social position they enjoy here and would like very much for it to continue." Tillie and Kate attended the fashionable New York Avenue Presbyterian Church, where they heard sermons by their old Indianapolis pastor, William A. Bartlett. Gresham attended less regularly. Although his earlier agnosticism had softened, he remained wary of organized religion and on one occasion dismissed a sermon by Bartlett on "the apparent conflict between science and religion" as "a flat talk."[6]

More to his liking were the visits from Justice John Marshall Harlan, who often dropped in at the Gresham house after church. Within a few blocks lived several Republican leaders with whom the Greshams enjoyed friendly relations: Senator John Sherman, General William T. Sherman, Navy Secretary William E. Chandler, and Senator Justin S. Morrill. Chief Justice Morrison R. Waite lived next door. Gresham soon found a place at the card tables at Chamberlain's restaurant, where he earned a reputation as a poker "sharp" as he relaxed with Matthew S. Quay, William Mahone, Henry Watterson, and others. He was soon described as "very *solid* with the President." Before leaving office, Gresham told Noble Butler that Arthur had said "that he had formed no friendship since he was twenty-five years of age equal to what he felt for me."[7]

Arthur left management of the Post Office Department largely to Gresham. As historian Leonard D. White aptly notes, that department was "par excellence the home of routine." With innovation limited to refinements and improvements in the basic postal machinery, the most the average postmaster general could hope for was to avoid scandal and to amass a record for competence as an administrator. Gresham did both. "This Department . . . is a very exacting one," he wrote after a year. "I work very hard, but have been accustomed to that all my life. My health is good, and I weigh 190 pounds—more than I ever weighed before."[8]

Although Gresham understood the political uses of department patronage, his record in the area of civil service reform was creditable. In early 1883 Congress had passed the Pendleton Civil Service Act, which marked the beginning of the merit system in the federal bureaucracy. It fell largely to Gresham to launch the new system in the Post Office Department, where he demanded strict adherence to the act's provisions and to departmental regulations. He vigorously enforced the ban on the circulation of political assessment letters within the department and promised to protect any postmaster in the field who refused to make a contribution solicited by such circulars. Moreover, although he did permit postmasters to serve on local political committees, he debarred their service on any such committee that accepted political contributions from federal employees.[9]

One of Gresham's main concerns was that postmasters' participation in politics not be detrimental to their duties. In Indiana he discouraged postmasters from outlying counties from serving on the Republican state committee because frequent trips to Indianapolis might lead them to neglect their offices. He even risked Arthur's displeasure by ordering Readjuster postmasters and other postal officials in Virginia to stop

making extended political speaking tours. These men had been appointed at the behest of Senator William Mahone, whose anti-Bourbon
coalition enjoyed the president's hearty support. Nonetheless, Gresham told them, "I cannot allow you liberties which are denied to other
postmasters. To do otherwise would be wrong, and would embarrass
the Department."[10]

Gresham also took considerable risk in firing Paul Vandervoort,
national commander of the Grand Army of the Republic (GAR), for
neglecting his duty as chief clerk of the Railway Mail Service at Omaha.
Vandervoort had made an arrangement with Gresham's predecessor
whereby he could be absent on GAR business and still collect his postal
salary, but Gresham refused to sanction the special treatment. The
dismissal set off a wave of protest from veterans and politicians alike.
As the first private to reach the office of grand commander, Vandervoort enjoyed enormous popularity with the GAR rank and file.
Gresham was unmoved, however, and told critics: "Good soldiers did
not like shirks during the war, nor do they believe in shirks in the civil
service."[11]

Gresham also resisted strong political pressure to dismiss employees whose services he valued. A few months after he took office several
clerks in the Railway Mail Service at Indianapolis clamored for the
removal of their division superintendent, C. Jay French, whom they
charged with favoritism and tyranny. French's chief fault seems to have
been making the clerks work; many of them, one reporter told Gresham, had come to view the mail service as "a sort of a political lying-in
hospital intended expressly for their pleasant leisure." Since many of
the complaining employees were Union veterans, their cause was
taken up by GAR leaders and Republican politicians and newspapermen. Gresham ignored warnings from the *Indianapolis Journal*'s John C.
New that keeping French in office would bring disaster to Hoosier
Republicans. He named a five-man investigating commission, which
after a month of hearings found no foundation for the allegations. An
efficient officer was thus saved, but Gresham reaped still more animosity among party regulars.[12]

Other actions Gresham took won praise from civil service reformers.
Over the protest of applicants he stuck to the rule that all clerkships in
the department at Washington must be filled by examination. He made
it an "invariable rule" not to interfere in local postmasters' selection of
their subordinates so that he could hold the postmasters responsible
for the management of their offices. In addition, he reduced the clerk
allowance for some of the nation's largest post offices and demanded
more efficient use of fewer employees. When he left the department,

Civil Service Commissioner Dorman Eaton, who had drafted the Pendleton Act, commended him for "the great value of the support which you gave to the cause of Civil Service Reform at its weakest stages. Your friendly encouragement, your rebuke of those who were willing to embarrass the commission, & your vigorous support of the extension of the rules in the P.O. Department were a great assistance."[13]

Gresham also took several steps to revamp department management and improve the country's mail service. For instance, he introduced competitive bidding for the purchase of supplies for local post offices. He secured an increase in the standard weight for first-class mail from one-half ounce to an ounce. Since only 6 percent of letters weighed more than half an ounce, there would be little loss of revenue, and that loss would be more than offset by patrons' sealing small packages formerly sent fourth class.[14]

Among the unfinished business inherited by the Arthur administration was the prosecution of the so-called Star Route Frauds, a conspiracy dating from the 1870s in which postal officials had allowed enormous increases in compensation to contractors for mail service in the sparsely settled West for little or no increase in service. Although the government met little success in prosecuting the alleged conspirators, Gresham sought to correct abuses in the Star Route service by regulating contracts more closely. Traditionally, speculators based in Washington would bid on and obtain numerous route contracts, which, to make a profit, they would then sublet to carriers at compensation so low as to make it virtually impossible for the subcontractors to provide adequate service. To curb this practice Gresham devised new regulations requiring contractors to obtain the postmaster general's permission for each subcontract, prescribing the form of the subcontract to be used, requiring the subcontractor to reside along the contract route, and banning subsubcontracts. His aim was to place greater responsibility on actual carriers. In addition, the department prepared legislation to require readvertisement for any so-called expedition of service, rather than merely increasing the contractor's compensation.[15]

Gresham considered his most important success in the Post Office Department to be the negotiation of revised railroad schedules to give greater speed to the mails between the East Coast and Chicago and points west. At 8:30 in the evening on March 8, 1884, the postmaster general boarded the first fast train out of New York, which reached Chicago the middle of the next night. The innovation met virulent criticism from midwestern newspapermen who feared competition from the large Chicago morning dailies. The New York train arrived in

Chicago at 12:40 A.M., and the outbound trains left at 3:00. Charging that the reason for the delay was to await the Chicago newspapers, the *Indianapolis Journal* labeled the new system a "screaming forty-mile-an-hour farce." But Gresham was not deterred, and the rapid mail transit shaved a day off delivery time between New York and San Francisco.[16]

The proposition that the federal government should assume control of the country's telegraph system had been debated ever since the invention of the instrument. In the 1880s the public's chief complaint against Western Union, which had acquired a near-monopoly, was the company's high rates, which it allegedly used to pay high dividends on masses of watered stock. The political potential of the issue was patent to observers such as James G. Blaine, who urged Gresham to advocate a government takeover. "Don't wait until everybody demands postal telegraphy," Blaine wrote. "Pioneer it and push it! No ambition is more legitimate than to secure popularity by doing the bold thing at the right time." The issue pulled Gresham two ways. He found reprehensible the monopoly control exercised by Western Union, which, he believed, charged "unreasonable" rates "solely for the purpose of making money." But he saw government takeover as a violation of the sacred precepts of frugality and limited government. Unlike Blaine, who conceived an activist role for government, Gresham clung to a more Jeffersonian view. "I am somewhat old-fashioned in my ideas about public affairs," he wrote John Foster as he rolled the matter over in his mind. "The great danger to popular institutions is extravagance."[17]

In his 1883 annual report Gresham defended the constitutionality of a government telegraph based on Congress's authority to establish post roads and regulate commerce, but he nonetheless opposed the scheme. A postal telegraph, he argued, would entail an increase in patronage so large as to "threaten the purity and duration of our institutions." Moreover, "in seasons of political excitement," such a system, "under the exclusive control of the dominant party, might be abused to promote partisan purposes and perpetuate the power of an administration." As a "first step in a dangerous direction," postal telegraphy might lead to federal incorporation, or even acquisition, of railroads and other companies. "The injurious tendency of such legislation cannot well be overestimated," he concluded. He believed a solution might lie in government regulation, including the setting of overall rates and the banning of future consolidations of private telegraph lines. As he continued to monitor Western Union, he admitted that "it may be that unless the company yields in some way, the Government will be impelled to intervene." Meanwhile, he did strike a blow for cheaper telegraphy; as the official responsible for setting the rates paid by the government, he cut those rates in half. "It may cause some friction," he said, "but I think the Western Union cannot afford to act ugly at this time."[18]

Gresham's most frustrating failure as postmaster general was his fight against the Louisiana Lottery Company. Unlike the telegraphy issue, here was a classic case of acceptable application of government power—the protection of citizens from "a business which is vicious and immoral, and which in the main preys upon the ignorant and the credulous."[19]

Under federal law the postmaster general could forbid delivery of registered letters or the payment of postal money orders to any person "conducting any fraudulent lottery." In 1879 Postmaster General David M. Key had issued such a ban against M.A. Dauphin, head of the Louisiana Lottery. Dauphin appealed the ban to the United States Supreme Court and, pending the outcome, presented Key with documents from Louisiana officials certifying that the lottery was not "fraudulent" under state law. Consequently, in February 1880, Key directed the "suspension" of the ban "until the case shall have been heard and determined by the supreme court." Early in the Garfield administration the lottery officials dropped the appeal on the grounds that Key had left office. In this legal limbo the business flourished until Gresham decided to challenge its use of the mails. Drawing on old habits, which prompted his former court clerk Noble Butler to note "how conspicuous the Judge is in the Postmaster General," he granted a hearing of arguments presented by lawyers for the lottery and for the government. He concluded that dropping the appeal had restored Key's original ban, and he again barred Dauphin from receiving registered letters and money orders.[20]

Dauphin immediately initiated a civil suit against Gresham, asking $100,000 damages for malicious interference with his legitimate business. More important, he advertised that all registered letters and money orders intended for him should be directed to the New Orleans National Bank. Gresham promptly ordered a similar ban against the bank, but the lottery's lawyers secured a court order enjoining the New Orleans postmaster from interfering with the bank's mail service. Federal Judge Don Pardee denied the validity of Gresham's order against Dauphin on the grounds that Key had revoked, not suspended, the original ban in 1880. Pardee also ruled that Gresham's order against the bank was "unsupported by law" because it was not aimed at a fraudulent lottery but at a "scheme to evade the orders of the postmaster general in relation to Dauphin's mail." Pardee's decision thus seemingly consigned the lottery to a legal never-never land beyond the reach of the postmaster general.[21]

Thus hamstrung, Gresham prodded the Justice Department to

bring criminal proceedings against Dauphin. Section 3894 of the federal statutes stipulated that "no letter or circular concerning lotteries" or other such schemes "shall be carried in the mail" and declared punishable "any person who shall knowingly deposit or send anything to be conveyed by mail in violation of this section." But the government's case was thrown out by federal Judge Edward Billings, who ruled that the law prohibited the carrying of lottery circulars "after the prohibited article has been deposited in the mail, and could not include the naked sending to the post office, which is alone charged in the informations." "Of course it is plain," the *New York Times*, noted sarcastically, "that the Department—and not Dauphin and the Louisiana Lottery Company— has been violating the law!" Sure that Billings had a personal stake in the lottery, Gresham told Supreme Court Justice John M. Harlan that the ruling was "perfectly preposterous." Nonetheless, an effort to secure a broader interpretation of the statute by the high court got nowhere.[22]

On the legislative front, Gresham asked Congress to strike the word "fraudulent" before "lottery" in the statutes so that Dauphin could no longer hide behind Louisiana law. He also asked for legislation banning from the mails newspapers and other publications carrying lottery advertisements—a recommendation that caused friction with his first assistant, Frank Hatton, whose *National Republican*, published in Washington, carried such advertisements. Opponents in Congress raised cries of states' rights and freedom of the press, and neither measure passed.[23]

Gresham looked on his fight against the Louisiana Lottery as a crusade against an enterprise that "the moral sense of the nation condemns." The crusade failed. Indeed, the 1880s proved one of the most prosperous periods for the concern. It did not fall until the 1890s, when it lost the protection of state law and Congress banned all lottery material not only from the mails but from all forms of interstate commerce.[24]

As postmaster general, Gresham showed himself to be an able administrator, but Arthur's original motive for appointing him probably had less to do with his administrative capacity than with political considerations. Although Arthur turned out to be a better president than his previous record had given most people cause to expect, he had failed to win much genuine popularity, either within his party or in the country at large. Blaine's Half-Breed faction could not forget that his accession to the presidency in the "lottery of assassination" had cut short its hopes for a brilliant administration under Garfield. On the other hand, the president's refusal to clear out Garfield's appointees wholesale had alienated such old Stalwart friends as Roscoe Conkling and Thomas C. Platt. And independents and reformers in the party still harbored reservations about Arthur's prepresidential record as a blatant spoilsman. In selecting Timothy Howe's replacement as postmaster general, the president hoped to make no more enemies and lose no more friends. Gresham was a longtime friend of General Grant, he had backed the reformer Benjamin Bristow in 1876, and Blaine had backed him for Garfield's cabinet. Hence his entrance into Arthur's cabinet seemed well suited to assuage intraparty animosities.[25]

But the appointment also had the effect of undercutting Gresham's Hoosier rival Benjamin Harrison, whose rapid rise posed a potential threat to any desire Arthur might have for the 1884 nomination. Since Arthur had assumed the presidency, Harrison had watched the patronage influence he had enjoyed under Garfield dwindle; the elevation of his chief antagonist to the government's most powerful job-dispensing office was the coup de grâce. Gresham did not hesitate to diminish the senator's influence. The first victory came in the selection of his own successor as district judge, when he persuaded Arthur to appoint another man over Harrison's Indianapolis law partner. Harrison soon found that the Post Office Department ignored his recommendations for the Railway Mail Service, one of the important bureaus untouched by the new Civil Service Act. He fared little better in other branches of the service and consequently withdrew from patronage matters. "As the old practice of referring these cases to the Senator for recommendations has been abandoned in my case," he explained to one frustrated officeseeker, "I should feel afraid to urge appointments." After a year in office Gresham understated the case when he told Noble Butler that "Harrison is growling a good deal." The tables had been turned, and with a vengeance.[26]

Gresham thus served Arthur well in checking Harrison, but ironically he himself rose in the public estimation as a potential rival to the president. A few weeks after his appointment, Supreme Court Justice John M. Harlan, traveling on the court circuit in the Midwest, reported that "there is in this section a wide-spread conviction that you may be selected to lead the Republican hosts in 1884." David Davis, Abraham Lincoln's manager in 1860, likewise wrote Gresham of his "strong faith that your selection will be deemed the wisest." Such talk was symptomatic of a widespread dissatisfaction with the current state of politics. As the *New York Times* put it, "It is as if the people, weary of looking over the familiar dreariness of the political landscape in which the same old 'landmarks' loom up, wearyingly persistent, hailed each freshly discovered and possible statesman with the cry, 'Why is not this the coming man?' " This feeling pervaded the Republican party, for recent setbacks augured disaster in 1884. In 1882 the Democrats had won 60 percent of the seats in the national House of Representatives—their largest majority since 1852. Especially ominous were Democratic victories in the former Republican bastions of Pennsylvania, Massachusetts, Michigan, Kansas, and Ohio. The onset of an economic slump dimmed party hopes still further. Arthur seemed an unlikely prospect to head a comeback, and Blaine, his chief rival, though widely popular, was distrusted by enough people to make his election doubtful. Hence, according to the *Times,* "People were delighted that another great man should have been found, and they began to ask, Why is not this the next President?"[27]

Gresham quite properly dismissed such talk and urged would-be supporters to turn their energies toward securing the nomination of President Arthur. To indulge aspirations of his own would be an act of disloyalty to his chief. But loyalty aside, he recognized that the nomination would most likely be an empty honor. Defeat in the October 1883 election in Ohio deepened the sense of gloom; there the Republican legislature's proposal of a prohibiton amendment to the state constitution had cost the party thousands of votes among the state's German immigrants. Gresham believed the efforts of temperance advocates to commit the party to prohibition could result only in further losses.[28]

Republican gains in New York and other states in the November elections brightened the party's prospects but did not alter Gresham's feelings on the presidential question. Indeed, at the end of 1883 he confessed, "The more I see of politics the less desire I have to remain in political life. It might not be so if great political questions separated the parties. Now there is little or nothing at stake which appeals to the judgment and conscience of the people." He toyed with the idea of returning to law practice when it came time to leave the cabinet, but what he wanted most was to succeed Judge Thomas Drummond on the federal circuit bench at Chicago. The timing of Drummond's resignation was crucial, however, for Arthur was reluctant to appoint a new postmaster general before the Republican convention in June, and other judicial aspirants were willing to don Drummond's robes at any time. In March Gresham and Drummond reached an understanding whereby Drummond would submit his resignation with the stipulation that it should take effect only upon the appointment of his successor. As it turned out, the judge took longer than expected to complete his work and did not resign until late June.[29]

Political enemies such as Benjamin Harrison naturally concluded that Gresham wanted to hold the judgeship "open to drop into if he gets no place on the national ticket." Even Noble Butler, who had always advocated Gresham's return to the bench, began to see a political motive creep into his friend's thinking, which Gresham was quick to disavow. "I have no aspirations for a Presidential nomination," he wrote in January. Even so, he continued to receive intimations of support that made his selection not inconceivable. In October Blaine had written encouragingly of his "political future," assuring Gresham that "you need not restrain your aspirations." In early 1884 the former secretary of state made what Gresham described as "a square proposition," offering his support for the nomination in exchange for his old cabinet post. Gresham replied that he could not consider such a deal.[30]

But he rejected the arrangement not merely out of loyalty to Arthur or repugnance for Blaine or lack of ambition. Although he remained loath to admit it, he was not immune to presidential fever. He realized, however, that any hope he had for the nomination lay not in jumping from Arthur's ship but in staying on and attracting second-choice support among the president's backers. Arthur was weak in the party, and Gresham might become, as the New York Times predicted, "the political heir of the Administration." The situation was delicate, and Gresham enlisted the assistance of John W. Foster, who offered to return from Madrid, ostensibly on State Department business but in reality "to aid in turning the tide." "Of course you understand that the President is anxious to succeed himself," Gresham told Foster. "I must say, however, that I do not believe he will be nominated. He will have a majority of the New York delegates, but the minority will be so active and resentful, that delegates from other states will be afraid of trouble in New York [Arthur's home state] if the President is made the standard bearer." Hence, said Gresham, "it is both my duty and my interest" to do "everything in my power to aid him in his aspirations." Foster agreed, and long before the minister arrived in April, Gresham had launched a campaign to round up support for Arthur or, in the event he should fail, for himself.[31]

For Gresham's purposes the most important base of support was Indiana. Not only was it his home state, but it also was, along with New York, one of the most important of the so-called "doubtful" states. Because it was a toss-up in any presidential election, party leaders fought especially hard to win its fifteen electoral votes, and many saw placing a Hoosier on the national ticket as a means to that end. But winning the state's delegation to the national convention would not be easy because Harrison was also considered a potential candidate. Moreover, Harrison was free to pursue his ambition openly, whereas

Gresham's commitment to Arthur required him to proceed by indirection. His proposed strategy was to work for delegates who were "thoughtful men," who would go to the Chicago convention "for consultation and with a determination to nominate a capable and at the same time the most available man." "If the interest of the party requires the nomination of some one out side of our own state," he told Foster's Evansville friend T.R. McFerson, "there should be no hesitation. Of course I hope the President may succeed." McFerson agreed: "Your friends all understand that you are not a candidate, but the time may come in the Chicago Convention when it may be advisable to make you one and we want men there who will be friendly to you and take advantage of it."[32]

This strategy collided with a similar one pursued by Harrison's backers, who sought delegates friendly to the senator's as yet unannounced candidacy. The spring witnessed a fierce contest between the two camps. Gresham's control of federal patronage proved a valuable asset, and Harrison's managers complained of losing supporters who "suffered from 'the Explosive force of a Post Office.'" But Harrison had the help of the *Indianapolis Journal*, whose proprietor John C. New had long disliked Gresham and hated him after his appointment as postmaster general had thwarted New's own cabinet ambitions. Harrison's law partner candidly admitted that the two were anxious "to see that Gresham is not foisted on the country as a representative of Indiana." The first test of strength came in the selection of delegates in the state's thirteen congressional districts. Neither Harrison nor Gresham could claim a clear victory in the district conventions. Each had the support of a loyal core among the twenty-six delegates, with the remainder apparently willing to go to either man if he should receive the support of other states. At the state level Gresham at first opposed Harrison's selection as a delegate-at-large because he would try to prevent Indiana from uniting behind Gresham in the event of Arthur's failure or might conduct himself so as to attract the favor of a deadlocked convention as Garfield had done in 1880. But on the eve of the state convention it was clear that Harrison could be kept off the delegation only with a fight, and Gresham told his supporters to offer no opposition. In the convention's only square contest between the two factions, Gresham's New Albany friend Morris McDonald defeated Harrison's man Will Cumback.[33]

Once the delegates had been chosen, Gresham and his allies set about wooing those who were wavering. He flattered them by soliciting their views and offering them railroad passes to visit Washington to discuss the "situation" face to face. For some, such visits even included interviews with the president, for it was, of course, for Arthur's benefit that Gresham labored. The work was not easy; former Postmaster General James N. Tyner reported that there was "very little support for Arthur in Indiana, or in our delegation." Gresham assured skeptical delegates that Arthur was "a sensible, self-respecting man," whose "justice towards all shades of opinion in the party" had saved it from "disruption and consequent ruin." He urged those who could not forget Arthur's years as a spoilsman in the New York machine to judge the president "by his public acts, rather than by what he said or did" before assuming office. "You would like the President better if you knew him better," he pleaded. Clear on where his own chances lay, Gresham continued to tell the Hoosiers, "I do hope we will be able to give Arthur a good vote in our state."[34]

Gresham also kept close account of other candidates. He considered Ohio's John Sherman "perhaps . . . the best equipped man in public life" and Vermont's Senator George F. Edmunds "a fit man—in every sense—for the office," but he knew neither commanded much serious support. He saw John A. Logan of Illinois as a pawn used by Blaine to keep votes from Arthur. Blaine posed the real threat. To delegates who leaned toward Blaine, Gresham cited the opposition to his candidacy in Massachusetts and New York and the unyielding hostility of Republican independents. In the South the administration placed great reliance on federal officeholders. Gresham joined in applying patronage in these rotten boroughs, although he believed "a large proportion" of the southern delegates to be "unmitigated scoundrels" who would sell their votes to the highest bidder in the convention.[35]

New York was crucial to Arthur's candidacy. Gresham had always suspected the president's support in his home state was "not as hearty as it should be," and in fact Arthur won only a plurality of its delegates. Blaine took almost as many, and a smaller but still substantial bloc went to the independents, who favored Edmunds. In the latter group Gresham himself probably enjoyed more support than the president. He hesitated to plead his own case to these men, however, for fear of doing "anything that would afford opportunity for saying that I am in the attitude of a candidate." Instead he suggested that "it might answer the purpose" if Foster met with them. Benjamin Bristow, Noble Butler, and Associated Press chief William Henry Smith all urged his merits on George William Curtis, a New York delegate. Although Curtis remained committed to Edmunds, he expressed friendliness for Gresham, and New York Evening Post editor Horace White said, "Gresham would suit us perfectly."[36]

While this work went forward, Gresham made a quick trip to the

Northeast to argue Arthur's case with delegates and party leaders. In
New York he found little support among the president's former col-
leagues in the party's Stalwart wing. Indeed, Stalwart leader Thomas
C. Platt told him that he intended to back Blaine. Since Platt and Roscoe
Conkling had an abiding hatred of Blaine, Gresham inferred that they
perversely were willing to see the party wrecked rather than support
Arthur, who they believed had betrayed them in matters of patronage.
Gresham had only somewhat better luck among the state's indepen-
dents. Still, he believed the tide was turning in Arthur's favor in New
York, especially among the city's businessmen. He helped organize a
businessmen's rally for the president and persuaded Bristow to address the gathering at Cooper Union. In Boston Gresham met with
Henry Cabot Lodge and other delegates but won few if any commitments to Arthur. But because Blaine had virtually no support in Massachusetts and several delegates were only lukewarm toward Edmunds,
Gresham believed there was hope for the president.[37]

As Gresham surveyed the nomination race in the last few weeks
before the national convention, all was confusion. On May 22 he wrote
Noble Butler that it "looks now like Arthur would be nominated on the
second ballot, if not the first." Yet on June 1, just two days before the
opening of the convention, he confessed to Butler, "I hope that Arthur
will pull through but I hardly expect him to have so much strength." In
the midst of the uncertainty, his own undeclared candidacy remained
alive as a second-choice compromise between Arthur's backers and the
independents. In the final preconvention week he and John W. Foster
assembled a discreet team to manage his interests in Chicago, including Butler, Charles W. Fairbanks, Robert G. Ingersoll, and John M.
Harlan. Gresham urged his Indiana supporters to turn out in force at
Chicago to demonstrate that Harrison was not "the only man in our
state."[38]

Yet even while engaging in these patently self-interested maneu-
vers, Gresham adhered to the position that nothing should be done
that "would afford any pretext for charging me with not keeping faith
with the President." He told newsmen that he "would as soon think of
picking the President's pocket as remaining a member of his official
household and scheming against him." Such statements were not
merely cynical or self-serving but indeed reflected Gresham's real
pangs of conscience and genuine discomfort. At no other time had his
ambition and resignation, his sense of destiny and his sense of propriety, torn at him so mercilessly. As the convention approached,
Noble Butler saw him sink into "nervous depression." In a letter to
William A. Woods, his successor as district judge, he lashed out at the

inanity and viciousness of political life: "I am not expecting the nomination, nor am I anxious about it. . . . I know there is no tranquility or
happiness for any self-respecting man while occupying the high office.
No great questions agitate the public mind; and there is little but sharp,
disagreeable and disgusting contests for place between men. The more
I see of political life at Washington, the less attractive it is to me. You
encounter insincerity and meanness every day."[39]

Nonetheless, when delegates and others poured into Chicago for
the convention, Gresham's name continued to appear on lists of possible nominees. Shop windows sported his picture among the hopefuls,
although because he had refused to release a more suitable pho-
tograph, one friend reported, his likeness was in the form of "some
hideous lithographs" whose "artist ought *to be shot*." From Chicago
Foster assured him that his supporters would do nothing "to compromise you with [the] President" and that they were giving Arthur
"earnest support" and resisting the "Harrison movement on that basis."[40]

Harrison's position, like Gresham's, was that of a potential dark
horse. The most important tactical question for the Harrison men was
whether to have Indiana present him as a formal candidate at the
outset. In the delegation's first caucus at Chicago, Gresham's managers
defeated such a proposal by a vote of sixteen to fourteen. But the next
day Harrison's men returned with a nonbinding resolution for the
senator's nomination, which passed, sixteen to fourteen, although
twelve Gresham delegates indicated they would not vote for Harrison.
The senator, believing he was to be placed in nomination, went home,
but the Gresham delegates persisted in their opposition. It was, however, the objection of the Blaine people that finally convinced Harrison's men to abandon an open candidacy. They had always expected
support from Blaine in the event of a deadlock, but Blaine's managers
complained that Harrison was keeping needed Indiana votes away
from the Maine leader. Gresham's supporters gleefully pronounced
Harrison "a dead cock in the pit," but in reality their victory was
Pyrrhic. They could not hope for a delegation united behind Gresham
after their humiliating treatment of the senator.[41]

In the convention's main contest, reporters' early polls showed
Blaine thirty or forty votes ahead of Arthur and less than a hundred
away from a majority. Arthur could still win with skillful management,
but that his convention forces lacked. Chief responsibility lay with
Assistant Postmaster General Frank Hatton and Commissioner of Internal Revenue Walter Evans. The convention was barely under way
when Gresham began receiving reports of their incompetence. They

bungled the selection of nominating speakers and failed to keep the president's southern base intact. Arthur's troubles might have inured to Gresham's benefit but for the dubious accessibility of his delegates even in the unlikely event that Hatton, who had little love for Gresham, should release them. A large number were impecunious southern officeholders, some of whom apparently fell under the sway of the Blaine men, who were rumored to have arrived in Chicago "loaded with money." The only other important source of potential support for Gresham was the independents, who arrived in Chicago still committed to Edmunds. These men took fierce pride in their resistance to disciplined organization and were thus less likely even than the Arthur delegates to be shifted en masse from their first choice to another candidate.[42]

On Friday, June 6, the convention took four ballots and Blaine led them all. Never did the Arthur men and the independents come close to a coalition. Meanwhile, at the White House it was meeting day for the cabinet, and attention focused on the telegraph. "The steady gains of Mr. Blaine on the third ballot," observed one reporter, "brought an evident shade of uneasiness over all faces, except perhaps that of the Postmaster General, who puffed his cigar with imperturbable coolness, occasionally exchanging a few words with the President and Secretary [of War Robert T.] Lincoln." Logan's withdrawal in Blaine's favor on the fourth ballot cinched his nomination.[43]

After Blaine's nomination Foster telegraphed Gresham: "Am pressed on all sides to authorize use of your name for Vice President. Shall we do so? Answer quick." He replied that he did "not want it in any event" and suggested that "Harrison would go well with Blaine." But the senator also declined, and the Blaine men turned to Logan, who won the nomination easily. Gresham later confessed that he would have accepted the second spot if tendered but said he could not have assumed the role of a candidate and become "liable to be defeated and humiliated."[44]

The long shot had not paid off for Gresham. He found solace in the claim that he had "kept faith" with Arthur "to the last degree." On the afternoon Blaine was nominated, Gresham recalled, the president "took me into a private room, thanked me for having stood by him, and said he did not believe many men in this selfish world would have been as loyal as I had under the same circumstances." Yet Arthur's gratitude did not change Gresham's belief that the president's "imbecile" managers had done him a great disservice in return. Once it had become clear that Arthur could not win, Gresham wrote David Davis, "if the President's forces had then been promptly thrown in favor of some one else," Blaine "might have been defeated," that is, Gresham might have been nominated. He also blamed his and Arthur's defeat on that "queer set," the independents: "Men of good, hard sense will take the best they can get when they are not able to get just what they want."[45]

But Gresham reserved his deepest resentment for Harrison, whose on-again, off-again candidacy, he charged, had been designed to prevent Gresham's emerging as a compromise nominee. The allegation was not groundless; after the convention Harrison wrote his manager, L.T. Michener: "I did not hope for success—but as I had often said to you, there was an Indiana aspect of the question in which I felt a very deep interest. I felt that had been taken care of—and was glad to have you give our state an advanced standing in securing the nomination of Mr. Blaine." Although Gresham's friends criticized Harrison for his "*hari kari* act in the clown's cap and bells," the Blaine men remembered his help and returned the favor four years later.[46]

Now that the administration's days were numbered, Gresham once again wrestled with career options. He might return to the circuit judgeship with its isolation from the uncertainties of politics. And yet the outcome at Chicago had left him with a residue of political ambition and desire for revenge. One friend urged him to "stay in politics and eat bean soup" if necessary "to get even with these cutthroats at Indianapolis who adhere to Harrison." While mulling over the judgeship, he wrote several friends that he soon expected to return to Indiana, practice law, "attend a few conventions," and generally "take some part in political matters." He flirted with the idea of running for governor until advisers warned him that injecting his name into an already well-defined field of candidates would be "a terrible mistake" that could end only in "a disgraceful defeat." He did not want to run for governor but later explained that he had not sent an absolute declination because "some of Mr. Blaine's friends suspect, or assume to suspect, the administration of not being entirely friendly to the national ticket. . . . If I had said I would not accept the nomination if it were offered me, evil-disposed persons might have had some grounds for charging that I was not willing to exert myself in behalf of the party."[47]

In fact, the Blaine people were justified in their suspicions. Gresham still thought Blaine appealed to "all the worst elements in the country," and he sympathized with "a widespread feeling among intelligent Republicans" that Democratic nominee Grover Cleveland was "a courageous, clean, well-meaning man." As a cabinet officer who had been prominently mentioned for the nomination, he felt "compelled" to "support the ticket as well as I can," but in fact he did very little. In mid-July he contemplated making a few speeches on the "outrages" in the

South, but he never did. Civil service reformers urged him to speak, and he "half agreed" to fill some campaign appointments in Massachusetts, but again he failed to follow through. He assured Maine Senator Eugene Hale that Blaine's protectionist arguments were popular with Indiana manufacturing interests, but he was less than candid, for his own beliefs inclined toward tariff reduction. A week later he confided to Noble Butler that if he spoke at all he was "against discussing the tariff issue." In late August both the chairman and the secretary of the Republican national committee and many others urged him to take to the stump, but he answered that official duties kept him in Washington.[48]

Try as he might, Gresham could not overcome his antipathy for Blaine. "I tried to write out something taking a charitable view of the [Mulligan] letters &c. but could not satisfy myself," he confessed to Butler. "I cannot defend his conduct." Nor did he marshal the vast resources of his department for the ticket. After the election former Postmaster General James N. Tyner complained that the Post Office Department, usually "second in importance and power only to a National Committee," had been "useless under Gresham."[49]

But whatever his feelings for Blaine, Gresham believed he had a legitimate justification for eschewing a public role in the campaign—the prospect of returning to the judiciary. He rejected several attractive offers to return to practice, including one to become chief counsel for the Chicago and North Western Railroad at a salary of $15,000. "I never realized what it was to be independent," he wrote Butler in early September. "I can't bear the idea of being a corporation's man—obliged to stand up [for] it right or wrong." Thus he was not totally disingenuous when he wrote Blaine that it was "the opinion of Judge Drummond & others whose judgment I respect, that I should not go upon the stump if, in a short time, I am to go upon the bench."[50]

But his decision to take Drummond's place was not to be acted on immediately, for the death of Treasury Secretary Charles J. Folger in early September raised a minor crisis in Arthur's cabinet. When he had difficulty finding someone to take the job for the administration's few remaining months, Arthur asked Gresham to assume the portfolio. Gresham preferred the judgeship, but when the president made it "a personal request," he yielded, with the stipulation that he be appointed judge within twenty days. Arthur agreed to continue his search for a permanent replacement. Gresham was sworn in as secretary of the treasury at eleven o'clock on the night of September 24, just an hour before the expiration of the time in which the president was legally bound to fill the vacancy.[51]

Although his transfer won general approval from businessmen, Gresham regarded it as "not a matter for congratulation." He had no time to learn the department's business and was still deluged with requests to make political speeches. The Blaine men, eager for some sign of administration support, especially called on him to address a businessmen's mass meeting in New York. He at first declined, but after intense pressure from party leaders he agreed to make a short speech.[52]

The occasion was a huge rally in the Wall Street district. Although other speakers glorified Blaine and protectionism, Gresham avoided the usual stump grandiloquence and made subtle departures from the platform's high-tariff position. "The public credit," he noted, "has been so firmly established and the debt so largely reduced that we can now safely reduce taxation. . . . The steady development of the country and the growth of its trade and commerce will increase the revenues under existing laws. There is, therefore, no necessity for maintaining our present rate of taxation." He conceded that in "revising our tariff laws and reducing our customs revenues, home interests should not be neglected." But, he added, "protection to our manufacturers and laborers can and should be afforded by taxing only such imports as come into real competition with them, and admitting others free." To some listeners, Gresham's ideas may have seemed more in line with the Democratic platform, but he assured them that it was "safer to trust" the Republicans to effect tariff reduction. "No intelligent man need be told that the weight of opinion in the Democratic party is decidedly opposed to the protective principle, but that if in full possession of the Government it would refuse to enact or maintain protective tariff laws." Having gone as far as he was willing to go in defense of protectionism, he added that it was not his "purpose to enter into an extended discussion of the tariff question." Perhaps crossing his fingers, he concluded by saying, "No man in the country is better equipped than Mr. Blaine to discharge the duties of the highest office in the gift of the people."[53]

Blaine was hardly comforted by Gresham's speech. In an anonymous letter to the *New York Tribune* after his defeat, he charged that "a few words once from Mr. Gresham" did not erase the "widespread impression . . . that the Administration was hostile to Mr. Blaine and did not sympathize with the canvass he was making for the cause of a protective tariff." Blaine also said that Arthur had dealt him a "deadly blow" by naming the "Free Trader" Hugh McCulloch to replace Gresham a week before the election. Arthur chose McCulloch, a Hoosier who had headed the Treasury Department under Andrew Johnson, largely at Gresham's urging, but Blaine charged that Arthur "threw the weight of his influence against Republican success" by "placing the Treasury under anti-Protection influences."[54]

Whatever its political impact, Gresham welcomed McCulloch's appointment because coupled with it was his own as circuit judge. He left Washington immediately, stopped at Indianapolis to vote, and then headed for Chicago, where he took up court duties without waiting to be confirmed by the Senate. The only hitch was threatened by Harrison, who was eager to resume control of the patronage in Indiana. Gresham had little stomach for a fight over a few offices in a dying administration, and the senator got his way. A few days after Congress convened in early December, the Senate approved Gresham's nomination without a division.[55]

Civil Service Commissioner Dorman Eaton lamented Gresham's move to the judgeship as "the loss of a first class administrator," but the less charitable *Indianapolis News* hailed it as removing a "mischief maker" who had "the temperament and sufficient power to be a source of constant trouble in political life." Gresham was overjoyed to be "giving up politics." Even before his appointment he had told friends that in arranging his future he would "not have political preferment in view." He had said such things before, and in reality his ambition was not completely dead. But his sojourn in national politics had reinforced that side of his nature that felt profound contempt for the game.[56]

Gresham accepted Blaine's defeat with equanimity. The loss only confirmed his conviction that there must "be a substantial reconstruction of political parties in this country before long." The Republican party had been in power so long that it was "full of disappointed and revengeful men," but the Democrats were so lacking in cohesion that Cleveland could have little hope of managing that party's "discordant elements." He predicted to Bristow that in 1888 a new party, or the Republican party "somewhat reformed," would rise to power. For the moment, however, he wanted no part of the work of political reform. Once again safely ensconced on the bench, Gresham took comfort from Senator Daniel Voorhees's kind word that he was at last "in out of the storm that rages."[57]

FIVE

PRESIDENTIAL CANDIDATE
Not Anxious for the Honor

When Gresham arrived in Chicago in late 1884, he found a vigorous, self-confident city whose population of over half a million exhibited a broad ethnic mix. The city had recovered remarkably from the great fire the previous decade and was now a leading industrial and transportation center. The new circuit judge moved easily into Chicago's elite, whose leaders included publisher Joseph Medill of the *Chicago Tribune*, George M. Pullman, banker John W. Doane, Senator Charles B. Farwell, merchant and real estate promoter Potter Palmer, and his wife, Bertha Honore Palmer, the city's premier hostess. Gresham had taken a 25 percent cut in pay on leaving the cabinet, but his $6,000 salary, small stockholdings, and proceeds from his farm in Indiana allowed him to live comfortably, if not quite in the grand style of many of his friends. He and Tillie took up residence in leased quarters in the Palmer House hotel, where they lived for several years. With them was Kate, who turned twenty-four in early 1885. Otto, then practicing law in the firm of Charles W. Fairbanks, remained in Indianapolis until 1890.[1]

Gresham found that "the judicial harness adjusted itself to me quite readily." He seemed determined to follow Justice John M. Harlan's advice to "fling away all ambition" and "forget all matters connected with the politics of the day." As circuit judge he encountered the same variety of cases he had seen on the district bench, but his jurisdiction now included Indiana, Illinois, and Wisconsin. "The work is hard," he told former cabinet colleague William E. Chandler, "but I like it."[2]

Once again, one of the important classes of litigation in his court involved alleged violations of the federal elections laws. In speeches he had often deplored fraud and corruption in the nation's politics, but in the courtroom, he found, the ideal of pure elections sometimes clashed with other important values, including the rights of defendants and the proper relation of federal and state power. Among the first cases he encountered was that of Joseph Mackin and others, Democrats, accused of altering the tally in a Cook County state senatorial election in 1884. The Democrats' alleged hope was to tip the balance in the evenly divided legislature and to elect a Democrat to replace United States Senator John A. Logan. The defendants were found guilty in district court. They immediately asked Gresham for a writ of error on the basis that they had been tried under an information filed by the district attorney rather than a grand jury indictment. Pending a hearing by the circuit court, Gresham granted a stay of sentence, which Mackin's Republican opponents denounced as "a cowardly, villainous act." At the subsequent hearing Gresham and Circuit Justice Harlan could not agree and certified the case to the Supreme Court, which eventually decided that, under the Fifth Amendment, the defendants could be tried only by grand jury indictment.[3]

A similar case grew out of the election of 1886 in Indiana. In Marion County (Indianapolis) the Democrats won the local elections, but Republicans charged that Democratic county chairman Simeon Coy and others had altered the tally sheets to give victory to the Democratic candidates for coroner and criminal judge. Three days after the election Gresham's successor as district judge, Republican William A. Woods, charged the grand jury to return indictments against Coy and his associates under various federal statutes that had been passed to combat intimidation of black voters in the South and granted federal jurisdiction in elections in which any representative in Congress was voted for. When the grand jurors found insufficient evidence to warrant an indictment, Woods dismissed them, and he and the prosecutors pursued the case by information. Gresham, who thought Woods had "ventured upon debatable ground," halted these proceedings by granting a writ of habeas corpus to one of the parties involved. "The mere fact that a representative in Congress is voted for at an election of state and county officers," he held, "does not authorize Congress to regulate such election in matters which in nowise relate to or affect the result so far as it concerns the United States." Undaunted, Woods impaneled a new grand jury, obtained indictments whose validity was sustained by Harlan, and proceeded to try and convict Coy and another defendant. Although Woods thus got around his objections, Gresham still feared that the logic of Woods's actions could lead the federal government to "assume the exclusive control of the election of state and county officers" and "oust the state courts of their jurisdiction." Many Republicans considered Gresham's position legal nitpicking. The pro-Harrison state central committee secretary Louis T. Michener claimed that it intensified "the anti-Gresham political sentiment in our party in Indiana."[4]

Although election cases attracted public attention, Gresham devoted far more time to railroad litigation. Chicago's location at the nation's great rail nexus made the seventh circuit court one of the busiest in the country. Overbuilding, intense competition, and bad management drove many railroads to dire financial straits, and to keep them operating their creditors often turned to the federal courts for the appointment of receivers. Gresham soon became expert in the arcana of railway finance and organization. In less than a year after his return to the bench, so respected were his managerial skills that a group of railroad presidents forming the Western Trunk Line Association asked him to become its chairman and "hold the organization with a firm grasp." Notwithstanding a proposed salary double that he earned as judge, he declined the offer. He also won the confidence of railroad workers. As he had done as district judge, he insisted that labor's claim on a road's revenue preceded that of bondholders. In the words of one receiver, "Frequent expressions of gratitude are heard for your promt [sic] action in ordering this payment and for the sturdy manner in which you handled the property."[5]

That Gresham was no mere chamberlain in service to railroad corporations was clear from his decision in a case involving Illinois's Granger Law of 1873, which empowered the state's Railroad and Warehouse Commission to set fair maximum rates. When the Chicago, Burlington, and Quincy claimed exemption from the prescribed rates, the judge upheld the commission's constitutional authority and accused the road of trying to deprive the public of its right of control over corporations. Whenever doubts existed as to the powers of corporations, he asserted, those doubts should be resolved in the public's favor.[6]

Gresham also displayed even-handedness between management and labor during the troubled spring of 1886, when thousands of American workers went on strike. A few railroad strikes led to litigation in his court, but none of them matched the near nationwide frustration of commerce during the 1877 strike. Gresham's response was far less aggressive than his antistrike activity that year. In early May, in the midst of the turmoil surrounding the bloody Haymarket Affair in Chicago, he refused to appoint special marshals to protect the Wabash Railroad, whose freighthandlers had struck. The Wabash was in receivership, but the receivers had been appointed by a judge in another circuit; Gresham based his refusal on the receivers' previous denial of his jurisdiction over the road and on their failure to be present in Chicago to manage it. In June, when switchmen struck the Lake Shore and Michigan Southern, lawyers for the road requested an injunction from Gresham, based on the road's legal designation as a bonded carrier of imported goods. Although this argument was little

more than a stratagem to kill the strike, Gresham did believe it war-
ranted a hearing and in the meantime issued a restraining order
against the strikers. Although such antistrike observers as the *Chicago
Tribune* welcomed this order as setting a precedent to halt strikes on
interstate railroads, Gresham had no such intent. As it happened, he
never held the hearing and never issued an injunction. The strike went
on despite his temporary order, but he apparently saw no need to take
further action. Compared with 1877, in 1886 Gresham was far less
disposed to make the federal courts the coadjutor of the railway companies in their struggles with their workmen.[7]

On the bench Gresham once again remained aloof from politics, but
he was not immune to scrutiny by Republicans casting about for
presidential material for 1888. Iowa's Senator William B. Allison described the judge as "a good, clean, strong candidate" with "splendid
presidential qualities." His balanced approach to labor problems
caught the attention of militant black editor T. Thomas Fortune, who
less than a month after the Haymarket bombing placed the legend "For
President, Walter Q. Gresham" atop the editorial column of his newspaper, the *New York Freeman*. Fortune saw Gresham as "a magnetic
man, a man of the people," and the likeliest candidate to rescue the
Republican party and the country. But Gresham told Fortune that he
was "out of politics with no expectation or desire of reentering the
political arena."[8]

The Republicans' dismal showing in the congressional elections in
November 1886 heightened their anxieties about 1888. Two weeks later,
as a pallbearer at the funeral of former President Arthur, Gresham
again stepped briefly into the national spotlight when he was greeted
warmly by Republicans who hoped to thwart a renomination of Blaine.
Newspapers carried stories of a mid-November planning session
among a half dozen party leaders at New York's Fifth Avenue Hotel,
which the Mugwump *New York Evening Post* welcomed as "a quiet
movement" in the judge's behalf. But again, Gresham was unwilling to
be used. "The thing has annoyed me," he told Noble Butler. "I am
satisfied with my present position and . . . it injures the influence and
therefore the usefulness of a judge if the impression gets out that he is
longing for political office."[9]

Ironically, just a few days after the letter to Butler, an action Gresham
took as judge gave even greater impetus to his presidential prospects.
On December 6, in a case concerning the receivership of the Wabash
Railroad, he issued an opinion that many viewed as a courageous
attack against cynical, self-serving corporate manipulation and as a
significant defeat for the arch-manipulator of the age, Jay Gould. The

case was one of the most complex and sordid examples of what was known in the parlance of the day as "railroad wrecking." The receivership, dating back to 1884, was originally conceived by the company's management as a means to avoid paying debts. Gould and other directors had given their personal endorsements on company promissory notes totaling over $2 million, but when the road did not produce enough revenue to pay the notes, they hit upon the scheme of securing the appointment of a receiver. For a debtor rather than a creditor to apply for a receiver was highly irregular, but Eighth Circuit Judge David J. Brewer, nephew of former Wabash president Cyrus Field, appointed as receivers Solon Humphreys and Thomas Tutt, two directors and large stockholders in the road. During their two years of control the receivers paid the Ellsworth Coal Company—also owned by Gould interests—rebates totaling more than the company's entire capital stock, while at the same time paying it exorbitant prices for coal.

The Wabash was a consolidated corporation, burdened by more than thirty mortgages with interest in arrears of $4 million. To head off foreclosure proceedings by the holders of bonds issued before the consolidation of 1879, the Gould interests themselves secured a foreclosure of the general mortgage of 1880. At the foreclosure sale a Gould-dominated purchasing committee bought the Wabash for $625,000. To avoid paying the accrued interest on pre-1880 bonds, the purchasing committee devised a plan whereby holders of the bonds, some bearing 6 or 7 percent would fund their interest into new 5 percent Wabash bonds. A majority of the bondholders acquiesced, but several of the senior bondholders refused to submit and turned to Gresham for relief, asking leave to foreclose their mortgages and demanding the removal of Humphreys and Tutt.

In a boldly worded opinion, Gresham ruled that the senior bondholders were entitled to foreclosure and that the Wabash would be taken from Humphreys and Tutt and "intrusted to someone who is capable and trustworthy." Casting suspicion on Judge Brewer, he added: "It is unusual and novel, to say the least, to entertain a bill filed *by* such a corporation against its creditors, and at once, without notice, place the property in the hands of one or more of the directors whose management has been unsuccessful." In addition, he denounced the "injustice" of the funding scheme, declaring, "Courts of equity should not refuse to protect the rights of minorities." As for Gould's coal company's charging his railroad high prices for coal and demanding rebates from it, Gresham noted, "Men with a proper appreciation of their rights and the rights of others—trustworthy men—are not apt to be found in such inconsistent relations. . . . It is going very far—

further than this court is willing to go—to enforce a secret contract for the rebate of freight paid to a railroad company." In later proceedings he appointed as receiver Thomas M. Cooley, one of the country's most respected jurists.[10]

The ruling met wide approval. Benjamin Bristow wrote Gresham that "in these days of tendency to vulgar money-worship & general disposition to treat lightly the moral delinquencies and crooked business methods of men of wealth, it is refreshing to read such courageous language." The *American Law Review*, the country's most influential legal journal, broke precedent and published the opinion in its entirety. The *New York Times* noted that the judge's "independence was everywhere applauded outside the circle [of] Gould dependents." Some of the abuses Gresham denounced were outlawed a few months later by the Interstate Commerce Act, and President Grover Cleveland had been so impressed by the opinion that he hoped to appoint the judge as one of the first commissioners to help "give the new law a good start." Although Gresham declined the offer, Cleveland selected as head of the commission Thomas M. Cooley, the Wabash receiver appointed by Gresham.[11]

After the decision, railroad managers were wary of entering Gresham's court, and he lost much of the goodwill they had borne him in his first year as circuit judge. More to their liking was another Wabash case in 1886, in which the Supreme Court invalidated Illinois's law governing long- and short-haul rail rates. This latter case, which marked a conservative trend in American jurisprudence, contravened Gresham's earlier decision upholding the state Railway Commission's power to set rates. Although his attitudes clearly ran counter to the tide of judicial opinion, Gresham continued to oppose "railroad wrecking" from the bench, but he never again confronted a case with the dramatic impact of the *Wabash* case.[12]

Whatever the long-term judicial effect of Gresham's *Wabash* decision, it had a significant impact on his political career. Jay Gould charged that the judge "must be suffering from a severe attack of the Presidential fever. . . . It doesn't cost much to call us names and these men with political aspirations think that it has great weight with the people." Gould spitefully misread Gresham's motives, for in fact he intended to stay on the bench permanently. In the summer of 1887 he told William E. Chandler that people should not connect his name with the presidency even "in a joking way."[13]

Yet as 1887 drew to a close, many of the men who had labored quietly for his nomination in 1884 were willing to roll up their sleeves again. They took heart from the results of the off-year elections in

November. The party did well in the Midwest but lost New York by over seventeen thousand votes. Since many observers had viewed the New York contest as a referendum on Blaine, the outcome cast serious doubt on his claim to a renomination. In less than a week Indianapolis lawyer William P. Fishback wrote John W. Foster, then practicing law in Washington, to initiate steps for a concerted effort in Gresham's behalf. But as one longtime southern Indiana friend told the judge, many of his old supporters would "not move until you actually say you want their services." Thus pressed, Gresham in mid-December wrote Charles W. Fairbanks, his chief Hoosier backer, that they should not make the effort "simply to gratify me." "My inclination is this—In view of the immense responsibility which the high position involves, let things drift, and if the call should then come (which is not probable) I will feel much better. Believe me when I tell you I am not anxious for the honor."[14]

Despite the judge's reluctance, over the next several months an informal network of supporters emerged to coordinate efforts in his behalf. In Indiana Fairbanks and Fishback worked with Noble Butler, former state party chairman John Overmyer, former Congressman W.H. Calkins, and other Gresham loyalists. In Illinois Senator Charles B. Farwell, *Chicago Tribune* publisher Joseph Medill, and former Whiskey Ring prosecutor Bluford Wilson looked after his interests. Others who played leading parts included Robert G. Ingersoll, Erastus Brainerd, editor of the *Philadelphia Daily News*, Philadelphia industrialist P.A.B. Widener, and Delaware Republican James Harrison Wilson, brother of Bluford. In New York Louis Howland of the Reform Club sought help from his fellow Mugwumps, and party regulars were courted by Richard Elmer, who had served under Gresham in the Post Office Department.

Gresham's initial grudging consent betrayed his sense that the task would not be easy. Blaine's supposedly dead candidacy was soon revived by his response to President Cleveland's December 6 annual message, which had called for substantial tariff reduction to alleviate a growing surplus in the treasury. Blaine denounced the message as a free-trade manifesto welcomed by the British, called for the maintenance of high protective duties, and advocated defense spending and a reduction of internal taxes on tobacco to reduce the surplus. His response not only breathed new life into his own presidential chances but also seemed to commit the Republican party to the doctrine of high protectionism, a circumstance equally troublesome for Gresham, who was identified with the low-tariff wing of the party.[15]

Another obstacle was the ambition of Benjamin Harrison, who

enjoyed a relatively stronger political standing than when the two men had clashed in 1884. Gresham no longer wielded the patronage he had held as postmaster general. The moment he had left Arthur's cabinet, Harrison had hastened to regain control over Indiana patronage, and after Cleveland's inauguration the senator earned a reputation as an outspoken defender of Republican appointees turned out of office by the Democrats. Moreover, he labored to mold the state Republican organization into a personal machine, making certain that only "men who will take a special interest in our plans" served as local and state party representatives. A Democratic reapportionment of Indiana's legislative districts jeopardized Harrison's reelection to the Senate in 1886, but he waged a desperate fight to retain his seat. He lost but was satisfied he had "come out of it with more friends & reputation than ever before." Early in 1888 Gresham and his associates found that Harrison's organization was still intact and "hard at work" in the quest for national convention delegates in Indiana.[16]

Facing an uphill fight, Gresham continued to feel doubts about his candidacy. In late January, Joseph Medill was about to "open up" for him and sent reporters to get details for a biography. "Embarrassed and annoyed," Gresham asked Noble Butler to work up a sketch of his early life. "The truth is I was poor—very poor. Even you don't know how things were, and I can't consent to seeing in print such details. But the Tribune people say that is just what the public wants. I know of no one else to turn to." Returning to a familiar theme, he wrote Butler that he was becoming "less ambitious" as he grew older. "I am almost ashamed to say to you that I have a strange feeling that something is impending. Something tragic." The tragedy, it turned out, was the utter futility of the Gresham campaign.[17]

By mid-February Gresham and his advisers agreed that the most they could hope for in Indiana was an uninstructed delegation, which would deny Harrison the certainty of thirty first-ballot votes and signify to Republicans elsewhere Harrison's weakness in his home state. This strategy proved hopeless, however, for just at that time Blaine's withdrawal from the race gave renewed impetus to the Harrison campaign. Stephen B. Elkins, Blaine's chief campaign lieutenant, had carried on a flirtation with Harrison for months and now told him that "in a quiet way, word is being passed around to the Blaine men that you are the choice of a great many of them." But Elkins cautioned, "It is very important that you have the solid Indiana delegation." Blaine himself thought Harrison would "make the best run." "Gresham is not acceptable," Blaine told Elkins, "I think he would not be strong. He is a disciple of Ingersoll in religion and has been a demagogue and iconoclast on the Bench. His unjust hostility to corporations would array the capital of the country against him before the canvass would be a month advanced." Republicans everywhere agreed that Blaine's supporters would wield great influence in the convention. As former Postmaster General James Tyner assured Harrison, Gresham had little chance "unless Blaine's friends are the most forgiving Christians yet discovered in politics."[18]

The day after Blaine withdrew, the *Indianapolis Journal* proclaimed Harrison "Indiana's Candidate." Through the spring his supporters did their utmost to make the claim a reality. Gresham's men soon found, as one newspaper editor reported to Fairbanks, that the "Harrison henchmen not only want a man to favor Benjamin but they want him to hate Gresham. They are unreasonable to the point of consummate cussedness." At the suggestion of the judge's son, Otto, Foster sought to kill off Harrison's candidacy by publicizing his vote twice as senator against legislation limiting Chinese immigration, a position unpopular with workingmen. Harrison's men replied that he had voted against the legislation because it violated existing treaties. The issue worried some of his eastern supporters but did not halt his campaign. Indeed, it inspired even greater efforts from his Indiana backers, who countered by emphasizing Gresham's unsoundness on the tariff and his passivity in the 1884 campaign.[19]

The bitterness between the two camps grew so intense that the Gresham men soon abandoned their hope even for an uncommitted delegation and adopted the strategy of going along with a favorite-son endorsement of Harrison. Believing that Gresham commanded much more support than Harrison outside the state, they were confident, as Robert G. Ingersoll put it, that "when Indiana gets into the convention with her favorite son, and no other state is willing to act as father—she will swap sons." The most skeptical critic of this strategy was Gresham himself, who doubted that the Harrison men would "act fair if you give them a solid delegation." Foster assured him that the plan called for securing enough places to "demand fair play," but getting the Harrison organization to accept "friendly" delegates proved enormously difficult. Throughout the state, Gresham men had to be extraordinarily discreet and even to "talk H. a little" to have any chance of being selected. Of the thirty delegates chosen at the district and state conventions, at most seven and probably no more than four could be regarded as Gresham men. Even these vowed to cast an initial vote for Harrison, "if there is a reasonable show for his nomination," although they added that the delegates should switch to the judge if he proved "more likely to succeed."[20]

94 Gilded Age Cato

Gresham fared better in his adopted state, Illinois, where he had the backing of the two most important Republican newspapers, the *Chicago Tribune* and the *Inter-Ocean*. His chief opposition came from Senator Shelby M. Cullom, who desired to become Illinois's favorite son and who regarded Gresham as a "jackass" and a "'tramp' not entitled to recognition as a citizen of our state." At the state convention Gresham's backers threw their support for the gubernatorial nomination to a Cullom ally, Joseph W. Fifer, who obliged by bringing his backers around to support Gresham instructions for the national convention delegates. Although Cullom remained disgruntled, the Illinois delegation was loyal to Gresham in the convention, casting forty of its forty-four votes for him even on the last ballot.[21]

Amid the spring's political turmoil, Gresham's duties as judge went on. Although he joined energetically in the hunt for delegates, he remained "fearful" that his effectiveness on the bench would be "damaged" by the newspaper booming and more public side of the campaign. He refused to attend a dinner in memory of General Grant because, he told Fairbanks, "it might be taken as evidence that I am anxious to help the boom." (Harrison, in contrast, did attend the Grant dinner in Pittsburgh, delivered what the Republican national chairman labeled an "excellent" address, and thereby gave a great boost to his candidacy.)[22]

But Gresham's actions in court could have significant political implications, and in an important railroad strike case he delivered an opinion that increased his popularity with labor. In early March engineers and firemen who had struck the Chicago, Burlington, and Quincy for a new wage formula launched a secondary boycott, requesting their fellow members of the brotherhoods employed on connecting lines to refuse to handle Burlington cars. The boycott went into effect on several western lines, sometimes with the acquiescence of managers who wished to avert strikes on their own roads. One such line was the Wabash. In response, attorneys for the Burlington petitioned Gresham to issue a "peremptory order" directing the Wabash receiver, John McNulta, to cease his refusal to exchange traffic, to enjoin the Brotherhood of Locomotive Engineers from issuing orders to its members against handling Burlington cars, and to order the brotherhood and its head, P.M. Arthur, to show why they should not be punished for contempt for interfering with property in the court's custody. Gresham issued no temporary order and agreed to hear arguments, but before the case came to a hearing receiver McNulta rescinded his orders against handling Burlington cars.

In court Gresham informed the Burlington lawyers that McNulta's action had removed any need for federal intervention. When the lawyers continued to press for some action on the contempt charge, the judge refused to punish either Arthur or the brotherhood. In a brief opinion he declared, "Lawless interference with the receiver and his employees in the discharge of their duty will not be tolerated." But, he noted, the engineers did "not desire to maintain an attitude of defiance to the law" and were "willing to aid the receiver in the lawful and successful administration of his trust." Hence he issued no injunction, and the Burlington's petition was merely placed on file. This outcome—ending the secondary boycott without applying coercion directly against labor—contrasted sharply with the broad injunctions against the Burlington engineers issued by federal judges elsewhere. Burlington president Charles Perkins called Gresham's ruling "a good decision," and the strikers' attorney hailed it as "the only decision the court could have rendered."[23]

Most important, Gresham survived the crisis with his reputation as a friend of labor intact. The *Minneapolis Journal* declared, "He has demonstrated repeatedly that the weak and the poor have just as good a chance for justice in his court as the wealthy and the powerful. His refusal to allow the power of the law to be used unjustly against the Burlington railroad engineers has not been overlooked by the workingmen." Gresham's managers were quick to publicize the statement by New York labor leader Thomas B. MacGuire that "of all the presidential candidates now before the people, Judge Gresham is the most acceptable to the Knights of Labor." They also cited his famous *Wabash* decision as proof that he was "a foe to unjust monopoly." In the words of the *Chicago Tribune,* opposition to the judge by corporations amounted to "Gouldism against Gresham."[24]

Gresham's opponents saw his candidacy as enough of a threat to raise a long list of objections to making him the party's nominee. They claimed that his firing of GAR commander Paul Vandervoort from the postal service while he was postmaster general had alienated thousands of normally Republican Union veterans. His Know-Nothing past returned to haunt him when Harrison supporters dredged up his allegedly anti-German speech of 1855 and sent copies to delegates throughout the country. In response, his son, Otto, and Noble Butler rushed to southern Indiana to assemble counteraffidavits from citizens denying that Gresham had used abusive language in the speech, and the *Chicago Tribune* defended him as one of "tens of thousands" of men who had "with the heedlessness and ardor of youth" joined the secret order as the only effective vehicle to oppose the Democrats in the 1850s. Even Gresham's religious views came under scrutiny, and he was accused of being an atheist. He had in truth never held very deep religious convictions, but it was his close relationship with and support from the noted agnostic Robert G. Ingersoll that cast most doubt on his Christian faith. The charge was damaging enough that the *Tribune*'s Joseph Medill felt it necessary to state publicly that Gresham was a regular churchgoer.[25]

The largest obstacle, however, was the tariff question, the most important issue of the 1888 campaign both before and after the convention. Gresham had always favored moderate tariff duties, but the campaign season was hardly under way before he was pinned with the odious "free trader" label. One Hoosier legislator told Harrison that the popularity Gresham had earned among workers for his court decisions was more than offset by his not being "regarded as sufficiently stalwart on the question of a protective tariff, a question of the most vital importance to the laboring man." Pennsylvania financier Wharton Barker, who published a weekly protectionist journal called the *American*, pointedly asked Gresham to "please let me know what rate of duties you advocate for iron ore, pig iron, bar iron, steel, steel rails, and wool" so that "we may act advisedly and have a gauge." Gresham thought Barker's letter "rather insolent" and did not answer it, but he did tell *Philadelphia Daily News* editor Erastus Brainerd that "no one who knows me thinks I am a free trader."[26]

The problem was compounded because most people knew him through his newspaper support, particularly that of the *Chicago Tribune*, whose publisher Medill was long associated with the low-tariff wing of the Republican party. The *Chicago Inter-Ocean* claimed that Gresham was "as good a protectionist as Blaine," but Gresham himself refused to discuss the subject publicly. Privately he wrote correspondents that he stood by what he had said in his New York subtreasury speech in 1884. His supporters distributed copies throughout the country, but as one Michigan editor told Fairbanks, a four-year-old speech could do little to reassure Republicans "uncertain about Gresham's present tariff belief." In truth, Gresham was out of step with the party on the issue. Although he had mentioned protection in his 1884 speech, he had placed greater emphasis on the need to lower rates to reduce the treasury surplus. If anything, he had moved farther away from protectionism in the intervening years. Exorbitant customs duties, he believed, placed an unfair burden on consumers, and the most that American industries could ask for was a tariff rate that made the price of foreign goods equal to the cost of producing American goods. Medill sought to allay protectionists' doubts by telling reporters that if Gresham "were to become the nominee of the Republican party, he would stand on the Republican platform," which would set "Republican policy in the campaign on the tariff." Such statements had little effect. A week before the convention Barker assured Harrison's men that they need have no "future fear from Gresham. The high tariff men will not have him."[27]

Closely related to the tariff issue was the attitude of the supporters of Blaine, the chief architect of the party's high protectionist position. Despite Blaine's February withdrawal, many of his backers clung to the hope of securing for him a nomination he could not refuse. Their strategy was to keep several candidates in the field with tentative offers of support; at the convention when no one of them would be able to secure a majority, the deadlocked delegates would turn to Blaine. "If there is such a scheme," Gresham told Fairbanks, "Harrison will join in it if he has not already done so." Harrison had indeed joined. Intimating support, Blaine man Stephen B. Elkins strung the former senator along with a twofold aim: to keep Harrison linked to the Blaine camp in case his votes should be needed to nominate Blaine, or, if Blaine were out and Harrison nominated, to make it clear to Harrison that he owed his success to the Blaine wing of the party. Over the months Blaine leaders cast a similar role for other candidates, including Chauncey Depew of New York, Russell Alger of Michigan, William Walter Phelps of New Jersey, and William B. Allison of Iowa, but none of them was courted with the same intensity accorded Harrison, who appeared to be the most acceptable candidate in the event the Blaine effort failed.[28]

Another advantage of the Harrison candidacy for the Blaine men was that it weakened Gresham, with whom their relations remained cool. "The talk about Gresham," snapped the *New York Tribune*'s Whitelaw Reid, "encounters the angry criticism of those Republicans who think that if Arthur's Cabinet had acted as Republicans ought to act, we should have had the missing 600 votes in this State in the last election." This hostility was aggravated when Mugwump journals such as *Harper's Weekly* hailed Gresham's candidacy as a "protest . . . against the spirit and tendency which were embodied in the candidacy of Mr. Blaine." The judge's managers saw the danger in being cast as "Blaine antagonizers," but when Medill and others sought to mollify the Blaine men with kind words for the Plumed Knight, they alienated other party members who, like Louis Howland of the New York Reform Club, denied that "in order to prove yourself a Republican you have got to slobber over Jim Blaine." In the end, Blaine's friends remained unmoved. "All oppose Gresham," Wharton Barker assured Harrison.[29]

Gresham enjoyed the support of some important party journals including the *Chicago Tribune,* the *Minneapolis Journal,* the *Philadelphia Daily News,* and the *St. Louis Globe-Democrat,* as well as William Henry Smith's Western Associated Press. But editorial support meant little to state party machine leaders. New York's "Easy Boss," Thomas C. Platt, told reporters that Mugwumps' "advocacy of Judge Gresham is what weighs him down more than any other one thing," and he also cited his early Know-Nothing connection and his views on the tariff as obstacles to his nomination and election. Similarly, Pennsylvania Senator Matthew S. Quay told John W. Foster that he did not think Gresham had "any chance" for the nomination. Although Foster and others sought to convince the two powerful leaders that a Gresham administration would treat them fairly in patronage, no arrangement ever materialized. Throughout the convention he received not one vote from New York or Pennsylvania.[30]

As so often in the past, the ambition that underlay Gresham's presidential bid in the spring of 1888 was confounded by his deep feeling of "embarrassment." In private he labored assiduously to round up convention support, but at the same time he claimed even to powerful would-be backers that he had no organization and was "making no effort to capture the nomination." Part of his reticence derived from his position on the bench, but the reasons ran deeper than judicial decorum. He continued to feel that "there is no agony like that of destroyed hope or ambition," and he feared becoming one of those men "who will be wretched so long as they live, simply because they were ambitious and failed." Not a few of his supporters were disturbed by his inclination, as one put it, to "draw out and deny his candidacy at the first indication of failure." But as the convention drew nearer, he made his disavowal of "fanciful ambition" more emphatic. To his long-time friend Benjamin Bristow he confided: "I am not anxious to be nominated here next month and do not expect to be. I know what forceful influences are at work against me. I must say I do not understand why the papers out here should be so anxious for my nomination and election. I think a majority of the delegates will be Blaine men at heart, & you know what that means. . . . While I am not an old man, I feel the sobering effect of age. I am not very ambitious." And yet during the convention Gresham's efforts in his own behalf continued to bespeak a man desperately, almost recklessly ambitious. He seemed at war with himself. His repeated denials were neither cynical nor calculated but instead pathetic expressions of the ambivalence and self-doubt that marked his entire political career. "I hardly understand myself," he confessed to Robert Ingersoll. "If it were to do over, I think I should act differently."[31]

Gresham headquarters were established at the Grand Pacific Hotel on June 12 to begin the last-minute wooing of delegates as they arrived in Chicago for the scheduled opening of the convention a week later. Despite the early start, problems continued to plague the Gresham campaign. Foster could not be present because of the death of a daughter. Fairbanks was left with most of the work, which was overwhelming; at one point Gresham ordered his exhausted manager to "take a strong drink of whiskey" and go to bed. The judge took an active part but probably did himself more harm than good. In keeping with the "proprieties," he at first left the convention city to stay at Judge Thomas Drummond's home at Wheaton, twenty-five miles away. But he was soon back in Chicago meeting delegation leaders in chambers and shaking hands in the hotels. Many considered such personal solicitation of support a gross breach of convention ethics. At least one easterner complained, "Had it been done by any other candidate, the mugwump-free trade press would have severely denounced it."[32]

Gresham's managers sought to allay the continued apprehension over his tariff views, but the effort seemed more farcical than efficacious. They issued a new campaign badge bearing the candidate's name sandwiched between the words "protection" and "victory." Claiming the judge was foursquare for the protection of labor, they staged a mass parade of "the tin-bucket brigade" during convention week to show his support among workingmen. This demonstration seemed less than convincing when opponents circulated rumors that a large proportion of the marchers were Democrats induced to make the free trip to Chicago by threats of dismissal by their employers at the Lafayette, Indiana, car works. The *Chicago Tribune* published an article in which reporter Walter Wellman claimed that Gresham had described himself in private conversation as "a firm believer in protection." That Gresham consented to the publication of the article is doubtful, however, for he absolutely forbade a similar representation by William Penn Nixon in the *Inter-Ocean*. Indeed, on the third day of the convention, when the delegates adopted a high tariff platform, Gresham drafted a letter to Illinois Senator Charles Farwell requesting him to withdraw his name. The alarmed Medill argued that if nominated he could clarify his views in his letter of acceptance and that a withdrawal now would be a great embarrassment to his supporters. Gresham reluctantly agreed not to send the letter to Farwell, but the party's unequivocal endorsement of high protectionism had rendered his chances of nomination all the more remote.[33]

Nor did the nominating speeches in his behalf help much. The Gresham men had originally planned to use Ingersoll, who had delivered the memorable "Plumed Knight" speech for Blaine in 1876, but objections to his defiant agnosticism made it clear he was the wrong man, as one Missouri Republican put it, "to invoke the blessing of Heaven on the movement." The honor then devolved upon Leonard Swett, an Illinois lawyer whose service as defense attorney for the Haymarket anarchists no doubt offended some delegates. With typical convention grandiloquence, Swett dwelt overlong on the history of the party, Gresham's early life, and a comparison of his candidate with Lincoln. He said very little about issues. Gresham's managers had scrutinized his text in advance and excised phrases like "tariff reform" and "the burthens under which the people groan." The only surviving reference to the tariff was a declaration that Gresham had "always stood with his party for the protection of American labor against foreign competition." The four seconders included black Mississippian John R. Lynch, whose remark that Gresham was "not presented as the first choice" of his home state of Indiana did little to aid the candidate. Similarly, Boston editor Samuel McCall raised the touchy question of Mugwump support, scolding those delegates who would "sacrifice so excellent a Republican as Judge Gresham, simply because he has received the praise of these men."[34]

Seven other men were nominated, but the candidate who appeared to have the largest bloc of potential support, Blaine, had gone unnamed. The first ballot on Friday, June 22, showed a wide dispersal of the 832 delegates' votes, which augured well for Blaine. Of fourteen men receiving votes, John Sherman led with 229. Thanks to Illinois's large vote, Gresham ranked second with 107, which also included eleven each from Minnesota and Missouri and handfuls from twenty-one other states, including one from Indiana. Two more ballots in the afternoon session brought no substantial move to anyone; Gresham remained second with 123 votes. The Blaine men's implicit strategy called for their strength to be divided among other candidates with a minor coalescing behind one or more in succession to test their strength, demonstrate their unpopularity, and eliminate them from consideration. The first "beneficiary" of this procedure was Harrison. After the Friday afternoon session, Platt's New York delegation decided to give three-quarters of its vote to the Hoosier in the evening, but the forces of the other candidates combined to force an adjournment of the evening session without a ballot. That the Blaine men were not reluctant to head off a Harrison stampede was evident in the support many of them gave to adjournment.[35]

Friday night brought the coup de grâce for Gresham. After adjourning, the lingering delegates, as a mass meeting, invited Ingersoll to speak. On the lookout all week for the chance to make "'the greatest effort of his life,'" Ingersoll delivered a rousing stump speech, which he climaxed by saying, "Now, being a Republican, being for the Republican party, being for protection, wishing and hoping for success, I am in favor of the nomination of Walter Q. Gresham." Pandemonium broke out immediately, but the greater portion of the noise was directed against Ingersoll's abuse of the delegates' invitation to make a nonpartisan speech. Charles Boutelle of Maine shouted: "Go home. It is an insult to the convention." The following morning Gresham generously wrote the chagrined Ingersoll, "I want to say I think you did just right last night and that I thank you for what you said." His son, Otto, later assured the orator that he preferred the speech just "as you spoke it than to have had the support of Mr. Platt and his friends." Nonetheless, Ingersoll had pronounced the funeral oration of the Gresham boom.[36]

The next day on the fourth ballot Gresham fell to fourth place with ninety-eight votes, while Harrison jumped to second place. On the next ballot, however, Harrison's total declined, and, as Walker Blaine noted, "Everybody thought Harrison beaten and everyone believed that father would be nominated that afternoon." But the anti-Blaine and anti-Harrison forces again forced an adjournment, and the weekend recess witnessed intense machinations. Fairbanks initiated the dispatch of telegrams from several points in Indiana urging the Hoosier delegation to switch to Gresham. The *Chicago Tribune* carried an interview with the Union Labor party's presidential nominee, who promised that if the Republicans nominated Gresham he would withdraw and Gresham would "pull the labor vote of the country." But these were acts of desperation with little effect. Front-runner John Sherman fairly begged that "New York do for me what she did for Indiana," but Platt and other Empire State leaders decided to stand by Harrison, especially after the arrival of Blaine's unequivocal refusal of a draft. On Monday, June 25, Harrison surpassed Sherman on the seventh ballot and took the nomination on the eighth. Gresham finished in fourth place with fifty-nine votes.[37]

Gresham was with Judge Drummond on the convention's last day, and those present noted that he received the news of Harrison's nomination "without a change upon his countenance." He shook hands with friends but declined to talk to reporters: "I have never been interviewed since the campaign commenced, and do not want to say anything now except to say that I am and always have been a Republican." Later he sent Harrison a one-sentence telegram: "It is hardly necessary that I should give you assurance of my earnest support."[38]

The gingerly wording of this customary congratulation reflected Gresham's bitterness at the triumph of his long-hated rival. "The evil influences were never so strong in any previous National Convention of either party," he protested to Noble Butler. "I will not undertake to tell you all the mean things that were resorted to by Harrison's friends." Convinced that the "railroad men were determined to beat me at all hazards" and that the Republican party was "largely controlled by unworthy and vicious men," he told Butler, "I am heartily glad that I was not nominated."[39]

Gresham's defeat sparked a cathartic crisis in his political career. Beyond his personal disappointment, he grew increasingly alarmed that the Republican party was becoming the tool of corporate interests. He had once been an uninhibited defender of property who had equated democracy with mob rule, but the labor strife of the 1880s and the corporate chicanery typified by the *Wabash* case had made him more inclined to side with workingmen and the victims of manipulation. Since his days in the Indiana legislature on the eve of the Civil War, he had often doubted that the country's political system accurately represented the people's will; now he began to suspect that in such manifestations as high protectionism, party leaders managed the system *against* the people's interest. "I am willing to stand a tariff equal to the difference in the cost of manufacture in this country and the other side," he told Butler, "but further than that I cannot and will not go. Clay & other Whig leaders went no further, and it is unjust and oppressive to take more from the people." He predicted that "many of the mechanics and laborers" would refuse to vote for Harrison.[40]

He would vote for the ticket, but he wanted no other role in the campaign. Ten days after the convention he left for a two-month vacation in Europe. He set out with Chicago banker and Democratic politician John W. Doane and a few other men but spent about half the trip wandering on his own. He took no one from his family and wrote few letters home. Except for an occasional encounter with a reporter, he isolated himself from happenings in America as he traveled through England, France, Belgium, Germany, Switzerland, and the north of Italy. He found the German people to be the most congenial he encountered—"a sincere, hospitable, good-hearted people, entirely free from pretense." On diplomatic questions he said relatively little, and on American relations with European powers, nothing at all. He did speculate on the possibility of new fighting between France and Germany, but as one who had seen war, he deplored the prospect.[41]

Gresham returned to the United States in mid-September, looking "a little stouter" and walking "a great deal livelier." He was soon back in court, but his labors were leavened by the preparations for the marriage of his daughter, Kate, on October 2 to a Chicago businessman. He also took time out to do honor to a prominent townsman, Democrat Melville W. Fuller, whom President Cleveland had appointed chief justice of the United States. At a banquet for Fuller, the recent presidential candidate just back from Europe stole a bit of the limelight and was described by one reporter as "this fine, stalwart figure, with the iron-gray hair and beard; this smiling, kindly face; this giant with strong, nervous hands which all were so eager to clasp." Greeted by hearty applause, Gresham spoke briefly on judicial responsibility. "Judges take a solemn obligation to administer equal and exact justice to the rich and the poor," he said, "and however able and rich in learning they may be they will fail in the discharge of this high duty if not endowed with courage and a robust sense of right."[42]

As the presidential campaign neared its close, Gresham came under increasing pressure to take part. One party official argued that "a letter in brief, strong & explicit terms *in your own handwriting* would influence hundreds, probably thousands of voters in Indiana and elsewhere." Gresham thought Harrison's managers were "pretty cheeky" to ask him for a public endorsement of the nominee, but he finally yielded and issued a public letter, in which he noted that it was "gratifying to know" that "my friends are supporting the ticket in good faith." "I do not think any fair-minded person doubts that I earnestly desire its success." But he added somewhat gratuitously, "The proprieties of the position which I occupy forbid my taking an active part in politics. . . . I could not actively participate in the campaign without exposing myself to just censure, and lowering myself in the estimation of right-thinking people." This was hardly the testimonial the Harrison men had hoped for.[43]

As the campaign wound down, charges of contemplated frauds flew between the Republican and Democratic camps. The near equality in strength of the two parties in Indiana, which meant that just a few voters could tip the balance, made that state a likelier field for corruption than most others. One week before the election Gresham spoke with Robert T. Lincoln, then practicing law in Chicago, who said that Harrison's law partner (and future attorney general) W.H.H. Miller and his son Russell Harrison had come to Chicago to solicit "money to buy votes" in Indiana and that he, Lincoln, was "in favor of chipping in." "Think of it!" Gresham wrote Noble Butler. "Harrison is so eager that he even sends his own son to beg money to ____. But that is not what disturbs me so much as the final outcome of such conduct. The purchase of voters is carried on by both parties with little effort at concealment. If the thing goes on unchecked a catastrophe is inevitable. What is to become of us?"[44]

The next day the Democratic *Indianapolis Sentinel* published a facsimile of a letter allegedly written by Republican national treasurer William W. Dudley, himself a Hoosier, to Indiana county chairmen, outlining a formula for the systematic purchase of votes. Republicans denied the charge and returned countercharges against the Democrats, but the incident seemed to confirm what Gresham had heard from Lincoln. Harrison won Indiana by four-tenths of a percent, New York by a margin almost as slim, and with them the election. The closeness of the outcome magnified the perceived significance of alleged purchased votes.[45]

Dudley's indiscretion embarrassed Harrison, and there was talk of making him the scapegoat for the alleged frauds. A week after the election, District Judge William A. Woods informed a grand jury that under federal statutes if "A attempts to bribe B, that is no offense . . . ; but if A advises B to attempt to bribe C, then the one who gives this advice is an offender." But Dudley was unwilling to submit quietly and threatened to implicate other men of prominence. As a result, Woods, a Republican, reconsidered and told the grand jury two months later that "the mere sending by one to another of a letter or document containing advice to bribe voters or setting forth a scheme for such bribery, however bold and reprehensible, is not indictable." After Harrison's inauguration Woods proceeded with a wholesale quashing of indictments against lesser figures. Severely criticized by the Democratic press, he sought to share responsibility for the partisan rulings by asking Gresham to "pass upon the questions." Gresham refused and simply told Woods that a judge must follow "his own mind and conscience." Privately Gresham told Noble Butler that Woods's "withers are wrung." Woods continued to quash indictments, and no one was ever convicted in the case.[46]

Dudley sued several newspapers for libel, and in return one of them, the *New York World*, launched a general investigation of corrupt election practices. One of the paper's reporters caught up with Gresham on court duty in Indianapolis, where he broke judicial silence to lash out at "the Pharisees who are doing this." With his preelection conversation with Lincoln in mind, he added, "It is men of prominence and respectability who raise these large sums of money knowing the use that they will be put to, men who deal openly in corruption one day and go to church the next. It is these men who bring disgrace upon the state."[47]

Thus Gresham ended the year once more embittered with the

Republican party. The party had rejected his leadership, and as so often in the past he explained his failure by the wickedness and knavery of others. "Evil influences" and "mean things" had nominated Harrison, "unworthy and vicious men" had taken control of the party, and in the end "Pharisees" bought the election. In 1888 Gresham's ambition had soared as high as it ever would, but the morality of his party had sunk low, or so he believed. In the years afterward it grew increasingly apparent that he was becoming a man without a party.

SIX

JEREMIAH

The Patriotism of Our
Revolutionary Sires

The fate of Gresham and his followers in the Harrison administration was a subject of speculation as soon as the election result was known. Some observers hoped that Harrison would follow Abraham Lincoln's example and appoint his chief competitors for the nomination to cabinet and other posts, with Gresham slated for a seat on the Supreme Court. Harrison did recognize his debt to James G. Blaine by inviting him back to his old post as head of the State Department, but he felt no similar obligation to his Hoosier rival.[1]

Less than three weeks into the new administration the death of Associate Justice Stanley Matthews turned speculation about a replacement to Gresham. The judge had significant support for the position, including that of Benjamin Bristow, Interstate Commerce Commission Chairman Thomas M. Cooley, and former Supreme Court reporter William T. Otto, who had been one of Gresham's mentors in the study of law nearly forty years before. But men who had opposed his nomination for president were equally unwilling to see his elevation to the high court. The secretary of the Boston Home Market Club wrote Harrison "to most earnestly protest such an appointment, or indeed that of any free trader or one who is not a pronounced protectionist." Of course, Supreme Court justices had little to say about tariff rates, but there was little danger of Gresham's appointment anyway. When Harrison let it be known that he would delay the appointment until the fall, it was clear he would make no magnanimous gesture. "Well as I thought I knew Harrison," Gresham wrote Noble Butler, "I did not believe he was so small." Perhaps not altogether candidly, he added: "In confidence, I don't care to go upon the Supreme Bench—indeed don't want to."[2]

Many of Gresham's erstwhile supporters fared better. Some won important appointments, including that of John Wanamaker as postmaster general. In Indiana Harrison appointed some Gresham men to local federal offices in an attempt to mollify the rival faction, but such recognition proved enormously irritating to men who had stood with Harrison from the beginning, and especially to those who failed to receive appointments. Within a few months Louis T. Michener, Harrison's 1888 manager, who superintended Indiana patronage, was convinced that it had been "very foolish" to waste favors on the Gresham people. Indeed, the president was soon out of favor with large numbers in both factions. Skillfully handled, the bestowal of offices could reinforce and augment a store of friendly feeling already extant, but it could do little to defuse old hostilities or create new support. There were too many supplicants and not enough soup. This fact coupled with Harrison's icy, blunt personality alienated Republicans high and low and cast doubt on his renomination almost before his term began. Before long disenchantment blossomed into a significant antiadministration faction in the president's own party.[3]

With few exceptions Gresham stayed out of patronage affairs, primarily because he believed he had little influence with Harrison but also because it seemed the "proper course" for a judge. He tended to matters in court and showed a continued solicitude for workingmen, particularly those who worked for railroads. In one receivership case he instructed Judge William J. Allen of the Southern Illinois district that laborers whose pay was in arrears "should not be required to be at the expense of employing counsel to prepare and file a petition for them." The judge should simply order the receiver to pay the labor claims, and "if he has not money enough to pay all, he should pay *pro rata* or perhaps those who are most necessitous, in full."[4]

A similar case in Indiana sparked anew the mutual animosity between Gresham and District Judge William A. Woods that had been smoldering since Woods's partisan handling of the Dudley affair earlier in the year. In a case involving the receivership of both the Illinois and Indiana portions of the Indianapolis, Decatur, and Springfield Railway, Gresham criticized Woods for appointing a receiver with jurisdiction beyond his district without first consulting the circuit judge. More important, he charged that the real purpose of the receivership was to allow the company "to get out of paying this indebtedness for labor and supplies." In a formal opinion he concluded that "the earnings of the property, which should have been first used in paying labor and supply claims, and other operating expenses, had been improperly and illegally paid to the holders of first mortgage bonds in satisfaction of interest, and that in order to maintain this unfair and illegal advantage for a time at least, a receiver was desired." He removed the receiver, a former Republican congressman, and nullified Woods's order.[5]

Some lawyers thought Gresham should have given Woods a chance to correct his mistake, but the *Evansville Courier* expressed the popular reaction: "At a time when every Department of the Government seems to be inspired by sordid considerations, or intimidated by the power of money, it is reassuring to know that there are still a few men in public station, who, like Judge Gresham, are uninfluenced either by the blandishments or threats of the Plutocrats." "It has materially added to his fame," reporter Walter Wellman wrote to Charles W. Fairbanks. "He is today the most popular, most respected man in the country." Perhaps so, but when Congress convened in December, Harrison sent to the Senate for the vacancy on the Supreme Court not Gresham's name but that of Judge David J. Brewer of the Eighth Circuit, the same judge who had appointed and assisted the Gould receivers Gresham had removed from control of the Wabash three years earlier. Gresham and his friends saw the choice as an ill-disguised rebuke. Indeed, Attorney General W.H.H. Miller seemed to have Gresham in mind when he defended the new justice as one who had the "courage" to decide in favor of "wealth and power and corporation" when "the law and justice of a case demand it," which was "courage of a kind which demagogues lack."[6]

Gresham would not be moving to Washington, but neither he nor his wife disliked the prospect of remaining in Chicago. They had been accepted in the city's social circles, and they were near their daughter, Kate, and her new husband. "Contentment is the secret of happiness," Gresham wrote to his niece. "I am now growing old (my head is almost white) and from observation I am convinced that people who are ambitious—immoderately so—to be rich or conspicuous, socially or otherwise, are not happy."[7]

Many of Gresham's old political supporters were anything but content, especially in Indiana, where a significant number of Republicans stood ready to challenge the Harrison organization. "Gresham in '92" was the rallying cry for many, and by mid-1890 newspapers carried reports of "a gigantic conspiracy" to "capture Indiana for Gresham." Annoyed by such talk, Gresham ordered his friends to "quit using my name in connection with politics" because it did not "do a judge any good." But he did encourage the antiadministration movement, telling its leader, Charles W. Fairbanks, that he would like "to see such a course pursued as would show that you and your friends in the State are a positive force." Assisting Fairbanks was the judge's son, Otto, who still had high hopes for his father's future and longed to avenge his loss to Harrison in 1888. "The boy's sagacity surprises me," Gresham wrote Fairbanks. "He schemes like an old politician."[8]

The first test of the movement came at the state convention in September 1890, where the platform was expected to be an index of the president's popularity. Noting that there was "a wide difference . . . between a mere endorsement and a hearty endorsement," Gresham passed along Otto's suggestion that Fairbanks and his friends should take control of the resolutions committee and "in effect censure the Administration by ignoring it or faintly praising it." After hours of wrangling, the committee issued a platform that simply "endorse[d]" the administration but "heartily approve[d]" the actions of congressional Republicans under "the brilliant and fearless leadership" of House Speaker Thomas B. Reed. The "anti's" had shown themselves to be a considerable force.[9]

Divisions aside, the Republican party's prospects in the upcoming congressional elections seemed grim. Many voters bridled at the large pension and other expenditures of the "Billion Dollar" Fifty-first Congress, and discussion of the Lodge "Force" bill calling for federal supervision of southern elections raised fears of a revival of Reconstruction. Like many others, Gresham saw the passage of the McKinley Tariff Act in October 1890 as the most damaging development. He had naively hoped for a "*liberal* reduction" of duties, but when House Ways and Means Chairman William McKinley's hearings in early 1890 showed a clear protectionist bias, Gresham realized anew why "many regard me [as] unsound as a republican." The final version of the act raised average rates to 49.5 percent and opened the way for Democratic charges of fostering high prices.[10]

McKinley faced an uphill fight for reelection, and Republicans throughout the country watched the Ohioan's race. In mid-October railroad car magnate George M. Pullman told Gresham that he had "secretly raised some money" to help McKinley's campaign. Gresham suspected the worst. Three weeks before the election, in a speech before a Chicago banquet honoring General Nelson A. Miles, he ruffled the audience of politicians and businessmen when he argued that "those who spend money in corrupting voters and bribing officers are more dangerous enemies to the Republic than were the men who engaged in unsuccessful rebellion against it." Pullman watched stonily as Gresham added, "Too many so-called respectable men think, or act as if they thought, that it was less disreputable to buy a vote than to sell a vote." With Chicago's Mayor Dewitt C. Cregier seated by his side, the judge went on to criticize the nation's "notoriously bad" municipal government as "largely intrusted to men who, if capable, are not trustworthy, many of them desiring loose and extravagant administration that they may profit thereby." Anticipating the arguments of twentieth-century Progressives, he saw the root of the problem in "the practice of electing municipal officers on political grounds."[11]

Gresham won plaudits from reformers such as Jacob D. Cox, who wrote that "every word from so influential a man as yourself which tends to waken the torpid conscience of the people . . . is worth its weight in gold." But his veiled reference to the Dudley scandal of 1888 did not endear him to the administration. Two days earlier the death of Justice Samuel F. Miller had opened another vacancy on the Supreme Court, but Harrison again bypassed Gresham and appointed District Judge Henry B. Brown of Michigan.[12]

In November the Republicans suffered a crushing defeat, winning fewer than a hundred seats in the national House. The causes varied. In Wisconsin, for instance, a Republican-sponsored law mandating the use of the English language in parochial as well as public schools turned many immigrants to the Democrats. Indiana state chairman Louis Michener found that among those "who contributed to our defeat [and] are telling why they did it . . . about nine-tenths of them were out of humor with the McKinley bill." Gresham agreed that the tariff issue was the paramount reason for the heavy losses. On court duty in Milwaukee after the election, he wrote Fairbanks that "thoughtful Republicans here say the state will remain democratic if our party do[es]n't tack on the tariff question." In the nation at large, he believed "republican prospects were never more gloomy than now. If the McKinley bill is made the test of republicans, and all who do not support it are treated as free traders, the party will go to pieces in '92."[13]

The 1890 outcome raised Gresham's personal political stock. T.R. McFerson, antiadministration leader in Evansville, reported to Fairbanks that the Republican club of that city "was unanimously agreed that Gresham was the only man we could elect President two years from now." McFerson had earlier said the reason for Gresham's strength was that "the people want a man for president who will set down hard on the trusts and monopolies." A month after the election Gresham added to that image when he issued a ruling compelling witnesses to testify before the Interstate Commerce Commission on pain of being held in contempt of court. Even allowing for McFerson's effusiveness, as 1890 drew to a close, a growing constituency both within and outside the Republican party looked to Gresham as one who might lead the country away from politics as usual.[14]

Early the next year discontent among Illinois farmers led to consideration of Gresham for election to the United States Senate. The 1890 election had given the Democrats 101 seats in the state legislature and the Republicans 100, with the balance of three seats going to members of the Farmers' Mutual Benefit Association (FMBA), one of many protest groups then springing up in reaction to economic distress in the West and South. Election to the Senate required 103 votes, and balloting between Republican Richard Oglesby and Democrat John M. Palmer remained deadlocked for several days. Even before the voting began, two of the FMBA members thought of throwing their support to Gresham as a way to break the impasse. They looked upon the judge as "one who has not actively engaged in politics," and more important, they were "impressed with the idea that Judge Gresham is a friend of the industrial classes." Gresham was "assured by leading republicans that when the republican vote w[oul]d elect me it w[oul]d be thrown solidly" and that he would receive the vote of "more than one democrat" as well. But he refused to court support for the place. When FMBA members sought a meeting with him to sound out his views, he declined to talk with them. In the end his name was not presented, and the legislature eventually elected Palmer amid veiled charges of bribery.[15]

Powerful personal reasons held Gresham back from the Senate race. He and Tillie were just then moving into a house of their own on Prairie Avenue, confirming their decision to remain in Chicago. Also, just at the time the FMBA men sought an interview, he was in bed with the "grippe." Most important, he could not be convinced to leave his lifetime position. "I could not make up my mind that it was the thing for me to do even if I could get it," he confessed to Fairbanks. Even so, the episode underscored the argument that any future prospects Gresham had in politics rested on his image as a representative of protest.[16]

There was some irony in Gresham's winning the notice of the farmers' protest group just as he was taking up residence on Prairie Avenue, one of Chicago's most fashionable streets. His salary plus the proceeds from his Indiana farm were hardly sufficient to purchase a house in such a wealthy neighborhood, but the move was apparently pushed by Mrs. Gresham, who had inherited money which she decided to put into real estate. Even so, Gresham had to take out a large mortgage. As for their rich neighbors, he had long before established a relationship with his friends in the city's business elite in which he scrupulously preserved his independence. On one occasion, banker John W. Doane, a close friend, purchased shares of Pullman stock for Gresham without his knowledge; when the first dividend check came in, the judge promptly returned it to the brokerage house. "Although these gentlemen are friends of mine and have endeavored to do me a kindness," he wrote, "I cannot accept the money." He continued to worry about his personal finances and remained a man of relatively modest means.[17]

Meanwhile, the antiadministration movement continued in Indiana. In early 1891 Fairbanks carried the banner into the contest for the Republican caucus nomination for U.S. senator. Gresham urged his friend to "fight to the finish," and the Harrison men were able to defeat him only by withdrawing their own candidate, Louis T. Michener, and throwing their support to Governor Alvin P. Hovey. Harrison's friends hoped Fairbanks's defeat would end "the racket & that henceforth the Greshamites . . . will remain quiet," but instead the hostility to the president intensified, not only in Indiana but around the country. For many, Secretary of State James G. Blaine, whose original warm relations with Harrison had grown cold, became a lodestone for the anti-Harrison feeling, especially outside Indiana. There was even some talk of a Blaine-Gresham ticket, not born of a new compatibility between the two men but instead reflecting their supporters' shared contempt for Harrison. In the summer of 1891 Fairbanks and Otto Gresham organized meetings of antiadministration leaders from around the country to map strategy. Genuinely alarmed, the president's men secured the help of long-time Gresham supporter John W. Foster, who had hopes of succeeding Blaine as secretary of state. Foster gave out an interview lauding Harrison as "a statesman of the first order" and warning Hoosier Republicans that they would only "dishonor themselves if they did not give him their enthusiastic support."[18]

Fairbanks clung to the hope that Gresham could be nominated for president in 1892, and his cousin, Associated Press newsman Delavan Smith, confronted the judge directly with the argument that "the nomination would have to be made by the Republican party in deference to the wishes of the farmers and laboring classes who believed him to be their friend." But Gresham told Smith he had no desire to be a candidate. His opposition to the president ranged beyond his personal ambition and his personal antipathy for Harrison. Gresham considered Harrison, as much as anyone else, responsible for the unfair exactions of the McKinley Tariff. On another level, he held Harrison ultimately culpable for the Dudley frauds of 1888 and, more important, believed the president had done nothing to raise the level of politics in the country. Though determined to stay out of politics, Gresham decided in the summer of 1891 to step forward, more than he had ever done before, to issue a warning of the dangers he saw threatening the republic.[19]

He saw his opportunity in his assignment as orator of the day at the unveiling of an equestrian statue of Grant in Chicago's Lincoln Park, to take place in October. Enlisting the help of Noble Butler in writing his speech, he intended to give a "direct and unequivocal statement of existing political abuses which are subversive of popular government." He would show that "our government was founded on the principle that neither one man nor a class of men, however wise or rich, can be trusted as a majority of the people" and that "the chief reliance of the nation is not the rich who are addicted to luxury and indolence but the great multitude engaged in business, industrial and hardy pursuits."[20]

The dedication of the Grant statue came during the annual reunion of the Society of the Army of the Tennessee. Gresham thus had a national newspaper audience and took full measure of his opportunity. Before a crowd of thousands he devoted the first two-thirds of his talk to Grant's military career, although he also praised Grant as president for "vetoing legislation which seriously threatened the public welfare." Then, moving to the heart of his message, he warned of "corrupt methods and practices in our politics which threaten to subvert free institutions." Men must rise up and "resist the aggressions of those who seek to make our politics both an art and a mystery, intelligible only to the adept and initiated, who assume the management of them by virtue of their capacity for the deft and artful manipulation of their fellows."[21]

Denunciation of corruption was not new in Gresham's jeremiads, but now he emphasized the political inequities of wealth and class. "The people are often cheated at the polls and in legislation, and prizes which should be the reward of honest merit are too frequently bestowed upon the cunning and unscrupulous rich." Men whose "greed and love of power are greater than their love of country," he warned, "may masquerade in the garb of righteousness, and address the people in the language of patriotism, but their virtues are assumed." The "shameless and insidious attacks on free institutions" by these "hypocrites and assassins of liberty" were "infinitely more dangerous than the revolutionary teachings and practices of a comparatively few visionary and misguided men and women in our large cities." Common laboring folk were "not enemies of law and order"; they would rush to the nation's defense "with unselfish and devoted patriotism." But they would do so only "so long as the powers of the nation are not perverted to their injury for the enrichment of a few."

At the climax of his address Gresham noted that "the patriotism of our revolutionary sires" had momentarily become "voiceless among the busy multitude, in the marts, on the farms and in the workshops," but "we must not think it has ceased to exist." To arouse it once again, he called for leaders "who have sprung from the people, with strong and resolute character, unspoiled by luxury, clear-minded and level-headed, able to see men and things as they really are, undeceived by outward show and conventionality." Such men would be "worth more to our nation than all its mere cunning, self-seeking politicians, its political theorists, or its plutocrats."

Although the speech fell short of a call for sweeping social change, it was, as the *New York Times* observed, "the sort of talk that makes Judge Gresham extremely unwelcome in high quarters" in the Republican party. The pro-Harrison *Indianapolis Journal* made no editorial comment and in reprinting the address omitted the section dealing with "revolutionary teachings." From the Democratic perspective, the *Chicago Herald* saw it as a "direct appeal on the one hand to the mugwump element in the republican party" and also an "obvious invitation to the farmers' independent movement to draw closer to one already high in alliance favor." The *Herald* asked pointedly, "What is the republican party going to do with this Cato?"[22]

That question engaged the attention of Harrison's men worried about the speech's impact on the antiadministration movement. Before long newspapers carried rumors of a bargain whereby Gresham would throw his support to the president for renomination in exchange for a promise of support for Gresham's nomination in 1896. The source remained unknown, but whether or not it was intended by Harrison's backers to smoke Gresham out, the report moved him to a public disavowal of any intention to challenge the president. "I cannot afford to stand before the country in the attitude of having dickered for the presidential nomination," he wrote Fairbanks indignantly. *"I cherish no political ambition and . . . will never be a candidate for president or any other office."* The young attorney faced a rising political career of his own, and Gresham assured him that if he chose to support Harrison, "it will not change my feelings for you." For himself, however, there could be no change. "The President's course towards me has been such that I cannot do anything to promote his political interests. I am not for him and shall not be. . . . I must be frank, I do not like him."[23]

The antiadministration movement in Indiana had generated much sound and fury, but it had failed to dislodge the Harrison men's hold on the party machinery. By the time the election year opened, they had begun to exercise more energetically the power of incumbency, calling federal officeholders into strategy sessions and pressing them to organize support for the president on the local level. In January they dominated a series of primaries to select party committeemen. Blaine's formal withdrawal from the race in February further discouraged the opposition, and in March Indiana's district and state conventions selected a solid Harrison delegation to the national convention.[24]

The administration exercised its organization muscle and duplicated this success in other states, although it could not completely extinguish the feeling among many Republicans that Harrison ought not to be renominated. But Gresham remained adamant that he was out of the running. In January Philadelphia industrialist P.A.B. Widener offered to coordinate a campaign with Harrison's Senate critics on his behalf. Gresham declined. Similar offers from Harrison Gray Otis of the *Los Angeles Times* likewise got nowhere, as did Thomas C. Platt's suggestion in late May of a Blaine-Gresham ticket. On the eve of the convention Gresham informed a group of Pennsylvania delegates who stopped in Chicago on their way to Minneapolis that "as an honest man" he could not accept the Republican nomination because of the party's commitment to the McKinley Tariff.[25]

By mid-spring Fairbanks was working in the Harrison campaign, but Gresham remained unreconciled. In one of his rare comments on foreign affairs before becoming secretary of state, he told Fairbanks that the administration's belligerent handling of a crisis with Chile over the murder of two American sailors in a Valparaiso saloon brawl had been designed primarily to shore up Harrison's renomination bid: "This fact will get into the minds of the people, and they will see that the President was just as bent on promoting his own political interests as he was on vindicating the nation's honor."[26]

Thanks to superior organization, Harrison had no trouble winning renomination at Minneapolis, and the convention adopted a platform endorsing the McKinley Tariff Act as "wise revenue legislation." As a consequence, Gresham found himself at a crossroads. He hated Harrison and thought the McKinley Act had been "designed to promote class interest and not the public welfare." In little over a week he told his old friend Benjamin Bristow, who was similarly troubled, that "the republican party of the past, with its high aims and purposes," had fallen to "a lot of selfish, tricky, unscrupulous men." "You are a better republican than I am," he concluded, "for you mean to stand by the party whether you can give a good reason for doing so or not."[27]

But where could he go? Gresham's labor decisions, his opposition to the McKinley Tariff, and his public denunciations of the "unscrupulous rich" all combined to catch the eye of many in the new Populist party, which would hold its first presidential nominating convention in less than two weeks. As early as the spring of 1891 an independent newspaper in Pittsburgh had touted him as a strong presidential candidate for the new party because he was a well-known public man who represented "none of its crankisms, but would attract a large independent vote outside the [Farmers] Alliance." In February 1892, he told one Hoosier Populist organizer: "You are not mistaken in supposing that I am a firm believer in popular government. The public welfare should be the aim of all legislation. A man who does not love the human race and desire the elevation of the masses is not to be trusted as a friend of free institutions." But, he added, "I do not express these views in the hope of recommending myself to you, and association with you in political action, as a fit person to lead your movement; I am not such a person."[28]

But there was enough ambiguity in this statement to lead many Populists to believe that he would accept a draft, and when Leonidas Polk, one of the front-runners in the nomination race, died suddenly on June 11, many more party members turned to Gresham. That he could draw significant strength from the major parties seemed confirmed by reports that Republican Robert Ingersoll and Hoosier Democratic Senator Daniel Voorhees would both be willing to campaign in his behalf. In late June he told Populist representatives that poor health, financial burdens, and family responsibilities would not permit him to make a campaign. Still, he added, "With the exception of your sub-treasury scheme, which to me is visionary and impractical, there is no difference [between us], unless it be that many entertain a stronger hope than I do that we are to escape a bloody revolution before this plutocracy of wealth surrenders its hold." In a similar vein he told a *Chicago Herald* reporter a few days later, "The most insidious of all forms of tyranny is that of a plutocracy. Thoughtful men see and admit that our country is becoming less and less democratic and more and more plutocratic." But he emphatically denied that he had told Populist leaders he would accept a draft nomination.[29]

When delegates arrived for the Omaha convention in early July, many of them still favored Gresham because they saw him as the likeliest candidate to broaden the third party's base of support. Opposing them were the backers of James B. Weaver of Iowa, James H. Kyle of South Dakota, Ben Terrell of Texas, and others who believed that the nomination should not go to some man outside the movement simply because he might attract more voters from the old parties. On the convention's third and final day, July 4, with the Gresham boom still very much alive, permanent chairman Henry L. Loucks opened the proceedings with a speech declaring that the nominee must be "a man who will meet with the approval of the people inside the party"—one who had "burned the bridge behind him." "We must know that he has been with us enough to have been found true, or he will find no place here."[30]

The Gresham enthusiasts were undaunted. The afternoon session was interrupted when national chairman Henry Taubeneck arrived waving a telegram from the Populist nominee for lieutenant governor

of Indiana: "I have seen Gresham. If unanimous he will not decline."
According to one reporter, "The effect of this telegram was electrical.
Thousands of people sprang instantly to their feet, and thousands of
voices cheered again and again for Gresham. There seemed no doubt
that among those wildly cheering enthusiasts were a majority of the
delegates." Loucks was hard pressed to head off a stampede for
Gresham and was aided by Weaver supporter Mary E. Lease and Paul
Vandervoort, whom Gresham had dismissed from the postal service a
decade earlier. Vandervoort offered a motion to adjourn until evening.
The intense arguing cooled somewhat after the arrival of Weaver, who,
though claiming that he was for Gresham if he would run on the
Populist platform, said that the judge ought not to be nominated until
his intentions were clear. After more wrangling, the motion to adjourn
carried.[31]

Meanwhile, a committee sent from Omaha met with Gresham in
Chicago. He told them that his declination was "final and irrevocable"
and wired the same message to party leaders at the convention. When
his telegram arrived during the evening session, the Gresham boom
ended, and the delegates proceeded to nominate Weaver. In Washington reporters noted a "sigh of relief" among Republicans and Democrats who had "been looking toward Omaha with a good deal of
anxiety." John W. Foster, who had replaced Blaine as secretary of state,
wrote Fairbanks that he was "glad to see our good friend Gresham was
not captured by the Alliance people." As the *Washington Post* put it, the
nomination of Weaver, who had long been associated with third-party
failures, had left the fall campaign "a square contest between the
Republican and Democratic parties."[32]

Thus Gresham's reprehension of the American political system
stopped short of assuming the leadership of a third party, but he had
no intention of returning to the Republican fold. By August 1 he had
decided to vote for Grover Cleveland. The Republican platform pointed to "prosperity in our fields, workshops, and mines" as proof of the
success of the high tariff, but that summer violence at the Homestead
steel plant and Idaho's Coeur d'Alene mining district belied the party's
claim that protectionism served the interests of workers. Gresham was
profoundly disturbed by the imbalanced relationship between labor
and capital those incidents illustrated. "The labor question has come to
stay," he wrote Indianapolis reformer Morris Ross; "it cannot be ignored."

We are living under new conditions, conditions utterly unlike anything in the
past. Labor-saving machinery has given capital an advantage that it never
possessed before. What is an equitable division of the joint product of capital

and labor, and who is to decide the question? I fear that the settlement of the controversy will be attended with serious consequences. The laboring men of this country have intelligence and courage, and they firmly believe that they are oppressed. They are growing stronger daily, and unless capital yields, we will have collisions more serious than the one which occurred at Homestead. The right to acquire and hold property must be recognized. No civilization of the past has amounted to anything that did not recognize that right. But those who employ labor seem to think that only property rights need protection, and that laborers are entitled to no more sympathy and consideration than the machinery which they tend. Employers go through their forms of worship in a perfunctory way, not heeding the injunction that we should love our neighbors as ourselves. It seems to me that labor will triumph in the near future, but will it use its power wisely?[33]

Of course, Cleveland was not offering a fundamental reordering of economic relationships, nor was Gresham clear as to how to bring about a more "equitable division of the joint product of capital and labor." But he did believe that Cleveland was "an honest, courageous, patriotic man," and the Democrats had long favored a lower tariff. Originally, he did not intend to announce his decision, but he was soon pressed by Democratic friends to do so. As the campaign got under way, many Democrats, especially Cleveland himself, were eager to win normally Republican states like Illinois and Wisconsin so as to diminish reliance on New York, where long-standing animosity between Cleveland and state party leaders cast serious doubt on his chances. Campaign leaders recognized the value of Gresham's conversion for their midwestern strategy. In mid-August Cleveland's manager, former Navy Secretary William C. Whitney, found Gresham vacationing in Connecticut and urged him to make a public declaration. Similar appeals came from Chicago Democrats, including Gresham's close friend Lambert Tree, who had served in the first Cleveland administration as minister to Belgium and to Russia. As a former judge, Tree understood Gresham's hesitancy and prompted fellow Chicagoan Chief Justice Melville Fuller to advise Gresham that there was no judicial impropriety in his issuing a public explanation of his change in political affiliation. Still he hesitated, prompting Cleveland to write Tree: "I am a little disappointed to learn that there is the least possibility of Judge Gresham's not pursuing the course which all of us have expected that he would follow, and was only awaiting his time to do so. I am exceedingly anxious that his friends and the people should hear from him, and I cannot appreciate any objection to his doing so."[34]

In early October Tree and District Judge William J. Allen stated publicly that Gresham would vote for Cleveland on the basis of the tariff issue and his belief that the Republican party had become a tool of the trusts. Democratic national chairman William F. Harrity immediately welcomed the help of "a statesman of so high a character and such great influence." Cleveland also was pleased although somewhat disappointed that the "Gresham matter came before the public in a very different shape from what I expected." As matters turned out, the Allen and Tree interviews set off speculation that left Gresham's intentions and motives more in doubt than ever, with Republicans charging that his failure to receive a Supreme Court appointment lay at the root of his switch.[35]

He tried to meet such criticism through private correspondence, claiming that "the President could have offered me no place that I would accept." He was especially eager to convince Fairbanks of his sincerity. "I think the tariff is the overshadowing question and I believe the republican party is wrong on it," he wrote his former manager. "I believe in 'government of the people, for the people, by the people' and as I see it the present leaders of the republican party do not believe in that kind of government." He would vote for Cleveland that year but did not know what he would do in future elections. "I have had no correspondence with him & have not heard from him in any way and want nothing from him. . . . I have no political ambition."[36]

Fairbanks accepted Gresham's explanation, but there was more truth in the charge of personal pique than Gresham wanted to admit. Moreover, rumors began to circulate that he was going to vote for Harrison. With less than two weeks left in the campaign, he finally agreed to issue a public letter addressed to Illinois Republican Bluford Wilson. In it he denied that he had wanted an office from Harrison, that he had wanted the presidential nomination in 1892, or that he had voted for Cleveland in 1888. He had, he said, "determined to vote for Mr. Cleveland this fall because I agree in the main with his views on the tariff." The McKinley Tariff, he charged, had been "passed in the interests of the favored classes and not for the benefit of the whole people." "Duties were imposed upon some articles so as to destroy competition and foster trusts and monopolies. . . . This was an abandonment of the doctrine of moderate incidental protection." "I think with you," he concluded, "that a Republican can vote for Mr. Cleveland without joining the Democratic party." Gresham was not alone; other prominent Republicans who announced for Cleveland included Thomas M. Cooley, Columbia University president Seth Low, and former Attorney General Wayne MacVeagh.[37]

Wilson sent Gresham's letter to Democratic headquarters in New York where campaign officials gave it to reporters. Republicans predictably branded him an "ingrate" and a "venomous traitor," who had "at last torn off the mask and gone into the Democratic party where he should have been years ago." On election day he was met at the polls by a *Chicago Tribune* reporter and took one more opportunity to defend his views. "The McKinley bill is not for the benefit of the poor," he said. "It makes the rich richer and the poor poorer." He argued that Democratic victory would "not mean free trade" but instead "a reduction without an entire loss of the protection theory." He pointed out that it took about $400 million each year to run the United States government and that "the only practical way" to raise such a sum was by customs duties. In so doing, "protection can be given to industries that need protecting," but rates "should not exceed the difference in the cost between the foreign countries and the United States." When the duties exceeded that difference, "the manufacturers in this country have the power to form a pool, a trust, and force the price above the real value as designated by the cost of production." He did, however, argue for free trade in raw materials so that manufacturers could produce their goods more cheaply and compete more effectively in foreign markets.[38]

The Democrats won Indiana, Illinois, Wisconsin, and the election. A week later Bluford Wilson congratulated Gresham on "the splendid effect of your great shot." The impact of Gresham's letter on the outcome is, of course, impossible to gauge, but its effect on his own career is easily discerned. The letter marked the end of his relationship with the Republican party, which for years had been tenuous at best. He had written Wilson that he could vote for Cleveland and still be a Republican, but he was fooling no one, least of all himself. In an age when party loyalty was the be all and end all for many politicians, such a step was looked upon as an act of betrayal. And a renunciation of party amounted to a declaration of political retirement. "I have no political ambition," he wrote his old friend and supporter Joseph Medill of the *Chicago Tribune*, "but if I had, no one realizes better than I do that I have committed political suicide. Some people are unable to understand that a man can deliberately do that."[39]

Ironically, that act of "political suicide" brought Gresham his greatest political distinction, appointment as secretary of state.

SEVEN

SECRETARY OF STATE
Proper Views of Things

Although Gresham's announcement in favor of Cleveland momentarily thrust him into the churning political currents, in the fall of 1892
he had every expectation of finishing out his public life as circuit judge.
"Nothing," he told Charles W. Fairbanks, "could tempt me to go into
politics."[1] In the fall court term the most important case before him
concerned the powers of the Interstate Commerce Commission, which
had been investigating charges that several railroads owned by the
Illinois Steel Company were guilty of unlawful discrimination in giving
rate preferences to the latter firm. When company officials refused to
answer questions or open company records, the commission asked
Gresham to compel them to comply on pain of being held in contempt
of court. The companies' lawyers replied that the commission was
engaged in a judicial inquiry which, as an administrative body, it could
not lawfully pursue.

The case presented Gresham with a dilemma. He sympathized
completely with the commission's efforts to reform railroading, but he
also felt genuine constitutional scruples about the separation of the
executive and judicial powers. In open court he expressed the fear that
if he threw out the commission's judicial power to examine witnesses,
its effectiveness would be wiped out. His decision, rendered in early
December, reflected an imperfect resolution of his conflicting concerns. He declared unconstitutional that part of the Interstate Commerce Act that required courts to "use their process" to aid the
commission's inquiries, on the grounds that "Congress can not make
the judicial department the mere adjunct or instrument of either of the
other departments of the government." But he also suggested a way
out of the problem. The act had been imperfectly drawn in that it
should have made it a criminal offense to refuse to cooperate with the
commission. "Undoubtedly," he said, "Congress may confer upon a
non-judicial body authority to obtain information for legitimate governmental purposes, and make refusal to appear and testify before it,
touching matters pertinent to any authorized inquiry, an offense
punishable by the court." Some observers regarded Gresham's reason-

ing as constitutional hair-splitting, and a year and a half later a divided Supreme Court reversed his decision.[2]

Outside of court, Gresham looked forward to the World's Columbian Exposition to be held in Chicago the next year as a way to publicize his and others' ideas on how to reform municipal government. He chaired a committee to organize a "world's congress on the government of cities" to meet in conjunction with the exposition. In a preliminary address announcing the project, he pointed to "the corruption, the inefficiency, and general mismanagement of government of many of the leading cities of the world and the consequent increase in them of crime, lawlessness, disease, insecurity, and danger." With the progressive's faith in scientific knowledge and experimentation, he noted that "new methods and systems of government have been tried in different cities throughout the world"; the proposed congress would "place the results of such practical tests within the knowledge and reach of all."[3]

For her part, Tillie Gresham looked forward to the social side of the world's fair. During inaugural ceremonies in October, she served as one of the patronesses at the ball presided over by Bertha Palmer, president of the Board of Lady Managers. Indeed, the future in general seemed bright to Mrs. Gresham. She later recalled, "I thought we were through with politics forever, so I was happy."[4]

Grover Cleveland had other ideas, however. On the day Gresham issued his Interstate Commerce Commission opinion, the president-elect sat down with his close adviser Daniel S. Lamont to discuss his cabinet. He surprised Lamont by suggesting Gresham for secretary of the treasury. "He is a Democrat as the parties are now divided and has been since 1888," Cleveland said. "He is an able, all-around man and would be of great service to me in the Cabinet." Moreover, he added, "The labor element have been very much attached to him by reason of some of his decisions—in which he of course did only his duty." Lamont replied that he doubted Gresham would accept for fear of "the imputation that he changed his politics for an office," and Cleveland answered that the judge was "too big a man for such a charge to lodge against." The next day William C. Whitney visited Cleveland and asked "if Gresham's name had ever occurred" to the president-elect. Cleveland said that it had, and after further discussion a preliminary roster of potential appointees emerged with John G. Carlisle at treasury and Gresham slated for secretary of the interior.[5]

Early in January Gresham was in New York and paid a brief call on Cleveland. The nature of their discussion was not recorded, but Gresham apparently withdrew himself from consideration and took the opportunity to press the claims of others. By mid-January Cleveland had arrived at a revised slate, and Gresham's name was not on it. The list was not final, however, and Cleveland was having particular trouble with the State Department. Around the first of the year he had offered the secretaryship to Chief Justice Melville Fuller, who had declined. A few weeks later the president-elect had "about determined" to offer the job to the secretary in his first term, Thomas F. Bayard. But Bayard was opposed by former Navy Secretary Whitney with whom he had battled for influence in the first administration. Along with Maryland Senator Arthur P. Gorman, Whitney revived consideration of Gresham. On January 25 Cleveland and Bayard reached an understanding that took Bayard out of the running for the cabinet. The same day Cleveland wrote Gresham inviting him to become secretary of state.[6]

Cleveland also dispatched former Postmaster General Don M. Dickinson to Chicago to try to allay the judge's apprehensions about accepting the appointment. Although he was inclined to turn it down, he promised to "deliberate" on the matter. The many friends he consulted were divided, but Mrs. Gresham and Otto opposed it, agreeing with Bluford Wilson that the judge should avoid even "the 'appearance of evil.' " On February 3 Gresham wrote Cleveland declining, citing demands of work and his household that he could not meet if he were to go to Washington.[7]

On the same day, however, Gresham wrote Dickinson that "some of the objections" he had mentioned in their conversations had "ceased to have weight" and that "I finally had a feeling (which has not left me) that I ought to go to Mr. Cleveland." The next day his Chicago friend John W. Doane wrote Whitney that if Gresham were made to feel it was "his duty to go to Washington, he would not hesitate a minute, but would accept." Gresham's and Doane's letters indicated a disposition on Gresham's part to be beseeched, but whether or not such was the case, Cleveland and other Democrats did fairly beg him to take the position. Dickinson wrote that Cleveland's "wish represents a great need" and that he had "never seen his heart and mind more fixed on anything." On February 7, still entertaining misgivings, Gresham yielded, although not without telling Cleveland to "feel perfectly free, even up to the last moment, to substitute someone else in my place should circumstances require it."[8]

Even after his acceptance Gresham still hoped Cleveland would "let me off," but he was impressed by the president-elect's "earnestness" and soon became reconciled to his decision. He knew that his identification as a Republican would cause a "row," but he had faith that "old

things are passing away." His apprehensions about entering a Democratic cabinet yielded to his confidence in the essential consonance of
his and Cleveland's views. Publicly, he told reporters that he had "no
desire to return to Washington" with its "shallowness" and "intrigues."
"I accepted simply because the office was urged upon me as a duty that
I owe to the American people."[9]

Foreign policy concerns had little bearing on Cleveland's selection of
Gresham. Indeed, the two men had apparently not exchanged ideas on
foreign affairs before the appointment was made. Princeton professor
Woodrow Wilson thought it seemed "a pity . . . to waste so fine a
Secretary of the Interior, as it seems certain Mr. Gresham would have
made, on the novel field of foreign affairs." In truth, it was Gresham's
stand on domestic issues such as the tariff plus political considerations
that originally drew Cleveland to him. John Bassett Moore, who had
served under Bayard in the first Cleveland administration, thought
Whitney had pushed Gresham for the top spot in the cabinet to keep
Bayard out. The political motives were broader, however. To many
observers, the Democratic landslide of 1892 had presaged a realignment of political parties; in constructing his new administration
Cleveland sought to further that realignment. Appointing Gresham
could help solidify support among the large independent element that
had voted for Cleveland in November, broaden the Democrats' appeal
to labor, and undermine the growing strength of the Populists. "You
are strong," Whitney told Gresham, "and represent a large class who
have not heretofore stood with our party." From the Republican perspective Albert J. Beveridge wrote that he feared that "this movement
upon the part of Mr. Cleveland & yourself may mean the breaking up of
old political lines and a general readjustment of parties."[10]

But speculation about a new political order did not make it a reality.
Although many Republicans praised Cleveland's good judgment in
selecting a capable adviser from their ranks, many more condemned
Gresham for his "apostacy." Most Democrats welcomed the new secretary as a valuable asset to their party, but a disturbing number denounced the appointment as an act of ingratitude to able and deserving
Democrats. In fact, during his two-year tenure Gresham proved to be
one of the most controversial figures in the administration. As one
writer presciently observed a few months after his appointment, "A
new party can be formed for success only upon some great and overshadowing issue; it cannot be done by a mere coalition between leaders."[11]

Ten days before the inauguration Gresham traveled east at Cleveland's request for a conference on problems facing the new administra-

tion. He went first to New York, where he met with outgoing Secretary of State John W. Foster, who briefed him on department business. He then went on to Cleveland's cottage at Lakewood, New Jersey, where he was joined by incoming Treasury Secretary John G. Carlisle. For four hours the three men discussed a variety of questions ranging from a treaty for the annexation of Hawaii pending in the Senate to the country's worsening economy. Afterward Gresham returned to Chicago to wind up affairs in his court before going on to Washington.[12]

He arrived in the capital on the evening of March 4 and was joined two weeks later by Tillie and Otto. The family took up residence at the Arlington Hotel in a suite of rooms that had been part of Charles Sumner's old house on Lafayette Square across from the White House. People of both political parties welcomed them back to the community they had left eight years before. Bayard, who was about to take up his post as ambassador to Great Britain, found Gresham "very attractive—so *direct* and honest. His nature is the direct opposite in every way from Blaine." Mrs. Gresham enjoyed being back in the Washington social world, attending state dinners and making new friends in the cabinet and diplomatic corps.[13]

Gresham and Cleveland took an instant liking to each other and soon established a close working relationship. Over the months the president became increasingly dependent on the secretary for counsel and support. Gresham quickly learned how to deal with Cleveland's stubbornly solipsistic approach to public questions. Cleveland rarely read books, he noted, but instead formulated his ideas on issues through conversation; once he had reached a judgment, his mind clamped shut. Gresham felt that "it was quite useless to attempt to advise him directly; that he seemed to repel any attempt of that kind; and that the only way you could reach him was to watch for an opportunity when he seemed to be inclining to views similar to your own, and then to endorse and support them, not as your own, but as his." But even with this need for indirection, Gresham acknowledged that he "got on very well" with the president. Cleveland reciprocated the feeling, writing Dickinson halfway through his term, "You don't know what a comfort Gresham is to me, with his hard sense, his patriotism, and loyalty. It is but little for me to say that I would trust my life or honor in his keeping at all times."[14]

Gresham took his oath of office on March 6, and that afternoon reporters found him "engrossed with the duties devolving upon him." His elaborately decorated offices were in the State, War, and Navy Building just west of the White House. For his secretary he chose Kenesaw Mountain Landis, a twenty-six-year-old lawyer whose family had supported Gresham in Indiana Republican politics. For the next two years the two men were rarely apart. A typical day found Gresham leaving the Arlington at eight o'clock with a cigar in his mouth and Landis in tow. They usually walked to the department and, reporters noted, the secretary frequently stopped to talk with acquaintances, "inviting fun by his cheerful tendency to allude to mirthful topics." Once he had reached his office, however, the fun was over. Until two o'clock he received diplomats, department personnel, newsmen, officeseekers, or others whose mission might or might not concern departmental business. After two, access was limited to those with appointments or members of the department, but even then frequent interruptions prevented prolonged concentration on business at hand. In the course of the day there would be a brief break for lunch and perhaps interruptions to consult with the president at the White House. Not until four o'clock could Gresham and Landis buckle down to sustained work. At six they would break for dinner back at the Arlington, taking with them bundles of papers over which they would work into the night. After a year Gresham described his office as "one of incessant toil," and Landis later recalled that the secretary "never rested."[15]

In attempting to become conversant in foreign affairs, one of the main difficulties Gresham confronted was the continuing distraction of domestic matters, ranging from congressional legislation to labor strife. One such diversion was relatively pleasant, when he and Tillie accompanied Cleveland and other cabinet officers to Chicago, where the president opened the world's fair on May 1. The fair was a monument to technological advance and prosperity, but before the end of its first week attention shifted to Wall Street, where stock prices fell precipitously to record lows. The Panic of 1893 had begun.

Ironically, the booming confidence the fair symbolized lay at the root of the disaster, for over the past several years businessmen of all kinds—railroad magnates, manufacturers, farmers—had overextended their enterprises, largely on borrowed money, staking their chances on an expanding economy. Most such speculative booms reach a point when returns appear unexpectedly meager, and confidence turns into doubt. That point had come in early 1893, and as winter wore into spring, a general collapse seemed inevitable. With the loss of confidence came a drive by investors and others to unload stocks, paper currency, and other assets for gold, leading to a severe drain on the gold reserve of the United States Treasury. In exchange for the reliable metal, people brought in Civil War–era greenbacks, silver coins, and treasury notes issued against the silver purchased by the government under the terms of the Sherman Silver Purchase Act of 1890. Before Cleveland took office, the gold reserve edged downward toward the $100 million level, generally regarded as the lowest level necessary to ensure the maintenance of a gold standard, the solvency of the government, and the economic well-being of the nation. On Inauguration Day the reserve stood at $100,982,410.[16]

In his Inaugural Address Cleveland hinted that he favored the repeal of the Silver Purchase Act as the key to renewed business confidence, but he took no immediate action. Even after the gold reserve dipped below $100 million on April 22, he delayed two more months before calling a special session, apparently to allow business demands for repeal to reach a crescendo that would make it easier to overcome pro-silver sentiment in Congress. Success would depend largely on the attitude of Senate Finance Committee Chairman Daniel W. Voorhees of Indiana, long known as a champion of expanded currency. It fell largely to Gresham as a fellow Hoosier to try to bring Voorhees around. Despite his general rule against becoming involved in Democratic patronage matters, he interceded with Cleveland on behalf of Voorhees's friends, including the senator's choice for district attorney for Indiana, who had been the only Democrat in the state legislature to vote against adoption of the Australian ballot and who now was opposed by both civil service reformers and organized labor. Although Gresham's "propitiating" Voorhees appalled reformers, the senator did agree to support the administration on the repeal question.[17]

On June 30 Cleveland called Congress into special session on August 7 to repeal the Sherman Act and thereby relieve the people of "present and impending danger and distress." Gresham welcomed the move, but he also frankly told Cleveland that "all this financial trouble is not due to the Sherman law." To be sure, much of the country's difficulty was "the result of senseless fright," and repeal "would do much good in getting rid of that fright." But more important, the administration must "keep its pledge on the tariff question." Gresham argued that Cleveland's message opening the special session should "at least refer to the tariff as something which will need attention" after silver repeal. He had an ally in former Navy Secretary William C. Whitney, who in late July attacked the high protective tariff as "essentially a tax upon the producing and industrial classes" and argued that as long as the present system continued, "the country's prosperity will never be permanently established." Moreover, because duties were levied primarily on necessities, Whitney said, "the general mass of the people . . . pay fifteen times as much tax in proportion to their means as the rich man. There lies the secret of national distress." "My views on the tariff coincide precisely with yours," Gresham wrote Whitney. "The Administration must show at the proper time unmistakably that in a contest between privilege and the people it is for the people."[18]

Before Congress convened, however, Gresham had little opportunity to press his views on Cleveland in person, because the president was at his summer home in Massachusetts recuperating from an operation to remove a cancerous growth in his mouth. The surgery had been kept a secret to avoid further disturbance to the country's financial markets. A week after Cleveland left Washington, Supreme Court Justice Samuel Blatchford died, and Attorney General Richard Olney and many others pushed Gresham as his replacement. But Cleveland had already come to regard him as indispensable in the cabinet. When most other members escaped Washington's summer heat, Gresham turned down vacation invitations to be on hand to do "all I can to secure passage of the repeal bill."[19]

In his message to the special session the president clung to his notion that the country's economic troubles were "principally chargeable" to the Sherman Act, whose repeal Congress should consider "at once and before all other subjects." Gresham continued his pressure on Voorhees, making sure "the riot act was read to him," whenever the senator appeared to be "wobbling." He also kept tabs on House members, urging, for instance, Chicago Congressman John C. Black's constituents to "prod him a little."[20]

Repeal passed the House easily on August 28. In little over a week Gresham believed that it was already having "a splendid effect on the country." The bill had majority support in the Senate, but when its opponents settled in for a long filibuster, Gresham once more saw the American republican experiment in peril: "The framers of our constitution expected the Senate to be a conservative body and act as a check against ill-advised legislation, but it has sadly degenerated; it is not patriotic. Quite a number of its members have secured their seats by corrupt means. The people are patient, but they will not much longer tolerate a body which instead of being useful impedes needed relief and reform. If the Senate persists in its course, our Government can not justly be called popular in form."[21]

Repeal did not pass the upper house until October 30. Gresham hailed the outcome as a "signal" triumph for the administration, but it was a Pyrrhic victory, bringing no real economic improvement. By the end of the year six hundred banks and fifteen thousand other businesses had declared bankruptcy, and American Federation of Labor president Samuel Gompers estimated that 3 million workers were unemployed. By January 1894, the gold reserve was down to $65 million, and the administration was forced to float the first of four unpopular bond issues. On the political front, repeal did nothing to help the Democrats avert landslide defeats in the November 1893 elections. Moreover, the silver struggle had left the party in Congress seriously divided for the tariff fight that still lay ahead.[22]

Preparation for that fight was already under way. The day after the House passed silver repeal, the Ways and Means Committee organized for the arduous task of writing a tariff bill with hundreds of complex rate schedules. When Congress reconvened in December, Chairman William L. Wilson introduced a bill which he estimated would lower overall rates from the McKinley Act level of near 50 percent to 30.31 percent. By no means calling for free trade, the proposal generally followed Democratic arguments for lower duties on raw materials, and it greatly expanded the free list. Decreased rates on manufactured items pleased the South. House members debated the bill during January 1894, adding a provision for a tax on incomes to compensate for lost revenues. With little other change it passed on February 1 by a comfortable margin.[23]

Gresham predicted Senate approval of the bill "substantially as it left the House," although without the income tax. He considered the new tax "just and equitable" but had doubts about instituting it in time of depression. As it turned out, the income tax survived, but nearly every other part of the bill came in for revision. Senators added 634 amendments, shunting aside the principle of free raw materials to give protection to industries in their home states. The Senate bill took more than forty items, including sugar, iron ore, and coal, from the Wilson bill's free list and raised the overall average rate eight percentage points.[24]

Leading in the gutting of the Wilson bill were several Democratic senators, many of whom Gresham believed were "gambling in sugar" with an eye to the Senate's restoration of a duty. He had, meanwhile, sold his own small amount of sugar stock to avoid any imputation of profiteering. But beyond motives of personal gain, Gresham thought many of the Democratic senators were out-and-out protectionists, who "if they were consistent . . . would be Republicans." They were Democrats, yet the administration had virtually no influence over them after squandering its leverage on the silver fight. Moreover, Cleveland had further alienated administration opponents by his disregard of senatorial courtesy in two Supreme Court nominations. Indeed, Gresham saw the party as in such "very bad shape" that he suggested that Cleveland sign the pending Silver Seigniorage Bill for the minting of the small amount of silver accumulated in the treasury. The bill posed no threat to the gold standard, and, Gresham argued, the president's approval "would be attended with good rather than injurious results" for the tariff fight. Nonetheless, Cleveland vetoed the measure in a message that shocked and angered prosilver Democrats.[25]

At the end of March Gresham still hoped a tariff bill would pass by the first of June. "The country is rich and prosperity will return," he wrote Bertha Palmer, "and with it there will be less dissatisfaction with the democratic party." But while Congress dallied, discontent among the unemployed grew and in some localities reached the flashpoint. Not only were "armies" of unemployed people forming to march to Washington, but unrest spread to workers who still had jobs, as the winter and spring witnessed a wave of strikes protesting wage cuts. Like many others, Gresham viewed all these developments with profound anxiety.[26]

The previous year Populist leader Henry Vincent had hailed his appointment as giving the "tin bucket brigade" a "friend at court." Now, however, Gresham found it increasingly difficult to fulfill that role in the siege mentality of the Cleveland White House. On May 1 five hundred out-of-work men under the leadership of Ohio businessman Jacob S. Coxey arrived in Washington to register support for a public works bill. Cleveland and Attorney General Richard Olney had planted secret service men in the group, and District of Columbia police, with federal troops in reserve, had little trouble dispersing "Coxey's Army" and arresting its leaders for minor trespass infractions. Gresham agreed with Cleveland and Olney that such disturbances represented "symptoms of revolution," but he was less inclined to believe that the simple application of force would make them go away. He thought Coxey was "an honest crank, as are most of his followers here," and that their movement addressed the fundamental problem he had decried for years. "If the very conditions of society are such that fair opportunity is denied honest men to support themselves and their families by their toil," he wrote Federal Judge Charles E. Dyer, "some change must be made or a catastrophe will be encountered. You ask what the change should be. I do not know. It may be necessary to have a more equitable division of the joint product of capital and labor. . . . Honest laboring men will not quietly see their families starve." Recognizing the radical tendencies of his words, Gresham added, "You must not infer that I am a socialist—much less an anarchist."[27]

Tariff legislation could help. "Our mills and factories can supply the home demand by running six or seven months of the year," and "this means enforced idleness for the balance of the year." Decreased duties on raw materials "would lower the cost of the manufactured article and enable our people to compete in foreign markets with Great Britain."

But free raw materials would only "improve our situation in this country to some extent." More important, general tariff reduction could curtail the power of the trusts with their arrogant disregard for the interests of workers and consumers. "We have gone too far in protecting special interests," Gresham wrote Dyer. "If men can be protected by tariff against foreign competition, and by trusts against home competition, they can do about as they please." On July 3, however, the Senate passed its version of the tariff bill, which, Gresham said, fell "far below what the country had a right to expect in view of the election of '92."[28]

On the labor front, meanwhile, the situation worsened. A strike that had begun in the Pullman Palace Car Works near Chicago in early May had by late June evolved into a general railroad strike disrupting traffic in two-thirds of the country. To handle the administration's response, Cleveland relied on Attorney General Olney, who had had long experience as a railroad lawyer. Gresham considered Olney "too much disposed to treat the present situation as if it were a case before a court in which he represented one of the litigants." Indeed, he feared that "the liberties of the people were in danger of being overridden in the desire for a hasty termination of trouble."[29]

Gresham denied the legality of Olney's two-pronged attack employing a court injunction and federal troops. He considered the sweeping injunction handed down by federal judges at Chicago an "abuse" of the court's equity powers and a usurpation of the jurisdiction of the criminal courts. He also thought that "in the absence of any statutory authority," it was illegal to employ military force "for the alleged protection of interstate commerce." The government could use troops to protect federal property from attack or to ensure the operation of railroads in receivership, but these conditions did not obtain. And although the charters of various railroads called for their designation as military roads in time of national necessity, no such necessity existed. Nor could the government legitimately invoke the "war statute" passed in 1861 to allow the president to use the army and navy "to enforce the faithful execution of the laws of the United States or to suppress . . . rebellion." The government could use troops for the protection of the mails, but Gresham doubted there was sufficient disruption to warrant invoking that authority; throughout the crisis he received letters and his daily newspaper mailed from Chicago. He was particularly alarmed that a military force was sent to Chicago over the objection of state authorities. Against such encroachments Gresham considered the maintenance of the power of local and state governments "vital to the safety and perpetuity of free institutions."[30]

On July 9 Cleveland issued a proclamation citing nearly all the grounds for federal intervention whose validity Gresham questioned. But the president did not ask his opinion, and the secretary offered none. Believing the proclamation to be "unlawful," he affixed his authenticating "By the President" signature as "merely a formal act." When Cleveland appeared "peculiarly willful" in the matter, Gresham considered resigning in protest. In the end, however, he accepted the counsel of State Department consultant John Bassett Moore that a cabinet member often "had to put up with and apparently submit to many things that were unpleasant and in conflict with his views." A rupture would only damage the administration's larger purposes. The secretary avoided an impasse with Cleveland when a federal grand jury indicted the strike's leaders and the strike petered out. In the aftermath, Gresham expressed his belief that "the destruction of society is not a remedy for anything," but he could not accept the view that the mere suppression of strikes could resolve the fundamental issues between labor and capital. He wrote one Chicago friend: "The laboring men of the country—I mean the honest ones (and a large majority of them are honest) firmly believe they are oppressed [and] that the powers of the Government have been perverted to their injury in the interest of the rich."[31]

Gresham's hopes for tariff reform were dashed a month later when the Senate-House conference reported a bill substantially like the Senate version, which became law without Cleveland's signature. "The people have been betrayed," Gresham wrote Louisville editor Henry Watterson. "Protected interests die hard, but they will die." In truth, advocates of protectionism became more deeply entrenched. In the fall congressional elections the Republicans, accusing the Democrats of a fatal inability to govern in the face of economic crisis, won landslide victories that presaged William McKinley's triumphant election to the presidency two years later. Cleveland's great crusade for tariff reduction, in which Gresham had enlisted in the fall of 1892, had ended in bitter disappointment, with political ramifications that lasted a generation.[32]

Despite the non-foreign policy reasons for his appointment and the great attention he gave to domestic policy, Gresham was secretary of state in fact as well as name. Cleveland relied on him not merely to administer the routine affairs of the State Department but to give substantive direction to the country's foreign relations. Yet his experience ill-equipped him for the task. His previous public service had been devoted exclusively to domestic concerns, and his private correspondence had carried almost no reference to foreign policy issues. As a result, he had to devote an inordinate amount of time to studying the background of diplomatic issues he confronted.[33]

He labored under several other handicaps as well. For one, his personality was not ideally suited for the diplomat's role. He sometimes showed a tactless impatience with the opinions of others, which did not help win them to his point of view. He often greeted foreign representatives in his shirt sleeves and otherwise displayed little regard for diplomatic niceties. In the words of one catty reporter, the secretary was "very Democratic in his manners, as you may judge from the fact that he pushes his food on to his fork with his thumb." Moreover, Gresham's lack of wealth deprived him of any diplomatic advantage that might come from expensive entertaining. And ill health continued to plague him. Overwork, irregular eating and sleeping habits, and heavy smoking contributed to a variety of ailments, ranging from severe colds and stomach troubles to pneumonia, which frequently kept him away from the department in 1894 and 1895.[34]

Moreover, his relationship with his subordinates was not all he might have desired. He had a low opinion of First Assistant Secretary Josiah Quincy, who distributed department patronage, and "did not wear crepe" when Quincy resigned after six months in office. Although he admired Second Assistant Secretary Alvey A. Adee's ability to frame a dispatch, he found him "sadly lacking in judgment." Gresham sought in vain to secure as first assistant Columbia University professor John Bassett Moore, whom he regarded as the country's foremost authority on international law. Though Moore refused a permanent appointment, he frequently advised the secretary as a special consultant. As for lower department patronage and officials in the field, Gresham wanted as little as possible to do with "the disagreeable duty of turning men out of office and putting others in." That decision proved a mistake, for he soon found himself saddled with a corps of diplomats who owed him bureaucratic fealty but no political obligation for their positions—a situation that gave some of them an overblown conception of their independence. At first not realizing how dependent he would be on representatives abroad, he came to regret some of the appointments made by Cleveland and Quincy.[35]

Gresham's party switch also undermined his effectiveness. Although he eventually adjusted to referring to Democrats as "we," he owed his influence as a Democrat entirely to Cleveland; he had no independent base within the party. As Moore recalled, "The Democrats who did not love Cleveland attacked him as a Republican who had not, in the Democratic sense, become fully naturalized." On the other hand, many Republicans, in the words of one department official, could "not forgive Mr. Gresham for having left them." They censured his "blundering foreign policy" and accused him of spitefully trying to overturn the achievements of his old rival Benjamin Harrison.[36]

That he had become a man without a party was clear in his relations with Congress. There such Republicans as George F. Hoar, Henry Cabot Lodge, Cushman K. Davis, and Charles A. Boutelle felt no sense of political kinship with him nor any hesitancy in damning him for nearly all his acts. Across the aisle the atmosphere was only slightly friendlier, for few Democrats were willing to take political risks to defend Gresham's policies. John T. Morgan, chairman of the Senate Foreign Relations Committee, disliked him, and the Secretary reciprocated, believing Morgan to be "insincere" and "in favor of jingoism and protection."[37] He was not without allies, including James B. McCreary and Isidor Raynor in the House and George Gray, Roger Q. Mills, and George G. Vest in the Senate. But even these men could not always be counted on to defend the administration. After two years of frustrating battles and abusive criticism, Gresham longed for March 4, 1895, "when this incompetent and unpatriotic Congress will disappear."[38]

For many years historians tended to dismiss Gresham as a do-nothing secretary of state, during whose tenure, according to Montgomery Schuyler, the State Department reached its "lowest ebb of activity" since the Civil War. That view was inaccurate. As one cabinet colleague put it, "In Judge Gresham's day there were so many foreign complications that our full sessions were often devoted to them alone."[39] Most scholars now recognize the great volume of business that confronted Gresham's department and the painstaking direction he gave to foreign policy.[40]

Foremost among the recent historians who emphasize Gresham's activity are those who see economic motivations at the root of American expansionism at the close of the nineteenth century. Led by Walter LaFeber and William A. Williams, these writers contend that American foreign policy in this period was fueled primarily by a quest for foreign markets and investment opportunities. In LaFeber's words, Gresham "provides the purest example of the economic expansionist, anti-colonial attitude of the new empire." That is, he sought all the economic advantages of expansion with none of the administrative difficulties that normally accompanied territorial acquisition. According to this view, Gresham believed that the expansion of American economic interests abroad, especially foreign markets to drain off surplus production, would cure the depression and save the country from a revolution by the unemployed.[41]

A close examination of Gresham's attitudes and actions reveals little foundation for this interpretation. Gresham did occasionally express anxiety at "symptoms of revolution," but he rarely drew a link between overseas economic expansion and the nation's labor troubles. He had been concerned about working people long before the Panic of 1893 and knew that the plight of labor derived not simply from overproduction but more fundamentally from a general maldistribution of wealth. Both before and after becoming secretary of state he wrote of the need for "a more equitable division of the joint product of capital and labor." Rather than advocating economic expansion, he believed that the solution to class difficulties must come through some change in the domestic economic system—a change he never seemed able to define.[42]

When Gresham arrived in Washington, he had no intention of using the office of secretary of state as the aggressive instrument James G. Blaine had sought to make it. He considered the "large policy" of the Harrison-Blaine era an aberration and deprecated "what is sometimes termed a magnificent or splendid Administration." His central aim was to try to "do something toward bringing the people back to proper views of things." Soon swamped with business, he found that his meager background forced him to treat each new problem on an ad hoc basis. He turned instinctively to well-established patterns of behavior. As a federal judge he had been an impartial arbiter adjusting questions brought to his attention; as secretary of state he recreated that role to a remarkable degree, relying upon international law, his understanding of traditional American interests, and his sense of justice and equity to guide his opinions. Significantly, the only activity in his previous career approaching experience in foreign affairs had been as a lecturer on international law at Northwestern University while on the bench in Chicago. Soon after taking over the State Department he wrote his wife that he "had plenty of work, but as the questions were all legal, they were easy." It was a judge's reverence for precedent, rather than any vision of territorial or economic expansion, that truly informed Gresham's conduct of foreign policy. But as John Bassett Moore observed, he "soon fell into trouble attempting to decide international questions judicially."[43]

Gresham's anti-imperialism showed most obviously in his opposition to annexation of Hawaii and his disapproval of American participation in the Samoan joint protectorate. Believing that "a free government cannot pursue an imperial policy," he was "unalterably opposed to stealing territory or annexing a people against their consent." Just as in domestic affairs, where he saw republicanism threatened by political venality and individual and corporate greed, he feared that if the United States departed from the "warnings of its founders and earlier statesmen" and entered "upon a career of foreign acquisition and colonization, the result will be disastrous" for American institutions. Similarly, he was "opposed to a large army and navy." He saw little need for a big navy for commercial or strategic purposes and feared that a burgeoning military establishment would threaten republican values.[44]

But this is not to say that his term as secretary of state marked a diminution of American interest in foreign affairs. The sheer volume and variety of problems that engaged the department required a substantial involvement. If the United States' emergence as a world power at the end of the century rested to some degree on accumulated experience, then by dint of heightened activity the Gresham period contributed to that eventuality. In no instance, however, did Gresham see his role as that of an innovator. He harbored no aspiration to write a new "doctrine" into American foreign policy but instead regarded himself as the defender of long-standing, and rather limited, American interests. At the start of his term he told the Russian minister that the Cleveland administration would be "inclined to be conservative in the way of adhering to the traditional policy of the Government." He saw little justification for or need to alter established patterns and deplored any tendency "to get away from the conservative teachings of the founders of our Government."[45]

But even though Gresham was not the economic expansionist portrayed by some writers, neither was he totally indifferent to American economic interests overseas. Indeed, as a traditionalist, he recognized that the long-standing functions of the State Department included intercession on behalf of such interests when foreign governments or individuals interfered with their legitimate pursuits. Yet his solicitude was generally defined and limited by the stipulations of existing treaties or the obligations of accepted international law and practice. With regard to *expanding* overseas economic opportunities, particularly in the field of trade, he and other administration officials sometimes shared in expansionist rhetoric but followed with effective action far less often.

Americans who ran into trouble doing business overseas frequently turned to the State Department for assistance, and like his predecessors, Gresham generally was willing to help. In the summer of 1893, for instance, he protested against a Brazilian government ban on overseas cipher telegrams as "an onerous fetter upon legitimate commerce and quite unusual in the intercourse of trading nations." The department also remonstrated against restrictions on American life insurance companies by Russia, American petroleum products by Austria-Hungary, and American grain by Belgium. And when a patent medicine firm reported rumors that the government of Turkey was going to exclude its products, Gresham agreed to investigate because, he said, "proprietary medicines form an important part of our export trade."[46]

Such actions were routine, but on many occasions Gresham and the department turned aside businessmen's pleas for intercession, most often when the requested action exceeded the bounds set by law, treaty, or custom. Not long after taking office, for example, Gresham received a complaint from the Standard Oil Company regarding regulations restricting the transit of petroleum through the Suez Canal. He refused to act in the matter because, he said, "the regulations afford no ground for diplomatic intervention by this Government." In different circumstances, when difficulties between France and Madagascar appeared to threaten American commercial interests in the latter country, Senator John T. Morgan urged the State Department to intervene, but Gresham replied that the 1881 treaty between the United States and Madagascar "gives this country no right or ground of intervention in the dispute, and the existence of commercial intercourse between the United States and Madagascar is not of itself a cause of mediation or friendly remonstrance with the French government."[47]

Businessmen frequently requested special assistance by consuls stationed abroad, but the department generally stuck to the rule articulated by Assistant Secretary Edwin F. Uhl that "the consul is a servant of the public, but not the agent of any individual citizen in the prosecution of private business." Hence consuls were not permitted to act as agents for American firms by advertising or procuring orders for their goods. The department usually rejected requests for consuls to make ad hoc investigations of market conditions in particular localities and instead referred correspondents to the regular monthly *Consular Reports*, which contained information of "sufficient interest" to be published "for the benefit of the public." In one notable case, New York Democratic leader William F. Sheehan, heading a syndicate of investors angling for concessions in Honduras, asked Gresham what protection they could expect from the United States if after they had spent "large sums of money" a revolution should occur in Honduras and jeopardize their investments. In reply, Gresham said that the department would "at all times endeavor to secure to our citizens in foreign lands the rights to which they may be entitled under international law and our treaties with other powers." But in typical judgelike fashion he added: "The general ground of diplomatic intervention, however, in behalf of private persons, is a denial of justice, and the question whether there has been, or is likely to be, such denial is one that can be determined only on the circumstances of each particular case as it may arise."[48]

Increasingly during the last third of the nineteenth century, many in the business community believed the department's economic function should extend beyond mere protection of overseas interests and em-

brace the active pursuit of new opportunities abroad, especially expanded markets. One month after Gresham took office the *North
American Review* published an influential article by Robert Adams, Jr.,
former United States minister to Brazil, which epitomized anxieties felt
by many. "The United States," Adams wrote, "has now reached a point
in its development where it raises more cereals than it consumes,
produces more goods than the people can wear, and more manufactured articles than the country needs. The necessity for foreign markets is pressing home to the people." On the level of rhetoric at least,
the Cleveland administration agreed. The president himself told Congress that "our products and manufactures should find markets in
every part of the habitable globe." In the words of Secretary of Agriculture J. Sterling Morton, "There is nothing of greater or more vital
importance to the farmers of the United States than the widening of the
markets for their products." Gresham said virtually nothing on the
subject publicly, but during the tariff fight in Congress he did note
privately that one of the important by-products of reform should be the
reduction of duties on raw materials, which "would lower the cost of
the manufactured article and enable our people to compete in foreign
markets with Great Britain."[49]

Indeed, tariff reduction formed the core of the Administration's
market expansion policy, primarily a negative approach, aimed more at
removing artificial, government-sponsored impediments to trade than
at offering positive action to increase it. This premise underlay the
administration-sponsored Wilson tariff bill. Although the final Wilson-
Gorman Act disappointed Cleveland and Gresham in many ways, it
did repeal Section Three of the McKinley Tariff under which the
Harrison administration had negotiated reciprocity agreements with
several foreign countries. By this approach, engineered largely by
Harrison's Secretary of State James G. Blaine, the United States had
won tariff concessions for the export of American products into foreign
countries, especially in Latin America, by offering reciprocal concessions on imports from those countries. The Democrats, believing,
in Gresham's words, that "legislation is preferable to an international
agreement," rejected this quid-pro-quo effort and instead sought a
generally freer trade, reducing American tariff rates with the confident
expectation that other countries would follow suit. Republicans dismissed such notions as naive and damaging to the country's economy.
Minnesota Senator Cushman K. Davis contended that "it was clearly
apparent that, if allowed to continue, [reciprocity] would within a few
years enormously increase our commerce."[50]

Nonetheless, following passage of the Wilson-Gorman Act Gresham lost little time in informing other nations that the agreements had ended. The next day, for instance, he informed the Brazilian minister in Washington that the arrangement with his country "exists no longer," and he rejected the minister's plea for an informal three-month extension. Indeed, the cancellation of Harrison's reciprocity arrangement with Spain for Cuba and Puerto Rico confirmed the Republicans' worst fears. Spanish customs officers began immediately to levy the maximum rate on imports from the United States. Gresham protested this action as unjustly discriminatory, but after a half year of difficult negotiations the most he was able to secure from Spain was treatment of American products on the most-favored-nation basis.[51]

A year and a half after passage of the Wilson-Gorman Act Cleveland had little more success to report to Congress than that Argentina, responding to the United States' elimination of a duty on wool, had "admitted certain products of the United States to entry at reduced rates." Nonetheless, he and others continued to defend the policy. In an anonymous article in the *Baltimore Sun* State Department official Frederic Emory argued that "nations do not take any more kindly than do individuals to the employment of force against them to induce them to trade." Republicans remained unconvinced. "Of all the blunders of the tariff," Henry Cabot Lodge said, none was "so deeply injurious to American interests" as the abrogation of the reciprocity agreements.[52]

The most irksome diplomatic difficulty stemming from the Wilson-Gorman Act involved Germany. Under reciprocity German sugar had entered the United States duty-free, but the new law imposed a duty of 40 percent ad valorem. In addition, because Germany paid a bounty to its producers on the sugar they exported, German sugar became subject to an extra duty of one-tenth of one cent per pound levied against sugar from bounty-paying countries. On the day the bill became law Germany lodged a formal protest charging that the discriminating rate violated the most-favored-nation clause of the existing commercial convention between the two countries. Gresham studied the German protest for more than a month before sending Cleveland an opinion based largely on the "legal aspects" of the question. The basis of the protest lay in the Treaty of 1828 with Prussia which, he wrote, conferred most-favored-nation status on the products of Germany as the successor to Prussia. Germany's sugar bounty was a purely domestic affair, and the Wilson-Gorman Act's discriminating duty constituted "an attempt to offset a domestic favor or encouragement to a certain industry by the very means forbidden by the treaty." He concluded that the duty ought to be repealed.[53]

Attorney General Richard Olney disagreed, arguing that the German sugar bounty was "a direct attack upon the sugar market of the United States." To protect itself from this act of "German aggression," he said, the United States was clearly justified in levying the extra duty.[54] But Gresham replied, "How can we defend ourselves against an accusation of treaty violation if we impose a duty on importation of German sugar one tenth of a cent per pound more than we impose upon such importations from another country?" Cleveland accepted Gresham's arguments and agreed to call for a repeal of the duty.[55]

Meanwhile, Germany had retaliated by banning the importation of American cattle and beef products, claiming that sanitary considerations prompted the action. The problem became still more acute when other countries, including Belgium, Denmark, and France, banned American beef, citing Germany's action as their reason for doing so. Gresham promised the German government that even though the United States considered its meat inspection "ample to protect Germany," it would adopt "even more rigid measures of inspection and control." He was all the more convinced of the need to eliminate the extra sugar tax, but a repeal bill died in the Senate, thus negating further diplomatic efforts for the lifting of the meat import ban. Indeed, Germany extended its prohibition to American beef merely transported through the country. The Department of Agriculture provided Gresham with evidence of the healthfulness of exported beef, which he marshaled in diplomatic representations to the other boycotting European countries, but he met no greater success in getting their restrictions removed.[56]

Criticism of Gresham's handling of commercial relations with Germany focused curiously not on the failure to secure the removal of the meat prohibition but instead on his "improvident" endorsement of the German protest against the sugar duty. But beef producers could find little more to praise in Gresham's policy, for his determination to push for repeal of the sugar duty regardless of German retaliation made the promise of repeal an ineffectual lever in negotiations to secure an end to retaliation. In his mind, the law of the case ultimately took precedence over the economics. Without demanding a lifting of the ban in return, he could do no more than hope that Germany would respond in kind.[57]

In addition to adjustment of the tariff rates, many businessmen and politicians looked to the corps of American consuls as a principal vehicle for the expansion of overseas trade. As diplomat Henry White put it, an indispensable part of the consul's job was "the promotion of our foreign trade by obtaining and sending home such information as is likely to be of assistance to our merchants." Since 1880 the department had published monthly *Consular Reports,* which during Gresham's time achieved a circulation of nearly five thousand copies to newspapers, journals, libraries, boards of trade, and individuals. Recognizing this service as one of the department's standard functions, Gresham worked for "as large a distribution as possible of these reports." In the spring of 1893 the second assistant secretary's office began sending them out weekly in abridged form to newspaper press associations around the country.[58]

Yet throughout Gresham's term criticism of the consular service mounted, the chief ground of complaint being the continuing connection of the service with the spoils system. Since consuls remained outside the civil service rules, their appointment still turned largely on political considerations, and most were party hacks of small ability and less training. Low salaries combined with uncertainty of tenure to deter more competent men from seeking consulships. With the accession of Cleveland and Gresham to office many reformers and businessmen expected an improved service, but in short order Assistant Secretary Josiah Quincy, to whom Gresham left the business of making appointments, began a wholesale removal of Republican consuls to make way for "deserving" Democrats.[59]

Gresham bore ultimate responsibility for Quincy's "consular debauch," but he was not totally indifferent to the quality of the service. He initiated an updating of the 1888 consular *Regulations* with the aim of making the book "more intelligible and easy of use." Moreover, he sent Congress a draft bill to fund an inspection with the threefold purpose of "detection and summary correction of abuses," "institution of uniform business methods," and "preparation for improved reorganization of the system." In pushing this legislation, however, he said nothing of the trade-expansion function of the consuls. Indeed, his call for eventual reorganization noted that "certain principal offices and Consular agencies can with profit be abolished."[60]

The inspection bill failed even to get out of committee, and many critics of the service found this approach inadequate to bring about true reform. Within Gresham's own department two clerks, Wilbur J. Carr and Francois Jones, decided to bypass the secretary and go directly to Foreign Relations Chairman John T. Morgan with legislation that would at last divorce the consular service from the spoils system. Morgan reported the bill favorably and urged its passage on the grounds, among others, that "our trade with many foreign countries would be greatly increased and rendered more secure." Republican Henry Cabot Lodge endorsed the reform as one that would truly enable the consular service to "promote the business interests of the United States." Yet the administration remained virtually silent on the subject except for vague references by Cleveland in his annual message to the need for consuls who were "men of character, intelligence, and ability." Without administration support the bill died without being seriously considered by either house. No real improvement in the consular service occurred during Gresham's term as secretary. With most of his time consumed by more significant diplomatic problems, he gave the issue relatively little attention. Effective reform did not come until after the turn of the century.[61]

Among those hoping for a more effective consular service was Secretary of Agriculture J. Sterling Morton, who considered the search for foreign markets part of his department's responsibility. He created a Section of Foreign Markets and sent special agents to engage in "missionary labors in the food-consuming fields of Europe." He also sought to exploit the State Department's personnel overseas as gatherers of market information, but with only mixed results. Gresham permitted consuls to answer ad hoc inquiries from the Agriculture Department on a limited basis but drew the line when Morton submitted a circular instruction to consuls to report directly to his own department on consumption and prices of farm products abroad. As a bureaucratic compromise, the State Department offered to prepare a circular instruction of its own and to permit stenographers from Agriculture to make copies of the consuls' replies. Morton accepted this arrangement.[62]

One other quasi-government entity concerned with the quest for overseas markets was the Commercial Bureau of the American Republics, which on balance Gresham considered more a nuisance than an asset. Founded in 1890 as an outgrowth of the first International American Congress, the bureau was an international agency headquartered in Washington and administered under the general supervision of the secretary of state. The bureau's principal function was the gathering and dissemination of commercial information relating to the nations of the Western Hemisphere. Clinton Furbish, the bureau's director appointed in the spring of 1893, generally shared the administration's small-government, low-tariff views. One method he recommended to promote trade expansion was "the establishment of permanent Commercial Museums where manufacturers and merchants may readily learn the needs of different markets, and where consumers may examine commodities they would purchase." "From such undertakings," he maintained, "the merchants of all countries will learn to look to individual enterprise rather than governmental aid for means of extending their trade."[63]

In this spirit Furbish sought to make the bureau's information pro-
gram self-sufficient. In October 1893, the bureau began charging a
small fee for its printed offerings, including its chief publication, the
Monthly Bulletin. Furbish's aim was to direct the documents to "those
who give proof of interest in the subject-matter by their willingness to
pay for what they need rather than appear in the guise of applicants for
free gifts from the Government." Furbish also began to solicit commercial advertising for the *Monthly Bulletin*. This move evoked strong
opposition from private periodicals such as the New York *Journal of
Commerce* whose publishers feared the competition from a publication
bearing the imprimatur of the United States government. Gresham
likewise disapproved this mixing of public and private business, which
at the least was of dubious legality, and promptly called a halt. Just at
that time he faced a recently passed congressional resolution asking
him to report on the "propriety of continuing" the Bureau of American
Republics, and he bluntly told Furbish, "I am not willing to recommend
its continuance on the basis of an advertising agency." Three months
later Gresham sent Congress a five-page report that included not one
line on any positive benefit performed by the bureau but instead
focused on the legalistic obligations of the United States' membership.
As long as a majority of the member nations contributed to its support,
he grudgingly concluded, "this Government can not in good faith
withdraw from the organization."[64]

This opinion epitomized Gresham's general attitude toward government-sponsored economic expansion. At a time when many in business and politics clamored for overseas markets to drain off the
country's excess production, Gresham pursued a relatively conservative policy. He did not believe the government was powerless to protect
businessmen's interests abroad or to help them find new opportunities, but he adhered to the precept that its actions should not
exceed the limits set by law, treaty stipulations, and standing practice
and custom. Indeed, in general as he charted the nation's foreign
policy, such considerations nearly always took precedence over economic concerns. His approach was widely criticized as too often resulting in chances missed and opportunities lost—in the words of Henry
Cabot Lodge, "everywhere a policy of retreat and surrender." Administration defenders disagreed. On the day before Gresham died, State
Department official Frederic Emory published an article asserting that
Cleveland and Gresham had put the nation "on the high road to that
great commercial expansion which is our natural and proper due." In
truth, however, Emory could point to little concrete action to substanti-
ate his claim. Instead he praised his chief for pursuing a policy actuated

by a "spirit of rectitude and fairness," which, he conceded, had "naturally drawn the fire of all the greedy interests that seek to profit by foreign entanglements." More important, Emory concluded, the administration had abjured "the 'jingo' policy of bluster" and had given the nation "peace with honor" in its relations with the rest of the world.[65]

Gresham's rejection of the "'jingo' policy" showed most clearly in his handling of relations with Hawaii—a problem he confronted the moment he was sworn in and probably the most nettlesome of his term.

EIGHT

HAWAII

There Is Such a Thing as
International Morality

The most perplexing problem Gresham dealt with as secretary of state, Hawaii, confronted him as soon as he took office and persisted throughout his term. In January 1893, in the waning days of the Harrison administration, Queen Liliuokalani was overthrown by a coup engineered by a group of nonnative, mostly American-descended lawyers, planters, and businessmen. Their chief complaint was her announced intention to reverse a past imbalance of political power under which foreigners had wielded much greater authority than her native Hawaiian subjects. Although the queen quickly backed down, the revolutionaries proceeded with their work, aided by the landing of United States troops and the hasty recognition of their provisional government by the American minister, John L. Stevens, who was a longtime advocate of annexation of Hawaii by the United States. The queen surrendered in the face of this American assistance to her enemies, although not without protest and not without submitting her case to the president of the United States. But Harrison ignored her personal plea and instead argued that the "overthrow of the monarchy was not in any way promoted" by the United States. He further held that the queen's restoration would be "undesirable" and would bring "serious disaster and the disorganization of all business interests." He concluded that annexation was the only course that would "adequately secure the interests of the United States." By February 14, 1893, a delegation of commissioners from the Hawaiian Provisional Government and Secretary of State John W. Foster had negotiated a treaty of annexation which Harrison promptly sent to the Senate.[1]

Among those watching these events closely were President-elect Cleveland and his prospective cabinet. In late February Gresham traveled east to meet with Cleveland and stopped in New York to talk with Foster at Foster's request. Foster later recalled that he had given Gresham "very full and detailed information of the state of business" in the State Department, and he also probably tried to predispose his successor to favor annexation. Afterward Gresham joined Cleveland and incoming Treasury Secretary John G. Carlisle at Lakewood, New Jersey. Cleveland had already received a letter from Queen Lili-uokalani asking his "friendly assistance in granting redress for a wrong which we claim has been done us" by the United States. Contemporary evidence is sketchy as to the content of the Lakewood discussions, but afterward newspapers reported that Cleveland wanted to appoint a commission to study the Hawaiian affair. Carlisle reportedly returned to Washington with a request from Cleveland to Democratic senators to block approval of the treaty. In fact, the Senate gave no attention to the treaty after February 22.[2]

Five days into his term Cleveland withdrew the treaty from the Senate for "reexamination." At that point his and Gresham's views were not yet settled. Needing a reliable source of information and unwilling to depend on Stevens, they sent James H. Blount, who had just retired as chairman of the House Committee on Foreign Affairs, as a special commissioner to investigate affairs in the islands.[3]

Foster and other Republicans charged that "Gresham's hostility for Harrison" led Cleveland to oppose annexation. The former president was mortified that the treaty, the crowning achievement of his admin-istration, should be "condemned as a hasty and botched piece of work by Gresham!" Partisan feeling may have had some influence on the new administration's policy, but it was not the deciding factor, for in the beginning at least Cleveland and Gresham were uncertain about what to do. A few days after taking office Gresham told ardently proannexa-tion Admiral George Brown that he feared that "some kind of a job might be mixed up in the matter," but Brown had the impression that "Gresham was thoroughly convinced of the advisability of annexation and would do all he could in favor of it." Although six days after Cleveland's inauguration Gresham was officially noncommittal with Hawaii's treaty commissioners, who were still in Washington, they too drew the conclusion that he was "heartily in sympathy with the annex-ation proposition." And a month later the Hawaiian minister reported to his government that after "a rather full conversation" with Gresham he had concluded that "the Secretary is disposed to annex the Is-lands—unless Mr. Blount's report shows insuperable obstacles." If Cleveland and Gresham had been set against annexation from the outset, there would have been no reason to go through the trouble and expense of the Blount mission. That their aim was to amass ammuni-tion against the previous administration—which had been repudiated in the November elections—is hardly credible. Cleveland wrote Carl

Schurz two weeks after taking office: "I do not now say that I should hold annexation in all circumstances and at any time unwise, but I am sure we ought to stop and look and think." The Blount investigation was to be just that—an investigation to ascertain the facts upon which the administration would determine its policy.[4]

Thus Gresham's attitudes and actions derived largely from what he learned from Blount, which in turn was determined by what he had asked. In essence he instructed Blount to answer two questions: To what extent had American officials participated in the overthrow of the queen? And to what extent was the provisional government supported by the Hawaiian people? Answers to the first would indicate whether the United States had violated international ethics. Answers to the second would show whether the new government was representative and, hence, whether it had the right to offer the islands for annexation. Gresham did not ask Blount to report on, nor did he otherwise display much interest in, the islands' resources, their commercial or strategic assets, or their general usefulness as an American possession. From the beginning he operated on a vague notion that the nation's interests in the matter depended more on its honor and moral rectitude than on its material or strategic advantages vis-à-vis other nations. Preserving republican virtue was more important than acquiring a base for the navy. Moreover, his peculiarly judicial approach locked him into a narrowly circumscribed pattern of response.[5]

Blount received no indication from Gresham or Cleveland that they favored restoring Liliuokalani to the throne or any other particular policy. Soon after his arrival in the islands he set about his investigation, collecting affidavits and conducting interviews with annexationists and royalists alike. Within a month he reluctantly accepted temporary appointment as Stevens's successor as minister.[6]

Gresham received reports from Blount from time to time, and over the next four months a belief in American culpability took shape in the secretary's mind. In mid-June the provisional government's minister in Washington, Lorrin Thurston, pressed him to reveal the administration's intentions. Although he refused to speak "more definitely," Gresham noted that "in determining what our action shall be we will not lose sight of the character of our own institutions, the manner in which the Provisional Government was established, nor to what extent it represents the wishes of the people of the Islands." Two days later he told Thurston,

You admit that a majority of the people of the Islands—certainly a majority of the qualified voters under the Constitution of 1887,—were loyal to the Queen

and her Government; that they did not wish to see that Government overthrown; that your Provisional Government was established against their consent; that they desire an independent government of their own, and are
opposed to annexation to the United States; and notwithstanding all this, the
United States, at the instance of the Provisional Government, should annex the
Islands and hold them by force if necessary against the will of the people.

Two months later Thurston called again. Armed with further facts from
Blount, Gresham charged that to secure Liliuokalani's surrender, the
annexationists had told her that Stevens had already recognized the
provisional government, that American troops had landed to assist the
revolutionaries, and that she could sign a protest that included the
understanding that the president of the United States would consider
her case. Thurston lamely denied this version of the events.[7]
      Gresham was disappointed that Blount's "hastily" prepared final
report, dated July 17, was not an airtight legal brief, but he had already
been convinced by the commissioner's earlier letters and documents.
He believed that the queen's assertion that she had surrendered only
"with the understanding . . . that her case would be fairly considered
by the President of the United States" gave the United States the right
to settle the controversy. Hence he turned immediately to thoughts of
restitution. Blount had "never dreamed of such a thing as the reinstatement of Liliuokalani," but when he returned to Washington in late
August, he found that the secretary's "inclination" was that "the circumstances created a moral obligation on the part of the United States
to reinstate her." Three weeks later Gresham asked Carl Schurz,
"Should not this great wrong be undone? 'Yes,' I say decidedly."[8]
      Gresham's proposal aroused much skepticism among his cabinet
colleagues, who considered it for a month before reaching a decision.
Although all agreed that the United States had wrongfully aided the
queen's overthrow, there was disagreement on how to make amends.
Gresham may have been willing to use force, but Attorney General
Richard Olney and others hesitated to endorse so drastic a move.
Olney argued that such action, if taken on the president's initiative
alone, would, as an act of war, be unconstitutional; second, the resulting fighting might reduce the country to "a poor substitute" for what
the queen had given up; and finally (and here Olney seemed to miss
one of Blount and Gresham's conclusions), the Hawaiian people might
now prefer the provisional government. Olney proposed instead that
the United States, on behalf of the queen, conduct negotiations with
the provisional government, in which the American representative
would hint at the use of force but do so without a potentially embar-

rassing deployment of troops. "It would be understood [by the provisionals] that the power of the United States was behind them [the negotiations], while there would be and need be no statement nor intimation of the necessity for the intervention of Congress, if it were found necessary to reenforce the negotiations by the use of the war power." That is, the American negotiator would permit the provisionals to believe that the United States would use force to restore the queen and omit telling them that the president felt powerless to act without the consent of Congress, which Congress was not likely to give. Before the negotiations, the United States would secure the queen's agreement to two conditions: she must recognize the provisional government's debts and pardon its members. This plan was substantially the one the administration followed. That it represented an interference in the internal affairs of Hawaii by a method as devious as Stevens's had been blatant seems not to have occurred to Olney, Gresham, or Cleveland.[9]

Success depended largely on the American minister in Hawaii, who would conduct the negotiations. Blount had never desired the position permanently and sent in a letter of resignation as soon as he received his appointment. The post was difficult to fill. Gresham urged the president to name Edward S. Bragg, minister to Mexico in Cleveland's first term. Gresham considered Bragg "a man of ability [and] an able lawyer" who possessed "decision of character." But Bragg's political opponents blocked his selection, and the appointment finally went to Albert S. Willis, a former Kentucky congressman with no diplomatic experience.[10]

Gresham gave Willis written instructions to "take advantage of an early opportunity" to meet with the queen so that he might "speedily obtain" her agreement to the conditions and then inform the provisional government that it was "expected to promptly relinquish to her her constitutional authority." In Washington Gresham described orally the procedures the minister should follow and told him to give the administration sufficient notice so that he might release Blount's report just before the consummation of the administration's policy and the changeover of government.[11]

Gresham also prepared a report to the president, bearing the same date as Willis's instructions, October 18. Intended to be kept secret until the queen's reinstatement, the secretary's report was designed as a public defense of the administration's course. Employing the style of a legal brief, Gresham detailed the evidence of American culpability and concluded that the annexation treaty should not go back to the Senate. As for the queen, he asked, "Should not the great wrong done

to a feeble but independent State by an abuse of the authority of the
United States be undone by restoring the legitimate government?
Anything short of that will not, I respectfully submit, satisfy the de-
mands of justice."[12]

After Willis arrived in Honolulu on November 4, he delayed nine
days before interviewing the queen. Confident of success, he telegraphed Gresham two days before the meeting that he could send
Blount's report to Congress. But the queen rejected the American
conditions and declared that the provisionals should be "beheaded and
their property confiscated." Willis gave her an opportunity to alter her
stance, but she would do no more than say that she might leave the
decision to her ministers. Since the administration's plan called for an
amnesty pledge before restoration and, hence, before the queen had
any "ministers," Willis considered this concession an effective refusal
of the conditions. Rather than press her to change her mind, he
suspended the negotiations until he could obtain further instructions,
thus delaying the negotiations another month.[13]

The first substantive word Gresham received from Willis was his
telegram about releasing Blount's report. When this message arrived
on November 18, he sent a copy to Olney as an indication that their
plan was working: "I infer that he has made headway. I hope so."[14]

Secrecy was essential, but as early as November 7 American newspapers reported that the administration had decided to reinstate the
queen. "Downright angry" over these leaks, Gresham told the
Hawaiian chargé d'affaires that the United States had not yet decided
on a policy. Although the stories were far from a blueprint of the
administration strategy, what angered Gresham most was their assertion that the United States would not resort to force. If the provisional
government knew that Cleveland had ruled out military action, Willis's
credibility would be destroyed and the provisionals could resist with
impunity his demands that they step down. The secretary's October 18
report explaining his policy had not ruled out the use of force, and,
apparently to bolster Willis's position, Gresham decided to release it to
the press.[15]

The publication backfired, however, for it led Hawaiian minister
Thurston to ask directly whether the United States planned an armed
intervention. Although Gresham tried to be ambiguous, the minister
went away with the clear impression that the United States would not
resort to force, or even if it did, that it would not do so to maintain the
queen on the throne. Hence he wired his government to "make every
preparation for resistance but not fire on American troops but compel
them to use actual force. . . . If force not already used no likelihood it

will be even if threatened or previously intended as overwhelming opposition will prevent it." In short, Thurston advised his government to call Willis's bluff.[16]

The advice proved sound, for the American public outcry that greeted Gresham's report made the use of troops a political impossibility and therefore rendered any veiled threat of force nugatory. Contrary to Gresham's intent, a bitter public debate erupted over whether the "Great Republic" should attempt to overthrow another "republic" and erect a monarchy in its place. "Was there no American spirit in the Cabinet when this policy of infamy was decreed?" asked the Democratic *New York Sun*. The Republican *Chicago Inter-Ocean*, one of Gresham's strongest backers in 1888, charged that the Secretary's "well-known personal animosity to the President under whom the Hawaiian revolution was effected" had led him into a "perversion of incontestable facts." (Harrison himself was pleased that the "newspapers seem to be taking good care of the old administration.") Even the proadministration *New York Herald* advocated letting the Hawaiians "settle their own disputes." Gresham was not without journalistic defenders, including the *Nation, Harper's Weekly,* and the *New York Post*, and he continued to maintain that "there is such a thing as international morality." But Thurston soon reported to his government that "the arbitrary harsh course proposed by the Gresham report has raised us up a host of friends who did not before exist, and, by stimulating interest in our affairs has given us a vantage ground which we could have reached in no other way." The provisionals fortified the government buildings, armed the citizens' guard, and demanded that Willis state whether or not the United States intended a military action.[17]

Willis refused to reveal American intentions, but he soon began to wonder whether the "peculiar difficulties" of the Hawaiian question could ever be surmounted or whether they were worth surmounting. Gresham ordered him to take "prompt action" and "insist" on the conditions with the queen, but instead of seeing her, he wrote a long, unofficial letter to the secretary complaining that the disclosures in the press and Thurston's assurances had "greatly increased the difficulty" of his carrying out the administration's plan. Moreover, he wrote, "Assuming the restoration of the queen with the temporary acquiescence of the Prov. Gov.," her government would soon "fall to pieces like a card house." "Would it be just to restore her & have another revolution at once—which seems probable?" Willis's concern focused on the fate of American interests after restoration. Until the revolution "American power behind the throne was greater than the throne," but now he doubted that this "paramount influence" could be "revived" under the queen. American interests, he implied, would be safer under the provisional government. Such views hardly comported with Gresham's conclusion that "anything short" of restoration would not "satisfy the demands of justice." Newspaper correspondent Charles Nordhoff wrote the secretary that the minister had been "completely captured by the 'genial' Provisionals" and had become "a mere tool in their hands." Nordhoff may have exaggerated, but clearly Willis was an unfortunate instrument for carrying out administration policy.[18]

On December 14 Willis received instructions from Gresham to tell the queen that if she continued to reject the American conditions the president would "cease interposition in her behalf." She finally relented and on December 18 gave him a proclamation accepting the conditions. Willis next met with the provisional government. He reviewed the American involvement in the revolution and the reasons for Cleveland's determination, submitted a copy of Liliuokalani's amnesty proclamation, and asked: "Are you willing to abide by the decision of the President?" Four days later the provisionals answered with an emphatic "No." President Sanford Dole contended that even if Blount were right and American officials had illegally assisted the revolution, that was "a private matter for discipline between the United States and its own officers," which did not confer "upon the United States authority over the internal affairs of this Government." In any case, he asserted, the revolution would have succeeded without the presence of American forces.[19]

Dole's rebuff to Willis ended the effort to restore the queen. Gresham thanked the minister, but privately he blamed Willis for the failure. If Edward Bragg had been minister, he told John Bassett Moore, "the Hawaiian programme would have gone through." Willis's failure to act immediately upon his arrival in Honolulu, coupled with his reluctance to act on his own initiative, proved fatal. Bragg, Gresham argued, "would have carried out the plans of the administration promptly, before they became known." It was only because of the "revelation of the plans . . . followed by an outcry in the U.S." that "the Provisional Government consequently assumed the attitude of resistance, which they would not have ventured to do otherwise." In the end, with no appreciation of the independent vitality of the provisional government, Gresham believed that the failure of his restoration plan lay not in its conception but in its dilatory and spiritless execution.[20]

Even before the denouement in Honolulu, developments in Washington had precluded restoration. Congress convened on December 4, and the press attacks that had greeted Gresham's and Blount's reports echoed in the legislative chambers. Although some Democrats defended the administration, most were as insistent as the Republicans in demanding copies of Willis's instructions and other documents. Congressional strictures focused on armed intervention, but it was obvious that neither house, though dominated by Democrats, would back the administration in any interference to restore the queen.[21]

In mid-December, with congressional criticism mounting and with no word yet from Willis that Liliuokalani had abandoned her hard line, Cleveland decided to send Congress a special message. Drafting had begun in November, one version being prepared by Gresham and Moore and another by Olney. Gresham was unwilling to relinquish executive control of the matter and called for a statement that the president was seeking such an "arrangement between the queen & the leaders in the revolution as would afford security to all, without the exclusion of any party from the government." Olney, however, believed the administration should cut its political losses by turning the matter over to Congress "for such action, if any," it might devise, the implication being that Congress would take no action at all. Cleveland was reluctant to go as far as Olney in abandoning the queen, but he did accept his general recommendation and adopted larger portions of his draft than of Gresham and Moore's. But, significantly, Cleveland and Olney both adhered to Gresham's perception of the issue as a judicial question. The bulk of Cleveland's message was a finely argued brief on the evidence of American responsibility for the revolution and on the justice of restoration, devoid of any mention of Hawaii's commercial or strategic desirability. Cleveland adopted Olney's language, but Gresham had stamped the administration's policy with his conception of the affair as an ethical rather than a "practical" question of American "interests." Cleveland made no specific recommendation but promised to "cooperate in any legislative plan . . . consistent with American honor, integrity, and morality."[22]

With apprehensions of an executive act of war allayed, Congress settled in for a long debate, although never with any real prospect of action. The ensuing arguments boiled down to partisan attacks or defenses of the contrasting policies of Harrison and Cleveland. Gresham followed these debates closely, hoping for vindication. He believed the Republicans were "embarrassed" by Stevens's actions and were trying "to obscure what was done prior to the 4th of March by making counter-charges against this Administration." In the House of Representatives, he was pleased to find, Democrats stood "practically as one man in support of the Administration." The House passed a resolution condemning Stevens, rejecting either annexation or a protectorate, approving Cleveland's affirmation (with respect to the January revolution at least) of the traditional American principle of non-interference in the domestic affairs of other countries, and asserting that the Hawaiians should have "absolute freedom and independence" to pursue "their own line of policy."[23]

In the Senate the sailing was less smooth. Gresham urged John M. Palmer to make a "telling speech on Blount's report" and to "talk just as if you were summing the case up to a jury." The upper house contained forceful Republicans, but to Gresham the "chief obstacle" was that several leading Democrats were "malevolent toward the President," especially Foreign Relations Chairman John T. Morgan. The Alabamian was in constant communication with the provisional government's representatives in Washington, and Thurston later wrote that the senator "could not have taken more interest in Hawaii if it had been a part of his own state." When Morgan's committee launched an investigation after Cleveland's special message, Gresham feared "mischief" and proadministration Senator George Gray soon reported that Morgan "examined the witnesses in a very partial and unfair way, evincing a disposition to aid the annexationists and injure the President."[24]

After a month and a half of hearings Morgan issued a report that asserted that conditions in Hawaii had made it "next to impossible" for Blount to "obtain a full, fair, and free declaration in respect of the facts." He excused Willis's negotiations as a proper exercise of American good offices to achieve a reconciliation between the Hawaiian factions but denounced the idea of restoration in no uncertain terms: "When a crown falls, in any kingdom of the Western Hemisphere, it is pulverized, and when a scepter departs, it departs forever; and American opinion cannot sustain any American ruler in the attempt to restore them, no matter how virtuous and sincere the reasons may be that seem to justify them." Morgan also inserted comments on the commercial and strategic value of the islands, contending that "all intelligent men in Hawaii and the United States, who have taken the pains to consider the subject," favored annexation. No other committee member signed Morgan's report, and Republicans and administration Democrats issued separate findings of their own.[25]

Senate Democrats, unlike their counterparts in the House, found it difficult to reach a consensus. After months of intermittent wrangling, the Senate passed a resolution that said nothing about annexation or restoration and declared "that of right it belongs wholly to the people of the Hawaiian Islands to establish and maintain their own form of government and domestic polity; [and] that the United States ought in no wise to interfere therewith." Although Gresham told Willis this resolution was "entirely satisfactory to the President," he could see little in it that endorsed the policy he had pursued.[26]

Despite the failure of restoration, Gresham was satisfied that at least "annexation is dead, whatever else may occur." He began to defend the administration's policy not only on grounds of international morality but also on grounds that Hawaii was unsuited to become an American possession. In the past, he argued, the United States had always acquired territory with the intention of receiving it into the Union as states; it could not now try to rule Hawaii as "Rome governed her provinces, by despotic rule." But since the islands' predominantly non-Anglo-Saxon people were inexperienced in the republican form of government that statehood would entail, the United States would end up with a "hotbed of corruption" on its hands. Moreover, acquisition of Hawaii would necessitate defending Honolulu and thus jeopardize the nation's security, since "[a] nation, like a chain, is no stronger than its weakest part." To those who saw Hawaii as an ideal base for the American navy, he replied that "a splendid naval establishment" was not "consistent with the early policy" of the republic and that "we do not need such a navy as European Governments maintain." Finally, annexation of Hawaii would beget annexation of other areas, and the nation would be launched on a "career of foreign acquisition and colonization." Such an "imperial" policy could yield only "disastrous" results. "Popular government will not long survive under such a policy."[27]

Reluctantly, Gresham reconciled himself to dealing with the provisional government. His actions betrayed a spiteful contempt that followed a pattern set in his earlier political career. In the past, when opponents such as Oliver P. Morton, Harrison, or Blaine had thwarted his aims, he had consoled himself with aspersions of their character. Now, viewing the failure of restoration as a miscarriage of justice, he looked upon the provisionals as miscreants who had escaped punishment and were worthy of only the barest diplomatic civility. Thurston later recalled that Gresham showed a "studied insolence and insult toward myself and the Government which I represented." The secretary expected Willis to exhibit the same attitude toward officials in Honolulu and reminded him that their "conduct" did "not entitle them to more than respectful treatment" and "dignified reserve."[28]

In Gresham's mind, the provisional government was an egregious affront to republican values—"a pure oligarchy, responsible to no one." He relished every sign of the regime's instability, and within the limits of his power to influence the situation, he seemed to tailor his actions to hasten its collapse.[29] In the spring of 1894, when the provisionals moved to establish a permanent government and permitted non-Hawaiian nationals to vote in elections for a constitutional convention, Gresham wired Willis that any American who took the provisional government's oath "contemplating participation in its affairs" abandoned the right as an American citizen to claim the protection of the United States. Although Willis did not receive this telegram until after the election, he reported that it created "a profound sensation" and would have deterred more than a third of the Americans from voting. When the Republic of Hawaii was proclaimed on July 4, 1894, Willis circumspectly granted the new government only provisional recognition subject to the approval of the president. Gresham regretted even this limited action and told Willis he should have merely "reported what occurred on the 4th, without recognizing the new government even in a qualified way." Following Willis's action, Cleveland did extend official recognition in early August.[30]

Gresham was equally disinclined to lend the Hawaiian government more tangible support by the presence of an American war vessel at Honolulu. Since April Rear Admiral John G. Walker had been sending Navy Secretary Hilary Herbert detailed reports on political conditions in Hawaii. Walker favored annexation, and his letters contained information Gresham did not care to see reported officially to Washington, where it became subject to congressional inquiry. He suggested to Willis that he tell Walker that the administration depended on the minister for political information, but Willis neglected to do so. Moreover, Walker fêted Dole and his cabinet on board his flagship and secured permission for American troops to drill on land, which, Willis reported, "smacked" of an American protectorate. On August 2 Walker received orders to return to the United States. Gresham and Cleveland concluded that it was not "necessary for our warships to remain at Honolulu," and no ship was sent to replace Walker's. The admiral's behavior thus served as an excuse to withdraw what many considered one of the main props under the antiroyalist regime.[31]

In early August Gresham met a delegation of the queen's supporters and, intentionally or not, tacitly encouraged them to attempt a coup. Samuel Parker, J.A. Cummins, and H.A. Widemann, all former royalist cabinet members, had come to Washington to obtain a final answer as to whether the United States would do anything to restore the queen. Gresham told them Cleveland could do nothing. They were anxious for a definite answer even if it were negative, Widemann noted, to "leave us free to pursue our own course" without incurring the opposition of the United States. In response Gresham promised, "You will encounter no opposition from this Government. We claim no right to meddle in the domestic affairs of your country." Parker asserted that it was "only a question of time" before the antiroyalist regime would "go to pieces" but that many royalists believed that the American ships had been present "to support the existing government in case it should need help." At this Gresham replied uneqivocally: "The attitude of this government ought to be understood at Honolulu. Our warships were sent there not to uphold the provisional government or its successor, but to afford protection to such of our own citizens as did not participate in the local strifes." "I am glad to hear you say that," Parker replied. "All our people desire to know is that the government of the United States is not on the side of the existing government and against them." Thus, although a few days later Gresham gave the royalists Cleveland's "absolute denial" of any help, they left Washington with the secretary's assurance that the United States would not block a royalist attempt at restoration.[32]

After the royalists' visit to Washington, rumors of a coup spread through Honolulu. Willis gave little credence to such talk until November 10, when Foreign Minister F.M. Hatch told him of reports that arms were about to be shipped to the royalists from San Francisco. At Hatch's request Willis wired this information to Gresham, who conveyed it to Olney for any action he thought necessary under the neutrality laws. But Gresham soon concluded that Willis had been duped by a Hawaiian government attempt to paint the Administration as sympathetic to the royalists. He asked Olney to hold off taking action. Two days after the arrival of Willis's telegram, Gresham asked Hawaii Chargé d'Affaires Frank Hastings to verify its contents. Although he had not investigated, he told Hastings that the administration had "no reason to credit" the report of an arms shipment. The chargé said he too had received no such information. Gresham's aim was not so much to elicit information as to put the best face on American inaction. He expected to see news reports from Honolulu alleging that even though informed by its own minister of a threatened arms shipment to the enemies of the Hawaiian government, the Cleveland administration, out of sympathy for the queen, had done nothing to enforce the neutrality laws. "I had this in mind," he wrote Willis, "when I sent for Mr. Hastings and permitted him to read your telegram." Scolding Willis for acting "without much reflection," Gresham reminded him of the United States' responsibility as a neutral: "Hawaii is not at war with any other power, we have no information of an insurrection against the present government, and we know of no statute which would authorize the President or the head of any Department to stop the shipment of arms from San Francisco. . . . Of course you understand we are maintaining no protectorate over Hawaii, and that we can do no more for her in the enforcement of our neutrality laws than we can for any other government."[33]

The absence of an American warship at Honolulu drew Congress's attention when it reconvened in early December 1894. Henry Cabot Lodge secured passage of a resolution instructing the secretary of the navy to transmit Admiral Walker's reports to the Senate—moving Gresham to conclude that Walker had "played his part" by sending copies to his "political friends." Lodge contended that the letters showed that "our true policy was the annexation of those islands," and he demanded that the administration explain why a warship should not be stationed at Honolulu. Others charged that Cleveland had ordered Walker's ship home in response to a request by the three royalist commissioners who had visited Washington. That Walker's orders antedated the royalists' visit by nearly a month was somehow lost in the debate. Republicans were determined to see collusion between the administration and the queen.[34]

In early January 1895, royalist forces launched an abortive insurrection. The fighting lasted only a few days and resulted in three deaths and scores of arrests. Willis reported that Dole was pleased that no foreign warships had been present during the disturbance, but Gresham wired back that Cleveland was dispatching a ship immediately. To head off criticism, the administration published both Gresham's telegram to Willis and Herbert's instructions to Rear Admiral L.A. Beardslee of the *Philadelphia*. United States forces were to give "no aid or support, moral or physical" to either party but only to protect the lives and property of American citizens who took no part in the disturbances. Any American, Herbert wrote, "who, during a revolution in a foreign country, participates in an attempt by force of arms or violence to maintain or overthrow the existing Government, cannot claim that the Government of the United States shall protect him against the consequences of such act."[35]

The brief fighting in Hawaii rekindled debate in Congress, and Gresham once more urged Democrats to "get even" with Republican critics. "Would it not be well," he asked Texas Senator Roger Q. Mills, "to let the laboring men in this country realize what manner of government now exists in Hawaii; how that government imports coolie laborers from Asia by ship load, under contract, etc.[?]" He urged Mills to raise the question of the government's finances and the fact that certain Republican senators were "very intimate with Thurston." Two days later Mills charged New England's Republican senators with favoring annexation because many of their constituents held Hawaiian government bonds. Lodge and others denied Mills's allegations. In the end, the Senate Democrats secured preliminary approval of a resolution (accepted as a substitute for another but never brought to a final vote), which affirmed the United States' policy of "absolute noninterference" and declared that "the Administration of President Cleveland in maintaining this policy as to our foreign relations deserves the approval and support of the American people."[36]

Gresham's subsequent action violated the spirit of this resolution and of Herbert's noninterference instructions to Beardslee. Several of the insurrectionists arrested by the Hawaiian government claimed American citizenship and sought the protection of American officials in Honolulu. When a military tribunal sentenced two of these men to be hanged, Willis remonstrated with the government ("of course in a *friendly* way," he told Gresham) and asked for a copy of the proceedings so that the United States might determine its "duty." Gresham approved Willis's action but criticized his lapse into cordiality. He ordered him to "demand" a delay in the executions and to forward to Washington the evidence used to support the death sentences. Should the government refuse to give him a copy of the proceedings and move to execute the Americans, Willis was to demand their custody and rely on the military force of the *Philadelphia* to back him up. The Hawaiian government did not share Gresham's appetite for a showdown. Never intending to carry out the executions, it soon reduced the Americans' sentences to imprisonment and before long set them free.[37]

Gresham also protested the Hawaiians' suspension of the writ of habeas corpus as it applied to aliens. Again drawing on his judicial experience, he told Willis, "The existence of martial law, while it may imply the suspension of the methods and guarantees by which justice is ordinarily secured, does not imply a suspension of justice itself." He ordered Willis to insist that all Americans imprisoned without charges be "promptly tried or promptly released." After protesting the summary imprisonment and deportation of one John Cranstoun, even though Cranstoun had apparently never been naturalized as an American citizen, the secretary was angered by Willis's failure to command Beardslee to take Cranstoun by force and hold him on the *Philadelphia* until instructed.[38]

In Congress Charles A. Boutelle charged that Gresham's actions showed "a very remarkable and striking change of public policy" since Beardslee's instructions a few weeks earlier. In truth, Gresham had acted consistently with his contempt for the Hawaiian government and was not much troubled by charges of inconsistency as to means. John Bassett Moore, who tried to moderate his actions, noted that the secretary was searching for "some handle against the Hawaiian authorities, whom he regards as administering a fraudulent government." He still considered the Republic of Hawaii "a travesty on popular or republican government" with no claim to "a place among the civilized nations of the world."[39]

For its part, the Hawaiian government was eager to blame the insurrection on the Cleveland administration and especially on Gresham. In late January it discovered that arms used by the royalists had indeed been shipped from San Francisco the previous November. The foreign minister told Thurston to give this information "to our friends in Congress so that they can draw from Gresham the fact of his failure to take any action." In February Thurston informed the secretary that American customs officials had seized the schooner *Wahlberg* and presented evidence of the ship's violation of the neutrality laws. Gresham promised to turn the evidence over to the Justice Department, but he also berated Thurston for what he still considered the Hawaiian government's false alarms in November about arms shipments. Although Thurston lodged repeated complaints about the *Wahlberg*, the administration took no action, and customs authorities released the ship without charges.[40]

Unable to obtain official satisfaction, Thurston leaked the *Wahlberg* accusations and other antiadministration material to the American press. Gresham discovered the source and confronted the minister, who confessed he had been guilty of "official impropriety" and offered his regret. But when Gresham asked him to put his apology in writing, he refused, and the secretary demanded his recall. In composing his instruction to Willis, Gresham took refuge on the high ground of self-righteousness that was so frequently his resort: "You will express the surprise and dissatisfaction with which this Government naturally regards the conduct of a foreign envoy who thus covertly uses his influence through the press to bias public opinion in the country whose hospitality he enjoys."[41]

Thurston's recall was about the only triumph Gresham scored over the Hawaiian government; the sum effect of his two years' effort was to block annexation. Except for the few times when Cleveland followed Olney's advice, Gresham took the lead in formulating the administration's policy toward the islands. During his first term Cleveland had spoken of the United States' "paramount influence" in Hawaii and of "a natural interdependency and mutuality of interest" between the two countries. Now, Gresham worked assiduously to prevent a return to that attitude. As Moore observed, the secretary "urged the President on and added all the fuel he could to his antagonism."[42]

Gresham's wife later wrote that his Hawaii policy was his "most creditable act" as secretary of state. Insofar as he conceived it as an act of justice to redress a wrong, the policy was highly creditable. He approached the problem as a case in court, weighed the evidence, and delivered his opinion in favor of restoration of the queen. Even as he began to argue the practical objections to annexation, he never abandoned his appeal to right and justice. Shortly before his death he wrote: "I think it was Franklin who said that if it is disgraceful for a single individual to steal it is no less disgraceful for a nation, an aggregate of individuals to steal. . . . I still have confidence in the ultimate triumph of the right. I believe that when the American people fully understand the Hawaiian matter, they will condemn the great wrong done to the natives by the missionaries and their descendants, supported by the United States." Americans, he believed, had no business imposing their will on others.[43]

But even though Gresham may have adhered to a moral standard higher than that of many of his contemporaries, he never fully realized that retribution as a goal in foreign policy had but limited application. The general proposition that revolutions never go backward was lost on him, nor did he ever appreciate that his attempt to depose the provisional government was a breach of faith differing only in degree from Stevens's original breach of faith with the queen. He had no sense of the irony in his effort to restore republican virtue at home by reviving a monarchy abroad. The provisional government's unwillingness to surrender and the public outcry in the United States did not alter Gresham's view but instead made him cling to it all the more tenaciously. Frustrated in his determination to reinstate the queen and angered by the impugning of his motives, he stood by his position with a pertinacity that transformed his attempted act of justice into an act of spite. His dealings with the Hawaiian leaders derived from a rational anti-imperialist formula but also from irrational personal pique. He anxiously expected the collapse of their regime as the final vindication of his course. That vindication never came. He succeeded only in postponing annexation, which finally occurred in 1898.

Politically, the policy was disastrous. It handed the Republicans an easily exploited issue and further weakened Cleveland's leadership of the Democratic party. It was equally devastating to Gresham's political position, alienating whatever Republican affection had remained to him and making him an embarrassing burden to the Democrats. In the early days of the administration there had been speculation that he might run for president in 1896 or that he might be appointed to the Supreme Court. His Hawaiian policy, resting as it seemed on resentment and spite, changed all that. With obvious relish, one New York Republican wrote Benjamin Harrison, "Gresham seems to be 'hating' himself out of public life."[44]

SAMOA

Affairs That Do Not
Specially Concern Us

At the same time Gresham blocked American imperialism in Hawaii, he sought to throw off the difficulties of empire already posed by the United States' complex relations with the South Pacific island nation of Samoa. A half decade earlier the United States had entered into a joint protectorate over Samoa with Great Britain and Germany. Gresham thought this condominium was wrong, and its entangling the United States with two European nations made him all the more eager to get out. Although in the end he failed to secure American withdrawal, he did successfully articulate an elaborate case against "the evils of interference in affairs that do not specially concern us."[1] His attempt to reverse the course of American expansion in the South Pacific proved an important foreshadowing of the anti-imperialism at the end of the 1890s.

When Gresham entered the State Department, American interests in Samoa dated back decades, although in substance they remained negligible. During the 1870s and 1880s growing British and German influence in the islands had led successive American administrations to overestimate the significance of American interests there and the need for government action to defend them. By the late 1880s rivalry over Samoa had taken Germany and the United States to the brink of war, but hostilities were averted in 1889, when they and Great Britain negotiated a settlement known as the General Act of Berlin. Under this treaty the United States joined with Great Britain and Germany to give minute superintendence to the islands' internal affairs. Designed to check international rivalry and ostensibly to guarantee Samoa's independence, the Berlin Act amounted to a cession of sovereignty in all but name to the three treaty powers. Under its provisions the powers appointed a chief justice, who was to be a nonnative, with jurisdiction over all questions arising under the act, including the election of the nominal king by the tribal chieftains. The act also established a municipal council for the port town of Apia, whose president was to be a nonnative and also principal adviser to the king. To raise revenue, the

General Act of Berlin set up a system of import and export duties, capitation taxes, licenses, and other duties. Considerable power rested with the American, British, and German consuls. In Gresham's view, this regime had been "inaccurately styled an 'autonomous government' " and was instead "a tripartite foreign government, imposed upon the natives and supported and administered jointly by the three treaty powers."[2]

Myriad problems plagued this government. The powers had difficulty finding suitable people to fill the posts of chief justice and municipal council president, and the natives resisted the regime. Especially troublesome was the long-standing bitter rivalry among native factions for the kingship. When the powers backed King Malietoa Laupepa, large numbers of natives under the leadership of the chief Mataafa defied the king and the foreign government until civil war erupted in July 1893. Greatly disturbed by this fighting, Gresham privately told Carl Schurz, "I do not like the treaty of Berlin, under which the three powers, England, Germany and the United States, obligated themselves to maintain the authority of the present King, Malietoa." Officially, he reluctantly conceded that "whether it was wise or unwise for the United States to enter into that treaty we must now in good faith share with the other powers the burdens and responsibilities we assumed." Hence the navy ordered the U.S.S. *Philadelphia* to Samoa to join German and British forces. Gresham hoped the powers would be able to overawe and defeat Mataafa and his followers without bloodshed, but before the *Philadelphia* could reach Samoa, Malietoa, supported by one British and two German ships, had defeated Mataafa with considerable loss of life. Mataafa and several chiefs were taken prisoner on board the foreign ships. The foreign consuls in Samoa suggested that the powers seize the opportunity to disarm all the natives, but Gresham was adamant that the United States would "take no part in disarming individuals." The powers subsequently decided to exile the rebel leaders to the German Marshall Islands, which to Gresham represented just one more burden for the powers. He opposed a permanent banishment; by February 1895, he thought the chiefs had suffered "ample punishment" and threatened to withdraw American support for their exile.[3]

The revolt spurred Gresham to suggest a conference with the German and British ambassadors in Washington to reconsider the future of Samoa and the condominium. This idea alarmed the American ambassador in London, Thomas F. Bayard, who feared that the inexperienced secretary might let Germany or Britain gain the upper hand. Bayard urged Gresham to read the documents from when he was secretary during Cleveland's first term, when he had insisted on the "independence and autonomy, or at least the absolute and secured neutrality" of the islands as the best defense of American interests. "With the penetration of the isthmus and its transit for commerce," Bayard wrote Gresham, "a main avenue to Australia and the islands of the South Seas, as well as to the East Indies, will conduct the current of commerce to the Samoan group." It was "of real interest to the United States to exert their full influence to prevent their passing under the exclusive domination of any single Nation." Gresham thanked Bayard for the advice but did not share his conception of America's interest in Samoa. "Our Government," he told Carl Schurz, "should not undertake to maintain a protectorate, either alone or in conjunction with other powers, in the South Seas or elsewhere." As it turned out, Germany rejected the proposed conference and called for even greater foreign interference in the Samoan government and for an American war vessel to help disarm all the natives. Refusing these proposals, Gresham told the Germans that the United States wanted nothing short of "such a consideration of the entire subject as may result in the substantial modification of obligations of the United States in the premises."[4]

After his proposal for a conference failed, Gresham worked to convince Cleveland of the need for a unilateral American withdrawal. In his first annual message in December 1893, the president recounted Mataafa's uprising and the banishment of its leaders at the treaty powers' expense. "This incident and the events leading up to it," he said, "signally illustrate the impolicy of entangling alliances with foreign powers." In language consistent with Gresham's ideas, he charged that the Berlin treaty marked a departure from American policy "consecrated by a century of observance." But in bringing Cleveland around, Gresham had had to play down the contrast between his proposed withdrawal and the Samoan policy of Cleveland's first administration. In 1889 the president had noted that the islands "lie in the direct highway of a growing and important commerce between Australia and the United States." He had called for a continuing American effort to guarantee "that the autonomy and independence of Samoa should be scrupulously preserved" from encroachment by other powers. The Berlin Act, although negotiated by the Harrison administration, was in fact the outgrowth of the Bayard-Cleveland policy.[5]

All this was pointed out to Gresham by John Bassett Moore, who had served as an assistant secretary of state under Bayard. "The real cause of our complicated relations to Samoa," Moore said, "is not the General Act of Berlin, but the policy of which it was the result, or the consummation." He noted that "unless we were ready to reconsider our policy and let Samoa alone, the termination of the General Act of Berlin would be inexplicable." This point did not deter Gresham, however, for it was precisely his aim to leave Samoa alone. When Moore sent him a memorandum which included quotations from Cleveland's statements during his first term, Gresham was "afraid" to show it to the president because he did "not want to present that aspect of the matter too prominently." He told Moore that "the President had complained that he had not understood the Samoan matter during his former administration, and that Mr. Bayard had gone further in the direction of intervention than he (the President) would have been willing to go, if he had been managing the business himself." Whenever Moore urged caution, the secretary "always answered that the President wanted to get out of" the Berlin condominium and was "now very vigorous in his opposition to our meddling with affairs at a distance." Cleveland "had become very full of this idea in the Hawaiian matter," Gresham asserted, and "wanted the Government to get out of such things and stay at home." In reality, these were Gresham's sentiments more than Cleveland's, for Moore noted that the secretary was "constantly working on the President to keep him in that frame of mind."[6]

Reports from Samoa aided Gresham's cause. American Land Commissioner William L. Chambers wrote Secretary of War Daniel S. Lamont in early 1894 that the natives had "much ground for discontent." Nearly all the country's revenues, he noted, went to pay the salaries of foreign officials who sent a considerable portion of the money to their homelands, yet the native officials, including the king, had not been paid in months. Discontent had increased after Mataafa's banishment, and Chambers predicted that other chiefs would soon launch "a bloody effort" to depose Malietoa and again force the powers to act to maintain the king. "What folly," Chambers wrote, "for three great governments to be worrying, and spending such amounts of money over so small and insignificant a country! The game is not worth the candle." The United States "should honorably disentangle itself from the alliance before difficulties arise that will, or may be regretted." Noting what the president had said in his annual message about the need to return to the successful isolationist policy of the past, Chambers warned that "after a while it may be too late, and it may be contended that 'consecrated principles' require our adherence to the subject beyond all American precedent." Lamont passed Chambers's letter on to Cleveland, and his apprehensions were underscored by Vice Consul-General William Blacklock, who predicted that 1894 would bring "bloody times again" to Samoa.[7]

As the prospect of new hostilities loomed, Gresham and Cleveland decided to initiate a public discussion of the Samoan issue. In April Senator George Gray, an administration ally, secured passage of a resolution requesting the president to send the Senate information about conditions in Samoa and all correspondence on the subject between the United States and the other treaty powers. Gresham enlisted Moore's help in drafting his report, and before they were finished the expected fighting resumed and added one more arrow to their quiver.[8]

Gresham's report was a finely argued warning about how even the smallest and seemingly most innocent undertakings abroad inevitably mired the country in complex troubles that forbearance in the first instance could have avoided. He began with the observation that since the General Act of Berlin had been in effect just about five years, "the present occasion is not inappropriate for a review of its results." Predictably, what followed sounded very much like an opinion from a judge on the bench:

It is in our relations to Samoa that we have made the first departure from our traditional and well-established policy of avoiding entangling alliances with foreign powers in relation to objects remote from this hemisphere. Like all other human transactions, the wisdom of that departure must be tested by its fruits. If the departure was justified there must be some evidence of detriment suffered before its adoption, or of advantage since gained, to demonstrate the fact. If no such evidence can be found we are confronted with the serious responsibility of having, without sufficient grounds, imperiled a policy which is not only coeval with our Government, but to which may, in great measure, be ascribed the peace, the prosperity, and the moral influence of the United States. Every nation, and especially every strong nation, must sometimes be conscious of an impulse to rush into difficulties that do not concern it, except in a highly imaginary way. To restrain the indulgence of such a propensity is not only the part of wisdom, but a duty we owe to the world as an example of the strength, the moderation, and the beneficence of popular government.[9]

After this introduction Gresham recounted American involvement before the Berlin Act. "Twenty years ago," he noted, "Samoa was, as to the United States, an unknown country." Not until 1873, when "certain 'highly respectable commercial persons' . . . represented the opportunities of increasing our commercial relations in that quarter of the globe" and the navy sought a coaling station, did the State Department dispatch an agent to gather information about the islands. That mission ended disastrously, for the agent, A.B. Steinberger, first violated his instructions by proclaiming a protectorate and then, after the State Department rejected that action, severed his connection with the United States and proceeded to rule the islands at the head of a government of his own concoction. In addition, it turned out that while representing the United States, he had been under contract to a German commercial firm to use his influence exclusively to aid that firm's business in Samoa. Steinberger was finally deported on a British warship, and, Gresham noted with undisguised sarcasm, "Thus closed the first chapter in the history of our relations to Samoa, and of the attempt by such relations to extend our commerce and influence in that quarter of the globe."

In 1877 a Samoan representative visited the United States to ask for a protectorate, but, Gresham said, Americans were still unconvinced "that 'their safety and prosperity' required the assumption of control over islands which were practically unknown to them" and "more than 4,000 miles distant from their shores." But in early 1878 the United States did agree to a treaty, the first formal definition of American relations with the islands, whereby the United States gained the right to establish a coaling station at Pago Pago in exchange for a promise to employ its "good offices" to help settle any differences that might arise between Samoa and other countries. Gresham argued that entrance into this treaty was inspired not by "any supposition that the character of our relations to Samoa greatly concerned us" or any "conception of the importance of the group" but "rather by an amiable desire on the part of our Government not to appear wholly insensible to the friendly advances of the Samoans." Indeed, "if the Samoans had not been incited by our local representatives to send an ambassador to Washington to obtain a treaty, none would have been made." Even so, it was this treaty, negotiated on grounds almost frivolous, that formed the basis for the serious entanglements to come.

The phrase "good offices" was "necessarily vague," and, Gresham asserted, it did not involve "the United States in the responsibilities of a protectorate." Indeed, on those occasions when American diplomats in Samoa had proclaimed protectorates, disregarding "the distinctive national policy which our Government had pursued since the days of Washington," their actions invariably had been disavowed. But in the late 1880s a perceived American obligation under the "good offices" clause almost led to an unnecessary war with Germany when that country committed acts that seemed to threaten Samoa's independence. "The United States had not consciously sought to participate in such a contest," Gresham wrote. "It had merely endeavored to fulfill a treaty stipulation which required nothing more than friendly interposition. But our first adventure in that direction afforded most signal and convincing proof that the only safeguard against *all* the evils of interference in affairs that do not specially concern us is to abstain from such interference altogether."

Thus, in the years before the Berlin Act, American involvement had evolved from a small and innocent beginning to an entanglement "fraught with so much peril to our 'safety and prosperity' [that] we look in vain for any compensating advantage." It had done nothing to improve the lot of the natives. The United States itself had reaped only "unmitigated disadvantage" from its "departure from our early and conservative policy." As for commercial rewards, he cited statistics to show that trade with the islands had remained "insignificant" and "scarcely appreciable." In any case, he added, "We have never found it to be necessary to interfere in the affairs of a foreign country in order to trade with it."

Gresham next outlined the Berlin Act by which the United States, in "pursuit of its new policy" of intervention, had committed itself to ensure the "so-called neutrality of these distant lands." He recounted the problems that had arisen under the treaty: the administrative difficulties, the natives' hostility, the insufficient revenues, and the continuing need for pecuniary support by the three powers. "Soberly surveying the history of our relations with Samoa," he concluded,

we well may inquire what we have gained by our departure from our estab-lished policy beyond the expenses, the responsibilities, and the entanglements that have so far been its only fruits. One of the greatest difficulties in dealing with matters that lie at a distance is the fact that the imagination is no longer restrained by the contemplation of objects in their real proportions. Our experi-ence in the case of Samoa serves to show that for our usual exemption from the consequences of this infirmity, we are indebted to the wise policy that had previously preserved us from such engagements as those embodied in the general act of Berlin, which, besides involving us in an entangling alliance, has utterly failed to correct, if indeed it has not aggravated, the very evils which it was designed to prevent.

Gresham did not call specifically for the abrogation of the Berlin treaty, and Congress made no response. Press reaction to his report divided largely along partisan lines. The Mugwump *Springfield Republican* agreed with Gresham that "jingoism has led us into a blunder in the Samoan business" and that the United States should "abandon it as quickly as possible." The Republican *Chicago Inter-Ocean*, on the other hand, denounced him as "an advocate of abandonment of all American policy that looks toward development of our foreign trade, or of our chances of naval supremacy in time of war." Again, opponents cited his anomalous political standing to cast doubt on the sincerity of his policy; the *New York Mail and Express* asked why Cleveland had abandoned the policy of his first term: "Has Gresham's malignant hatred of President Harrison and Secretary Blaine found lodgment in the heart of Cleveland?"[10]

Undaunted, Gresham in early July sent Congress further Samoan correspondence, which, he claimed, provided "abundant confirmation" of his views. Again Congress took no action. On August 10 Cleveland joined the issue squarely in a secret message to the Senate, urging American withdrawal from the Berlin Act. He noted that since the inception of the foreign regime the islands had suffered disorder "requiring the constant intervention of the treaty powers." The United States had reached a crossroads: either it must join the other powers in "more effective measures" for "the suppression and disablement of the native opposition" or it must end its participation in the protectorate. He asked the Senate to decide whether it would "concur in the termination of the general act of Berlin, if such termination could be brought about on acceptable terms." Congress adjourned before the Senate could take action.[11]

Meanwhile, because the United States had sent no warship to Samoa, British and German naval forces had to quell the native rebels, who had risen again in the spring. They surrendered only after the loss of many lives on both sides. Since the peace thus achieved was no less shaky than previous ones, it appeared that lasting tranquillity would require the continuous presence of the powers' warships. From Apia the new consul-general, James H. Mulligan, wrote a private letter to Gresham deploring the island administration as "a travesty on government and common sense" and "laughable, if it were not serious." Facing the prospect of unending "sacrifice of life and treasure" to prop up this regime, Cleveland raised the subject of withdrawal publicly when Congress reconvened in December. Echoing Gresham's views, he declared that the tripartite government had "utterly failed to correct," if indeed it had not "aggravated, the very evils it was intended to prevent." American participation in the joint protectorate, he said, had done nothing to stimulate commerce with the islands and had been "in plain defiance of the conservative teachings and warnings of the wise and patriotic men who laid the foundations of our free institutions." Again, he urged Congress to issue its judgment on the question of unilateral withdrawal.[12]

At last the Foreign Relations Committee undertook deliberations on the subject. The administration had learned from the British and German ambassadors that their governments would probably accept American withdrawal, but the biggest stumbling block proved to be the committee chairman, John T. Morgan. Morgan feared that withdrawal from the condominium would jeopardize American rights to a naval coaling station at Pago Pago. Gresham cared little for such bases and privately scoffed at talk of "a splendid naval establishment," but to win Morgan's approval of the withdrawal scheme he assured the senator that American harbor rights antedated the Berlin treaty and were guaranteed by the 1878 treaty with Samoa. Morgan remained unconvinced, however, and joined the Republican minority on his committee to kill Cleveland and Gresham's proposal.[13]

Thus Gresham failed to secure an end to American participation in the protectorate. Even so, he continued to resist any broadening of the foreign domination of the islands' government. He rejected numerous German pleas that the control of expenditures be taken out of native hands and assigned to the president of the municipal council. Adhering to a strict construction of the Berlin Act, he told the German ambassador that even though the United States might sympathize with the "general purpose of preventing the native Government from squandering its revenues," the foreign officials in the Samoan government had no right to "exercise powers forbidden them by the act." Similarly, when the foreign officials drew up a proposed prohibition of the importation and sale of arms, he refused his assent because the new law contained "certain ancillary provisions" that went beyond the treaty and would "require an exercise of legislative power which [the State] Department does not possess."[14]

After Morgan's committee defeated withdrawal, little remained for the administration but to try to put the best face on its policy. Gresham believed the Republicans were "afraid of Samoa" and urged Moore to write newspaper articles defending the administration's position. In the Senate Democrat Roger Q. Mills drew embarrassing contrasts between the Republicans' position on Hawaii in which they denounced monarchy in support of republicanism and their support of the Berlin treaty by which they had obligated the United States to maintain a king in power against the wishes of his subjects. It was "Republican monarchy," Mills argued, that held the "enslaved peoples of the Samoan Islands . . . in subjection."[15]

As in the case of Hawaii, Republicans contended that an American presence in Samoa was "of serious consequence to our military and commercial interests in the Pacific." Henry Cabot Lodge spoke for many when, in an article entitled "Our Blundering Foreign Policy," he castigated Gresham and Cleveland for failing to see "the wisdom of maintaining not only a naval station, but our commercial influence in the Samoan group." "The effort of this Administration," Lodge charged, "has been to . . . give up our hold and to abandon Samoa . . . [and] to leave our interests without protection."[16]

Gresham would have accepted that characterization of his policy with equanimity, except that he would have denied that the United States had any significant interests in Samoa that required protection. American trade in the group was minuscule, but whatever its volume, he argued that it should be carried on without meddling in the islands' affairs. Militarily, Samoa was not an asset but a liability, requiring constant armed intervention by the United States and the other powers to suppress native discontent. Moreover, although he focused on the entanglement of the Berlin treaty as most lamentable, he recognized that the United States' difficulties in Samoa stemmed ultimately from its own unilateral involvement beginning in the 1870s. That he referred cynically to pressure for that involvement by "certain 'highly respectable commercial persons'" and generally denigrated American commercial interests in the islands revealed how little concerned he was with economic expansion. Indeed, the compelling lesson he believed the Samoan problem taught was that chasing after the chimera of commerce could lead to burdensome commitments and trouble. Most important, Samoa was just the sort of "Roman province" Gresham had sought to avoid in Hawaii. He believed the United States' strength as a nation derived largely from its compact, albeit large, territory and its relatively homogeneous population. To ignore the conservative teachings of the Founders and extend American responsibility into the far-flung regions of the globe with their alien peoples was to sap the vitality of the republic and court its downfall. Americans should "stay at home and attend to their own business," he declared, for otherwise "they would go to hell as fast as possible."[17]

TEN

THE ORIENT AND THE LEVANT
No Departure from the Wise Policy

As Gresham's policy toward Samoa clearly showed, he generally took the view that the United States' interests on the far side of the Pacific rim were minimal. And yet, events in the Orient during his tenure as secretary of state consumed a great deal of his time and energy. In advocating American withdrawal from Samoa he argued forcefully that "the only safeguard against *all* the evils of interference in affairs that do not specially concern us is to abstain from such interference altogether." Yet at that very time a war between China and Japan in 1894-95 posed a severe test of his adherence to that principle. And as in the case of Samoa, long-standing treaty obligations initially drew the United States and Gresham in.[1]

Age-old rivalry between China and Japan over the status of Korea provided the backdrop for the war, precipitated by an uprising in the Hermit Kingdom in the spring of 1894. Although the Korean government suppressed the rebellion, both China and Japan dispatched troops to Korea, and each subsequently refused to withdraw first.[2] The United States recognized Korean independence, and the Shufeldt Treaty of 1882 obligated the American government to exert its good offices if other nations dealt "unjustly or oppressively" with Korea. Before the outbreak of fighting, the State Department honored a Korean request and instructed the American minister at Seoul "to use every possible effort for the preservation of peaceful conditions." But when the Korean minister pressed for further help, Gresham informed him that the United States would maintain "impartial neutrality" and exert its influence with Japan "only in a friendly way" and "in no event" intervene jointly with other powers.[3]

Reluctant to see the United States embroiled in the controversy, Gresham and Cleveland adhered to the position that the Far Eastern war endangered no American "policy." But they also recognized that armed conflict could jeopardize American commerce with both China and Japan and endanger the lives of American missionaries in China. Moreover, Gresham suspected that if Japan waged a successful war against China, the European powers would intervene, leading to a possible disruption of the balance of power in the Orient. That possibility was of little direct American concern, but Gresham nonetheless warned Japanese Minister Gozo Tateno, "While you would not, in any event, encounter us, you might encounter strong European Powers, with deplorable consequences." Tateno said his government appreciated the risks involved, and he admitted that the real reason for Japan's aggressive stance was the government's desire to quell opposition to its rule at home. This frank admission outraged Gresham's moral sense. After his conversation with Tateno he sent a strongly worded telegraphic instruction to the American minister to Japan, Edwin Dun, "to say to the Government at Tokyo that the President will be painfully disappointed should Japan visit upon her feeble and defenseless neighbor the horrors of an unjust war." In reply the Japanese government claimed that it sought only to ensure "peace, order, good government, and independent sovereignty" in Korea and contended that China's frustration of Korean reform was the real threat to peace.[4]

Gresham's telegram to Dun was as far as he was prepared to go to prevent hostilities between Japan and China. With the "entangling alliance" of Samoa fresh in his mind, he rejected a British suggestion of a joint Anglo-American offer of good offices. He likewise told the Chinese minister, Yang Yu, that the United States was "unwilling to run the risk of taking the first step jointly with other Powers" and that it could do no more to prevent war than it had already done. On July 18 newspapers published the substance of his instruction to Dun. The sympathies of the American people lay predominantly with the Japanese, and when critics charged that the secretary had "practically taken the side of China" and jeopardized "much that we have gained from Japan by diplomacy," he made no further efforts to deter Japan from launching a war.[5]

Japan initiated hostilities in late July and soon amassed victory after victory. Gresham feared that a Japanese triumph would weaken authority throughout the Chinese provinces, causing "the foreign-hating natives" to threaten the lives of American missionaries. To protect Americans in China the navy increased its Asiatic fleet from five to eight vessels. Gresham suggested to Navy Secretary Hilary Herbert that "small ships, able to run up the rivers, might be very useful" for greater accessibility to Americans in the interior. But such apprehensions notwithstanding, in early October he rejected another British proposal for a joint diplomatic intervention with Germany, France, and Russia, all of whom he deemed "more immediately affected by the war" than was the United States. Making another veiled reference to Samoa, he observed that with "few exceptions" American diplomatic history showed "no departure from the wise policy of avoiding foreign alliances and embarrassing participation in guaranteeing the independence of distant states."[6]

As the war proceeded, the Chinese registered repeated pleas for help under the good-offices clause of the 1858 Sino-American Treaty, and in November 1894, Cleveland and Gresham yielded. In instructions to Dun offering American good offices, Gresham repeated the administration's position that the "deplorable war between Japan and China endangers no policy of the United States." But he again warned that "other powers having interests in that quarter may demand a settlement not favorable to Japan's future security and well-being." Confirming his suspicions a week later, the Russian minister at Washington informed Gresham that if Peking fell Russia might, "owing to its large interests in Asia, feel obliged to call a halt" and that Japan would not be allowed to acquire control of Korea or any Chinese territory. Still, Gresham and Cleveland once more refused a proposed intervention with Britain, Germany, France, Russia, and Italy. Gresham especially emphasized that the United States would play no part, "either alone or jointly with other powers, in a mediation or intervention which contemplated the use of force against either belligerent."[7]

China accepted the American offer of good offices, but Japan saw no reason to allow third-party interference. Japan was, however, willing to receive peace overtures from China conveyed through the American ministers at Peking and Tokyo. Thus began a process whereby the two belligerents communicated on the subject of an armistice and the initiation of a peace conference, employing the United States envoys not as mediators but as intermediaries. This arrangement was entirely consistent with Gresham's desire to keep the American role at a minimum. He was not above occasionally applying pressure on the Chinese; when China balked at naming a plenipotentiary, for example, he reminded Yang Yu that it was China who was asking for peace and should name an imperial envoy without delay. But for the most part, he tried to remain neutral, cautioning Dun and American minister to China Charles Denby to do so, too. Denby was more prone to violate this injunction than Dun, and the secretary had to remind him that the American ministers were "merely neutral channels of communication between China and Japan with no authority to conduct peace negotiations" and he should "do nothing that will even appear to compromise in any degree this Government's position of impartial neutrality."[8]

Denby hoped that "the influence secured by diplomatic work" could "assist our country in securing commercial privileges." He told China's chief negotiator, Li Hung Chang, that the only way China could pay its war indemnity was to sell concessions for railroad construction, banking, and mining and that the United States had plenty of men who were "competent to engage in the work of reform." Gresham promptly admonished Denby for giving such advice to Li. He warned the minister that he would "likely be beset by Americans anxious for valuable concessions" and that he should not permit his "generous and obliging nature" to get out of hand. Denby nonetheless persisted, advising the secretary that "the glory of greatly increasing and spreading American interests in China" would crown his administration of the State Department. Gresham died before this last expression of Denby's ardor reached Washington, but his successor, Richard Olney, instructed Denby to "abstain from using your diplomatic position" to promote American financial and business interests in China.[9]

Eventually, in the spring of 1895, China and Japan negotiated a treaty whereby China recognized Korea's independence, agreed to pay a war indemnity secured by its customs revenue, granted broader commercial privileges to Japan, and ceded the Liao Tung Peninsula, Formosa, and the Pescadores Islands to Japan. As Gresham had suspected, Russia, France, and Germany objected to Japan's acquisition of territory on the Chinese mainland and forced her to retrocede the Liao Tung Peninsula.[10]

Denby had confidently predicted that American participation in the peace negotiations, however limited, would greatly increase the United States' prestige in the Far East. At home, however, Americans demonstrated less enthusiasm for what some denounced as another anti-Japanese move and a front for the protection of British interests in China.[11] In fact, the American role in the search for peace was almost completely overshadowed by a sensational incident at the beginning of the war which aroused a great outcry in the United States and colored all subsequent public opinion about Gresham's Far Eastern policy.

At the beginning of hostilities the United States agreed to use its good offices to render unofficial protection to the nationals of each country in the territory of the other. In August two Japanese alleged to be spies were arrested in the French concession at Shanghai and delivered by the French consul-general to the American consul-general, T.R. Jernigan. Jernigan and Chargé d'Affaires Charles Denby, Jr., son of the American minister, refused to relinquish these men to Chinese authorities, who thereupon took the case to Gresham. The secretary ordered Denby and Jernigan to hand over the two Japanese; the exercise of unofficial good offices did not mean the American legations and consulates could be made asylum for Japanese who violated local laws or committed belligerent acts. To ensure "ample opportunity for investigation and deliberation," Gresham secured a promise from the Chinese minister in Washington that the alleged spies would not be tried until after Denby, Sr., who had been home on leave, arrived at Peking.[12]

Jernigan and Denby defended their action on grounds of humanity and local usage at Shanghai, which stipulated that accused foreigners should be tried not by local Chinese authorities but by a "mixed court" of a Chinese magistrate and a foreign "assessor." Not terribly well-versed in the law of international extraterritoriality, Gresham asked John Bassett Moore for help. "Is the situation or condition of China so exceptional that she cannot, without the consent of other powers, arrest and punish spies?" he asked Moore. "If we are to first determine whether or not the evidence is sufficient to put an alleged spie [sic] on trial, our jurisdiction is paramount to that of China even in time of war." Moore incorporated these views into a draft dispatch which stated that with the opening of hostilities Japanese and Chinese became "wholly subject" to the jurisdiction of local courts.[13]

Public interest in the case might have died down, but the execution of the two Japanese two weeks before the elder Denby's return revived its sensational treatment in the American press. When Gresham heard of the execution in mid-November, he complained to Yang Yu that the Chinese government's violation of its promise to delay the trial had put him in "a very awkward position, and as you say, 'I lose face.' " He hinted that it might "be as well if we ceased endeavoring to assist China any more in the matter of mediating with Japan." Yang replied that the evidence against the Japanese was so overwhelming that it did not seem necessary to await the return of the American minister, whose only valid object was to see that they received a fair trial, not to prevent their execution. Moreover, he wrote Gresham, the Chinese government had never promised to delay the trial. This assertion so took the secretary aback that he was "afraid to trust" himself to draft a reply, and he asked Moore to do it. Desiring no rupture in Sino-American relations, however, he cautioned Moore to phrase the response "as softly as possible without omitting what is essential." He accepted Moore's draft, which reminded Yang that their interviews also included the third assistant secretary, who concurred in Gresham's understanding of the promise. Yang then expressed his regret at the misunderstanding, and the matter was dropped.[14]

The incident attained a significance in domestic politics far out of proportion to its diplomatic importance. The spies had been tortured, correspondent Julian Ralph claimed in a gruesome report for *Harper's Weekly* complete with details about extracted fingernails and crushed genitals. The State Department had received no evidence of torture, and Gresham suggested that Ralph "evidently hopes to create a sensation." Other newspapers repeated the story, however, and the cry was soon heard that the blood of the "tortured and murdered Japs" was on Gresham's hands. He defended his return of the spies as the only action open to him under international law, but critics labeled him a heartless "stickler for technicalities." Theodore Roosevelt accused him of "brutal stupidity and cowardice" and called for his impeachment. Moore wrote newspaper articles defending Gresham, and Cleveland sought to dismiss the issue as the result of "misapprehension" on the part of American diplomats in China.[15]

But the issue would not die. Prompted by Roosevelt, Henry Cabot Lodge introduced a resolution requesting the president to transmit all diplomatic correspondence relating to the incident and to inform the Senate whether or not the Japanese had been tortured. Fearful that further publicity might endanger the peace feelers between China and Japan for which the United States was acting as intermediary, Chairman John T. Morgan and Republican John Sherman had Lodge's resolution referred to the Foreign Relations Committee. Gresham particularly feared that the resolution would jeopardize new bilateral treaties he had negotiated with China and Japan. Cleveland had just sent a new Japanese commercial treaty to the Senate, which had not yet ratified it. In the case of China, although both nations had ratified a new immigration treaty, the Chinese had yet to deliver their ratification in Washington. To forestall precipitate action on Lodge's resolution, Gresham invited Morgan and Sherman to the department to read the material in private. The tactic worked; the Chinese ratification was received a few days later, and the resolution did not emerge from committee until after the New Year's recess. Gresham considered his position to have been "unassailable," but he knew the correspondence would be "seized upon by the Republicans in their effort to damage the State Department." In fact, publication of the documents in mid-January 1895 did rekindle press criticism of the "shameful and sickening affair," which continued to overshadow all other aspects of his Far Eastern policy. In March Republican Senator Cushman K. Davis published in the *North American Review* a damning appraisal of Gresham's general performance as secretary of state and devoted over half of his discussion to the spy incident.[16]

Davis made no mention whatever of Gresham's treaties with China and Japan, which formed perhaps the most important and enduring part of his dealings with those nations. Although Gresham had been content with the treaty system as he had inherited it and was reluctant to enter into treaty negotiations with either country, once the pacts were finally written he was anxious that they be approved.

The problem of immigration had plagued Sino-American relations for decades. The Angell Treaty of 1880 empowered the United States to "suspend" but "not absolutely prohibit" the immigration of Chinese laborers, and the Exclusion Act of 1882 "suspended" such immigration for ten years. In 1892 the Geary Act extended the ban another ten years and added stringent regulations including one requiring all Chinese laborers in the United States to obtain certificates of residence on pain of deportation. By the time Gresham became secretary the Chinese government had decided to test the constitutionality of this law, and the Cleveland administration helped expedite a hearing before the Supreme Court. Gresham assured the Chinese that the registration requirement would not be enforced until after the Court had passed on its validity. In addition, at considerable political risk to the administration, he asked Pacific Coast governors to employ all means to protect the Chinese from violence when the law was scheduled to take effect May 6, 1893.

In late May the Court upheld the law, but Gresham again assured the Chinese minister that insufficient appropriations would preclude its rigid enforcement before the regular session of Congress, at which time the law would most likely be amended. With Gresham's support the Geary Law was amended by the McCreary Act, which extended the registration period six months. But the new law also required two photographs of the registered laborer and defined "laborers" broadly while defining "merchants," who were permitted to immigrate, narrowly. Minister Yang Yu complained against these "additional objectionable provisions." Contending that the restrictive acts violated the Angell Treaty's guarantee of most-favored-nation treatment for Chinese in America, Yang suggested that the time had come to correct the anomalous situation by negotiating a new treaty.[17]

After Yang pressed the matter, Gresham agreed to discussions but left it to Yang to submit a working draft. The minister offered a modified version of the unratified Bayard-Chang convention of 1888, which had "absolutely prohibited" the immigration of Chinese laborers for twenty years. In addition to a preamble nullifying the restrictive legislation passed in and since 1888, Yang's draft reduced the prohibition to ten years and permitted the immigration of wives and children of laborers already in the United States. It also contained an extradition clause and a "special article of reciprocity," which, to balance the Geary Act, would permit China to register all citizens of the United States residing in China. Two weeks passed, and Yang found it necessary to prod Gresham, who in late January 1894 replied that he found "certain recitals and provisions" objectionable and proposed to defer further discussions until after the expiration of the registration period in May. Yang protested vigorously, however, and Gresham agreed to proceed with negotiations.[18]

He accepted the reduction to ten years, but the clauses on extradition and laborers' families were eliminated. The article relating to the registration of Americans in China was altered to permit the registration of laborers only (of whom there were none) and to stipulate that the United States should provide the Chinese government with the Americans' names. The only real contention in the negotiations surrounded the problem of Chinese laborers who had gone back to China and wished to return to the United States. In 1888 the Senate had amended the Bayard Treaty to prohibit the return of such laborers. Now Yang proposed a guarantee of their right to return to the United States. Gresham refused, but rather than repeat the obnoxious Senate amendment, he merely inserted the word "registered" to delimit those who would be allowed to return. Since none or few of those returned Chinese laborers then in China could have registered under the Geary Act, this insertion had the same effect as the Senate amendment but with less offense to the Chinese.[19]

Gresham and Yang signed the treaty on March 17, the secretary's sixty-second birthday. The press generally applauded, although critics on the West Coast said the return provision "throws wide open the gates, breaks down the barriers, and offers a premium to an incursion of coolie labor." The convention lay in the Senate for months, its consideration impeded by debates on the tariff, which the administration said should have the "right of way." In July 1894, the Senate had still taken no action, and Gresham told Morgan that the Chinese government was growing "very anxious." A month later the Senate gave its consent by a vote of forty-five to twenty. At this juncture California Senator Stephen M. White introduced legislation to stiffen the requirements for admission by nonlaborers to prevent fraudulent entry by laborers. Again prodded by Yang, Gresham protested, and White's bill died in committee.[20]

Once the Senate had approved the treaty, Gresham was eager to exchange ratifications, lest it suffer the same fate as Bayard's 1888 agreement. In December 1894, a year after negotiations had begun, he and Yang exchanged ratifications, congratulating each other for at last placing Sino-American relations "on a firm basis of equal rights and perfect good feeling." With more than modesty Gresham told the minister: "You have made the treaty. . . . All praise is due you."[21]

Gresham's treaty negotiations with the Japanese came as part of a general effort by Japan to undo the so-called unequal treaty system which for years had bound Japan to a position of inferiority in its dealings with Western powers. Pressed by domestic political opposition, the Japanese government sought general revision of its commercial treaties to elevate its status more toward one of equality. The Japanese began revision discussions with the British in late 1893, and the following March Minister Gozo Tateno asked Gresham if the United States would enter similar negotiations. Gresham was slow to respond to Tateno's appeals, hoping to delay talks until after the outcome of the Anglo-Japanese negotiations to ensure that the United States would relinquish no more to Japan than did Britain, its chief competitor for Japanese commerce. Moreover, Gresham was wary of Japan's proposal to make reciprocal the rights of the citizens of each of the two countries to enter, travel, reside, or hold property anywhere within the territory of the other. The United States had never sought an extension of residential privileges for Americans in Japan, he claimed, and any treaty permitting unrestricted immigration of Japanese laborers to the United States would likely fail in the Senate. Not until early July did he finally agree to sit down with the Japanese, but he delayed serious discussion until he had received a copy of the final Anglo-Japanese treaty signed on July 16.[22]

Gresham and Shinichiro Kurino (who had replaced Tateno as minister chiefly because of Tateno's failure to secure a new treaty) used the British agreement as a model and made few changes in its provisions granting Japan equal status in a number of matters relating to commerce and navigation. To overcome American objections to immigration of laborers, the Japanese offered a clause noting that the stipulations regarding reciprocity in admission, travel, residency, and so forth did "not in any way affect the special laws, ordinances and regulations with regard to trade, police and public security in force in each of the two countries and applicable to all foreigners in general." Gresham insisted on including among the exemptions laws relating to the immigration of laborers and laws that might be enacted in the future. He also pressed for the elimination of the phrase "applicable to all foreigners in general." When he and Kurino had ironed out the differences over this clause, their work was essentially complete. The only other significant difference between the British and American treaties was that Britain retained the right to establish Japanese import quotas on some British goods by convention, while the United States agreed to leave American products subject wholly to the statutory tariff of Japan.[23]

Gresham urged Senator Morgan to take "speedy action" on the pact, noting that Japan regarded "the final consummation of the treaty as a matter of supreme importance" and the British, who feared American commercial competition, were "exceedingly anxious" that it fail. An effort by White of California to insert a reference to the "exclusion" of Japanese laborers failed, and in early February 1895, the Senate gave its unanimous consent to the treaty.[24]

Although problems in the Orient occupied much of Gresham's time, he showed no inclination to preside over an extension of American responsibility in East Asia. Though recognizing the dangers dismemberment of China might bring to American interests, he never translated his vague apprehensions into a vigorous policy statement like the Open Door Notes Secretary of State John Hay issued a few years later. His efforts at mediation in the Sino-Japanese War were extremely cautious. His approach to the spy incident was legalistic and illustrated his opposition to American diplomats' assuming unwarranted and unwonted responsibility, even though perhaps justified on humanitarian grounds. Similarly, he gave little encouragement to those diplomats' efforts to further American economic interests in the East. His treaty negotiations with China and Japan revealed no great eagerness to reorder relations with those countries. Indeed, as Yang Yu repeatedly told his government, Gresham seemed to lack a clearly defined notion of affairs in the Far East.[25] But this imperfection in his thinking was not so much a failure of his understanding as it was a reflection of his belief that that distant quarter of the globe lay outside America's particular interest.

Gresham brought a similar attitude to his handling of relations with the Middle East. Here the most troublesome problem was the defense of the legitimate rights of Americans sojourning in the Ottoman Empire, where Christian missionaries and others suffered harassment from Turkish officials and Moslem marauders. Americans' rights in Turkey dated back to the Treaty of 1830, which guaranteed United States citizens against molestation and granted them the right to be tried for offenses by the American minister or consul rather than by local authorities. This extraterritorial status was modified somewhat by the Protocol of 1874, which also secured to Americans the same rights as Ottoman subjects in the possession of real estate. During the last quarter of the nineteenth century, during the reign of Sultan Abdul Hamid II, American missionaries suffered continuing annoyance, and intercession in their behalf became a routine State Department function. In the early 1890s this annoyance appeared to be increasing, and the champions of the missionaries grew more insistent in calling for government help. Soon after Gresham took office, one of the first reports he received from the Diplomatic Bureau called for sending an American warship to the eastern Mediterranean. The American Board of Commissioners of Foreign Missions also sent the new secretary a copy of its pamphlet, *The Treaty Rights of American Missionaries in Turkey,* and for the next two years maintained a barrage of letters and telegrams requesting intervention.[26]

In this atmosphere Gresham vigorously carried forward the department's traditional defense of Americans' treaty rights. In one instance, when incendiaries destroyed a building at an American college at Marsovan, he demanded full restitution, a decree of future protection, a permit to rebuild, and punishment for the offending parties. Similarly, when an American missionary was assaulted in Kurdistan, he called for "an immediate and thorough investigation" by Turkish authorities, "adequate punishment" of those found guilty, and a guarantee of "future protection" of American missionaries. He even protested the Turkish government's "vexatious" arrest of native subjects "necessarily employed" by American missions and schools, when such arrests seemed designed as a deliberate "hindrance and molestation" of those institutions' activities.[27]

But Gresham was not inclined to go beyond treaty limits. Americans in Turkey, including missionaries, often purchased property in the name of a Turkish subject to avoid the higher prices charged foreigners. Gresham hesitated to invoke the Protocol of 1874 to defend such property because American property rights could be "better asserted and more practically defended" only when ownership was actually recorded in an American name. In another class of cases, in the absence of a naturalization treaty between the United States and Turkey, numerous problems arose when Armenian Christians who had become naturalized Americans sought to reenter Turkey, a privilege the sultan generally denied to subjects who had alienated their allegiance. The United States held that once subjects of Turkey had acquired American citizenship they deserved the same protection by the American government as any other citizen. Gresham protested the punishment of returning Armenians as criminals simply because they had become United States citizens. But at the same time he recognized that as "an attribute of sovereignty," the Turkish government had "the right to expel them and, incidentally, to arrest them for the purpose of expulsion." Moreover, should a returning Armenian reassert his Turkish citizenship to gain entry into the country and then claim the protection of American citizenship once inside the empire, the State Department would refuse to countenance such "duplicity"; once a Turk had reverted to allegiance to the sultan, he had "clearly dissolve[d] the obligation of his adopted country to protect him longer as a citizen."[28]

In the mid-1890s Christians in both Europe and America focused their concern on the plight of Armenians in Turkey. Under the Treaty of Berlin of 1878 several European powers had assumed a measure of responsibility for the protection of this Christian minority. But balance-of-power factors as well as humanitarian considerations governed the Europeans' interest, and Gresham was loath to see the United States become involved in the matter, especially since it was not a signatory to the treaty. Thus the State Department ordered its officers in Turkey not to convey in official dispatches any "unconfirmed and improbable reports" of atrocities committed against Armenians. In September 1894, Minister Alexander W. Terrell reported that he had "entirely reliable" information that a massacre of Armenians had just occurred in the interior. Gresham took no action on this report, and when Congress later called for "any information" on alleged cruelties against Armenians, he withheld several of Terrell's dispatches relating to the incident.[29]

Before long reports of Armenian massacres appeared in Western newspapers, and mass meetings of Armenians and their sympathizers urged the State Department as well as European powers to enforce the Treaty of Berlin. Still, Gresham did nothing regarding the treaty, although he now requested Terrell to "inform the Department as fully as possible" about alleged massacres. Terrell reported that the sultan had appointed a Turkish commission to investigate the affair and would like an American consul to serve as a member. Cleveland and Gresham declined the sultan's request, but within a few days Great Britain, a signatory of the Berlin Treaty, suggested that an American travel with the commission. In addition, Congress began to voice concern regarding the alleged atrocities. Bowing to this pressure, Gresham reluctantly agreed to let American consul Milo Jewett "accompany" the commission, stipulating that Jewett could not be a "member" and must report only to his own government. The sultan refused this arrangement. Gresham had no regrets over this refusal but wired Terrell that it would be "unfortunate" if Jewett were not permitted to proceed. When this mild remonstrance brought no change in the sultan's position, the secretary ordered Terrell to drop the question: "This Government cannot be supposed to take any part in the fulfillment of the engagements of the Treaty of Berlin by the signatories." Privately, he thought the United States was "better out of the matter than in it."[30]

Gresham was satisfied that he was pursuing "our well-known policy of non-interference in the internal affairs of Europe," but interventionist-minded critics denounced his handling of the Jewett mission.

"In Armenia," wrote Henry Cabot Lodge, "we did enough to be laughed at and too little to be effective." Criticism focused on Minister Terrell, whom missionaries considered a reluctant champion of their rights. Gresham also was displeased with Terrell but because he thought the minister "impudent" in his representations to the sultan's government. He enjoined Terrell to exercise "increased prudence and reserve in discussing questions of continental policy in order to avoid possible embarrassments and misconstructions of the policy and motives of your government."[31]

As criticism from missionaries mounted, Gresham sought to allay the Christians' apprehensions but also to resist their pressure for more vigorous intervention. He assured Terrell that "what the missionary element may think of the attitude of this Government, or of your acts as its representative, seems no adequate reason for your transfer to another mission." But he also warned Terrell against adding to the "impression unfortunately already existing in some quarters that you are disposed to appear as the Sultan's apologist or advocate." Similarly, he assured the missionaries that Terrell would adjure the Turkish government to provide "adequate protection of their lives and property in case of need," but he also frankly told them that the United States was "seriously handicapped in dealing with this class of questions by the indiscretions attributed to some American missionaries" who openly sympathized with the Armenian revolutionary movement opposing the sultan.[32]

Still leery of Terrell, the missionaries called for the creation of a permanent American naval station at Smyrna in the eastern Mediterranean. The administration rejected this proposal as "contrary to the practice of this Government." At the State Department's request, however, the navy dispatched two ships to the area to ascertain the validity of the missionaries' anxiety and to intimate to Turkish authorities that the United States would see that its citizens were protected "under the guarantees of treaties." Gresham assured the Turkish minister in Washington that the visit of the ships was friendly. Indeed, the mission was more shadow than substance and was probably aimed more at quieting American public opinion than at intimidating the sultan. As one naval officer put it, "The governor of Massachusetts is as much liable for the murder of settlers by the Apaches as is the governor of Smyrna for the murder of the Armenians by the Koords." Terrell was an embarrassment to the administration. Sending warships symbolized disapproval of him, while serving notice that the United States intended to protect its citizens.[33]

Terrell had called for ships, but when their officers held discussions with Turkish officials, he chafed under this obvious rebuke to his diplomatic methods. He argued that if the missionaries would stop taking their complaints directly to the State Department and start dealing with him and the consuls in the field, "much circumlocution" and confusion could be avoided in ensuring their protection. The department heartily agreed. In May 1895, a few days after Gresham became fatally ill, Acting Secretary Edwin F. Uhl informed the head of the Foreign Missions Board that he should "instruct" his missionaries in Turkey to apply for aid directly to the nearest American consular offices rather than to Washington. All cases in which Americans were entitled to diplomatic intercession under treaty guarantees were covered by general instructions, and when complaints came to the department directly, it could "at best merely repeat directions with which the consuls are familiar."[34]

Thus, when the direction of American policy in Turkey passed out of Gresham's hands, that policy was no broader in scope than when he had assumed office two years earlier. He had inherited nettlesome problems in Turkey. That he was driven by genuine sympathy for the Christians as well as by a vociferous missionary lobby to render an emphatic defense of American rights within treaty guidelines was evident from his diplomatic instructions. Equally evident, however, was his belief that no amount of sympathy for slaughtered foreign Christians should be permitted to entangle the United States in affairs essentially European. But in charting this course—a strong defense of legitimate treaty rights but no more—he was ill-served by an erratic, self-important minister, whose appointment he regretted. He made no move to dismiss Terrell, however, and, forced either to defend him or to reprove him, he variously did both. As a result, despite Gresham's own notion of the limits of American responsibility, the American policy in Turkey seemed at times timid, at times meddlesome, but often ill-defined and unpredictable.

ELEVEN

THE WESTERN HEMISPHERE
The Consistent Policy Pursued

At the time of Gresham's tenure in the State Department in the mid-1890s, American diplomatic concern rarely extended beyond the Western Hemisphere, and, indeed, a great deal of the diplomatic intercourse between the United States and European nations pertained not to matters in continental Europe but to European involvement in the American hemisphere. The United States carried on more diplomatic exchange with Great Britain than any other European country, and more often than not that intercourse focused on questions in the New World. Among the most time-consuming and convoluted of these issues was the Bering Sea fur seal controversy.

Like most other problems during Gresham's term, the question was an inherited one with a long history. It centered on the preservation of the fur-bearing seal that inhabited the Bering Sea. Late each spring the seal returned to their rookeries on the Pribilof Islands, which were part of Alaska. Pups were born soon after the females' arrival. During the nurturing season, lasting through the summer, the mothers might swim up to two hundred miles from the islands in search of food for their young. Over the years the furry skins of these creatures had showed a steady rise in value, commanding $30 each by 1890.[1]

Soon after the Alaskan purchase in 1867, to eliminate destructive competition, the secretary of the treasury granted a monopoly for fur-sealing on the Pribilof Islands to the Alaska Commercial Company, whose dazzling financial success soon attracted others into seal-hunting. These other sealers took their catch from the sea, and before long this pelagic sealing threatened to make the herd extinct. The Alaska Company limited its take to young "bachelors," males under four years old without mates. In the water, however, discrimination as to sex was impossible, and the killing of a female during the nurturing season entailed not only her own death but that of her just-born young back on the islands as well. Moreover, because the seal sank rapidly on being killed, estimates placed as high as ten the number destroyed in the water for each one actually secured.[2]

An 1868 statute prohibited the killing of fur seal "within the limits of the Alaska territory, or in the waters thereof," but the government took no action until the first Cleveland administration, when revenue cutters captured several Canadian sealing vessels. When the British government protested, divided counsels inhibited an emphatic response, but toward the end of the term Secretary of State Thomas F. Bayard favored an international arrangement over unilateral American action to preserve the seal. Harrison's secretary of state, James G. Blaine, drew the issue more sharply in defense of a presumed right of the United States to prohibit sealing in international waters. The resulting impasse led the two powers to submit the matter to arbitration.[3]

They agreed to submit five questions to a tribunal of two members from each of the interested countries and three appointed by other governments. The first question asked what exclusive jurisdiction in the Bering Sea and exclusive rights to the seal fisheries Russia had claimed and exercised before ceding Alaska. Second, how far had Britain conceded Russia's claims, and, third, to what extant had Russia's rights passed "unimpaired" to the United States when it acquired Alaska? Fourth, was the Bering Sea subsumed under the phrase "Pacific Ocean" in the Anglo-Russian Treaty of 1825 by which Russia had renounced any right to interfere with foreign fishing or navigation in the Pacific Ocean? (Blaine had contended that it was not.) And, last, did the United States have any right of property in the seal when they ventured beyond the three-mile limit? The treaty also empowered the tribunal, in the event it should deny the United States' claim to jurisdictional rights in the Bering Sea and property rights in the seal, to issue concurrent regulations to enable Britain and the United States to protect the seal outside their territorial limits.[4]

At the Paris Tribunal of Arbitration, John W. Foster headed the American commission which presented the formal written version of the American case before Cleveland's inauguration. All that remained after Gresham became secretary was the presentation of the oral arguments. Gresham regarded the American case as a "transparent blunder," but because proceedings were so far along he decided that he could not revise it or do anything but support the commission.[5]

That support seemed less than full when newspapers carried reports that he had complained to Treasury Secretary John G. Carlisle that as secretary of state Foster had been "very free" with the money appropriated for the commission he would head as agent, especially as to the salary of its disbursing officer, Elijah W. Halford. As editor of the *Indianapolis Journal*, Halford had bitterly opposed Gresham in Indiana Republican politics; during the Harrison administration he had served as the president's private secretary. Now working for the commission, he received his regular salary as a major in the army plus a daily allowance of $15, making his total pay nearly equal to that of a cabinet officer. Foster accepted Gresham's explanation that the stories originated in the Treasury Department, but Republicans in the United States saw partisan malice in the reports. Ohio Congressman Charles H. Grosvenor charged that Gresham's "disparag[ing] the Harrison administration in its diplomatic action . . . has aided and abetted the enemy in the Behring Sea contest." Harrison himself told Foster he had never known anyone "so given to aspersing the motives of other people" as Gresham.[6]

Nonetheless, the incident did not undermine the commissioners' effectiveness. The American case failed for substantive, not bureaucratic reasons. While the tribunal was still sitting, Russia made an agreement with Great Britain implicitly renouncing all claim to exclusive jurisdiction over the fur seal on the high seas in the western half of the Bering Sea. As Gresham told the Russian minister in Washington, this action was "both surprising and displeasing" to the United States, for it undermined the American assertions of control of seal-hunting in the eastern Bering Sea, which were based upon prior Russian assertions. Although the Anglo-Russian modus vivendi probably did not have a determining influence on the arbitrators, it rendered the weak American case all the less tenable.[7]

On August 15, 1893, the tribunal rejected four of the five American contentions. The United States possessed no extraordinary jurisdiction in the Bering Sea and no property rights in the seal outside the three-mile limit surrounding the Pribilof Islands. The tribunal did find that Russia's rights had passed unimpaired to the United States, but since it ruled against the American claim regarding the substance of those rights the finding was without significance. Thus the United States was powerless to take unilateral action to protect the seal in international waters. But the tribunal also issued a set of regulations for the protection of the seal "outside the jurisdictional limits" of the two countries. These regulations prohibited pelagic sealing within sixty miles of the Pribilofs at any time and in the American half of the Pacific Ocean north of thirty-five degrees latitude from May 1 to July 31. They also limited fur-sealing to nonmotorized ships and outlawed the use of nets, explosives, or firearms, except shotguns, which could be used only outside the Bering Sea. These regulations might prove effective, but they would take effect only when the two powers had agreed on means to enforce them.[8]

Foster contended that because the proposed regulations would protect the seal, the outcome of the arbitration should not be regarded "as anything but a success for the United States." Gresham disagreed. As he saw it, "our right of property in the fur seals and our right to protect them were the most important questions submitted to the Tribunal, and . . . if the award had been in our favor on those questions there would have been little necessity of regulations." But he agreed that the important task now was to secure British cooperation "in an honest effort to enforce the regulations in spirit as well as letter."[9]

Since the first seizures of Canadian ships in the mid-1880s the British had hoped to keep the issue from damaging their country's growing amity with the United States. At the same time the imperial government was under constant pressure from Canada to defend the interests of pelagic sealers who denied that they were exterminating the herd. In 1886 these sealers had taken fifty thousand skins valued at $350,000; by 1892 Canada's sealing fleet numbered sixty ships, over twice the number of American vessels. The British admitted the risks of pelagic sealing, but as Foreign Secretary Lord Salisbury had earlier noted, "pleasing Canada is the whole object of all we have been doing." This attitude persisted in the struggle to put the Paris regulations into effect.[10]

Gresham was content to assign the task to American Ambassador Thomas F. Bayard, whose familiarity with the complex question, dating back to his own term as secretary, exceeded Gresham's. Moreover, holding the talks in London would perhaps render them more immune to pressures from the Canadians. But the British government urged that the talks be shifted to Washington because of an "overwhelming" load of work at the Foreign Office and because of British Ambassador Sir Julian Pauncefote's experience with the question. Gresham informed Pauncefote that his need to supplement his own knowledge would result in "delay which both Governments desire to avoid," but the British insisted, and Bayard advised Gresham to accede to their request. The secretary was somewhat miffed by his ambassador's "generosity," but he reluctantly agreed to pursue the negotiations. In doing so, he drew heavily on John Bassett Moore's services.[11]

Nearly four months after the Paris award Gresham entered into discussions with the British ambassador, rejecting a British proposal that Canada be admitted as a party. Bayard had forwarded a draft of a convention embodying verbatim the regulations handed down by the tribunal, but Pauncefote now asserted that a convention was not necessary and that the two countries could regulate pelagic sealing by legislation. Gresham insisted on a bilateral agreement, but as he feared, Pauncefote intimated that Britain would make no agreement without first reaching an understanding about control of sealing on American islands. Although Gresham believed that the seal should be protected for several years "both on land and sea," he reminded the ambassador that the "first object to be accomplished" was giving "immediate effect" to the regulations, which were "designed to attain the principal end which the parties to the arbitration had in view—that of putting an end to the destructive and indiscriminate slaughter of seals on the high seas." Any "supplementary rules" could be agreed on later.[12]

In early 1894 the talks remained stalled while Pauncefote claimed he was waiting for more definite instructions, but meanwhile a new sealing season was getting under way. Senate Foreign Relations Chairman John T. Morgan, who, as one of the Paris arbitrators, had voted to uphold the American contentions and still believed in an American property right in the seal, proposed that, to "stimulate the British Government" to reach an agreement, Congress should pass a law enabling American officials to arrest British sealers and try them in American courts. At first Gresham discouraged such legislation, but as the May 1 starting date of the proposed closed season drew near, he finally admitted that he and the ambassador could not reach an agreement and that it was time to "proceed at once with all dispatch in obtaining needed legislation."[13]

Gresham and Pauncefote could not agree even on a modus vivendi to remain in force until Congress and Parliament could enact their respective laws, and so prompt action by those bodies was made all the more necessary. Foreseeing this contingency, Gresham had already sent draft legislation to Congress. On April 2 he abandoned negotiations with Pauncefote, and the same day Morgan introduced the bill, which reproduced the nine regulations written by the arbitrators. An additional section stipulated that American citizens on vessels violating the regulations could be arrested by British officers and turned over for trial in American courts, provided that Britain enacted similar legislation. Four days after its introduction, Cleveland signed Morgan's bill into law. Less expeditiously and just two weeks before the start of the closed season, Parliament overrode fierce opposition from the Canadians and passed its law.[14]

In the original arbitration treaty Britain and the United States had agreed "to cooperate in securing the adhesion of other powers" to any regulations resulting from the Paris tribunal. In August 1894, the two nations sent identical notes to several countries requesting them to enforce the regulations with respect to their own citizens. The response was discouraging; only Italy and Germany registered unqualified willingness to comply, and the latter country noted that none of its shipping had ever taken part in seal-hunting. Gresham was especially concerned to secure the cooperation of Russia and Japan, but neither was eager to accept the Paris regulations in the eastern half of the Pacific and the Bering Sea without assurances that their own sealing grounds would be protected from depredations by Americans and Canadians. Arduous negotiations, described by Gresham in the case of Russia as "unpleasant and fruitless," resulted in only limited agreements with the two Asian powers. But, in fact, no citizens of either had ever taken seal in the American half of the ocean. Thus, feeling bound by treaty to obtain the "adhesion of other powers," Gresham had expended great time and effort pursuing a diplomatic goal of little practical significance.[15]

A more tangible question concerned British claims arising out of the seizure of Canadian sealing vessels by American revenue cutters during the first Cleveland and the Harrison administrations. The Paris tribunal had determined the facts of the seizures but left the two parties to determine the compensation to be paid by the United States. Britain estimated claims at over $540,000 and suggested that both countries appoint commissioners to settle the issue. Gresham insisted that a convention would be required to define such a commission's responsibilities. This insistence led to another round of irksome negotiations with the British ambassador. By mid-August 1894, Pauncefote and Gresham were on the verge of signing an agreement when Cleveland and Gresham, apparently concerned over the expense of a commission, offered to settle by paying a lump sum of $425,000. The British promptly accepted, but in Congress the necessary appropriation bill met opposition from Morgan, who claimed that "not one shilling" was due Great Britain. The senator charged that Gresham was evading "his constitutional duty" and a treaty mandate to arrive at a figure by "negotiation." Congress refused to make the appropriation. Bayard reported the British government's disappointment and expressed his own view, with which Gresham no doubt agreed, that Morgan was "the most wholly and dangerously unreliable person" in public life. After Gresham's death a bilateral commission finally awarded Britain $473,151.26, nearly $50,000 more than Cleveland and Gresham had offered.[16]

The confidence that observers had placed in the Paris regulations rested largely on their prohibition of the use of guns. But according to Treasury Department figures, the 1894 season showed a substantial increase in the pelagic catch over those of previous years. The ban on firearms had forced sealers to employ Indian crews whose use of spears did not warn nearby seal as did gunfire and consequently allowed for more concentrated and efficient hunting. Britain disputed the significance of the United States' statistics, but nonetheless the calculations for the covered waters showed a doubling of the catch of 1893.[17]

Gresham fed resolutions of inquiry to congressmen to publicize the failure of the sealing rules. In early 1895 he addressed a note to Pauncefote citing the "startling increase in the pelagic slaughter" and calling for "a speedy change in regulations." He proposed that the United States and Britain join with Russia and Japan to appoint a commission to arrive at suitable measures for the preservation of the herds. Pending the commission's report, he called for a modus vivendi absolutely prohibiting pelagic sealing in the Bering Sea. To force the British to negotiate, he sponsored legislation stipulating that if Britain failed "to cooperate with the United States in such measures as, in the judgment of the President, will prevent the extermination" of the herds, the secretary of the treasury should order the killing of all seal on the Pribilof Islands and sell them for the profit of the United States. This piece of diplomatic extortion actually passed the House but was blocked in the Senate, ironically by Morgan, who, despite his Anglo-phobia, would not admit the failure of the regulations he had helped to write at Paris.[18]

In the end, Britain refused to adopt more stringent controls on pelagic sealing, and during the 1895 season only two British vessels patrolled the covered waters. The fur seal herds continued to diminish. By 1911, when the United States, Great Britain, Russia, and Japan finally agreed to ban all pelagic sealing, fewer than 150,000 seal remained.[19]

Although conservationists might argue the importance of preserving the fur seal, the international controversy achieved dimensions clearly out of proportion to its importance. Fewer than five hundred Americans earned their living in catching seal, and none did so in treating their skins, which was carried on exclusively in London. The fees collected by the United States from the Pribilof concessionaires hardly covered the cost of maintaining a fleet to combat pelagic sealers. Nonetheless, Blaine and other American officials had seemed willing to jeopardize the hard-won and time-honored principle of freedom of the seas, all in the name of the seal. Gresham did not initiate a more realistic approach. He continued to avow that the United States and Britain were "deeply interested in the preservation of the seal herd" and that the "interests of the two countries" were "intimately involved" in the matter. In retrospect, the great expenditure of time, effort, and concern that he and others devoted to the issue seem more a mockery of diplomacy than the real thing.[20]

The long-run significance of the affair lay not in the fate of the seal but in the development of Anglo-American relations. The issue served as an irritant that could have impeded the growth of closer ties between the two countries. At times, when mired in the frustrating negotiations with Pauncefote, Gresham's distrust of Britain's sincerity and good intentions rivaled that of the most rabid Anglophobe. But at the same time, the Paris arbitration illustrated the possibilities for amicable settlement of apparently irresolvable disputes. Although Gresham considered the Paris award an American defeat, he could also say that the United States had not "wholly failed" because "the settlement of an embarrassing controversy with Great Britain by arbitration is enough of itself to justify the expenditure of the time and money." Even though the Paris regulations proved of little effect, he was willing to see the principle of arbitration given wider application. A few months before his death he and Pauncefote began discussions for a general Anglo-American arbitration agreement that eventually resulted in the (unratified) Olney-Pauncefote Treaty of 1897. Thus, even though the United States could claim few diplomatic victories in the fur seal dispute while Gresham presided over American foreign policy, the quest for cooperation over confrontation inched the two countries forward toward the general rapprochement they enjoyed during the twentieth century.[21]

Affairs in Latin America, it seemed to Gresham, were much more the "special concern" of the United States than were those of Europe or Asia. Here the United States had a long-standing, if ill-defined, policy in the Monroe Doctrine. Gresham subscribed to that doctrine insofar as it aimed to reduce European influence in the Western Hemisphere, but he refrained from permitting a defense of its precepts to go so far as to flout the higher dictates of international law. Nor did he agree with those who saw the doctrine as a vehicle for expanding United States influence in Latin America. He would defend the United States' legitimate rights, but as European influence in the hemisphere declined, he rejected the argument that the logical concomitant was a broadening of American responsibility.

In the fall of 1893 a revolt in the Brazilian navy against the government of acting president Floriano Peixoto required Gresham to attempt to define the United States' prerogatives and responsibilities under the Monroe Doctrine and particularly the government's responsibility to protect American commerce. In the ensuing months his course was clearly more legalistic than expansionist. Since taking office he had shown no particular solicitude for the expansion of the export trade with Brazil, despite a reciprocity arrangement in existence since 1891.

That agreement, like others negotiated under the McKinley Tariff Act, ended with the passage of the Wilson-Gorman Act. Gresham promptly informed the Brazilian minister in Washington, Salvador de Mendonca, that the agreement was dead and rejected the minister's pleas that it continue an additional three months. Although Gresham was not completely indifferent to the prospects for increased trade with Brazil, those prospects did not dictate his policy toward the naval revolt. He protected legitimate American interests as he saw them, but in attempting to pursue a neutral course in the affair, he relied on long-standing diplomatic tradition and international law in framing his policies regarding questions of safety for noncombatants, nonrecognition of the insurgents, neutrality, and the protection of American neutral commerce.[22]

The revolt had a variety of causes: personal animosities in the ruling elite, friction in federal-state relations and between the president and the congress, militarism, government extravagance, army-navy rivalry, and some lingering monarchical sentiments following the overthrow of the empire in 1889. In early September 1893, officers of the navy, led by Rear Admiral Custodio de Mello, commandeered several vessels in the harbor at Rio de Janeiro from which they threatened to bombard the city unless President Peixoto resigned. A similar move two years earlier had forced the ouster of President Deodoro da Fonseca, but Peixoto was made of sterner stuff. With the army on his side he was determined to maintain his post, and open warfare ensued in the harbor.[23]

At the request of the American minister, Thomas L. Thompson, the United States sent the U.S.S. *Charleston* to Rio, where it was later joined by other American ships. Several noncombatants died in the early fighting, and Thompson wired Washington that further bombardment would endanger American lives and property in Rio, which had no defenses. The State Department ordered Thompson and the American naval commander on the scene, Captain Henry F. Picking, to use "every possible effort" to protect Americans and their property and "all the moral force of our Government . . . by protest and otherwise to prevent further destruction and bloodshed." Through intermediation by the ministers and naval commanders of those foreign powers represented by warships in the harbor, an understanding was reached whereby the insurgents would not bombard the city so long as the government offered no provocation by fortifying it.[24]

Meanwhile, fighting continued between the rebel ships and government fortifications at other points around Rio bay. Navy Secretary Hilary Herbert cautioned Picking to "constantly bear in mind that intervening force against insurgents should be resorted to only to prevent bombardment of a city so not defended or otherwise situated as to make such bombardment contrary to dictates of humanity or in accordance with the rules of civilized warfare." The agreement regarding Rio proper proved not entirely effective, but because of repeated infractions by the government as well as the insurgents, the foreign naval commanders hesitated to intercede further to prevent Mello's firing on the city. Through Thompson, Peixoto complained of this nonintervention to Gresham, but the secretary took no action. Finally, the government's placement of batteries on several hills within the city led the naval commanders to cease intercession altogether in early January. Herbert approved Picking's stand, and Gresham also believed that the government's violations of the agreement "justify this conclusion." Moreover, he said, the United States had "no desire to intervene to restrict the operations of either party."[25]

Gresham's policy regarding American commerce followed traditional concepts of the protection of neutral trade. On October 11 he instructed Thompson to "endeavor to favor legitimate entry and export of American owned merchandize and innocent trade of American ships." The minister, after consultation with Picking, had already posted a notice to all Americans that they fly the U.S. flag on all launches, lighters, barges, or other vessels used in loading or unloading American freight. He reported that there had been no interference with such conveyances.[26]

Nevertheless, over the next few weeks Brazilian owners of barges and other small craft grew reluctant to rent them to foreign shippers for fear that Mello's forces would capture them. Hence Thompson cabled Gresham for authority to protect "with force when necessary" American goods carried in these vessels between merchant ships and the city's docks. On November 1 Gresham replied that since the insurgents had no recognition as belligerents and posed no "pretense" of a blockade, any attempt to seize such conveyances carrying American cargo "can and should be resisted." But he avoided the specific sanction of "force," simply ordering Thompson to show the instruction to the rebel commander. Moreover, he stipulated that protection could be given only to barges and lighters that did "not cross or otherwise interfere with Mello's line of fire." Similarly, he told inquiring American shippers that their goods would be protected from seizure provided only that "you do not cross the line of fire or otherwise interfere with the military operations of the insurgents." This neutral position remained the core of Gresham's policy throughout the revolt. After the commanders of other foreign naval forces at Rio adopted the same stance and so informed the insurgents on November 6, Thompson assured Gresham that "we shall have no serious difficulty" with commerce.[27]

On the question of granting the insurgents recognition as belligerents, Gresham fell back on his judicial experience, formulating his policy in strict accordance with the dictates of international law. Opposition to the Peixoto government was not limited to the navy but also included revolutionaries in the southern states of Santa Catarina and Rio Grande do Sul. On October 23 Mello claimed that a provisional government had been established at Desterro, Santa Catarina. This regime consisted of three naval officers, one calling himself chief of the provisional government and the other two each assuming three cabinet posts. On this basis Mello applied to foreign governments for belligerent status.[28]

To frame his response, Gresham turned to Richard Henry Dana's 1866 edition of Henry Wheaton's *Elements of International Law*, which, he later noted, set forth "a very correct statement of the principle by which neutrals should be governed in the recognition of an insurgent or *de facto* Power as a belligerent." Dana said that among the tests for recognition was "the existence of a *de facto* political organization of the insurgents, sufficient in character, population and resources, to constitute it, if left to itself, a State among the nations, reasonably capable of discharging the duties of a State." The Brazilian rebels failed to meet that test, Gresham believed. Moreover, recognition of belligerency would signify the right of the insurgents to establish a blockade, a concession directly contradictory to the position the United States had maintained during its own Civil War. Gresham borrowed several phrases verbatim from Dana and Wheaton when he wired Thompson that the insurgents had not "put on foot and maintained a political organization which would justify the United States in recognizing them as belligerents and recognition would be a gratuitous demonstration of moral support to the rebellion and an unfriendly act towards Brazil." Invoking strict neutrality, he enjoined the minister to act as "an indifferent spectator." Over the next several months Gresham twice again refused the insurgents' request for belligerent status, and no power ever granted them such recognition.[29]

The United States' refusal to recognize the insurgents appeared to lend "moral support" to the Peixoto government, an impression strengthened by an incident that occurred just as Gresham was instructing Thompson to "espouse the cause of neither side." Rear Admiral Oscar F. Stanton, upon arrival at Rio aboard the U.S.S. *Newark*, exchanged visits with and fired a salute to the rebel Admiral Mello. These acts, contravening long-standing navy practice, bewildered the Washington officials who were attempting to maintain neutrality. Gresham thought Stanton had "practically recognize[d] the insurgents as belligerents," and Herbert recalled him immediately.[30] Embarrassed by the admiral's indiscretion, both Gresham and Thompson turned aside Brazilian expressions of gratitude. When Mendonca thanked Gresham for Stanton's removal as "one more proof of the sincere friendship of the Government of the United States towards Brazil and its republican institutions," the secretary delayed a month before replying. The American government, he told the minister, was simply "acting upon established precepts of international law." Again quoting directly from Dana and Wheaton, he noted that Stanton had been recalled to "dispel any inference that the United States were disposed to afford a gratuitous demonstration of moral support to the insurgent force, or to pass censure upon the Government of Brazil." The American position, he reiterated, was "one of impartial observation, although holding friendly intercourse with the existing government."[31]

Stanton's recall grew out of a complaint from Brazil's minister in Washington, which administration officials could not ignore. Thompson, "not being informed of the circumstances of the recall," assured Gresham that he "saw nothing whatever to indicate partiality on the part of Admiral Stanton." The dismissal bore no relation to American policy regarding the protection of commerce. Had there been any interference with American shipping, Stanton would have given the required protection. He explained to Navy Secretary Herbert that one of the reasons he had made contact with the rebel leader was "a probability of necessary communication with Admiral Mello" in the event lighters conveying American goods were disturbed. Stanton was in command at Rio for all of one week, during which time there was no such interference. On November 14 Thompson reported "no losses to this date either in life, property, or commerce."[32]

In December the question of protection of commerce led to a dispute between Thompson and Captain Picking, the temporary commander of American forces in the harbor. On December 7 the Brazilian government ordered foreign merchant ships out of the area bounded by Enxadas, Cobras, and Santa Barbara islands—virtually all of the waterfront loading zone—so that its forces might fire on the insurgents from the mainland. The merchant vessels complied, but the government quickly realized that clearing the docks had exposed its own troops on shore to fire from the rebel ships. Within two days the government again permitted and encouraged merchantmen to dock at the wharves. In the interim, however, the two sides had begun firing in this zone, and Picking joined his fellow foreign commanders in refusing to protect merchant vessels desiring to dock. Picking believed the authorities were trying to use the merchantmen as a shield. Protecting them from gunfire at the wharves, he asserted, would break neutrality and "assist on one side."[33]

Thompson, along with the American consul and masters of eight of the nine American merchant ships in the harbor, telegraphed Gresham that the captain was refusing to protect American merchantmen with permits to dock. Herbert asked for an explanation from Picking, who replied that his position rested on Gresham's November 1 instruction calling for protection of only that commerce not interfering with the line of fire. "I desire to protect absolutely all the United States commerce," he wrote, "but cannot do this in the discharging berths without affording aid materially to the side of the Brazilian Government and interfering with operations of insurgents." It was not a question of the rebels' capturing American goods, for Picking wrote, "they will not seize cargo." Instead, the problem was that the loading zone was "frequently under fire" from both sides. "I cannot," he explained, "protect life of the crew or prevent accidental damage to vessels, which is demanded."[34]

Disagreeing with Picking's idea of a line of fire, Thompson cabled Gresham that firing was "desultory" and scattered. He predicted "serious impediments to our commerce." Even so, the officials at Washington gave Picking no order to escort vessels to the docks.[35] Moreover, the State Department told merchants who complained of Picking's stance that he was "extending to the ships of our citizens at Rio the same protection as is granted by any and all of the other powers to their nationals at that port." Adopting the captain's very words, the department said that "in the present state of affairs, the protection which this Government can grant cannot extend to the lives of the crews or prevention of accidental damage to vessels while in the discharging berths."[36]

Thompson's dispatches betrayed an increasing antipathy for the insurgents. Gresham did not regard him as an entirely creditable reporter and ordered him at one point to "send facts not rumors." The minister had taken up residence at Petropolis, over twenty-five miles north of Rio, which made coordination of diplomatic and naval actions difficult. Finally, at Picking's request, Gresham directed Thompson to stay at Rio.[37]

From the beginning of the revolt Thompson sent occasional reports of rumors that the insurgents intended to restore the Brazilian monarchy and were receiving aid from Europeans to do so. Gresham paid little heed to these stories until mid-December, when Thompson cabled that the allegedly monarchist Admiral Luiz Phillipe de Saldanha da Gama had assumed leadership of the revolt, that British naval officers had withdrawn protection of British commerce, and that the British commander at Rio had offered munitions to the insurgents. These allegations, coupled wth pressure from Mendonca, who,

Gresham noted, "professes to have information that several of the most influential governments of Europe . . . are affording the insurgents material aid," moved the secretary to prepare a precautionary instruction to Bayard in London. He directed the ambassador to exercise "watchfulness" regarding Britain's Brazilian policy and to take "prompt and discreet action in case the course of events should warrant timely intimation of the concern that would be here aroused by any interference by Great Britain in the affairs of this continent." Nothing beyond this mild note was required, for Bayard replied that Britain and other European governments were too concerned with affairs on their side of the Atlantic to pay much attention to the form of government in Brazil. In addition, Thompson sent word that da Gama had repudiated his previously reported position of favoring a return to the empire. Thus by January 6 Gresham could write confidently, "I do not think the European Powers will venture upon steps for the re-establishment of the monarchy."[38]

Nor did businessmen's complaints move Gresham to alter his cautious, neutral policy regarding protection of commerce. In reply to New York merchant Isidor Straus, he made no promise of any new action but instead vaguely noted that the "Administration has not neglected anything necessary for the protection of American interests at Rio." He wrote to W.H. Crossman that the United States had been "watchful" from the start of the insurrection and that American warships had already received ample instructions to "afford all needful protection to our merchant vessels." William Rockefeller, president of Standard Oil of New York, registered the specific complaint that the insurgents were preventing the transfer of his company's goods, worth over $5,000, from an island in the bay to the wharves, thereby causing heavy loss from leakage. Gresham apparently perceived no urgency, for the State Department informed Rockefeller that standing instructions to the naval forces "in regard to discharge of cargo by lighterage or otherwise, seem to cover the facts stated by you." The department did send a copy of Rockefeller's letter to the secretary of the navy, not with a request for new instructions but with the observation that "instructions [sent through Thompson in November] already given to Captain Picking in regard to discharge of cargo by lighterage or otherwise" were sufficient to "cover the facts mentioned in the Standard Oil Company's letter." None of these statements signified any change in policy. Indeed, it was not until several months after the revolt had been suppressed by Brazilian authorities that Gresham received word from Standard Oil that it had recovered its goods.[39]

After the agreement protecting Rio from bombardment ended in early January, Washington officials felt some anxiety that a broadened area of fighting might inhibit commerce. Hence Herbert suggested to Picking that he and Thompson reassure both sides that the United States did "not desire to interfere" but also request them to designate a time and place for loading and unloading of cargo "to be interrupted only by notice of the actual intention to bombard." Picking replied that in light of the insurgents' hope of reducing the government's revenue derived from customs duties, he doubted that they would interrupt their military operations in the interest of commerce. Even so, Herbert requested the captain to "invite" the other foreign commanders to join him in addressing the insurgents. At the same time, Gresham directed Thompson to work with Picking to try to get the rebels to "designate a place, if there be such a place, where neutral vessels may receive and discharge cargoes in safety without interference with military operations." The careful wording of Gresham's instruction made it clear that he had no intention of using protection of American commerce as a device to defeat the revolt. As it happened, several diplomats at Rio refused to address communications to the insurgents, and, as Picking reported, the situation was such that they "did not consider relief to commerce necessary." Consequently, the matter of a designated loading zone was dropped in both Rio and Washington. The question was academic in any case because Thompson observed on January 12 that several American ships, at their own risk, had ventured to the docks and discharged and taken on cargo "without interference."[40]

At this time Gresham sent Thompson a letter restating the American position regarding commerce at Rio. The United States, he said, had "no desire to intervene to restrict the operations of either party at the expense of its effective conduct of systematic measures against the other." But "no substantial interference with our vessels" would be "acquiesced in unless . . . made effective in pursuance of some tangible plan of orderly military operations." Clearly, Gresham felt some concern that the insurgents might attempt a de facto blockade by firing randomly about the harbor, but he obviously saw no urgency in the situation, for rather than telegraphing the minister he sent the instruction by mail, which took at least a month to reach Brazil.[41]

This January 10 instruction marked no departure in policy.[42] As department consultant John Bassett Moore later wrote, it was "intended merely as an amplified and explanatory restatement of the position held by the United States from the beginning." Second Assistant Secretary Alvey Adee, who drafted the note, said it "was the constant mixing up, in the harbor, of the aggressive and defensive operations of actual war, with questions of interference with foreign commerce referable only to the international code of the high seas, that worried Mr. Gresham." Following international law, Gresham had maintained throughout the revolt that the United States would not honor a paper or piecemeal blockade. According to Adee, this instruction attempted to cast that position in "an acceptable formula which should not interfere with the ordinary prerogatives of war." In sending a copy to the Navy Department, Gresham requested no new naval instructions but merely observed that it referred to the protection of commerce "in the event" of bombardment or blockade.[43]

Nor did Admiral A.E.K. Benham's arrival with the U.S.S. *San Francisco* at Rio on January 12 reflect a change in administration policy. After reviewing Stanton's case, Herbert apparently concluded that the easiest way to deal with the veteran officer, whose retirement was imminent, was to have him trade commands with Benham. Stanton took over the North Atlantic Station and Benham assumed command of the South Atlantic Station at Rio, held temporarily by Picking. These orders in mid-December coincided with the Navy Department's decision to send another warship, probably as an added precaution after Thompson's allegations of material European help to the insurgents and his then unfounded report that the new insurgent leader da Gama intended to block the landing of merchandise. The change of command did not connote any disagreement with Picking's stance. Herbert assured the captain that "sending the 'San Francisco' necessarily included Admiral. No reflection on you."[44]

For the first few weeks of Benham's command the situation remained unchanged. Benham told merchant captains that goods in lighters carrying the American flag would be protected, but this was "intended only to cover protection from seizure and not from the fire of the Government or Insurgent forces" against each other—exactly Picking's position. As late as January 26 Thompson reported no "serious interference" with American commerce, but Benham had already had intimations that the insurgents were going to adopt new tactics. On January 24 he received a complaint from an American merchant captain that the rebels had leveled rifle fire against his vessel en route to the upper part of the bay. Benham protested to da Gama, reminding him that the insurgents had no recognition as belligerents and thus no right of blockade. Da Gama denied that he intended to blockade and claimed the shots—"always given without ball"—had been fired to warn the ship out of the danger zone. Benham accepted this explanation but asked that future warnings be conveyed by boat rather than by shots.[45]

The next day, however, he received word that the rebels had fired on another American merchant ship—this time with "ball cartridges"—to prevent it from going to the wharf. Benham demanded an end to this direct interference, although he adhered to the established policy of neutrality and assured da Gama, "This demand is not intended to restrict or hamper in any way the prosecution of your military or naval operations. American Ship-Masters have been warned of the risk they incur from accidental or stray shots by going to the wharves of the city." When da Gama failed to reply, Benham decided to offer an armed escort for merchantmen to the wharves. In this operation on January 29, the U.S.S. *Detroit* exchanged a few shots with the ships of the rebels, who consequently agreed to cease direct molestation of ships going to the discharging berths. Benham's action was limited, defensive, and in reaction to direct fire by the insurgents. It reflected a heightened aggressiveness on the part of the rebels, not of the Americans, and Picking reported to Herbert that Benham had been "perfectly right." Afterward the status quo ante was resumed. Benham assured da Gama that once again American merchant ships would have to "take the consequences of getting in the line of fire."[46]

The incident surprised administration officials, who requested explanations from both Benham and Thompson. Gresham asked Thompson to report whether Benham's attitude was different from Picking's and "if different, in what respect and why." Both men explained the defensive nature of the action and made clear that it had not interfered with the military operations of either side. The admiral said he had "acted on principles of international law, that unless rights of belligerents are conceded to them, they cannot use force toward neutral vessels." Apprehensive that Benham's action might isolate the United States in its defense of neutrality and move the European naval commanders toward the insurgents, the Washington officials asked if he were at odds with his foreign counterparts. Benham reported that he had "notified" them of his intention, and Thompson noted that they had acquiesced, after the fact. Thus satisfied that the incident had raised no complications with either the Europeans or da Gama, Herbert wired Benham: "We are satisfied entirely with the prudence and judgment with which you have carried out instructions and protected American commerce." Less enthusiastically, Gresham told Thompson the admiral had "acted within his instructions."[47]

Circumstances at Rio, attributable more to the rebels than to Benham or his superiors, provided one of the few widely applauded events of Gresham's tenure at State. With the disastrous attempt to reinstate Queen Liliuokalani still fresh in the public mind, it was politically impossible for Gresham or Herbert to quibble over the precise limits of Benham's prerogative. "It is so much more agreeable," observed the Democratic *Cincinnati Enquirer,* "to praise a Democratic Administration for wise and good acts than to criticize it for mistakes, that the *Enquirer* takes great pleasure in calling attention to this energetic policy of our Government in Brazilian waters." Even the Republican *New York Tribune,* whose criticism of Gresham was normally a reflex, commended Benham for reminding the world that the United States was "yet both ready and able to defend its rights wherever they may be assailed." Seizing the sorely needed political capital, the administration gave the correspondence covering the affair to the press and had it read in Congress, where resolutions praising Benham were introduced. In his annual report Herbert boasted that Benham's "decided action" would "have a far-reaching and wholesome influence in quite a number of countries where revolutions are so frequent as to almost constantly imperil the rights of American citizens."[48]

Many observers attributed the downfall of the revolt to American initiative, particularly to Benham's action in late January.[49] In truth, however, the fighting continued for nearly two more months. Picking reported that the "sharpest contest" yet took place on February 9, almost two weeks later.[50] The naval insurgents were not defeated until the government had assembled a new navy and erected large guns within Rio from which it launched a decisive attack on the rebel fleet in mid-March. It took the government another month to subdue the rebellion in the southern states, and sporadic fighting continued for a year after that. No doubt Benham's action gave the impression of aggressiveness against the insurgents, but that impression was unwarranted.[51]

The essential feature of the American position throughout the revolt was not opposition to the insurgents but "watchfulness" in the interest of legitimate American trade and against possible European intervention. Cleveland was entirely sincere in his later claim that the United States had maintained a "firm attitude of neutrality." When the rebels, who had no standing as belligerents even among European powers sympathetic to their cause, seemed to threaten trade with mainland Brazil, Gresham believed the United States had no choice under international law but to announce its determination to safeguard the neutral commerce of its nationals. When the threat became more tangible in late January, so also did the American response. To their ultimate disservice, the rebels had so defined the situation that the United States appeared, so to speak, to wage neutrality against them. Even after the Benham incident, however, Gresham clung to the notion that America's role was narrow, nonaggressive, and based squarely on tradition and international law. He did not set out with the purpose of defeating the insurgents. Any injury to their chances of success that may have resulted was incidental to—not the purpose of—American policy.[52]

Not long after the Benham episode, events in Nicaragua challenged Gresham again to formulate some conception of American interests in Latin America, especially as they involved economic concerns and the Monroe Doctrine. In contrast to the Brazilian affair, American commercial interests in Nicaragua seemed to run at cross purposes with the Monroe Doctrine. The issue centered upon control of the Mosquito Indian Reserve on the Atlantic coast, where American business interests, which predominated in the area, favored the continuance of a local regime more or less guaranteed by a British protectorate in preference to the assertion of sovereign control by the Nicaraguan government. Following long-standing policy, Gresham deemed the Monroe Doctrine and treaty engagements paramount to economic considerations, and he gave consistent support to Nicaragua's sovereignty in the face of British "pretensions."

The Mosquito Reserve had been a sore point in Anglo-American relations for more than half a century, particularly since it included the eastern end of a projected transisthmian canal. By the Clayton-Bulwer Treaty of 1850 the United States and Great Britain had each disavowed exclusive control over such a canal and agreed that neither would ever "occupy, or fortify, or colonize, or assume, or exercise any dominion over Nicaragua, Costa Rica, the Mosquito Coast, or any part of Central America." Ten years later, in the Treaty of Managua between Nicaragua and Britain, the latter relinquished its protectorate over the Mosquito Reserve and recognized Nicaraguan sovereignty there. But this treaty also stipulated that the Mosquito Indians should have the right of local self-government over "themselves and all persons residing within such district," "according to their own customs and . . . not inconsistent with the sovereign rights of the Republic of Nicaragua." The United States welcomed the Managua Treaty as bringing an end to British interference, but this proved premature, for Britain continued to claim a right to intercede for the Indians in their relations with the Nicaraguan government. This claim was essentially affirmed in an arbitration decision delivered by the emperor of Austria in 1881, which rendered the Mosquito Reserve practically independent and limited Nicaragua's "sovereignty" to flying its flag in the area and appointing a commissioner to look after its "sovereign rights." This decision denied to Nicaragua and gave to the Mosquito government the right to grant concessions, regulate trade, and levy import and export duties. The United States was not a party to this arbitration and refused to be bound by it.[53]

American economic exploitation of the reserve began in the 1880s and mainly consisted of the extraction and exportation of hides, mahogany, gold dust, rubber, and fruit, especially bananas. Relying on concessions from the reserve government and its easy trade and tax policies, Americans prospered and by 1893 conducted over 90 percent of the reserve's commerce. Although the government was ostensibly in the hands of the Mosquitoes, actual authority rested with foreigners, mostly British and Americans, who, according to one American diplomat, were "thoroughly inoculated with the idea of their local independence of the sovereign," Nicaragua, and considered themselves "under the special protection of Great Britain." American businessmen disliked the corrupt local regime dominated by black British subjects from Jamaica, but they dreaded control by the Nicaraguan authorities, who they feared would rescind their economic privileges.[54]

Under the Treaty of Managua the Mosquitoes had the option of abandoning self-government and accepting Nicaraguan rule. In late 1893 the government made a diplomatic effort to persuade them to give up home rule, but they refused. Early the following year the government took stronger measures, dispatching troops to Bluefields, the reserve's chief town, and inaugurating martial law. In response, the Mosquito chief sought help from the British consul, who wired to Jamaica for a British warship. The consul also persuaded the Nicaraguan commissioner to remove all but twenty of his troops and to form a provisional council. When a provisional police force failed to prevent disorder, the commissioner consented to the landing of British marines.[55]

Officials in Washington, apprehensive over a possible violation of the Clayton-Bulwer Treaty and the Monroe Doctrine, viewed this landing with alarm. Gresham wired the American minister in Nicaragua, Lewis Baker, to ascertain whether the British troops had landed to assert a "right of sovereignty" of the Mosquitoes or only to protect British lives and property. He also ordered Bayard in London to obtain an explanation from the British. Baker, who was in Managua and was himself poorly informed about affairs in the Mosquito Strip, reported his understanding that the British had claimed that the local Indian government was sovereign in the reserve. Bayard, however, relayed the British foreign secretary's disavowal of a protectorate and noted that the marines had been landed only to "extend safety to residents and check violence." In response to a Senate inquiry, Gresham reported Bayard's version of British intentions, apparently in an attempt to quiet congressional anxiety.[56]

Meanwhile, Americans in the reserve, disagreeing with the State Department, tendered "sincere thanks" to the British soldiers. As

Consul S.C. Braida reported, the Americans were "afraid of Nicaraguan cupidity and tyranny" and insisted that those living in the
reserve "should be left free to create their own local regime" without
interference from the Nicaraguans. Fearing the "well-known caprices
of a Latin-American government," American businessmen beseeched
American consuls to request the new Nicaraguan authorities to "give
pledges and guaranties that the interests, vested rights, rights and
privileges enjoyed by citizens of the United States shall remain intact
and shall not be interfered with." When no satisfactory assurance was
forthcoming, American Consular Agent B.B. Seat joined a delegation
that went to Washington to present the Americans' case to the administration. Similarly, Consul Braida warned his superiors that Nicaraguan rule would spell "the utter ruin of all that American capital and
energy has [sic] accomplished and built up here."[57]

Gresham brushed these warnings aside. Instead of rushing to aid
threatened American business interests, he ordered American diplomats "not [to] meddle in political affairs in Mosquito." He disavowed
any participation by American officers with Nicaraguan authorities
and British representatives in the creation of the provisional government. Such participation—even in defense of American economic
interests—would appear to lend approval to British assertions dero-
gating Nicaraguan sovereignty over the reserve and would thus run
counter to standing American policy. The core of that policy remained
the recognition of Nicaragua's indisputable sovereignty and the denial
of any right of Great Britain to intervene in reserve affairs.[58]

Gresham's stance squared with the standing American interpretation of the Treaty of Managua as ending any British right to interfere.
The most forceful statement of that view had appeared during the first
Cleveland administration in an instruction from then Secretary of State
Bayard to the American minister in London, E.J. Phelps. Bayard had
written that any effort by Britain to reassert influence in Nicaragua
would violate both the Monroe Doctrine and the Clayton-Bulwer
Treaty. Accepting this precedent, Gresham wrote Bayard: "I have read
many times your admirable instruction of November 23 '88 to Mr.
Phelps, and have said to the President that I think the Administration
should stand by it."[59]

Gresham considered the reports from the biased American diplomats in Nicaragua "confused" and thus delayed an "intelligent review"
of the affair until he had received the report of a navy officer dispatched
to the reserve. That report confirmed the British claim that troops had
landed only to protect life and property, but it also detailed British
participation in the provisional government, the focus of U. S. concern.

Hence Gresham sent Bayard a strongly worded dispatch asserting that the "joint assumption of authority by British and Nicaraguan agents of powers to enact and administer a local government" rested "upon no sound basis of existing right." Such action was not "compatible" with the Treaty of Managua, "by which all intervention by Great Britain in the affairs of the Reservation was renounced." He instructed Bayard to "express to [Foreign Secretary] Lord Kimberley the President's hope and expectation that the anomalous situation now disclosed may speedily cease."[60]

In response, Kimberley suggested joint intervention by the United States and Great Britain "to guard against apprehended Nicaraguan violence to American and British interests." Gresham rejected the idea as against "the consistent policy pursued by previous Administrations in dealing with Central American questions." The United States could "neither participate in nor sanction any device" to impair Nicaragua's "unquestionable" sovereignty. "So far as American rights of person and property in the reservation are concerned," he told Bayard, "should they be invaded, we could only look to [Nicaragua] the territorial sovereign for redress." It was true that foreigners had dominated the reserve government, but "no matter how conspicuous the American or other alien interests which have grown up under the fiction of Indian self-government, neither the United States nor Great Britain can fairly sanction or uphold this colorable abuse of the sovereignty of Nicaragua."[61]

British Ambassador Julian Pauncefote told Gresham the Treaty of Managua obligated Britain not to abandon the Indians to the "cruel, brutal" Nicaraguans, but he also confessed that the British found the job "distasteful" and "would be glad to step out and let the United States deal with the Nicaraguans and the Indians." Gresham saw this proposal as equally detrimental to Nicaraguan sovereignty. "Can we hold that republic responsible for acts done at Bluefields," he asked, "and deny to it the right to exercise such force as may be necessary to maintain authority and order at that place?" Nicaragua's sovereignty must not be undermined by either British or Americans in the name of the Mosquitoes, even for the sake of protecting British or American "interests."[62]

Meanwhile, Gresham continued to receive pleas for help from Americans in the reserve. Minister Lewis Baker encouraged opposition to Nicaraguan rule and urged American businessmen to put their complaints in writing for forwarding to Washington. Baker painted a dire picture of the future under Nicaraguan control: military despotism, unpunished crime, disorder, crushing taxation, forced loans, the loss of concessions, and the general destruction of American interests. He told Gresham the Americans believed they had a "right to appeal to the Government of the United States" to secure "to them a local government which shall protect them and their families in their persons and property." He called for a virtual American protectorate in the area—directly contradicting American policy. Gresham ordered him "to do or say nothing tending to disparage Nicaragua's rightful claim to paramount sovereignty or to encourage pretensions to autonomous rights inconsistent therewith." Baker ignored this order and tried to pressure the Nicaraguan government to remove its soldiers from Bluefields. Once more Gresham rebuked the minister: "Recognizing, as this Government does, the paramount rights of the Republic in that region, it ill becomes the representative of the United States to interfere to restrain the Nicaraguan Government in the exercise of those sovereign rights." Baker's refractoriness was a prime example of the problems Gresham encountered after he had abstained from superintending State Department patronage. Baker was "a vain, weak man" and an "unfortunate" representative, whose recall might be necessary.[63]

Defending Nicaragua's sovereign rights would have been easier had that government been more careful in meeting its sovereign responsibilities. In the spring of 1894 the murder of an American citizen by a local police officer intensified the Americans' opposition to a Nicaraguan takeover of the reserve. After negligence by Nicaraguan officials twice permitted the escape of the alleged culprit, Gresham and Baker pressed the Nicaraguan government to recapture the murderer, to discipline officials responsible for his escape, and to "adopt such measures as will leave no doubt of its sincere purpose and ability to protect the lives and interests" of American citizens. These representations followed traditional diplomatic usage regarding the protection of nationals abroad. Although acting Secretary of the Navy William McAdoo added a bit of bluster in ordering an American navy commander on the scene to "use all the force" at his command to reinforce Baker, no force was used, and Baker later admitted that he had "not protest[ed] too vigorously." In any event, the Nicaraguans remained cavalier. They "declined" Baker's protest, lied about the culpability of the officer responsible for the murderer's second escape, and finally failed to recapture him before he left the country. Such inaction made a mockery of American demands, but Gresham shrank from registering further protest. Although Baker was annoyed that the case was subsequently "virtually ignored by this [Nicaraguan] Government and apparently dropped by ours," Gresham hesitated to pursue the protest to the point of interfering with Nicaragua's right to administer its internal affairs.[64]

Meanwhile, canal champions such as John T. Morgan saw the Mosquito crisis as an opportunity to abrogate the Clayton-Bulwer Treaty and clear the way for completion of an American-controlled waterway. Morgan was sponsoring legislation whereby the U.S. government would guarantee $70 million worth of bonds of the financially straitened Maritime Canal Company. When Britain originally landed troops at Bluefields, he wrote Gresham that the time was "ripe" in Congress to take "vigorous action" for a "firm denial" of British pretensions. But Gresham had little sympathy for Morgan's financing scheme and even less for the assault on the 1850 treaty, which he regarded as the one sure basis for denying British assertions in Central America. Although Morgan's bill passed the Senate, Cleveland threatened a veto if it passed the House.[65]

In general, Gresham showed no great solicitude for an American canal. On one occasion, when the Nicaraguan government seized property belonging to the American-owned Maritime Canal Company, he refused to take action and instead told company officials to seek redress in the courts of Nicaragua. When the government threatened to terminate the concession, he did invoke standard diplomatic procedure to assert the company's legitimate contractural rights, but evidence indicates that the withdrawal of the forfeiture was attributable primarily to successful negotiations between Nicaragua and company officials. Moreover, when Baker intimated to Nicaraguan officials that the United States would guarantee the company's credit and lend its aid to finish construction, the secretary ordered him to disavow any such intention. As in other parts of the world, in Nicaragua Gresham betrayed no great eagerness to see the State Department become the pliant servant of American economic interests.[66]

Gresham opposed exclusive control of the canal by the United States or any other single country. Influenced by John Bassett Moore, he favored neutralization of the canal, which he believed "the world would demand and insist upon." He envisioned an international agreement similar in terms to the Clayton-Bulwer Treaty, to be signed by all the major maritime powers. He managed to bring Cleveland around to this idea and held preliminary discussions with Pauncefote, but the neutralization concept went no further.[67]

Meanwhile, in the reserve, despite the original foreign influence in the provisional government, Nicaraguan authorities soon took control. But in July an uprising by Indians and foreigners, including some Americans and British, overthrew the Nicaraguan commissioner and forced the removal of government soldiers from Bluefields. Chief Robert Henry Clarence reinstated a local Indian government again dominated by foreigners, including at least two Americans. At the request of the American consul and with the consent of the commissioner, Navy Commander Charles O'Neil landed troops to preserve order and protect American lives and property. But O'Neil did not restore the commissioner and instead advised Americans to remain neutral, which in effect was a warning not to aid the Mosquito-foreign faction. Baker advised them to respect Nicaraguan sovereignty, and Gresham added his warning against "unlawful interference of citizens of the United States in a matter which only concerns the Nicaraguan Government and the Indians dwelling in its territory."[68]

It was only a matter of time before the Nicaraguan government could reassert its control over the reserve. Pauncefote, fearing a "collision," urged that the United States and Britain tell Nicaragua "that she must not resort to violence and bloodshed." Gresham rejected such a representation as tantamount to "an endorsement of the recent outbreak at Bluefields and the ousting of the existing authority." The United States would protect the "legitimate rights" of Americans, but it would not act to deny Nicaragua's right to reestablish its authority. The implication was clear: Britain should likewise refrain from interfering. In London Bayard secured Kimberley's assurance that Britain would not sanction the use of the Mosquitoes as a "shield" for foreigners fighting Nicaraguan rule.[69]

In August Nicaragua retook Bluefields with no British opposition. Still, Bayard and Gresham agreed that the only way to prevent further intervention was to eliminate Britain's purported right to intercede on the Indians' behalf. They told the Nicaraguans that the Mosquitoes should be "induced" to surrender self-government and incorporate themselves into the republic. "Induced" or not, the Indians voted for incorporation on November 20, 1894. Gresham welcomed this removal of "the last pretext of Great Britain to interfere in the political affairs of Mosquito." According to Bayard, the British were pleased at "the prospect of having 'Clarence' and his fortunes eliminated from their political responsibility."[70]

A final lingering problem irritated relations between Nicaragua and the two powers. In retaking Bluefields the Nicaraguans had arrested and deported without trial several foreigners, including two Americans, suspected of aiding the July uprising. The Americans had held office in Clarence's government. Privately Gresham believed there was "scarcely room for doubt" that Nicaragua had "good ground" for expelling them. Officially, however, he deplored their summary treatment. In framing his protest, he was careful not to deny Nicaragua's sovereignty but instead based it on the provisions of the 1867 Nicaraguan-American Treaty governing the rights of nationals of one country residing in the other. Even so, the Nicaraguan government continued to refuse the deported Americans a trial, although it did permit them to return temporarily to Bluefields to settle their affairs. The issue ended when this permission was soon made permanent, so long as the men obeyed Nicaraguan law.[71]

Twelve of the deportees were British, including the proconsul at Bluefields, E.D. Hatch. Gresham had "no doubt" that Hatch had committed "acts inimical to N[icaragua]'s authority in the Strip" and had "instigate[d] others to resist that authority," but he recognized that the involvement of a diplomat rendered the British case more delicate than that of the two Americans. He advised Horatio Guzman, Nicaraguan minister in Washington, that his government ought to revoke the banishment and send Britain a note "regretting the arrest and expulsion of her subjects, and apologizing, etc." But the Nicaraguans were slow to respond. After nearly half a year of waiting for a satisfactory reply, the British demanded an indemnity of $75,000 and the appointment of a commission to award personal damages to the deportees. Pending the settlement, Great Britain refused to discuss with Nicaragua "any question with regard to the treaty of Managua and the recent proceedings in the Mosquito Reserve." The Nicaraguans looked to the United States to champion their cause in the name of the Monroe Doctrine. But even though Gresham considered Britain's demands harsh, he made it clear the Nicaraguans must answer the British directly. The Monroe Doctrine, he maintained, could not be so construed as to have the United States deny Great Britain its right to call a Latin American country to account for an affront. Nicaragua then told Britain that a revocation of the banishment was unnecessary because it had pardoned the deportees. She suggested that the indemnity as well as damages be submitted to arbitration. When Britain declined to modify its demands, Gresham again had "Doctor Guzman on my back." Again he told the minister that the United States "exercised no protectorate over his country" and would do nothing "as the controversy now stood."[72]

Although refusing to take the Nicaraguans' quarrel "off their hands," Gresham nonetheless feared that their failure to pay might lead to a British demand for territory, which, as a violation of the Clayton-Bulwer Treaty, would concern the United States. He considered Lord Kimberley "somewhat of a Jingoist" who might use the incident to reopen the Mosquito question. Should Britain occupy Nicaragua to enforce the collection of the indemnity, he fully expected Congress to declare war. Advising Bayard that the department had "conclusive evidence" that "Hatch was largely responsible for the uprising against Nicaragua," he expressed the hope that Kimberley would "avoid action which will embarrass us here."[73]

Nonetheless, British troops did land in Nicaragua, although, significantly, at Corinto—as far from Mosquito as possible. Gresham had urged Britain to delay the landing to permit Nicaragua to meet the demands, and Cleveland now urged Britain to give Nicaragua the opportunity to settle on the condition of withdrawing the troops. In the end, the crisis was resolved anticlimactically when neighboring El Salvador came to Nicaragua's rescue by offering to guarantee payment of the indemnity.[74]

The Hatch incident and the landing of British troops at Corinto brought renewed denunciations of Gresham's foreign policy. To the Republican *Boston Journal*, American inaction meant "the Monroe Doctrine is not worth the paper it is written on." To counter such attacks the State Department published an authoritative edition of the doctrine as it first appeared unembellished in Monroe's 1823 Annual Message. The department also distributed an exposition on the doctrine by John Bassett Moore, demonstrating its inapplicability to the Hatch incident.[75]

In fact, the Monroe Doctrine had formed the basis of Gresham's attitude toward Nicaragua, but once again he held a strict constructionist view of a standing American policy, and the Corinto landing lay outside that conception. Nor was he willing to see the doctrine distorted in the interest of American commercial interests. As Cleveland summarized the administration's policy, "Although the alien interests arrayed against Nicaragua in these transactions have been largely American and the commerce of that region for some time has been and still is chiefly controlled by our citizens, we can not for that reason challenge the rightful sovereignty of Nicaragua over this important part of her domain." Ridding Nicaragua of unwarranted British interference in the Mosquito Reserve lay at the heart of Gresham's purpose, and the final incorporation of the Indians under Nicaraguan rule sealed the triumph of a decades-old American policy. As Gresham reported to his old Indiana friend Noble Butler, when Great Britain was thus "rooted out of the Mosquito Reservation," a "question which had annoyed our Government for fifty years [was] finally settled."[76]

TWELVE

LAST CRISIS
The Clouds Had About All Cleared

The growing anxiety over economic expansion in the 1890s mirrored a general quickening of nationalistic spirit in the United States. Writing in May 1895, E.L. Godkin observed that "Jingoes" around the nation seemed to "treat even the extension of our commerce as a military operation." "Profoundly dissatisfied" with isolation, they looked forward to a war "with a certain exultation." Godkin's comments appeared in a piece titled "Diplomacy and the Newspaper" in which he decried the "daily abuse of the Secretary of State" by those who mistook the "common politeness in his despatches" as "base truckling to foreigners." Godkin defended Gresham for "following the rules of civilized diplomatic intercourse and trying to keep the peace," but his was a lonely voice. Indeed, the spring of 1895 witnessed a mounting "jingoist" criticism of Gresham's conduct of the State Department as weak and pusillanimous. In March Henry Cabot Lodge published his *Forum* article blasting American foreign policy as "blundering" and Republican Senator Cushman Davis cataloged the alleged failures of two years of Democratic diplomacy in the *North American Review*. Even in Cleveland's home state the legislature passed a resolution condemning the administration for its "supineness, dilatoriness and lack of National and patriotic spirit."[1]

At Gresham's behest, John Bassett Moore ghostwrote a defense of the administration called "Two Years of American Diplomacy" published in April under the name of Democratic Senator George Gray. In conversations with Moore, Gresham spoke of his fear of a growing "war spirit in the U.S." Newspapers and other sources of public opinion seemed to indicate that the American people were "ready for a conflict & [would] demand positive if not aggressive policies." Even his old Chicago friend and former diplomat Lambert Tree was "saying that we needed a war to straighten things out." Facing a host of problems that made him "anxious as to the future," the secretary felt profound disquietude at the incipient warmongering taking hold of the public consciousness in the final months of his tenure.[2]

Gresham inadvertently contributed to this "war spirit" by his quick and seemingly aggressive response to a minor incident growing out of a revolt recently launched against Spanish rule in Cuba. On March 8 a Spanish warship fired on, but missed, the American merchantman *Alliance* while it was passing between Cuba and Haiti. When the news reached Washington, Gresham ordered American Minister Hannis Taylor to tell the government in Madrid that the United States would "expect prompt disavowal of the unauthorized act and due expression of regret on the part of Spain" as well as "immediate and positive orders . . . to Spanish naval commanders not to interfere with legitimate American commerce passing through that channel." These instructions marked one of the few times Gresham won enthusiastic approval from "jingoist" editors and politicians, who, in the words of the *New York Sun*, believed the incident offered the administration "a chance to redeem itself, at least in some degree."[3]

But Gresham was uncomfortable with praise from such quarters. Almost immediately he set about lowering the belligerent tone. He had not written the original telegram to Taylor but had accepted a draft from Second Assistant Secretary Alvey Adee, which he later decided had "gone too far." When the Spanish promised merely to study the case, Gresham replied, almost sweetly, that the "President . . . does not permit himself to doubt that [the] *Alliance* incident will be satisfactorily adjusted in due time without disturbance of the friendly relations between the two Governments." When a month had passed with no substantive answer, he adopted no stronger language than that the "delay is not understood" and "the President deprecates further delay." Spain eventually sent a completely satisfactory reply. Gresham had expected such an answer all along, and except for the department's original outburst, he refused to allow this minor issue to undermine Spanish-American relations. Likewise, he pursued a hands-off policy with regard to the Cuban revolt, adhering to strict enforcement of the neutrality laws and advising at least one would-be American filibuster to "remain at home" because "the Government of the United States could not shield you from punishment."[4]

More significant in contributing to the "war spirit" of 1895 was a festering boundary dispute between Venezuela and British Guiana. Although this quarrel had little more bearing on the vital interests of the United States than had the *Alliance* firing, the truculent approach taken later by Cleveland and Gresham's successor, Richard Olney, transformed it into the most important incident in the foreign policy of the second Cleveland administration, with the possible exception of Hawaii, and one of the most important in all of the nineteenth century. Had Gresham lived, the American response would probably have been far less bellicose than that offered by Olney.

The dispute was an old one whose origins lay in the indefiniteness of boundary and title of the original Spanish and Dutch territories to which Venezuela and Britain had succeeded. For the past twenty years Venezuela had sought American help in the name of the Monroe Doctrine with no substantial success, although the United States had on occasion advocated arbitration. In the fall of 1893 Venezuelan Chargé David Lobo gave Gresham a short history of the conflict and asked for a renewal of the "friendly services" of the United States in his country's behalf. Gresham took no action, but Cleveland's annual message in December did note that a restoration of diplomatic relations between Venezuela and Great Britain (which Venezuela had broken off in 1887) and a reference of the question to arbitration would be "a most gratifying consummation."[5]

In March 1894, Minister José Andrade gave Gresham a detailed history of the Anglo-Venezuelan negotiations and again requested the United States to try to persuade Britain to submit to arbitration. (Neither Britain nor Venezuela had rejected arbitration outright, but each insisted on certain precedent conditions which the other refused.) The minister suggested that under the Monroe Doctrine the United States' "own rights and interests" were at stake. He expressed the hope that, as guarantor of the hemisphere, the United States government would "find sufficient reasons of political convenience, even of moral obligation" to adopt such a "tone . . . as may convince Great Britain" to concede Venezuela's claim. But Gresham delayed over three months before sending a copy of Andrade's statement to Ambassador Thomas F. Bayard in London. Nor did he employ the "convincing tone" the Venezuelans had hoped for. "The President," he said, "is inspired by a desire for a peaceable and honorable adjustment" and "would be glad to see the reestablishment of such diplomatic relations" as would achieve that end. He reiterated the United States' support for arbitration and its willingness to "do what it can to further a determination in that sense." But instead of ordering Bayard to press the Foreign Office, he left it entirely to the ambassador's discretion "to avail yourself of any convenient opportunity to advance the adjustment of the dispute in question."[6]

The Anglophile Bayard showed little disposition to prod the English. His attitude did not particularly distress the State Department, however, for during a visit home in the summer and fall of 1894, he apparently received no new promptings from Gresham or Cleveland to pursue the issue more vigorously. Nearly six months after his original instructions to Bayard, Gresham had received no report of progress toward a settlement.[7]

Meanwhile, the Venezuelans turned to the vehicle of public opinion to try to bring the Cleveland administration around to a more aggressive espousal of their cause. In the summer of 1894 they hired former American minister to Caracas William L. Scruggs as a publicity agent and lobbyist. Scruggs promised them a "campaign of education" that would arouse the American people "to a reassertion and maintenance of the Monroe Doctrine." In October he published the pamphlet *British Aggressions in Venezuela, or the Monroe Doctrine on Trial*, designed to convey the idea that the boundary dispute directly affected American interests. Scruggs raised the specter of a British assault on American commercial interests and American honor. Should Britain gain control of the Orinoco River—"the key to more than a quarter of the whole continent"—she would soon "work radical changes in the commercial relations" dependent upon that avenue. Failure by the United States to halt this "extension of her colonial system" would mean an "explicit abandonment" of the Monroe Doctrine "at once and forever; and this would involve a sacrifice of principle, and a surrender of international prestige and influence, which no first-class power can afford to make." "The people of this country," Scruggs solemnly avowed, "would never ratify such an act of pusillanimity." The pamphlet achieved wide circulation, and by late fall 1894, newspapers throughout the United States had begun to give it favorable notice.[8]

The degree to which this heightened press interest influenced Cleveland or Gresham is impossible to determine, but December did see a slight intensifying of administration concern. Gresham told Bayard that he hoped Britain would not adhere to her refusal to arbitrate except on the condition that Venezuela recognize a portion of the British claim. Nudging the ambassador a bit, he said, "It is not doubted that you will discreetly exert your influence in favor of some plan of honorable settlement." At the same time Cleveland's annual message promised renewed efforts to bring about a restoration of diplomatic relations and arbitration. And a month later, in early January 1895, Gresham requested Bayard to "ascertain unofficially" whether Britain would agree to receive a Venezuelan minister. Although Bayard broached the subject to Foreign Secretary Lord Kimberley in late January and again in February, he did not bother to report on the meetings to Gresham until April. In the meantime, he merely remarked that the "efficiency" of American calls for arbitration was "greatly weakened" by Congress's failure to pay the $425,000 settlement resulting from the Bering Sea arbitration.[9]

Scruggs knew nothing of Gresham's instructions or Bayard's efforts. With only the president's message to gauge the administration's attitude, he soon determined upon the need to add congressional endorsement to Cleveland's still mild call for arbitration. Encountering much "indifference" in Congress, he finally turned to his own representative, Leonidas Livingston of Georgia, who had little experience or interest in foreign affairs. On January 10 Livingston submitted a resolution, written by Scruggs, praising the principles of arbitration, depicting the dispute as a danger to "American public law and traditions"—that is, the Monroe Doctrine—and commending Cleveland's call for arbitration. The administration showed little interest. In answer to an inquiry from the Committee on Foreign Affairs, Gresham refused to draw a distinction between the merits of Livingston's resolution and a substitute considered by the committee. For his part, Livingston supported his measure in a rousing, pro-Venezuela speech written by Scruggs. The resolution passed the House without a division, passed the Senate with minor changes, and received Cleveland's signature on February 20. Gresham still assigned little importance to the resolution, however, and did not send a copy to Bayard, who was supposedly urging arbitration on the British, until April 9.[10]

Scruggs sought to put personal pressure on Gresham, but he found the secretary unwilling to go beyond the position that Venezuela ought to reopen relations with Britain. Scruggs detected that Gresham had given little attention to the substance of the dispute. No doubt embarrassed by his lack of knowledge, Gresham was not the least inclined to yield to the entreaties of this insistent, rather annoying lobbyist whose bribery of the Venezuelan president in a claims case had led to his dismissal as minister to Caracas several years earlier. Moreover, Gresham was on the verge of serious illness—"tired, fagged out, worried and cross," as Scruggs described him—and thus unable to concentrate on the legal minutiae of the issue. Once called away by Cleveland from a session with Scruggs, he growled, "Damn it, I'm not made of iron; I must have sleep." Scruggs concluded that the secretary "neither knew anything about the question nor cared anything about it."[11]

In March a severe stomach ailment incapacitated Gresham until the latter half of the month, when he finally began "carefully studying" the boundary dispute. At first he was guided by the statement submitted by Venezuelan Minister Andrade the previous year, which, he believed, showed "quite clearly, and I suppose in the main correctly, how G.B. has from time to time demanded territory which she had not previously claimed." He concluded that Britain's position was "contradictory and palpably unjust" and wrote unofficially to Bayard that if she "undertakes to maintain her present position on that question, we will be obliged, in view of the almost uniform attitude and policy of our government, to call a halt."[12]

Gresham made similar observations to John Bassett Moore, whom he asked to draft an instruction to Bayard again calling for arbitration with "some allusion to the interest which this government has in the question and its settlement." But Moore became alarmed that the secretary was moving toward championing the Venezuelan claim and applying the Monroe Doctrine to a case which Moore considered inappropriate. He apparently succeeded in checking Gresham's incipient bellicosity, for the April 9 instruction to Bayard was couched in language nearly as mild as that of previous ones. Gresham once more recommended "impartial arbitration" but made it clear that the United States had always "refrained from entering into the merits of the controversy" and would continue to do so. The instruction concluded: "While we do not assume to dictate to those [Latin American] States, or to exercise an undue influence over them, as to what their relations with other powers of the world shall be, yet their fortunes have always been an object of solicitude, and we cannot view without anxiety the continuance of disputes in which their peace and happiness are deeply involved." Such language was a far cry from Olney's later declaration that "the United States is practically sovereign on this continent, and its fiat is law upon the subjects to which it confines its interposition."[13]

Moore, who considered Andrade's statement "preposterous," provided Gresham with English histories of British Guiana. By mid-April he had receded from his momentary anti-British position. "The more I study the case," he told Moore, "the clearer it becomes to me that Venezuela's pretensions are largely unfounded in right." He concluded that Venezuela "had better settle if she can" on the basis of the line drawn by British engineer Robert Schomburgk in 1841, because, "in view of the facts," she could not justify her extreme claim to a boundary on the Essequibo River.

But not merely the facts impressed Gresham. He grew more and more irritated by the way Venezuela was seeking to win American support. When Andrade inquired about Bayard's progress in London, Gresham frankly told him that the controversy was between Venezuela and Britain and that the United States "sustained no such relation to his Government as made it our duty to take its place in the dispute." Moreover, he disliked Scruggs's efforts to "manufacture sentiment in this country in her favor and thereby to bring pressure to bear upon this Administration." He deprecated Venezuela's recent grant of concessions in the disputed territory to American citizens as just one more part of "the general plan of forcing the U.S. to espouse the cause of Venezuela." He also suspected that the Venezuelan propaganda campaign was receiving aid from congressional Republicans, who, he said, had "no higher purpose than embarrassing this Administration." Gresham advised Andrade that his country should restore relations with Britain immediately and "proceed in the regular way" to reach a solution. He was determined that Venezuela should not be allowed to "dump the controversy upon us" in the name of the Monroe Doctrine.[14]

In early May Gresham was again incapacitated by an illness, which turned out to be his last. Although he was thus removed as an effective force in policy, the restrained course he had fashioned continued for a time. Cleveland apparently harbored no desire to precipitate a crisis with Britain, for he wrote the ailing secretary on May 4 that "matters are straightening out in our foreign relations . . . and the 'jingoes' are hunting for good back seats." On May 25 Acting Secretary Edwin F. Uhl told the Venezuelans that Cleveland's mind was "unchanged" as to the "necessity of resuming diplomatic relations" to bring about an agreement for arbitration. Similarly, on June 5, Uhl advised Bayard that an "unconditional resumption" of relations was a "proper and necessary step" toward a settlement, and the United States would do nothing until that step had been taken.[15]

Whether Gresham could have held the administration to this course had he lived is impossible to say. Increasing political pressure, as exemplified by Henry Cabot Lodge's article "England, Venezuela, and the Monroe Doctrine" in the June North American Review, pointed to the need for some bold stroke to dispel criticism of the administration, especially before the convening of the Fifty-fourth Congress in December. Moreover, as Cleveland later testified, he was becoming convinced that he should take a resolute stand on the basis of the Monroe Doctrine. Certainly by the time he read the draft of Olney's July 20 note to the British, the president was ready to endorse its vigor as "the best thing of the kind I have ever read." In the last weeks of his service as secretary, Gresham had concluded that the United States was "simply being made a catspaw" by the Venezuelans, accepting and espousing their version of the conflict more or less unquestioningly. If the United States were to avoid coming out a "fool," he believed, it must make its own investigation of the claims. Once more betraying his judicial cast of mind, Gresham hoped thus to arrive at an "intelligent opinion" on the case and act accordingly.[16]

Most certainly he would not have favored the stance assumed by Olney's note, which proclaimed the United States' right to interfere and demand arbitration on the basis of the Monroe Doctrine. Although it appears that Olney himself may have doubted the applicability of the doctrine, he yielded to Cleveland's insistence and framed an instruction to Bayard reasserting it and American rights under it with unprecedented vigor. He expected the British to back down and was shocked by their rejection of the right of the United States to intervene. As a result, he was forced to resort to low-key, undramatic negotiations for an arbitration agreement, which Gresham probably would have pursued all along. Meanwhile, to gain time and disarm critics spoiling for war, the president appointed an American commission to study the boundary dispute. Whether or not Cleveland and Olney were influenced directly by Gresham's original proposition for an independent investigation, the appointment of the commission seemed an endorsement of his idea that the United States must be armed with facts of its own finding before making any substantive representations to Great Britain. That Olney had tried to force the British to the arbitrating table before such an investigation appeared to some critics to be approaching the problem "backend foremost." In the end Olney was aided in securing an arbitration by European developments that left Britain increasingly less disposed to be involved in a serious dispute in the Western Hemisphere. In 1899 an arbitration tribunal at Paris drew a boundary not far from the Schomburgk line, which four years earlier Gresham had said was about all the Venezuelans could expect.[17]

Gresham's Venezuelan policy typified his unwillingness to claim new American prerogatives in foreign affairs. Once more he defended traditional American rights, narrowly defined. Many saw the controversy as an important step by the United States onto the stage as a world power, but Gresham denied the need or the propriety of such a step. Characteristically, he approached the problem judicially, weighing the evidence and making his recommendation on the basis of longstanding policy. As was true throughout his two-year tenure, he shunned unwarranted interventionism or expansion of American responsibilities but instead consulted the conservative interests of the country as revealed to him by tradition, international law, and the dictates of simple justice.

In early May 1895, Gresham fell ill with pleurisy. Although the Venezuelan matter was still pending, he anticipated no trouble, and for the first time in two years he felt "hopeful as to the future." He told his secretary, Kenesaw Mountain Landis, that at last "'the clouds had about all cleared away.'" He never recovered. In late May his illness developed into pneumonia. He died at 1:15 on the morning of May 28, 1895, in his rooms at the Arlington Hotel. In Landis's words, "the work in the State Department killed him," and Mrs. Gresham agreed that he simply "wore himself out." His body lay in state at the White House, and after a brief funeral ceremony Cleveland and the cabinet accompanied it to Chicago for burial. A year later it was reinterred at Arlington National Cemetery.[18]

Tillie Gresham was "overwhelmed with the blow." "I had fought so long by his side," she wrote John Bassett Moore, "I did not think he would leave me." She remained in Chicago for a time after leaving Washington and then moved to Indianapolis, where she lived with her son Otto. She died in 1930 at the age of ninety-one.[19]

Cleveland likewise considered Gresham's death "a great affliction." "His companionship and constant loyalty," the president wrote a friend, "largely constituted all the comfort that came to my official life." No condolence Cleveland received was more appropriate than that from Bayard who wrote that the secretary "was penetrated by the belief, and always acted upon it, that in the present era the United States [is] quietly conserving and augmenting the elements and resources of material and moral power which the enormous armaments and feverish anxieties are draining away from other nations. We have liberated all sorts of forces in the United States—and those of conscience and unselfish patriotism have their essential parts in the struggle for supremacy."[20]

But if Gresham was motivated by "conscience and unselfish patriotism," expansionist critics condemned his policy of "quietly conserving" as backward. As the Literary Digest noted at his death, "His foreign policy has been denounced as un-American, unpatriotic, and treacherous, and his record for the two years of service in the State Department has been represented as humiliating and unsuccessful." He was reviled by men of both parties, and the sting of criticism affected him deeply. "The wound in the leg received by him on the battlefield," wrote one department official, "did not cause near as much pain as the continued shower of envenomed shafts attacking every action of his since he accepted the President's invitation to take charge of the State Department."[21]

In a political sense the furor and denunciation that marked Gresham's two years as secretary of state formed a predictable last chapter in a lifetime of political alienation. Throughout his career he had decried dangers of one sort or another that threatened the handiwork of the Revolutionary Founders. As a Know-Nothing in the 1850s, he saw the republic imperiled by ignorant immigrants unschooled in the ways of democracy. In the 1860s southern rebels sought to wreck the government, and in the following decades spoilsmen took possession of it and turned it to their own venal purposes. In 1877 railroad strikers seemed bent on rule by the mob, but worse, the 1880s saw the rise of an insidious plutocracy that would smother civic virtue with greed. But the 1890s brought perhaps the gravest threat of all: warmongering jingoes who would subvert the republic and create an empire. It was perfectly fitting that Gresham's chief aim as secretary of state was to "do something toward bringing the people back to proper views of things." It had been the occupation of a lifetime.[22]

But outside of the department and his small circle of associates, few agreed with or even understood Gresham's "small" policy, rooted as it was in old republican notions of virtue, justice, morality, and fair play. "His great principle was *right*," recalled department clerk Wilbur J. Carr, "and he spoke the word *right* with impressive earnestness." In the words of the independent *Philadelphia Telegraph*, "He scorned Jingoism, and, while profoundly believing in the maintenance of what he regarded as a true and dignified American policy, he refused to become the ally or supporter of irresponsible adventurers and political speculators in any part of the New or the Old World." According to the *Nation*, Gresham had chosen to "walk in the beaten and honorable path of American diplomacy, and not go wandering in the by and forbidden ways of ignorant bullying that thinks itself statesmanship."[23]

But such a diplomacy ill comported with the increasingly perfervid nationalism of the 1890s. As Moore later observed, during Gresham's tenure the United States was already "entering upon the era of the 'big stick.' " His calls for a return to traditional republicanism and "the conservative teachings of the founders of our government" seemed more and more out of place. Indeed, the great irony and ultimate significance of his foreign policy was that it spurred an impassioned public controversy that gave enormous impetus to the growing expansionist sentiment in the country. Denouncing Gresham's often quixotic diplomacy in Hawaii, Samoa, and Latin America was easy and constituted the first lesson in the training of many an American imperialist. Henry Cabot Lodge spoke for many when he remarked, "If the humiliating foreign policy of the present Administration has served to call attention to these questions . . . it will perhaps prove to have been a blessing in disguise." When Lodge and others moved the country closer to formal empire in the second half of the decade, Gresham seemed in retrospect even more a beleaguered defender of a rapidly fading past.[24]

ABBREVIATIONS

ASW-FC	Albert S. Willis Papers, Collections of the Filson Club, Louisville
BB-LC	Benjamin H. Bristow Papers, Library of Congress
BH-LC	Benjamin Harrison Papers, Library of Congress
CS-LC	Carl Schurz Papers, Library of Congress
CWF-LL	Charles W. Fairbanks Papers, Lilly Library, Indiana University
DAB	*Dictionary of American Biography*
DD-ISHL	David Davis Papers, Illinois State Historical Library
DMD-LC	Don M. Dickinson Papers, Library of Congress
DSL-LC	Daniel S. Lamont Papers, Library of Congress
FRUS	*Papers Relating to the Foreign Relations of the United States*
GC-LC	Grover Cleveland Papers, Library of Congress
HSL-LL	Henry S. Lane Papers, Lilly Library, Indiana University
HW-LC	Henry Watterson Papers, Library of Congress
IHSL	Indiana Historical Society Library
IMH	*Indiana Magazine of History*
ISHL	Illinois State Historical Library
ISL	Indiana State Library
JAG-LC	James A. Garfield Papers, Library of Congress
JAH	*Journal of American History*
JBM-LC	John Bassett Moore Papers, Library of Congress
JGB-LC	James G. Blaine Papers, Library of Congress
JMH-LC	John Marshall Harlan Papers, Library of Congress
JMH-UL	John Marshall Harlan Papers, Law School Library, University of Louisville
JS-LC	John Sherman Papers, Library of Congress
JTM-LC	John T. Morgan Papers, Library of Congress
JWF-LC	John W. Foster Papers, Library of Congress
LC	Library of Congress
LL	Lilly Library, Indiana University
LTM-LC	Louis T. Michener Papers, Library of Congress
LT-NL	Lambert Tree Papers, Newberry Library, Chicago
MVHR	*Mississippi Valley Historical Review*
NA	National Archives
NCB-IHSL	Noble C. Butler Papers, Indiana Historical Society Library
NL	Newberry Library
OR	*The War of the Rebellion: A Compilation of the Official Records of the Union and Confederate Armies*
OS-LC	Oscar Straus Papers, Library of Congress
PHR	*Pacific Historical Review*
RBH	Rutherford B. Hayes Papers, Hayes Library, Fremont, Ohio
RGI-ISHL	Robert G. Ingersoll Papers, Illinois State Historical Library
RG28-NA	General Records of the Post Office Department, Record Group 28, National Archives

RG45-NA   General Records of the Navy Department, Record Group 45, National Archives

RG59-NA   General Records of the Department of State, Record Group 59, National Archives

RG60-NA   General Records of the Department of Justice, Record Group 60, National Archives

RG94-NA   General Records of the Office of the Adjutant General, Record Group 94, National Archives

RO-LC   Richard Olney Papers, Library of Congress

RST-ISL   Robert S. Taylor Papers, Indiana Division, Indiana State Library

SMC-ISHL   Shelby M. Cullom Papers, Illinois State Historical Library

TFB-LC   Thomas F. Bayard Papers, Library of Congress

THA-UM   Transcripts from the Diplomatic Correspondence in the Hawaiian Archives, Thomas M. Spaulding Collection, Department of Rare Books and Special Collections, University of Michigan Library

WB-LC   Wharton Barker Papers, Library of Congress

WCW-LC   William C. Whitney Papers, Library of Congress.

WHS-IHSL   William Henry Smith Papers, Indiana Historical Society Library

WHS-OHSL   William Henry Smith Papers, Ohio Historical Society Library

WLS-LC   William L. Scruggs Papers, Library of Congress.

WR-LC   Whitelaw Reid Papers, Library of Congress

WQG-LC   Walter Q. Gresham Papers, Library of Congress

53RC   53d Indiana Infantry, Regimental Correspondence, Archives Division, Indiana State Library

NOTES

INTRODUCTION

1. Lewis L. Gould, "Walter Quintin Gresham," in John A. Garraty and Jerome L. Sternstein, eds., *Encyclopedia of American Biography* (New York, 1975), 454-55; Thomas C. Slaughter to Walter Q. Gresham, July 10, 1878, WQG-LC.

2. Gresham to Slaughter, November 29, 1877 [misfiled under March 29, 1877], November 14, 1868, WQG-LC.

3. See, for example, Henry Adams, *Democracy* (New York, 1880), and *The Education of Henry Adams* (Boston, 1918). E.L. Godkin's attitudes are probably best represented in the *Nation*, of which he was editor from 1865 to 1899. See also William M. Armstrong, ed., *The Gilded Age Letters of E. L. Godkin* (Albany, 1974). For examples of the Progressive School attitude, see Vernon Louis Parrington, *Main Currents in American Thought* (New York, 1927, 1930), Vol. 3, *1860-1920: The Beginnings of Critical Realism in America*, 7-31; Matthew Josephson, *The Robber Barons* (New York, 1934), and *The Politicos* (New York, 1938); Charles A. Beard and Mary R. Beard, *The Rise of American Civilization* (New York, 1930), chap. 23. See also Richard Hofstadter, *The American Political Tradition and the Men Who Made It* (New York, 1948), chap. 7.

4. See, for example, H. Wayne Morgan, *From Hayes to McKinley: National Party Politics, 1877-1896* (Syracuse, 1969), and Morgan, ed., *The Gilded Age* (1963, Rev. and enlarged ed., Syracuse, 1970), 129-48, 171-87; R. Hal Williams, *Years of Decision: American Politics in the 1890s* (New York, 1978).

5. Thomas C. Reeves, *Gentleman Boss: The Life of Chester Alan Arthur* (New York, 1975), 370; Josephson, *Politicos*, 113; Allan Peskin, *Garfield* (Kent, Ohio, 1978), 128, 322. See also H. Wayne Morgan, *William McKinley and His America* (Syracuse, 1963); Robert Kelley, *The Transatlantic Persuasion: The Liberal-Democratic Mind in the Age of Gladstone* (New York, 1969), chaps. 7 and 8; Richard E. Welch, Jr., *George Frisbie Hoar and the Half-Breed Republicans* (Cambridge, Mass., 1971); Lewis L. Gould, *The Presidency of William McKinley* (Lawrence, Kan., 1980); Justus D. Doenecke, *The Presidencies of James A. Garfield and Chester A. Arthur* (Lawrence, Kan., 1981); Geoffrey Blodgett, "The Political Leadership of Grover Cleveland," *South Atlantic Quarterly* 82 (1983): 288-99.

6. Morton Keller, *Affairs of State: Public Life in Late Nineteenth Century America* (Cambridge, Mass., 1977), chap. 7; Walter Q. Gresham, *Address of Judge Walter Q. Gresham at the Unveiling of the Grant Statue, Chicago, October 7, 1891* (Chicago, 1893), 8; Geoffrey Blodgett, "The Mugwump Reputation, 1870 to the Present," *JAH* 66 (1980): 882, 884; Gresham to E.B. Martindale, February 15, 1884, WQG-LC.

7. Sherman is quoted in an undated note by Charles W. Fairbanks, CWF-LL.

8. Benjamin Harrison to John W. Foster, May 1, 1893, BH-LC.

9. Gresham to Alvin P. Hovey, December 10, 1883, WQG-LC.

10. Gresham, *Address at the Unveiling of the Grant Statue*, 10.

11. Harry Thurston Peck, *Twenty Years of the Republic, 1885-1905* (New York, 1917), 308. See also, for example, Montgomery Schuyler, "Walter Quintin Gresham," in Samuel Flagg Bemis, ed., *The American Secretaries of State and Their Diplomacy*, 10 vols. (New York, 1927-29), 8:269; Allan Nevins, *Grover Cleveland: A Study in Courage* (New York, 1932), 511; Richard W. Leopold, *The Growth of American Foreign Policy: A History* (New York, 1962), 109.

12. See, for example, Jeffrey M. Dorwart, *The Pigtail War: American Involvement in the Sino-Japanese War of 1894-1895* (Amherst, Mass., 1975), and "Walter Quintin Gresham and East Asia, 1894-1895: A Reappraisal," *Asian Forum* 5 (1973): 55-63; Eugene Goll, "The Diplomacy of Walter Q. Gresham, Secretary of State, 1893-1895" (Ph.D. dissertation, Pennsylvania State University, 1974); George E. Paulsen, "The Gresham-Yang Treaty," *PHR* 37 (1968): 281-97; and Paulsen, "Secretary Gresham, Senator Lodge, and American Good Offices in China, 1894," *PHR* 36 (1967): 123-42.

13. Walter LaFeber, *The New Empire: An Interpretation of American Expansion, 1860-1898* (Ithaca, 1963), 197-229; William Appleman Williams, *The Roots of the Modern American Empire* (New York, 1969), 38, 365-66, 371-72.

14. Gresham to Morris Ross, August 1, 1892, to Charles E. Dyer, May 2, 1894, to Wayne MacVeagh, May 7, 1894, WQG-LC.

15. Gresham to John Overmyer, July 25, 1894, to William G. Shearman, March 5, 1895, WQG-LC; John Bassett Moore, Diary Memoranda, May 1894, JBM-LC.

16. Robert H. Wiebe, *The Search for Order, 1877-1920* (New York, 1967); Gresham to William G. Shearman, March 5, 1895, WQG-LC.

Chapter 1. APPRENTICE

1. *Abstract of the Returns of the Fifth Census* (Washington, D.C., 1832), 34-35; *Statistical View of the United States . . . A Compendium of the Seventh Census* (New York, 1970), 226, 229; James H. Madison, *The Indiana Way: A State History* (Bloomington, 1986), 57-142; John M. Gresham and Company, comp., *Biographical and Historical Souvenir for the Counties of Clark, Crawford, Harrison, Floyd, Jefferson, Jennings, Scott, and Washington, Indiana* (Chicago, 1899), 115-21.

2. Matilda Gresham, *Life of Walter Quintin Gresham, 1832-1895*, 2 vols. (Chicago, 1919), 1:8-9; *Chicago Tribune*, February 25, 1888.

3. Gresham, *Gresham*, 1:9; *Chicago Tribune*, February 25, 1888.

4. Gresham to Noble C. Butler, January 30, 1888, NCB-IHSL; Gresham to Charles W. Fairbanks, February 4, 1888, CWF-LL.

5. Untitled, undated sketch of Gresham, NCB-IHSL; Gresham, *Gresham*, 1:12; Gresham to Mrs. Walter Q. Gresham, December 26, 1863, May 14, 1864, WQG-LC.

6. Gresham, *Gresham*, 1:9-25, 47; Charles W. Calhoun et al., comps. and eds., *A Biographical Directory of the Indiana General Assembly*, Vol. 1, *1816-1899* (Indianapolis, 1980), 311.

7. Gresham, *Gresham*, 1:10-13; Gresham to Butler, December 30, 1891, NCB-IHSL.

8. Gresham, *Gresham*, 1:26-27. Otto served as assistant secretary of the interior under Abraham Lincoln and as Supreme Court reporter from 1875 to 1883. Outliving Gresham by ten years, he was a lifelong friend and counselor (*DAB*, 14:110).

9. Gresham, *Gresham*, 1:26-27; Samuel Bannister Harding, ed., *Indiana University, 1820-1904* (Bloomington, 1904), 149-52; Theophilus A. Wylie, *Indiana University, Its History from 1820, When Founded, to 1890* (Indianapolis, 1890), 211, 410.

10. Gresham, *Gresham*, 1:27-29, 36; Gresham, comp., *Biographical and Historical Souvenir*, 143-144.

11. Gresham, *Gresham*, 1:7, 28-29, 67.

12. Gresham to Thomas C. Slaughter, January 14, 1876, WQG-LC; Gresham to William H. English, November 13, 1885, Dennis Pennington File, English Legislator Collection, IHSL; Gresham, *Gresham*, 1:30.

13. Richard P. McCormick, *The Second American Party System: Party Formation in the Jacksonian Era* (Chapel Hill, 1966), 270-77; Dorothy Riker and Gayle Thornbrough, comps., *Indiana Election Returns, 1816-1851* (Indianapolis, 1960), passim; Dale Beeler, "The Election of 1852," *IMH* 12 (1916): 45-52.

14. Emma Lou Thornbrough, *Indiana in the Civil War Era, 1850-1880* (Indianapolis, 1965), 3, 13-15.

15. Gresham, *Gresham*, 1:49, 52, 54-55.

16. Thornbrough, *Indiana in the Civil War Era*, 61-64; Charles Zimmerman, "The Origin and Rise of the Republican Party in Indiana from 1854 to 1860," *IMH* 13 (1917): 212-19, 232-38; Roger H. Van Bolt, "Fusion Out of Confusion, 1854," *IMH* 49 (1953): 353-90.

17. Carl Fremont Brand, "The History of the Know Nothing Party in Indiana," *IMH* 18 (1922): 61, 67-68; Gresham to S. Wolf, May 24, 1888, Walter Q. Gresham Papers, Indiana Division, ISL; *Chicago Tribune*, May 24, 1888; Gresham, *Gresham*, 1:59, 65-66. Although there is some discrepancy in the evidence as to when Gresham joined the Know-Nothings, his own recollection to Wolf that he joined sometime during 1854 seems most reliable.

18. *New Albany Weekly Ledger*, September 25, 1855; *New Albany Ledger*, August 23, 1866; *Chicago Tribune*, May 31, 1888. There is no evidence to confirm Mrs. Gresham's later claim (Gresham, *Gresham*, 1:66) that Gresham entered the Know-Nothing organization blind and that "as soon as he learned that party's narrowness and proscriptive nature, he at once abandoned it." Gresham himself recalled that he had been a member for about a year (Gresham to S. Wolf, May 24, 1888, Gresham Papers, Indiana Division, ISL).

19. Roger H. Van Bolt, "The Rise of the Republican Party in Indiana, 1855-1856," *IMH* 51 (1955): 198; Gresham, *Gresham*, 1:29, 54-55.

20. *New Albany Ledger*, August 30, 31, October 16, 19, 1854; Godlove Orth to Schuyler Colfax, September 25, 1854, in J. Herman Schauinger, ed., "The Letters of Godlove S. Orth, Hoosier American," *IMH* 40 (1944): 55; Gresham, *Gresham*, 1:36, 59-60; Thornbrough, *Indiana in the Civil War Era*, 66-67; Zimmerman, "Origin and Rise," 244-45.

21. Brand, "Know Nothing Party," 79-80, 182-83, 186-90, 203, 206; Slaughter to Daniel D. Pratt, September 7, 1855, quoted in Van Bolt, "Rise of the Republican Party," 198; Gresham, *Gresham*, 1:62-63; New Albany *Weekly Ledger*, September 25, 1855.

22. The "GREASY DUTCH" speech dogged Gresham's later political career. The language quoted was embodied in an affidavit printed in a Democratic newspaper during his 1866 campaign for Congress. In the presidential campaign of 1888 his opponents reprinted the article as a flyer and sent it to delegates to the Republican national convention. Gresham asserted that a "democratic politician prepared the certificate . . . and caused his political friends to sign it five years after the alleged speech was made." Copies of the flyer may be found in H.C. Payne to Gresham, May 18, 1888, CWF-LL; Gresham to S. Wolf, May 24, 1888, Gresham Papers, Indiana Division, ISL; *Chicago Tribune*, May 31, 1888; New Albany *Weekly Ledger*, September 25, 1888; Gresham, *Gresham*, 1:65-66.

23. Gresham, *Gresham*, 1:63-65.

24. *New Albany Ledger*, October 16, 1855.

25. Zimmerman, "Origin and Rise," 259; Gresham, *Gresham*, 1:69; E. Duane Elbert, "Southern Indiana Politics on the Eve of the Civil War" (Ph.D. dissertation, Indiana University, 1967), 239.

26. David M. Potter, *The Impending Crisis, 1848-1861* (New York, 1976), 323-25; Russell

M. Seeds, ed., *History of the Republican Party of Indiana* (Indianapolis, 1899), 27-28; Thornbrough, *Indiana in the Civil War Era*, 81-83; Gresham, *Gresham*, 1:75-77; Zimmerman, "Origin and Rise," 367-71; Gresham to Henry S. Lane, September 23, 1858, HSL-LL.

27. Gresham, *Gresham*, 1:31, 78.

28. Gresham, *Gresham*, 1:1, 3, 4, 60, 61, 66-68, 72.

29. Gresham, *Gresham*, 1:72-74.

30. Kenneth M. Stampp, *Indiana Politics during the Civil War* (Indianapolis, 1949), 26-27, 32; Seeds, ed., *Republican Party of Indiana*, 29-30; Brand, "Know-Nothing Party," 290-91; *Indianapolis Journal*, January 30, February 10, 1860; William T. Otto to Henry S. Lane, January 31, 1860, HSL-LL.

31. *Indianapolis Journal*, February 6, 1860; Otto to Lane, January 31, 1860, HSL-LL; Slaughter to Daniel D. Pratt, January 31, 1860, Daniel D. Pratt Papers, Indiana Division, ISL.

32. *Indianapolis Journal*, February 23, 1860; Stampp, *Indiana Politics*, 27-28; Seeds, ed., *Republican Party of Indiana*, 29-30; Thornbrough, *Indiana in the Civil War Era*, 87, n. 4.

33. Otto to Lane, January 31, 1860, HSL-LL. Mrs. Gresham's biography of her husband does not mention his seeking the clerkship nomination.

34. Seeds, ed., *Republican Party of Indiana*, 30; Stampp, *Indiana Politics*, 29-30, 40. Mrs. Gresham's book (1:110) contends that Gresham favored Chase's nomination. I have found no contemporary evidence to confirm this assertion, which in light of Gresham's political associations and his own moderation seems unlikely. *New Albany Weekly Ledger*, July 4, 1860.

35. *New Albany Weekly Ledger*, July 25, 1860; *New Albany Tribune*, July 20, 1860; Gresham, comp., *Biographical and Historical Souvenir*, 79-80.

36. James Sutherland, *Biographical Sketches of the Members of the Forty-first General Assembly of the State of Indiana* (Indianapolis, 1861), 11; Gresham, *Gresham*, 1:120.

37. Thornbrough, *Indiana in the Civil War Era*, 91-95; New Albany *Weekly Ledger*, October 17, November 21, 1860. In this period voters routinely split a ticket by pasting a sticker with the desired candidate's name onto a printed ballot furnished by the opposing party. Thirty years later, when Gresham was appointed secretary of state by Democrat Grover Cleveland, Republicans charged that he had won in 1860 by giving adjusted ballots to unsuspecting German Democrats. Men who had worked in the campaign denied the charge, asserting they had "explained fully to each voter how the ticket was fixed" (W.N. Tracewell to Gresham, March 8, 1893, WQG-LC).

Chapter 2. PRESERVING THE UNION

1. Gresham, *Gresham*, 1:122-25.

2. Gresham to Mrs. Walter Q. Gresham, January 7, 18, 1861, WQG-LC.

3. Indiana, *House Journal*, 1861, pp. 665-66, 995, 1066; Ariel Drapier and William Drapier, comps. *Brevier Legislative Reports*, 1861, p. 306; Indiana, *Senate Journal*, 1861, pp. 703-4, 711, 744-45, 889.

4. Indiana, *House Journal*, 1861, pp. 25-26, 99; Drapier and Drapier, comps., *Brevier Legislative Reports*, 1861, pp. 84, 168-69.

5. Indiana, *House Journal*, 1861, pp. 145-46; Drapier and Drapier, comps., *Brevier Legislative Reports*, 1861, pp. 58-59, 83-84, 127-28, 141-45; *Indianapolis Journal*, January 23, 1861; *Laws of Indiana*, 1861, pp. 184-85, 188-89; William Dudley Foulke, *Life of Oliver P. Morton*, 2 vols. (Indianapolis, 1899), 1:102-5; Cyrus Allen to Abraham Lincoln, January

25, 1861, Morton to Lincoln, January 29, 1861, Abraham Lincoln Papers, LC; Indiana, *Senate Journal*, 1861, pp. 220-22; Gresham to Mrs. Gresham, February 3, 1861, WQG-LC; Stampp, *Indiana Politics*, 64.

6. Gresham to Mrs. Gresham, February 24, 1861, WQG-LC.

7. Gresham to Mrs. Gresham, March 1, 1861, WQG-LC; Robert Gray Gunderson, *Old Gentlemen's Convention: The Washington Peace Conference of 1861* (Madison, 1961), 89-91; Indiana, *House Journal*, 1861, pp. 1040, 1073-74; Drapier and Drapier, comps.,*Brevier Legislative Reports*, 1861, p. 373; *Indianapolis Journal*, March 12, 1861.

8. *Indianapolis Journal*, February 5, 1861; *Chicago Tribune*, February 25, 1888.

9. Joseph A. Parsons, Jr., "Indiana and the Call for Volunteers, April, 1861," *IMH* 54 (1958): 1-2; Foulke, *Morton*, 1:110; Indiana, *House Journal*, 1861, p. 205.

10. Indiana, *House Journal*, 1861, pp. 200, 257, 311-12, 630-41, 746, 768, 808-46; Drapier and Drapier, comps., *Brevier Legislative Reports*, 1861, pp. 110, 173, 299, 326, 342-48; Stampp, *Indiana Politics*, 66-67; Foulke, *Morton*, 1:110-11.

11. Gresham, *Gresham*, 1:137-38; Indiana, *House Journal*, 1861, pp. 21, 143, 164-66, 351-52, 641-42; Drapier and Drapier, comps., *Brevier Legislative Reports*, 1861, pp. 13, 83, 93-94, 197-98, 289-91, 350.

12. Gresham to Mrs. Gresham, January 16, 18, 30, February 3, 24, March 1, 6, 1861, WQG-LC.

13. Gresham to Oliver P. Morton, April 15, 1861, Oliver P. Morton Papers, Archives Division, ISL; Drapier and Drapier, comps., *Brevier Legislative Reports*, Special Session, 1861, p. 66; Gresham to Mrs. Gresham, April 25, 28, 1861, WQG-LC.

14. Horace Bell to Otto Gresham, April 26, 27, 1897, WQG-LC; Drapier and Drapier, comps., *Brevier Legislative Reports*, Special Session, 1861, pp. 33, 52, 57-61, 72, 80-83, 89-93, 100; *Laws of Indiana*, Special Session, 1861, pp. 9, 16-17, 22.

15. Indiana, *House Journal*, Special Session, 1861, pp. 60, 66, 101, 144-47, 162; Drapier and Drapier, comps., *Brevier Legislative Reports*, Special Session, 1861, pp. 33, 64-67, 93-99.

16. Drapier and Drapier, comps., *Brevier Legislative Reports*, Special Session, 1861, pp. 41, 111, 148-50, 156, 165, 175-79, 190-92, 206-9, 243-46, 262-63; *Laws of Indiana*, Special Session, 1861, pp. 85-87; Stampp, *Indiana Politics*, 83-85; Foulke, *Morton*, 1:150-52; Gresham, *Gresham*, 1:144.

17. Gresham to Mrs. Gresham, April 28, May 31, June 2, 1861, WQG-LC.

18. Ibid., September 27, 1861; Gresham, *Gresham*, 1:138, 144, 146, 149; Caleb B. Smith to the adjutant general, May 21, 1861, Letters Received, General Records of the Adjutant General, Compiled Military Service—Walter Q. Gresham, Generals' Reports of Service—Walter Q. Gresham, RG94-NA.

19. Gresham to Mrs. Gresham, September 24, 27, 30, October 6, 16, November 3, 8, 1861, April 23, 1862, WQG-LC.

20. Ibid., October 6, 16, 24, November 3, 24, 1861.

21. Ibid., December 7, 10, 15, 1861, Horace Bell to Otto Gresham, May 27, 1897; Gresham to Morton, December 8, 1861, to William H. Schlater, December 8, 1861, 53RC; Gresham, *Gresham*, 1:168-69.

22. Gresham to Morton, January 22, 27, 1862, Charles Collins to Morton, January 29, 1862, 53RC; *New Albany Ledger*, February 12, 1862; Gresham to Mrs. Gresham, March 1, 3, 9, 15, 1862, WQG-LC; Gresham, *Gresham*, 1:170-72.

23. Gresham to Mrs. Gresham, March 20, 22, 29, April 3, 8, 12, 1862, WQG-LC; Gresham, *Gresham*, 1:182-85; Generals' Reports of Service—Gresham, RG94-NA.

24. Gresham to Mrs. Gresham, May 31, June 10, July 8, September 15, 1862, WQG-LC.

25. C.B. Smith to Edwin Stanton, August 29, 1862, Compiled Military Service—

Gresham, RG94-NA; C.T. Nixon to Gresham, September 17, 1862, WQG-LC; *New Albany Ledger*, October 3, 1862.

26. *OR*, 17:pt. 1, 330-31; Gresham to Mrs. Gresham, October 26, November 2, 20, 21, 1862, WQG-LC.

27. Gresham to Morton, August 15, 1862, T.C. Slaughter and D.M. Jones to Morton, April 22, 1863, 53RC; Schuyler Colfax to Lincoln, December 17, 1862, Compiled Military Service—Gresham, RG94-NA; Morton to Lincoln, January 14, 1863, Lincoln Papers, LC; W.T. Otto to Gresham, February 28, 1863, Gresham to Mrs. Gresham, April 1, 1863, WQG-LC; Gresham, *Gresham*, 1:212-15, 2:826-34.

28. Gresham to Mrs. Gresham, March 24, April 20, May 27, December 5, 1862, WQG-LC; Gresham, *Gresham*, 1:200-206.

29. Gresham, *Gresham*, 1:171, 203-5; Gresham to Mrs. Gresham, June 24, July 2, 1863, WQG-LC; Gresham to Lazarus Noble, March 25, 1863, 53RC; Gresham to Morton, May 30, 1863, Morton Papers, Archives Division, ISL; General Orders No. 4, March 19, 1863, Order Book, Regimental Books, Fifty-third Indiana Volunteer Infantry, RG94-NA.

30. Gresham to Mrs. Gresham, May 15, 23, June 1, 6, 18, 19, 24, 28, 1863, WQG-LC; *OR*, 24:pt. 2, 289; Generals' Reports of Service—Gresham, RG94-NA.

31. Gresham to Mrs. Gresham, November 2, 21, 1862, June 18, 24, 1863, Gresham to T.S. Ralston, January 30, 1863, WQG-LC; Gresham to Ralston, January 13, 1863, Letterbook, Regimental Books, Fifty-third Indiana Volunteer Infantry, RG94-NA.

32. OR, 52:pt. 1, 419; Gresham to Mrs. Gresham, May 20, June 30, 1862, July 27, August 7, 1863, WQG-LC.

33. Gresham, *Gresham*, 2:834-35; Compiled Military Service—Gresham, RG94-NA.

34. Gresham, *Gresham*, 1:257-64; OR:31, pt. 3, 478-79, 32:pt. 2, 158; General Orders No. 7, November 5, 1863, General and Specific Orders, Gresham to Lt. Col. G.H. English, December 19, 1863, Letters Sent, Special Order No. 12, January 11, 1864, Special Orders, Third Brigade, Fourth Division, Seventeenth Army Corps, RG94-NA.

35. Louis S. Gerteis, *From Contraband to Freedmen: Federal Policy toward Southern Blacks, 1861-1865* (Westport, Conn., 1973); Special Orders No. 1, December 13, 1863, No. 7, December 19, 1863, No. 11, January 10, 1864, Special Orders, Gresham to Col. B.G. Farrar, January 22, 1864, Letters Sent, Third Brigade, Fourth Division, Seventeenth Army Corps, RG94-NA; Gresham, *Gresham*, 1:245, 256-57.

36. Gresham to English, December 19, 1863, Letters Sent, Third Brigade, Fourth Division, Seventeenth Army Corps, RG94-NA; Gresham, *Gresham*, 1:264; Gresham to Mrs. Gresham, November 25, 1863, January 25, 1864, and passim, WQG-LC.

37. *OR*, 32:pt. 1, 242-48, pt. 2, 765, 52:pt. 1, 520, 522; Ann Turner, *Guide to Indiana Civil War Manuscripts* (Indianapolis, 1965), 122; Gresham, *Gresham*, 1:288-93; Gresham to W.R. Holloway, March 20, 1864, RC53; Generals' Reports of Service—Gresham, RG94-NA.

38. Generals' Reports of Service—Gresham, RG94-NA; Gresham to Mrs. Gresham, April 27, May 12, 16, 20, 1864, WQG-LC.

39. *OR*, 38:pt. 3, 551-52, 578-79; Generals' Reports of Service—Gresham, RG94-NA; Gresham to Mrs. Gresham, May 27, June 7, 14, 1864, WQG-LC.

40. Slaughter to Gresham, June 18, 1864, F.W. Mathis to Gresham, July 8, 1864, Gresham to Mrs. Gresham, June 12, 14, July 8, 10, 12, 1864, WQG-LC; Generals' Reports of Service—Gresham, RG94-NA; *OR*, 38:pt. 3, 577-80.

41. *OR*, 38:pt. 3, 542-43, 579-80, 590, pt. 5, 218; Generals' Reports of Service—Gresham, Declaration for Invalid Army Pension, May 1866, Pension Record—Walter Q. Gresham, RG94-NA.

42. Gresham to Mrs. Gresham, April 12, 1862, WQG-LC; Gresham, *Gresham*, 1:302-6, 312; Surgeon's Certificate, September 13, 1875, Pension Record—Gresham, RG94-NA.

43. Gresham to Lorenzo Thomas, May 12, 1865, Gresham to Otto, May 17, 1865, Otto to U.S. Grant, May 19, 1865, W.W. Belknap to F.P. Blair, Jr., December ? 1865, Conrad Baker et al. to the president, n.d., Compiled Military Service—Gresham, Gresham to Thomas, December 1, 1864, Letters Received by the Adjutant General, Special Orders No. 51, February 1, 1865, No. 151, March 29, 1865, No. 262, May 29, 1865, Generals' Papers—Walter Q. Gresham, RG94-NA; Otto to Gresham, April 22, 27, 1866, Service Pension No. 65627, June 15, 1866, WQG-LC.

44. Gresham to Mrs. Gresham, June 7, 1864, WQG-LC.

45. Invalid Pension Certificate No. 65627, June 15, 1866, Gresham to Slaughter, November 6, 1865, WQG-LC; Victor M. Bogle, "New Albany: Mid-Century Economic Expansion," *IMH* 53 (1957): 127-46; Gresham to John H. Butler, December 6, 1865, Noble C. Butler to George I. Reed, September 1, 1899, NCB-IHSL; Gresham, *Gresham*, 1:341.

46. Thornbrough, *Indiana in the Civil War Era*, 225-26; Gresham to Henry S. Lane, April 23, 1866, HSL-LL.

47. Thornbrough, *Indiana in the Civil War Era*, 228-33; Seeds, ed., *Republican Party of Indiana*, 35-36; Gresham to Lane, April 23, 1866, HSL-LL; Gresham to Slaughter, October 10, 1867, WQG-LC.

48. *New Albany Commercial*, July 12, 13, 1866; *New Albany Weekly Ledger*, July 18, 1866; Gresham, *Gresham*, 1:333-34.

49. *New Albany Commercial*, July 21, August 30, 1866; Gresham, *Gresham*, 1:334-35.

50. *New Albany Commercial*, July 30, August 30, October 8, 1866.

51. *New Albany Weekly Ledger*, July 25, August 1, 8, 29, September 5, 12, 19, 26, October 3, 24, 1866; *New Albany Commercial*, August 30, September 19, October 1, 4, 9, 1866; Gresham, *Gresham*, 1:337-38; Thornbrough, *Indiana in the Civil War Era*, 238.

52. *New Albany Commercial*, October 15, 17, 1866; Gresham, *Gresham*, 1:339; *Biennial Report of the Agent of State of the State of Indiana, January 1, 1869 to the Legislature* (Indianapolis, 1869).

53. Thornbrough, *Indiana in the Civil War Era*, 237-38; Charles H. Mason, Gresham, et al. to Lane, December 8, 1866, HSL-LL; Gresham to Slaughter, October 10, 1867, WQG-LC; Gresham, *Gresham*, 1:422-23; William G. Carleton, "The Money Question in Indiana Politics, 1865-1890," *IMH* 42 (1946): 109.

54. Gresham to Conrad Baker, January 11, 1868, Conrad Baker Papers, IHSL; *Indianapolis Journal*, January 29, February 21, July 17, 18, 1868; Seeds, ed., *Republican Party of Indiana*, 39; *New Albany Weekly Ledger*, July 22, 1868.

55. *Indianapolis Journal*, July 18, August 6, 13, 22, September 9, October 10, 22, November 2, 1868; Slaughter and Gresham to Morton and Daniel D. Pratt, March 1, 1869, Daniel D. Pratt Papers, Indiana Division, ISL; Gresham to Baker, January 11, 1868, Baker Papers, IHSL; *New Albany Ledger*, October 26, 30, 1868; Gresham, *Gresham*, 1:343-45.

56. *Indianapolis Journal*, November 10, December 9, 11, 19, 1868, January 15, 1869; Gresham to Baker, November 10, 1868, Baker Papers, IHSL; Gresham to Slaughter, November 14, 1868, WQG-LC.

57. Gresham to Slaughter, November 14, 1868, WQG-LC.

58. B.F. Scribner to Col. ?, March 2, 1869, B.F. Scribner Papers, IHSL; John A. Rawlins to Gresham, January 27, February 22, 1869, Grant to Gresham, February 11, 1869, Gresham to Slaughter, February 26, 1869, WQG-LC; *New York Times*, January 31, February 10, 26, 27, 1869; Gresham, *Gresham*, 1:346-47.

59. Gresham to Slaughter, June 23, 1869, WQG-LC.

60. Gresham to David Davis, October 17, 1869, DD-ISHL; *New Albany Ledger*, August 26, 1869; J.J. Hayden to Pratt, September 2, 1869, Pratt Papers, Indiana Division, ISL; *Indianapolis Journal*, September 3, 1869; *Indianapolis Sentinel*, September 3, 1869.

61. Gresham to Davis, October 17, 1869, DD-ISHL; Flora McDonald Ketcham, "David McDonald," *IMH* 28 (1932): 180-87; Gresham, *Gresham*, 1:349.

Chapter 3. DISTRICT JUDGE

1. Gresham to David Davis, October 17, 1869, John D. Howland to Davis, October 2, 1869, DD-ISHL; Gresham, *Gresham*, 1:349-50.

2. Gresham to Conrad Baker, May 19, 1870, Conrad Baker Papers, IHSL; Gresham to A.W. Hendricks, May 30, 1870, A.W. Hendricks Papers, Indiana Division, ISL; Gresham to Mrs. Gresham, April 22, 1871, to Thomas C. Slaughter, April 10, 1872, May 6, 18, September 11, 1874, WQG-LC; Howland to Davis, March 9, 1872, Gresham to Davis, August 13, September 4, 1872, September 15, 1874, March 9, 1875, to Howland, November 22, 1874, DD-ISHL; J.H. McNeely to Daniel D. Pratt, December 14, 1874, Daniel D. Pratt Papers, Indiana Division, ISL; Gresham, *Gresham*, 1:352.

3. *In re* Carter, 3 Bissell 195; *St. Louis, Alton, and Terre Haute Railroad Co.* v. *Indianapolis and St. Louis Railroad Co. et al.*, 9 Bissell 99; Gresham, *Gresham*, 1:349-78. Bissell's *Reports*, volumes 2 through 11, and the *Federal Reporter*, volumes 2 through 17, cover the period Gresham served as district judge.

4. Gresham to Davis, September 13, 1872, DD-ISHL; *Congressional Record*, 42d Cong., 2d sess., 522-24, 528-29; Gresham to Slaughter, April 10, July 22, 1872, WQG-LC.

5. Irwin Unger, *The Greenback Era: A Social and Political History of American Finance, 1865-1879* (Princeton, 1964), 213-48; Gresham to Benjamin Bristow, June ? 1874, BB-LC; Carleton, "Money Question," 121.

6. Gresham, *Gresham*, 1:420, 425-28; Carleton, "Money Question," 121-23.

7. Gresham to Slaughter, May 6, 18, August 15, September 11, November 21, 1874, WQG-LC; Gresham to Davis, September 15, 1874, DD-ISHL.

8. Gresham to Davis, September 15, 1874, DD-ISHL; Gresham to Slaughter, August 15, September 11, November 21, 1874, WQG-LC.

9. Gresham to Slaughter, November 21, 1874, WQG-LC; Gresham to Howland, November 22, 1874, DD-ISHL.

10. Gresham to Harlan, June 20, 1874, JMH-LC; Gresham to Bristow, June 1, 1874, BB-LC; Ross A. Webb, *Benjamin Helm Bristow: Border State Politician* (Lexington, 1969), chap. 8.

11. Webb, *Bristow*, 207, 212; Gresham, *Gresham*, 2:441-51; *United States* v. *Distillery No. Twenty-eight et al.*, 6 Bissell 483; *Indianapolis Journal*, January 11-15, 17-22, 24-26, February 1, 2, 1876; Harry J. Sievers, *Benjamin Harrison: Hoosier Statesman* (New York, 1959), 87-92.

12. Gresham to Slaughter, October 21, December 5, 1875, April 2, May 2, 1876, WQG-LC; Thornbrough, *Indiana in the Civil War Era*, 559, n. 50, 561, n 56; Sievers, *Harrison: Hoosier Statesman*, 163; *National Cyclopedia of American Biography*, 48:397.

13. Gresham to Harlan, January 9, 1876, JMH-LC; Gresham to Noble C. Butler, December 25, 1875, NCB-IHSL; *Indianapolis Journal*, October 16, 1875.

14. Gresham to Slaughter, October 21, 1875, to Thomas Drummond, November 4, 1875, WQG-LC; Gresham to Davis, November 13, 1875, DD-ISHL.

15. Gresham to Slaughter, November 24, 29, December 5, 1875, WQG-LC; Howland to Davis, December 5, 1875, DD-ISHL; Benjamin Harrison to L.M. Campbell, December 1, 1875, BH-LC.

16. Gresham to Slaughter, November 29, 1875, January 14, 1876, WQG-LC.

17. Keith Ian Polakoff, *The Politics of Inertia: The Election of 1876 and the End of Reconstruction* (Baton Rouge, 1973), 16-36.

18. Gresham to Harlan, January 9, 22, March 11, 1876, JMH-LC; Gresham to Slaughter, March 4, 12, 1876, WQG-LC; Gresham to Bristow, December 20, 1875, BB-LC.

19. Gresham to Harlan, January 9, 22, March 11, May 11, 15, 17, 27, 1876, JMH-LC; Gresham to Slaughter, February 9, March 4, 12, May 2, 18, 1876, WQG-LC; Webb, *Bristow*, 206-7, 217-19.

20. J. H. Wilson to Gresham, March 29, 1876, Gresham to Slaughter, April 2, 22, 1876, William Cullen Bryant et al. to Gresham, April 6, 1876, WQG-LC; Gresham to Bristow, June 10, 1876, BB-LC; Polakoff, *Politics of Inertia*, 39-44.

21. Gresham to Harlan, March 11, 1876, JMH-LC; Gresham to Slaughter, March 12, April 2, 1876, WQG-LC. The Mulligan letters were named for James H. Mulligan, who revealed their existence to a congressional investigating committee.

22. J.H. Wilson to Gresham, March 29, 1876, Gresham to Slaughter, April 2, 1876, WQG-LC; *Indianapolis Sentinel*, April 11, 1876; *Indianapolis Journal*, April 17, 1876; W.R. Holloway to W.H. Smith, April 11, 14, 1876, Richard Smith to W.H. Smith, April 18, 1876, WHS-IHSL. Besides the circumstantial clues, the best evidence that Gresham gave the story to the *Sentinel* is the close similarity between the wording in the paper's account and that in Gresham's April 2 letter to Slaughter.

23. Gresham to Harlan, June 3, 1876, JMH-LC; David Saville Muzzey, *James G. Blaine: A Political Idol of Other Days* (New York, 1934), 90-99.

24. Gresham to Bristow, May 25, June 10, 16, 1876, BB-LC; Gresham to Slaughter, May 23, 28, June 19, 1876, WQG-LC; Gresham to Harlan, June 3, 25, 1876, JMH-LC; *New Albany Ledger-Standard*, June 14, 1876; Richard C. Bain and Judith H. Parris, *Convention Decisions and Voting Records* (Washington, D.C., 1973), Appendix C.

25. Gresham to Slaughter, March 4, October 19, 1876, WQG-LC; Russell H. Conwell, *Life and Public Services of Gov. Rutherford B. Hayes* (Boston, 1876), 302-08; Foulke, *Morton*, 2:415-25; Sievers, *Harrison: Hoosier Statesman*, 98-119.

26. Gresham to Slaughter, October 19, 1876, and fragment, n.d., [October-November, 1876], WQG-LC; Gresham, *Gresham*, 2:459-60.

27. The other disputed vote was from Oregon. For discussions of this election, see C. Vann Woodward, *Reunion and Reaction: The Compromise of 1877 and the End of Reconstruction* (Boston, 1951), and Polakoff, *Politics of Inertia*, chaps. 6-8.

28. Gresham to Slaughter, December 7, 1876, January 28, February 1, 1877, WQG-LC; *Congressional Record*, 44th Cong., 2d sess., 869-70, 878-79; *Indianapolis Journal*, January 25, 30, 1877; J.R. Robinson to Morton, January 26, 1877, Oliver P. Morton Papers, Indiana Division, ISL; Foulke, *Morton*, 2:441-59.

29. Gresham to Slaughter, December 7, 1876, January 28, March 3, 1877, WQG-LC; *Indianapolis News*, May 8, 1877; George B. Wright to Hayes, March 8, 1877, Gresham to Stanley Matthews, March 30, 1877, RBH.

30. Robinson to Morton, January 26, 1877, Morton Papers, Indiana Division, ISL.

31. *Indianapolis News*, May 8, 9, 14, 1877; Morton to Hayes, February 25, March ? 1877, Morton to E.B. Martindale, March 10, 1877, RBH; Gresham to Carl Schurz, April 2, 1877, Morton to Schurz, April 20, 1877, to Hayes, April 20, June 1, 6, 12, 1877, W.H.H. Terrell to Hayes, May 9, 1877, Records Relating to Pension Agents, Appointments Division, Records of the Office of the Secretary of the Interior, Record Group 48, NA; Gresham to Slaughter, May 20, 1877, WQG-LC.

32. Gresham to Slaughter, April 23, 1877, WQG-LC.

33. Gresham to Slaughter, August 6, 1877, WQG-LC. For general treatments of the strike see, for example, Robert V. Bruce, *1877: Year of Violence* (Indianapolis, 1959); Philip S. Foner, *The Great Labor Uprising of 1877* (New York, 1977). See also Gresham, *Gresham*, 1:379-408.

34. *Indianapolis News*, July 23, 24, 1877; *Indianapolis Journal*, July 24, 1877; Sergeant Wappenhaus to chief signal officer, July 24 (telegram), 25 (four telegrams), 26 (telegram), 1877, Albert J. Myer, chief signal officer, to the president and secretary of war, July 28 (two telegrams), 29 (two telegrams), 30 (telegram), 1877, RBH.

35. *Indianapolis Journal*, July 24, 27, 1877; Gresham to Thomas Drummond, July 24, 1877 (telegram), Drummond to Gresham, July 24, 1877 (telegram), WQG-LC; *Indianapolis News*, July 25, 1877; Charles Devens to Benjamin Spooner, July 26, 1877 (telegram), Letters Sent to Marshals and Attorneys, RG60–NA.

36. *Indianapolis News*, July 25-27, 1877; Gresham to Devens, July 24, 1877 (telegram), Spooner to Devens, July 24 (telegram), 25 (telegram), 1877, Indiana File, Letters Received, Devens to Spooner, July 25 (telegram), 26 (telegram), 1877, Letters to Marshals and Attorneys, RG60–NA; Gresham to Hayes, July 25, 1877 (telegram, spelling and punctuation corrected), RBH; Minutes of the Meeting of the Committee of Public Safety, July [26], 1877, A.W. Hendricks Papers, Indiana Division, ISL; *Indianapolis Journal*, July 27, 1877.

37. Minutes of the Meeting of the Committee of Public Safety, July [27], 1877, Hendricks Papers, Indiana Division, ISL; Indianapolis, *Proceedings of the Common Council, Called Session*, July 27, 1877, pp. 283-86; *Indianapolis News*, July 27, 28, 1877; *Indianapolis Journal*, July 28, 1877; Gresham to Devens, July 27, 1877 (telegram), Indiana File, Letters Received, RG60–NA.

38. *Indianapolis News*, July 30, August 3, 4, 1877; Gresham to Drummond, [July 1877] (draft telegram), Drummond to Gresham, July 30 (three telegrams), 31 (two telegrams), 1877, WQG-LC; *Indianapolis Journal*, August 2, 1877; *King v. O. & M. Railroad Co.*, 7 Bissell 529.

39. Walter Nelles, "A Strike and Its Legal Consequences—An Examination of the Receivership Precedent for the Labor Injunction," *Yale Law Journal* 40 (1931): 507-54; Gerald G. Eggert, *Railroad Labor Disputes: The Beginnings of Federal Strike Policy* (Ann Arbor, 1967), 35-41, 52-53; John Bassett Moore, Diary Memoranda, July 1894, JBM-LC.

40. Gresham to Slaughter, January 28, August 6, 1877, WQG-LC.

41. Thornbrough, *Indiana in the Civil War Era*, 305-9; Gresham to James A. Garfield, November 25, 1877, JAG-LC; Gresham to Slaughter, August 6, 1877, March 10, May 31, September 3, 1878, WQG-LC.

42. Gresham to Slaughter, November 29, 1877 (misfiled under March 29, 1877), WQG-LC.

43. Slaughter to Noble C. Butler, February 12, 1878, with enclosure, "The Senatorship," NCB-IHSL; Gresham to Slaughter, March 10, May 31, 1878, Slaughter to Gresham, July 10, 1878, WQG-LC.

44. Sievers, *Harrison: Hoosier Statesman*, 154-55, 159-62; Gresham to Slaughter, September 3, 1878, WQG-LC.

45. Gresham to Harlan, May 26, 1879, JMH-UL; Gresham, *Gresham*, 2:473-83.

46. W.T. Sherman to Gresham, August 6, 1878, WQG-LC; Gresham to Hayes, September 25, 1878, RBH; Gresham, *Gresham*, 2:462-68; J. D. Defrees to Harrison, October 13, 1879, BH-LC; Gresham to N.C. Butler, March 24, 1879, J.H. Butler to N.C. Butler, November 18, 1879, NCB-IHSL.

47. This material and quotations in the next five paragraphs are from *Report of the Proceedings of the Society of the Army of the Tennessee at the Thirteenth Annual Meeting Held at Chicago, Illinois, November 12 and 13, 1879* (Chicago, 1879), 25-42; *Chicago Tribune*, November 13, 1879.

48. J.H. Butler to N.C. Butler, November 18, 1879, NCB-IHSL; Gresham to Slaughter, August 6, 1877, September 3, 1878, WQG-LC; Morgan, *From Hayes to McKinley*, 57-74.

49. Morgan, *From Hayes to McKinley*, 59-62; *Chicago Tribune*, November 13, 1879.

50. Benjamin F. Babcock, *The Presidential Favorites* (Chicago, 1884), 53-54; *Indianapolis Journal*, May 31, June 2, 6, 1880; Morgan, *From Hayes to McKinley*, 88-93; J.M. Butler to Harlan, June 2, 1880, JMH-UL; Gresham to Harrison, June 8, 1880, BH-LC.

51. D.W. Voyles to Gresham, November 3, 1879, NCB-IHSL; B.F. Claypool to Gresham, May 27, 1880, WQG-LC; *Indianapolis Journal*, May 14, June 16, 17, 18, 1880; Gresham to Robert S. Taylor, September 19, 1880, RST-ISL; James N. Tyner to Stephen W. Dorsey, February 3, 1881, JAG-LC; Gresham, *Gresham*, 2:488; Paul Tincher Smith, "Indiana's Last October Campaign," *IMH* 19 (1923): 332-45.

52. *Indianapolis Journal*, October 12, 1880.

53. Sievers, *Harrison: Hoosier Statesman*, 173-80; *Indianapolis News*, October 14, 1880; Schuyler Colfax to Harrison, November 5, 1880, Harrison to R.W. Thompson, December 4, 1880, Thompson to Harrison, December 6, 1880, BH-LC; Gresham to George F. Chittenden, November 16, 1880, George F. Chittenden Papers, Indiana Division, ISL; S. Stansifer to Butler, October 28, 1880, NCB-IHSL; and NCB-IHSL, October-December 1880, passim.

54. William Armstrong to Butler, October 26, 1880, H.C. Hartman to Butler, November 1, 1880, NCB-IHSL; Harrison to Taylor, October 16, November 13, December 2, 4, 1880, BH-LC; Gresham to Taylor, November 2, 1880, RST-ISL; *Indianapolis Journal*, December 5, 1880; Gresham to Chittenden, December 10, 1880, Chittenden Papers, Indiana Division, ISL.

55. Gresham to Chittenden, December 10, 1880, Chittenden Papers, Indiana Division, ISL; D.W. Voyles to Butler, December 14, 1880, NCB-IHSL.

56. Voyles to Butler, December 14, 1880, NCB-IHSL; J.H. Woodard to D.G. Swaim, February 1, 1881, Charles Foster to Garfield, n.d. [1881], Harrison to Garfield, February 1, 1881, Tyner to Dorsey, February 3, 1881, W.W. Dudley to Garfield, February 1, 23, 1881, Ben Butterworth to Garfield, February 23, 1881, JAG-LC; *Indianapolis News*, April 20, 1881.

57. Harrison to Garfield, January 28, February 1, 14, 1881, BH-LC.

58. Gresham to Slaughter, April 2, 1876, WQG-LC; Blaine to Garfield, January 18, 1881, R.G. Ingersoll to Garfield, March 3, 1881, Garfield Diary entries, March 2, 3, 1881, Dorsey to Garfield, March 4, 1881, JAG-LC.

59. Blaine to Garfield, [March 4, 1881], Garfield to Blaine, March 4, 1881, Garfield Diary entries, March 4, 5, 1881, JAG-LC; Gresham to Davis, March 27, 1881, DD-ISHL.

60. Gresham to Davis, March 27, 1881, DD-ISHL; *Report of the Proceedings of the Society of the Army of the Tennessee at the Fourteenth Annual Meeting held at Cincinnati, Ohio, April 6th and 7th, 1881* (Cincinnati, 1885), 156.

61. Gresham to Davis, March 27, 1881, DD-ISHL.

Chapter 4. POSTMASTER GENERAL

1. Benjamin Harrison to N.C. Butler, January 30, February 10, 1882, Butler to Harrison, February 6, 1882, R.B.F. Pierce to Butler, March 13, 1882, NCB-IHSL; Gresham, *Gresham*, 2:489.

2. John W. Foster to Gresham, March 31, 1883, WQG-LC.

3. *New York Times*, March 26, 28, 30, 31, April 1-4, 1883; Foster to Gresham, April 3, 1883, WQG-LC; Chester A. Arthur to Harrison, April 3, 1883 (telegram), Harrison to Gresham, April 3 (telegram), 4 (telegram), 1883, Gresham to Harrison, April 4, 1883 (two telegrams), Foster to Harrison, April 8, 1883, BH-LC.

4. *New York Times*, April 12, 1883; *Nation*, April 12, 1883; *Indianapolis Journal*, April 7, 1883.

5. Alfred Harrison to Gresham, April (misdated "March") 10, 1883, WQG-LC; *Indianapolis Journal*, April 11, 1883; *New York Times*, April 14, 1883.

6. Gresham to N.C. Butler, May 7, 1883, J.H. Butler to N.C. Butler, February 19, 1884, NCB-IHSL; Gresham to D.W. Voyles, October 19, 1883, to Laura Ream, February 27, 1884, WQG-LC; *National Cyclopedia of American Biography*, 48:397; Gresham, *Gresham*, 2:491, 494-95.

7. Gresham, *Gresham*, 2:490-91; *Chicago Tribune*, May 12, 1886; C.M. Walker to Butler, July 18, 1883, Gresham to Butler, September 15, 1884, NCB-IHSL.

8. Leonard D. White, *The Republican Era: A Study in Administrative History, 1869-1901* (New York, 1958), 259; Gresham to George W. Stubbs, March 22, 1884, WQG-LC.

9. *House Executive Document 48*, 48th Cong., 1st sess.; *Indianapolis News*, January 8, 1884; *Indianapolis Sentinel*, May 3, 1884; Gresham to W.D. Lewis, January 5, 1884, to W.W. Hart, August 8, 1884, to W.R. Hoole, August 11, 1884, WQG-LC.

10. Gresham to Stephen Lawley, February 21, 1884, to A.C. Harris, July 19, 1884, to C.E. Wilson, December 14, 1883, Butler to Gresham, June 4, 1883, WQG-LC; Gresham to R.P.W. Morris, October [17], 1883, Letters Sent, RG28-NA; Stanley P. Hirshson, *Farewell to the Bloody Shirt: Northern Republicans and the Southern Negro, 1877-1893* (Bloomington, 1962), 105-22.

11. Mary R. Dearing, *Veterans in Politics: The Story of the G.A.R.* (Baton Rouge, 1952), 271; Gresham to R.S. Robertson, January 2, 1884, John McNulta to Gresham, September 10, 1883, Gresham to James F. Pitts, September 18, 1883, WQG-LC.

12. C.S. Elder to Gresham, June 21, 1883, Fred Knefler to Gresham, October 16, 1883, J.H. Woodard to Gresham, January 25, 1884, Gresham to John C. New, January 28, 1884, New to Gresham, January 30, 1884, WQG-LC; Gresham to Lorenzo Myers, Letters Sent, January 19, 1884, RG28-NA; *Indianapolis Journal*, January 25, 26, 28, 31, February 2, 20, March 6, April 3, 1884.

13. Gresham to Dorman B. Eaton, March 19, 1884, Eaton to Gresham, March 19, November 1, 1884, Gresham to W.W. Tuttle, December 8, 1883, to J.M. Shackelford, December 15, 1883, to F.V. Luse, April 16, 1884, to John A. Logan, October 3, 1883, WQG-LC; "Chief Clerk" to Butler, August 13, 1883, NCB-IHSL; Gresham to J.A. Wildman, December 6, 1883, Letters Sent, RG28-NA; *Annual Report of the Postmaster General, 1883*, 10-12; *Indianapolis Journal*, November 15, 1883.

14. *Annual Report of the Postmaster General, 1883*, 12, 27-29; *Annual Report of the Postmaster General, 1884*, 14-15; Gresham to James G. Blaine, October 24, 1883, WQG-LC; 23 *U.S. Statutes at Large*, 386-87.

15. J. Martin Klotsche, "The Star Route Cases," *MVHR* 22 (1935): 407-18; *Annual Report of the Postmaster General, 1883*, 13-15, 123, *Annual Report of the Postmaster General, 1884*, 21-22, 96-101.

16. Gresham to W.E. Chandler, June 14, 1886, William E. Chandler Papers, LC; *Chicago Inter-Ocean*, March 13, 1884; Gresham to J.S. Dickerson, March 21, 1884, WQG-LC; *Indianapolis Journal*, March 20, 25, 1884; *Annual Report of the Postmaster General, 1884*, 25.

17. *Indianapolis Journal*, August 29, 1883; Blaine to Gresham, October 19, 1883, Gresham to Foster, November 10, 1883, WQG-LC; *Annual Report of the Postmaster General, 1883*, 37.

18. *Annual Report of the Postmaster General, 1883*, 33-37; Gresham to Blaine, October 24, 1883, to A.A. Sprague, January 21, 1884, to John M. Harlan, September 6, 1884, WQG-LC.

19. *Annual Report of the Postmaster General, 1883*, 32, 56.

20. *New Orleans National Bank* v. *Merchant*, 18 Fed. Rep. 841; C.W. Moulton to Gresham, July 6, 1883, Butler to Gresham, July 19, 1883, WQG-LC; *New York Times*, July 6, 8, 9, 1883.

21. *Annual Report of the Postmaster General, 1883*, 31-32, 56; Gresham to W. P. Fishback, November 3, 1883, WQG-LC; W.B. Merchant to Gresham, September 21, 1883, Letters Received, RG60–NA; *New Orleans National Bank* v. *Merchant*, 18 Fed. Rep. 841.

22. Gresham to B.H. Brewster, October 19, November 22, 1883, January 21, 1884, Letters Sent, RG28-NA; 19 *U.S. Statutes at Large* 90; *United States* v. *Dauphin*, 20 Fed. Rep. 625; *New York Times*, May 25, 1884; Gresham to Harlan, May 26, 1884, WQG-LC.

23. *Annual Report of the Postmaster General, 1883*, 32-33; *Senate Journal*, 48th Cong., 1st sess., 139, 350, 405, 678-79; *Congressional Record*, 48th Cong., 1st sess., 3520, 4180-81, 4380-84, 4735, 2d sess., 104-5; *Senate Reports 233* and *288*, 48th Cong., 1st sess; *House Journal*, 48th Cong., 1st sess., 188, 651-52, 736, 860, 2d sess., 55; *House Reports 472* and *826*, 48th Cong., 1st sess.; *New York Times*, November 12, December 3, 1883.

24. *Annual Report of the Postmaster General, 1883*, 33; John Samuel Ezell, *Fortune's Merry Wheel: The Lottery in America* (Cambridge, Mass., 1960), 248-49, 255-71. The civil suits brought against Gresham by Dauphin and the New Orleans bank dragged on until late 1890, when the plaintiffs dropped them (W.H.H. Miller to Gresham, April 25, 1891, WQG-LC).

25. Reeves, *Gentleman Boss;* 313-14, 371; *Indianapolis Journal*, April 7, 1883; *Harper's Weekly*, April 14, 1883; Blaine to Gresham, October 19, 1883, WQG-LC.

26. Butler to Gresham, May 3, 1883, John A. Henry to Gresham, May 3, 1883, Harrison to W.B. Thompson, August 30, 1883, WQG-LC; Harrison to Judge Chase, April 28, 1883 (telegram), Harrison to H.L. Brooks, May 19, 1884, BH-LC; Harrison to Lucius Embree, May 5, 1883, Lucius Embree Papers, Indiana Division, ISL; Gresham to Butler, May 19, 1884, NCB-IHSL.

27. Harlan to Gresham, June 9, 1883, David Davis to Gresham, July 19, 1883, WQG-LC; *New York Times*, April 12, 1883; Thomas V. Cooper and Hector T. Fenton, *American Politics*, 14th ed., rev. (Boston, 1890), Bk. 1, 304-7, 314.

28. *Indianapolis Journal*, June ? 1883, clipping in BH-LC; R.A. Cameron to Gresham, June 18, 1883, Gresham to E.B. Martindale, October 26, 1883, to Foster, October 12, 1883, WQG-LC; John Sherman, *Recollections of Forty Years in the House, Senate and Cabinet*, 2 vols. (Chicago, 1895), 2:860-61, 864, 866-67.

29. Gresham to Charles L. Henry, December 3, 1883, to A.P. Hovey, December 10, 1883, Drummond to Gresham, December 20, 1883, February 9, 12, June 16, 20, 1884, Gresham to Drummond, February 27, 1884, to Davis, March 24, 1884, WQG-LC; *Indianapolis Journal*, March 10, 1884.

30. Harrison to Will Cumback, March 5, 1884, Will Cumback Papers, LL; Butler to Gresham, January 18, 25, 1884, Blaine to Gresham, October 19, 1883, J.H. Woodard to Gresham, January 5, 1884, WQG-LC; Gresham to Butler, January 21, 1884, NCB-IHSL; Gresham to Davis, March 7, 1884, DD-ISHL; Gresham to Benjamin Bristow, May 5, 1884, BB-LC; Gresham, *Gresham*, 2:495.

31. *New York Times*, February 4, 1884; Foster to Gresham, February 11, 1884, Gresham to Foster, February 27, March 20, 1884, WQG-LC.

32. Gresham to John Overmyer, March 21, 1884, to T.R. McFerson, April 5, 1884, McFerson to Gresham, April 10, 1884, WQG-LC.

33. Gresham to H.S. Bennett, March 4, 1884, O.W. Nixon to Gresham, March 28, 1884, Gresham to Foster, March 20, April 19, 1884, Gresham to J.V. Hadley, March 6, 1884, WQG-LC; James E. Rose to Harrison, April 12, 1884, W.H.H. Miller to Harrison,

April 22, 1884, BH-LC; *Indianapolis Journal*, April 11, 1884; *New York Times*, April 11, 1884. Numerous reports on the district conventions are in WQG-LC, April 10, 1884ff., passim, and BH-LC, April 10, 1884ff., passim.

34. Gresham to G.G. Reiley, May 3, 14, 20, 1884, to J.B. Kenner, May 15, 1884, to O.A. Simons, May 19, 1884, to W.R. Gardiner, May 20, 1884, to F.M. Posey, May 20, 1884, to J.C. Veatch, May 22, 1884, to A.P. Charles, May 23, 1884, to D.M. Alspaugh, May 23, 1884, to F.J. Phillips, May 5, 1884, J.N. Tyner to Gresham, April 18, 1884, Gresham to W.A. Montgomery, May 2, 1884, Reiley to Gresham, May 9, 1884, Gresham to E.B. Martindale, May 19, 1884, WQG-LC.

35. Gresham to O.W. Nixon, March 31, 1884, to Foster, March 20, 1884, to Veatch, May 22, 1884, to Montgomery, May 2, 1884, to Reiley, May 3, 1884, to Frank Hatton, April 21, 1884, to E. Rosewater, April 24, 1884, to S.F. Miller, April 2, 1884, to Davis, May 23, 1884, WQG-LC; Gresham to Davis, March 7, 1884, DD-ISHL; Gresham to C.W. Fairbanks, May 14, 1884, CWF-LL.

36. Gresham to Davis, March 24, 1884, DD-ISHL; Bain and Parris, *Convention Decisions*, Appendix C; Gresham to A.C. Harris, May 3, 1884, Gresham to Bristow, May 3, 1884, WQG-LC; G.W. Curtis to Butler, May 11, 1884, NCB-IHSL; W.H. Smith to Curtis, May 3, 1884, RBH; Horace White to Smith, May 6, 1884, WHS-OHSL.

37. Gresham to Veatch, May 22, 1884, Bristow to Gresham, May 14, 22, 1884, Gresham to Bristow, May 15, 1884, WQG-LC.

38. Gresham to Butler, May 22, June 1, 1884, Foster to Butler, May 28, 1884, NCB-IHSL; Gresham to Fairbanks, May 23, 1884, CWF-LL; Fairbanks to Gresham, May 25, 1884, Gresham to Harlan, May 26, 1884, Harlan to Gresham, May 31, June 1, 1884, WQG-LC; *New Albany Ledger*, June 6, 1884.

39. Gresham to C.H. Aldrich, May 22, 1884, to G.G. Langsdale, May 28, 1884, Butler to Gresham, May 29, 1884, Gresham to W.A. Woods, May 26, 1884, WQG-LC.

40. *Chicago Tribune*, June 1, 1884; D.P. Baldwin to Gresham, June 5, 1884, Foster to Gresham, June 2, 1884 (two telegrams), WQG-LC.

41. G.W. Steele to Gresham, May 31, 1884, D.W. Voyles to Gresham, June 1, 1884, Foster to Gresham, June 1 (telegram), 2 (three telegrams), 3 (telegram), 5, 1884, Baldwin to Gresham, June 5, 1884, WQG-LC; *Indianapolis Journal*, June 3, 4, 6, 1884; *New Albany Ledger*, June 3-5, 1884; *Chicago Tribune*, May 22, June 3-5, 1884, *New York Times*, June 3, 5, 1884.

42. *New York Times*, June 2, 3, 1884; W.P. Nixon to Gresham, June 2, 1884, Walter Evans to Gresham, June 3, 1884 (telegram), J.M. Brown to Gresham, June 8, 1884, Gresham to Brown, June 12, 1884, Harlan to Gresham, June 1, 1884, W.H. Bradley to Gresham, June 2, 1884, J.M. Scovel to Gresham, June 11, 1884, Bristow to Gresham, June 3, 1884, WQG-LC; Bain and Parris, *Convention Decisions*, Appendix C.

43. *Proceedings of the Eighth Republican National Convention . . . 1884* (Chicago, 1884), 97-128, 138-64; *Chicago Tribune*, June 7, 1884.

44. Foster to Gresham, June 6, 1884 (two telegrams), Gresham to Foster, June 6, 1884 (telegram), to Morris McDonald, June 9, 1884, WQG-LC.

45. Gresham to McDonald, June 9, 1884, to Drummond, June 13, 1884, to Davis, June 12, 1884, to O.W. Nixon, June 12, 1884, WQG-LC.

46. Gresham to A.C. Harris, June 9, 1884, Harris to Gresham, June 7, 1884, WQG-LC; Harrison to L.T. Michener, June 11, 1884, BH-LC.

47. Gresham to Drummond, June 13, 1884, Voyles to Gresham, June 14, 1884, Gresham to Martindale, June 13, 1884, to Voyles, June 17, 1884, to J.W. Hayden, June 14, 1884, to Langsdale, June 16, 1884, R.S. Foster to Gresham, June 18, 1884 (telegram), T.W. Bennett to Gresham, June 18, 1884 (telegram), Gresham to A.C. Harris, June 18 (telegram), 23, 1884, WQG-LC; *New York Times*, June 18, 19, 1884.

48. Gresham to Drummond, June 19, 1884, to J.M. Brown, June 12, 1884, to Bristow, June 12, 1884, to Davis, June 12, 1884, to J.M. Butler, July 13, 1884, to W.W. Phelps, August 22, 1884, to G.I. Reed, July 19, 1884, to Harris, July 10, 1884, to Eugene Hale, August 4, 1884, to Samuel Fessenden, August 21, 1884, to B.F. Jones, August 25, 1884, WQG-LC; Gresham to N.C. Butler, August 11, 21, 1884, NCB-IHSL.

49. Gresham to Butler, September 7, 1884, NCB-IHSL; Tyner to James S. Clarkson, November 23, 1884, James S. Clarkson Papers, LC.

50. Gresham to Butler, September 7, 1884, NCB-IHSL; Gresham to W.C. Goudy, September 18, 1884, to Blaine, September 22, 1884, WQG-LC.

51. Gresham to Butler, September 15, 1884, NCB-IHSL; Gresham to Davis, September 16, 1884, WQG-LC; *New York Times*, September 25, 26, 1884.

52. *Chicago Tribune*, September 26, 1884; Gresham to Bristow, September 28, 1884, BB-LC; C.A.T. Collins to Gresham, October 16, 1884 (telegram), S.B. Elkins to Gresham, October 18, 1884 (telegram), J.D. Warren to Gresham, October 17 (telegram), 18 (telegram), 1884, WQG-LC.

53. *New York Tribune*, October 21, 1884.

54. "Protectionist" to the editor of the *Tribune*, December 6, 1884, in *New York Tribune*, December 8, 1884. Blaine's draft of his letter is in WR-LC.

55. Gresham, *Gresham*, 2:504; Harrison to M.M. Hurley, November 22, December 2, 1884, BH-LC; *Journal of the Executive Proceedings of the Senate*, 48th Cong., 2d sess., 349, 351, 376.

56. Eaton to Gresham, November 1, 1884, Gresham to William Mahone, October 28, 1884, to Aldrich, August 22, 1884, WQG-LC; *Indianapolis News*, October 29, 1884.

57. Gresham to Bristow, November 21, 1884, BB-LC; Gresham to Aldrich, August 22, 1884, D.W. Voorhees to Gresham, November 28, 1884, WQG-LC; Gresham to Chandler, November 25, 1884, Chandler Papers, LC.

Chapter 5. PRESIDENTIAL CANDIDATE

1. Bessie L. Pierce, *A History of Chicago*, 3 vols. (New York, 1937-57), volume 3, *The Rise of the Modern City, 1871-1893*; Gresham to N.C. Butler, December 6, 24, 1884, to Ben Miller, February 23, 1887, NCB-IHSL; Gresham to C.W. Fairbanks, January 7, 1886, CWF-LL.

2. Gresham to W.E. Chandler, November 25, 1884, W.E. Chandler Papers, LC; John M. Harlan to Gresham, December 3, 1884, WQG-LC.

3. *Mackin v. United States*, 23 Fed. Rep. 334; "S.T." to Gresham, March 24, 1885, WQG-LC; *Chicago Legal News*, May 23, 1885; *Chicago Tribune*, May 22, 23, 1885, January 2, 1887; *Mackin v. United States*, 117 U.S. 348; Gresham, *Gresham*, 2:484-88.

4. *Indianapolis Journal*, November 6, 1886; Gresham to Butler, November 7, 1886, NCB-IHSL; Simeon Coy, *The Great Cnspiracy: A Complete History of the Famous Tally-Sheet Cases* (Indianapolis, 1889), 33-35, 157; *Ex Parte* Perkins, 29 Fed. Rep. 900; W. A. Woods to Harlan, May 22, 1887, JMH-UL; *United States v. Coy and others*, 32 Fed. Rep. 538; *In re* Coy, 31 Fed. Rep. 794; *In re* Coy, 127 U.S. 731; L.T. Michener to E.G. Hay, August 11, 1887, Eugene Gano Hay Papers, LC.

5. Gresham to N.C. Butler, April 23, 1887, NCB-IHSL; Fairbanks to Gresham, June 20, 1885, Gresham to J.M. Butler, December 12, 1884 (telegram), John McNulta to Gresham, February 26, 1886, WQG-LC; Gresham to Fairbanks, June 22, 1885, CWF-LL.

6. *Chicago Tribune*, September 19, 1885; George H. Miller, *Railroads and the Granger Laws* (Madison, 1971), 93.

7. Gresham to Solon Humphreys and T.E. Tutt, May 4, 1886 (telegram), Humphreys and Tutt to Gresham, May 5, 1886 (telegram and letter), Wager Swayne to Gresham, May 7, 1886 (telegram), Tutt to Gresham, May [7, later misdated May 6], 1886, WQG-LC; *Chicago Tribune*, June 24, 26, 29, 30, and July, passim, 1886. Gerald Eggert (*Railroad Labor Disputes;* 68-69) contends that Gresham's temporary order in the *Lake Shore* case was a "significant portent for the future" for the development of the federal court labor injunction. Such seems not to be the case, however, for a judge who had issued a state court injunction at the time later wrote to Gresham, "I don't remember, if I ever knew, how you have, when on the bench, ruled with reference to" strike injunctions (Henry M. Shepard to Gresham, July 14, 1894, WQG-LC).

8. *Public Opinion*, September 11, 1886; *New York Freeman*, May 29, 1886; Gresham to Butler, June 2, 3, 1886, NCB-IHSL.

9. *New York Times*, November 23, 1886; *Chicago Tribune*, November 24, 1886; *Public Opinion*, November 27, December 4, 11, 1886; Gresham to Butler, December 1, 1886, NCB-IHSL.

10. *Atkins* v. *Wabash, St. L. & P. Ry. Co.*, 29 Fed. Rep. 161; "A Chapter of Wabash," *North American Review* 146 (February 1888): 178-93.

11. Benjamin Bristow to Gresham, December 8, 1886, February 9, 1887, WQG-LC; "The Wabash Receivership Case," *American Law Review* 21 (January-February 1887): 104-20, 141; *New York Times*, December 9, 1886; Bristow to Gresham, February 14, 1887, NCB-IHSL.

12. *New York Times*, March 4, 1887; *Wabash, St. L. & P. Ry. Co.* v. *Illinois*, 118 U.S. 557; Arnold M. Paul, *Conservative Crisis and the Rule of Law: Attitudes of Bench and Bar, 1887-1895* (New York, 1960); *Chicago Legal News*, September 7, 1889; Gresham to Woods, September 28, 1889, WQG-LC.

13. *New York Tribune*, December 9, 1886; Gresham to Chandler, July 21, 1887, Chandler Papers, LC.

14. *New York Times*, November 9, 15, 1887; W.P. Fishback to J.W. Foster, November 12, 1887, Foster to Fishback, November 25, 1887, to Fairbanks, November 25, 1887, Gresham to Fairbanks, December 14, 1887, CWF-LL; D.W. Voyles to Gresham, November 18, 1887, WQG-LC.

15. James D. Richardson, *A Compilation of the Messages and Papers of the Presidents*, 10 vols. (Washington, D.C., 1903), 8:580-91; *New York Tribune*, December 8, 1887; J.H. Wilson to Bluford Wilson, December 11, 1887, CWF-LL.

16. Sievers, *Harrison: Hoosier Statesman*, chaps. 17-18; Harrison to Michener, December 22, 1885, to "Cos Mag," November 12, 1886, BH-LC; Foster to Gresham, February 14, 1888, WQG-LC.

17. Gresham to Butler, January 30, 1888, NCB-IHSL.

18. *Chicago Tribune*, February 17, 1888; Sievers, *Harrison: Hoosier Statesman*, 310-11, 317; S.B. Elkins to Harrison, February 11, 14, 27, 1888, J.N. Tyner to Harrison, February 20, 1888, BH-LC; James G. Blaine to Elkins, March 1, 1888, in Oscar Doane Lambert, *Stephen Benton Elkins: American Foursquare* (Pittsburgh, 1955), 120.

19. *Indianapolis Journal*, February 14, 28, 29, 1888; C.B. Landis to Fairbanks, February 20, 1888, Otto Gresham to Fairbanks, February 11, 1888, Foster to Fairbanks, February 22, 1888, CWF-LL; Sievers, *Harrison: Hoosier Statesman*, 222-24, 322-23; *New York Herald*, February 22, 1888; Elkins to Harrison, March 3, 1888, BH-LC.

20. W.H. Smith to Fairbanks, February 27, 1888, with note, Fairbanks to Gresham, February 29, 1888, Gresham to Fairbanks, March 11, 1888, E.H. Bundy to Fairbanks, March 15, 1888, CWF-LL; Robert G. Ingersoll to Gresham, May 17, 1888, RGI-ISHL; Foster to Gresham, March 16, 1888, WQG- LC; Michener to E.F. Tibbott, October 1, 1895,

BH-LC; "The Harrison Campaign for the Nomination in 1888," Memorandum, LTM-LC; *Chicago Tribune*, April 21, 1888.

21. *Chicago Tribune*, February-June 1888, passim; *Chicago Inter-Ocean*, February-June 1888, passim; S.M. Cullom to J.R. Tanner, April 10, 1888, SMC-ISHL; Michener to E.W. Halford, May 17, 1889, BH-LC; Joseph Medill to J.W. Fifer, June 6, 1888, Joseph W. Fifer Papers, ISHL; Bain and Parris, *Convention Decisions*, Appendix C.

22. Gresham to Ingersoll, March 11, 1888, RGI-ISHL; Gresham to Fairbanks, March 14, 1888, CWF-LL; Sievers, *Harrison: Hoosier Statesman*, 326.

23. *Chicago Tribune*, March 9, 10, 13-15, 1888; *Beers* v. *Wabash, St. L. and P. Ry. Co.*, 34 Fed. Rep. 244; Eggert, *Railroad Labor Disputes*, 84-90; Donald McMurry, *The Great Burlington Strike of 1888* (Cambridge, Mass., 1958), 124, 128. The Burlington brought two other cases before Gresham, demanding an exchange of its cars by roads not in receivership. The Rock Island's management denied it was refusing to handle Burlington cars, and Gresham issued no injunction, although he kept the petition on file. The Chicago Belt Line offered no argument against the Burlington's application, and a temporary injunction was issued more or less automatically by consent of both parties. As it happened, this injunction was not needed to enforce the handling of the cars and was never made permanent (*Chicago Tribune*, March 16, 25, April 4, 5, 1888; *New York Times*, April 4, 5, 1888).

24. *Minneapolis Journal*, June 4, 1888, quoted in *Public Opinion*, June 9, 1888; W.J. Freany to W.A. Van Buren, February 26, 1888, CWF-LL; *South Bend Tribune*, March 24, 1888; *Chicago Tribune*, June 10, 1888.

25. *New York Times*, February 20, 1888; *Indianapolis Sentinel*, March 15, 1888; C.B. Farwell to Gresham, June 5, 1888, J.H. Wilson to Gresham, June 6, 1888, WQG-LC; *Chicago Tribune*, May 24, 31, June 3, 7, 1888; M.M. Hurley to H.C. Payne, May 15, 1888, enclosed in Payne to Gresham, May 18, 1888, Frederick King to Gresham, May 21, 1888, Morris McDonald to Fairbanks, "Sunday P.M." [May 27?], 1888, CWF-LL; Gresham to S. Wolf, May 24, 1888, Walter Q. Gresham Papers, Indiana Division, ISL; R.W. Patterson to Butler, May 29, 1888 (telegram), Gresham to Butler, May 31, 1888, NCB-IHSL.

26. Jake Covert to Harrison, February 26, 1888, BH-LC; *New York Evening Post*, March 20, 1888, quoted in *Public Opinion*, March 24, 1888; Wharton Barker to Gresham, May 25, 1888, WB-LC; Gresham to A.P. Brown, June 10, 1888, Walter Q. Gresham Papers, IHSL; Gresham to Erastus Brainerd, March 17, 1888, WQG-LC.

27. *South Bend Tribune*, March 28, 1888; *Chicago Inter-Ocean*, March 16, 1888; Gresham to Brainerd, March 17, 1888, WQG-LC; *Chicago Tribune*, March 16, June 7, 1888; J.E. Jones to Fairbanks, June 14, 1888, CWF-LL; *New York Tribune*, October 21, 1888; Gresham to Butler, September 21, 1888, NCB-IHSL; Barker to R.S. Taylor, June 11, 1888, RST-ISL.

28. Whitelaw Reid to John Hay, March 20, 1888, WR-LC; Gresham to Fairbanks, March 18, 1888, CWF-LL; Robert D. Marcus, *Grand Old Party: Political Structure in the Gilded Age* (New York, 1971), 107-8; Elkins to Harrison, February 14, 27, March 15, 18, April 6, May 7, 1888, BH-LC.

29. Reid to C.F. Crocker, April 23, 1888, WR-LC; *Harper's Weekly*, June 9, 1888; C.B. Landis to Gresham, May 21, 1888, CWF-LL; Louis Howland to Butler, June 5, 1888, NCB-IHSL; Barker to Harrison, June 4, 1888, BH-LC.

30. *Harper's Weekly*, June 16, 1888; Foster to Fairbanks, April 24, 28, 29, 1888, Richard Elmer to Fairbanks, June 6, 1888, Gresham to Fairbanks, June 20, 1888, CWF-LL; Foster to Gresham, April 28, 29, 1888, Elmer to Foster, May 3, 1888, Farwell to Gresham, June 5 1888, WQG-LC; *Indianapolis Journal*, June 2, 1888; Bain and Parris, *Convention Decisions*, Appendix C.

31. Gresham to Brainerd, March 8, 1888, John Prout Papers, Indiana Division, ISL;

Gresham to Ingersoll, March 11, May 1, 1888, RGI-ISHL; *New Albany Weekly Ledger,* March 28, 1888; Voyles to Butler, April 8, 1888, NCB-IHSL; Gresham to Benjamin Bristow, May 23, 1888, BB-LC.

32. Foster to Gresham, June 10, 1888, C.E. Dyer to Gresham, June 15, 1888, WQG-LC; Gresham to Fairbanks, June 17, 1888 (telegram), and n.d. [1888], CWF-LL; Butler to Mrs. N.C. Butler, June 20, 1888, NCB-IHSL; *Indianapolis Journal,* June 17, 19, 1888; *Indianapolis News,* June 19, 1888; *Chicago Tribune,* June 13, 21, 1888; Herbert Radclyffe to Harrison, March 23, 1889, BH-LC.

33. *New York Times,* June 21, 1888, November 6, 1892; *Chicago Tribune,* June 17, 21, 22, 25, 1888, February 16, 1893; *Indianapolis Journal,* June 18, 19, 21, 22, 1888; *New Albany Ledger,* June 20, 1888; *Indianapolis News,* June 21, 1888; *Proceedings of the Ninth Republican National Convention* (Chicago, 1888), 108; Gresham to Medill, November 7, 1892, WQG-LC; Gresham to Bristow, November 5, 1892, BB-LC.

34. J.H. Chase to Gresham, June 6, 1888, NCB-IHSL; Paul Avrich, *The Haymarket Tragedy* (Princeton, 1984), 300; O. Nixon to Gresham, n.d. [1888], WQG-LC; *Proceedings of the Ninth Republican National Convention,* 113-21.

35. *Proceedings of the Ninth Republican National Convention,* 163-67, 170-73; *New York Times,* June 23, 1888; A.M. Jones to John Sherman, June 21, 1888 (telegram), JS-LC; Chauncey Depew to Cyrenus Cole, September 22, 1922, Chauncey Depew Papers, Yale University Library, New Haven.

36. *Indianapolis Journal,* June 15, 1888; *New York Times,* June 23, 1888; *Chicago Tribune,* June 23, 1888; Gresham to Ingersoll, June 23, 1888, Otto Gresham to Ingersoll, July 6, 1888, RGI-ISHL.

37. *Proceedings of the Ninth Republican National Convention,* 178-79, 183-86, 188-89, 195-205; Walker Blaine to Mrs. James G. Blaine, July 5, 1888, JGB-LC; G.W. Wilson to Fairbanks, June 24, 1888 (telegram), CWF-LL; *Chicago Tribune,* June 25, 1888; Sherman to Warner Miller, [June 24, 1888] (telegram), JS-LC; Michener to Barker, June 24, 1888 (telegram), WB-LC; *Indianapolis Journal,* June 26, 1888.

38. *Indianapolis Journal,* June 26, 1888; Gresham to Harrison, June 25, 1888 (telegram), BH-LC.

39. Gresham to Butler, July 5, 1888, NCB-IHSL.

40. Gresham to Butler, July 5, September 21, 1888, NCB-IHSL.

41. Gresham to Fairbanks, July 5, 1888 (telegram), CWF-LL; *Chicago Tribune,* September 3, 19, 1888; *Chicago Inter-Ocean,* September 18, 1888. In no letter in the manuscript collections I consulted did Gresham record his impressions of his European trip, and Mrs. Gresham's biography of her husband is silent on the subject.

42. *Chicago Inter-Ocean,* September 18, 1888; *Chicago Tribune,* September 25, October 3, 1888.

43. Walter Evans to Gresham, October 19, 23, 27, 1888, WQG-LC; Gresham to Fairbanks, September 30, 1888, CWF-LL; Gresham to W.H. Calkins, October 23, 1888, in *Indianapolis Journal,* October 25, 1888.

44. Gresham to Butler, October 30, 1888, NCB-IHSL.

45. *Indianapolis Sentinel,* October 31, 1888; *Indianapolis Journal,* November 1, 3, 1888; *New York Times,* November 1, 1888; W. Dean Burnham, *Presidential Ballots, 1836-1892* (Baltimore, 1955), 391, 633.

46. Sievers, *Harrison: Hoosier Statesman,* 419-21; Gresham, *Gresham,* 2:606-18; *Chicago Legal News,* February 2, 1889; *Indianapolis Journal,* March 29, 30, April 2, 1889; Gresham to Butler, April 3, 1889, NCB-IHSL.

47. Gresham, *Gresham,* 2:606-7; *New York World,* November 28, 1888.

Chapter 6. JEREMIAH

1. *Chicago Tribune*, November 11, 12, 1888, May 29, 1888; *New York Times*, February 26, 1889.

2. *Chicago Tribune*, March 23, April 14, 27, 1889; Benjamin Bristow to Gresham, March 25, April 1, May 19, June 4, 1889, T.M. Cooley to Gresham, March 23, 1889; W.T. Otto to Gresham, March 22, 1889 (telegram), WQG-LC; Herbert Radclyffe to Benjamin Harrison, March 23, 1889, BH-LC; *Indianapolis Journal*, March 23, 29, 1889; Gresham to Noble Butler, April 3, 1889, NCB-IHSL.

3. Wharton Barker to Harrison, February 8, 1889, L.T. Michener to E.W. Halford, April 6, June 8, 22, September 10, 1889, BH-LC; Walter Wellman to C.W. Fairbanks, April 5, 1889, CWF-LL; Harry J. Sievers, *Benjamin Harrison: Hoosier President* (Indianapolis, 1968), 41-43; Morgan, *From Hayes to McKinley;* 328-31.

4. *New York Times*, October 5, 1889; Gresham to W.J. Allen, August 1, 1889, CWF-LL.

5. *Indianapolis Journal*, August 9, 13, 14, 1889; W.A. Woods to J.M. Harlan, August 11, 1889, JMH-LC; Gresham to Woods, September 28, 1889, NCB-IHSL; *New York Times*, August 13, 1889; *Chicago Legal News*, September 7, October 5, 1889.

6. A.C. Harris to Gresham, October 18, 1889, W.T. Otto to Gresham, December 7, 1889, February 15, 1890, *Evansville Courier*, clipping, n.d., WQG-LC; Wellman to Fairbanks, August 17, 1889, CWF-LL; *New York Times*, August 13, 1889; Sievers, *Harrison: Hoosier President*, 137-38.

7. *Chicago Tribune*, December 9, 23, 1888, January 17, February 23, 1889; Gresham to Zetta, February 9, 1890, WQG-LC.

8. *Indianapolis News*, January 23, July 14, 1890; *Indianapolis Sentinel*, January 24, 1890; *New York Times*, July 15, 1890; Gresham to Butler, July 21, 1890, NCB-IHSL; Bristow to Gresham, July 15, 1890, WQG-LC; Gresham to Fairbanks, August 7, September 2, 1890, Otto Gresham to Fairbanks, September 17, 1889, January 23, May 22, July 17 (telegram), 1890, CWF-LL.

9. Gresham to Fairbanks, August 7, September 2, 1890, CWF-LL; *Indianapolis News*, September 10, 1890.

10. Gresham to Erastus Brainerd, December 10, 1888, Walter Q. Gresham Papers, Indiana Division, ISL; Gresham to Zetta, February 9, 1890, WQG-LC.

11. Gresham to Butler, October 16, 1890, with text of speech, NCB-IHSL.

12. J.D. Cox to Gresham, October 31, 1890, W.T. Otto to Gresham, October 23, 1890, M.L. Bundy to Gresham, December 24, 1890, WQG-LC.

13. Paul Kleppner, *The Cross of Culture* (New York, 1970), 143-71; Richard Jensen, *The Winning of the Midwest* (Chicago, 1971), chap. 5; Michener to Halford, November 8, 1890, BH-LC; Gresham to Fairbanks, November 7, December 7, 1890, CWF-LL.

14. T.R. McFerson to Fairbanks, November 4, 1889, November 5, 1890, CWF-LL; *In re* Counselman, 44 Fed. Rep. 268; *In re* Peasely, 44 Fed. Rep. 271; "The Gresham March," by S. Francis, printed sheet music, Indiana Division, ISL.

15. *Chicago Tribune*, January 16, 21, February 11, 14, March 12, 1891; Bluford Wilson to Fairbanks, January 1, 1891, E. Callahan to Fairbanks, January 12, 20, 1891, Gresham to Fairbanks, February 11, 1891, CWF-LL.

16. Gresham to Fairbanks, December 7, 1890, February 11, April 11, 1891, CWF-LL; Reuben H. Donnelly, comp., *The Lakeside Annual Directory of the City of Chicago, 1891* (Chicago, 1891), 924.

17. Gresham, *Gresham*, 2:633, 634, 635; Gresham to Edward L. Brewster & Co., September 29, 1888, WQG-LC; *New York Times*, June 25, 1892.

18. Gresham to Fairbanks, January 9, 12, 14, 17, 19, 1891, CWF-LL; *Indianapolis*

Sentinel, January 19, 20, June 12, 13, 14, 1891; *Indianapolis News*, January 19, 20, June 12, 22, 1891; *Indianapolis Journal*, January 20, 1891; S.J. Peelle to Halford, January 21, 1891 [filed 1892], Peelle to Michener, August 10, 12, 1891, *Evansville Standard* clipping, n.d., Scrapbook No. 21, BH-LC; Fairbanks to Brainerd, December 27, 1890, John McNulta to Fairbanks, June 2, 1891, handwritten resolution with names, dated June 11, 1891, T.R. McFerson to Fairbanks, June 15, 1891, CWF-LL.

19. Delavan Smith to Fairbanks, June 14, 1891, CWF-LL; Gresham to Butler, July 21, 1890, August 6, 27, 1891, NCB-IHSL.

20. Gresham to Butler, August 6, 27, 1891, NCB-IHSL.

21. Quotations here and in the next two paragraphs are from *Report of the Proceedings of the Society of the Army of the Tennessee at the Twenty-third Meeting Held at Chicago, Ill., October 7th and 8th, 1891* (Cincinnati, 1893), 430-46; *Address at the Unveiling of the Grant Statue*, 1-12.

22. *New York Times*, October 8, 1891; *Indianapolis Journal*, October 8, 1891; *Chicago Herald*, October 9, 1891.

23. *Chicago Herald*, October 9, 1891; *Indianapolis News*, October 22, November 28, 1891; *Indianapolis Journal*, October 23, 1891; Gresham to Fairbanks, October 23, 1891, Fairbanks to Gresham, October 24, 1891, CWF-LL.

24. Peelle to Halford, December 5, 1891, January 11, 29, February 3, 13, March 5, 11, 1892, B. Wilson Smith to Halford, February 19, 1892, John K. Gowdy to Halford, February 13, 1892, BH-LC.

25. Marcus, *Grand Old Party*, 151-74; P.A.B. Widener to Gresham, January 15, June 3, 1892, J.H. Woodard to Gresham, April 14, 1892, H.S. Kindekoper to Gresham, June 4, 1892, WQG-LC; Woodard to Fairbanks, April 14, 1892, CWF-LL; *New York Times*, May 25, 1892, February 14, 1893.

26. Fairbanks to "My dear Patchell," April 11, 1892, Gresham to Fairbanks, January 30, May 18, 1892, CWF-LL.

27. Donald Bruce Johnson and Kirk H. Porter, comps., *National Party Platforms, 1840-1972* (Urbana, 1975), 93; Gresham to Wharton Barker, July 12, 1892, WB-LC; Gresham to Bristow, June 21, 1892, BB-LC.

28. *Pittsburgh Dispatch*, May 3, 1891, in *Public Opinion*, May 9, 1891; Gresham to C. A. Power, February 16, 1892, quoted in Gresham, *Gresham*, 2:659-60.

29. John D. Hicks, *The Populist Revolt: A History of the Farmers' Alliance and the People's Party* (Minneapolis, 1931), 233; S.R. Davis to Gresham, May 23, 1893, WQG-LC; *New York Times*, June 25, 27, July 2, 1892; *American Non-Conformist*, June 23, 1892; *Chicago Herald*, June 27, 1892, clipping, Scrapbook 22, BH-LC.

30. *New York Times*, July 2-4, 1892; E.A. Allen, *The Life and Public Services of James Baird Weaver* (n.p.: [People's Party Publishing Company], 1892), 77-83, 88-89.

31. Allen, *Weaver*, 102-6; *New York Times*, July 5, 1892.

32. *Chicago Tribune*, July 5, 1892; *New York Times*, July 5, 1892; *Washington Star*, July 5, 1892, quoted in *Public Opinion*, July 9, 1892; John W. Foster to Fairbanks, July 6, 1892, CWF-LL; *Washington Post*, July 6, 1892.

33. Johnson and Porter, comps., *National Party Platforms*, 93; Gresham to Morris Ross, August 1, 1892, WQG-LC.

34. Gresham to Ross, August 1, 1892, WQG-LC; Grover Cleveland to Wilson S. Bissell, July 24, 1892, Cleveland to Lambert Tree, "undated; about September 20, 1892," in Allan Nevins, ed., *The Letters of Grover Cleveland, 1850-1908* (Boston, 1933), 295-96, 309; John Bassett Moore, Diary Memoranda, May 1894, JBM-LC; Tree to Cleveland, September 15, 1892, GC-LC.

35. Unidentified newspaper clipping, n.d. (dateline October 2), "Mr. Halstead's Correspondence," unidentified clipping, Scrapbook 23, BH-LC; *New York Times*, October

3, 4, 1892; *South Bend Tribune*, October 23, 1892; *New Albany Daily Ledger*, October 5, 1892; Cleveland to Tree, October 7, 1892, LT-NL; W.B. Slemons to Gresham, October 3, 1892, WQG-LC.

36. Gresham to Slemons, October 6, 1892, WQG-LC; Gresham to Fairbanks, October 14, 1892, CWF-LL.

37. Fairbanks to Gresham, October 28, 1892, Walter Wellman to Gresham, October 30, 1892, Bluford Wilson to Gresham, October 25, 1892, WQG-LC; *South Bend Tribune*, October 20, 1892; Gresham to Wilson, October 27, 1892, in Gresham, *Gresham*, 2:672-73.

38. *New York Times*, November 11, 1892; Patrick Ford to Harrison, November 3, 1892, J.A. Wildman to Halford, October 5, 1892, BH-LC; *Milwaukee Telegraph*, November 5, 1892, clipping, GC-LC; J.W. Doane to William C. Whitney, October 15, 1892, WCW-LC; *Chicago Tribune*, November 9, 1892.

39. Bluford Wilson to Gresham, November 16, 1892, Gresham to Joseph Medill, November 7, 1892, WQG-LC.

Chapter 7. SECRETARY OF STATE

1. Gresham to Charles W. Fairbanks, October 14, 1892, CWF-LL.

2. *Chicago Tribune*, September 23, 1892; *In re* Interstate Commerce Commission, 53 Fed. Rep. 476; *Chicago Legal News*, December 17, 1892; *Interstate Commerce Commission* v. *Brimson*, 154 U.S. 447.

3. *Chicago Tribune*, September 28, 1892.

4. Ibid., October 19, 1892; Gresham, *Gresham*, 2:678.

5. Daniel S. Lamont, Memoranda on Cabinet, December 7, 9, 1892, DSL-LC.

6. Although there is no direct evidence, one may speculate that perhaps Cleveland offered the State Department to Fuller in order to open the chief justice position for Gresham. *New York Times*, February 10, 1893; Lamont, Memoranda on Cabinet, January 4, 16, 1893, DSL-LC; John Bassett Moore, Diary Memoranda, 1894, JBM-LC; Grover Cleveland to L. Clarke Davis, January 25, 1893, in Nevins, ed., *Letters of Cleveland*, 315; Cleveland to Gresham, January 25, 1893, WQG-LC.

7. Don M. Dickinson to Gresham, January 27, 1893 (telegram), Bluford Wilson to Gresham, January 30, 1893, Gresham to Cleveland, February 3, 1893, WQG-LC; John W. Doane to William C. Whitney, February 4, 1893, WCW-LC; Gresham, *Gresham*, 2:679-80.

8. Gresham to Dickinson, February 3, 1893, DMD-LC; Doane to Whitney, February 4, 1893, WCW-LC; Lamont to Gresham, February 5, 1893 (telegram), "D" to Gresham, February 6, 1893 (telegram), Whitney to Gresham, in Lamont to Gresham, February 6, 1893 (telegram), Cleveland to Gresham, February 6, 1893 (telegram), Gresham to Cleveland, February 7, 1893, WQG-LC.

9. Gresham to W.H. Smith, February 16, 1893, WHS-OHSL; Gresham to Noble C. Butler, [February 10, 1893], NCB-IHSL; *Philadelphia Ledger*, February 22, 1893, quoted in *Literary Digest*, March 4, 1893.

10. Lamont, Memoranda on Cabinet, December 7, 1892, DSL-LC; Woodrow Wilson, "Mr. Cleveland's Cabinet," *Review of Reviews* 8 (April 1893), in Arthur S. Link, ed., *The Papers of Woodrow Wilson*, 44 vols. to date (Princeton, 1966–), 8:164; Moore, Diary Memoranda, 1894, JBM-LC; *Public Opinion*, February 25, March 4, 1893; *Literary Digest*, February 25, 1893; Whitney to Gresham, in Lamont to Gresham, February 6, 1893 (telegram), Albert J. Beveridge to Gresham, February 16, 1893, WQG-LC.

11. *Public Opinion*, February 25, March 4, 1893; *Literary Digest*, February 25, 1893; Richard H. McDonald, Jr., "The Ambition of Mr. Cleveland," *Literary Digest*, July 15, 1893.

12. Cleveland to Gresham, February 9, 1893, Cleveland to Lamont, February 23, 1893, Nevins, ed., *Letters of Cleveland*, 317, 319; John W. Foster, *Diplomatic Memoirs*, 2 vols. (Boston, 1909), 2:273; *New York Times*, February 24, 25, 26, 1893; Gresham, *Gresham*, 2:684-85, 712. The Gresham biography misdates the Lakewood conference as taking place February 22.

13. *New York Times*, March 5, 6, 1893; Gresham, *Gresham*, 2:688-93, 696-97, 813-15; Thomas F. Bayard to Moore, April 14, 1893, JBM-LC.

14. Moore, Diary Memoranda, 1894, JBM-LC; Cleveland to Dickinson, March 20, 1895, Nevins, ed., *Letters of Cleveland*, 319.

15. *New York Times*, March 5, October 8, 1893; Gresham, *Gresham*, 2:580; Gresham to Mrs. Potter Palmer, March 26, 1894, Walter Q. Gresham Papers, Chicago Historical Society; K.M. Landis to Moore, August 14, 1895, JBM-LC.

16. Gresham, *Gresham*, 2:699-700; Williams, *Years of Decision*, 71-76.

17. Richardson, *Messages and Papers*, 9:390; Williams, *Years of Decision*, 75-76, 78-79; Daniel W. Voorhees to Cleveland, March 10, 20, August 14, 1893, Carl Schurz to Cleveland, March 30, 1893, GC-LC; Gresham to Horace White, April 3, 1893, WQG-LC; Cleveland to Schurz, March 31, 1893, White to Schurz, April 4, 1893, CS-LC; White to Lucius Swift, April 4, 1893, Swift to "My Dearest," April 24, 1893, Lucius Swift Papers, Indiana Division, ISL; *Literary Digest*, April 1, 1893.

18. Richardson, *Messages and Papers*, 9:396; Gresham to Cleveland, July 3, 1893, GC-LC; Gresham to F.P. Schmitt, August 16, 1893, WQG-LC; Gresham to Lamont, July 24, 1893, DSL-LC; *New York Times*, July 28, 1893; Gresham to Whitney, July 28, 1893, WCW-LC.

19. Williams, *Years of Decision*, 79; Moore, Diary Memoranda, 1894, JBM-LC; J.R. Doolittle to Cleveland, July 15, 1893, GC-LC; Gresham to Butler, July 17, 1893, NCB-IHSL; Gresham to M.E. Ingalls, August 25, 1893, WQG-LC.

20. Richardson, *Messages and Papers*, 9:401-5; Gresham to Whitney, July 28, 1893, WCW-LC; Voorhees to Cleveland, August 14, 1893, GC-LC; Gresham to W.J. Allen, August 14, 1893, to Doane, August 17, 1893, to Franklin MacVeagh, August 31, 1893, WQG-LC.

21. Gresham to Bayard, September 7, 1893, to Alexander C. Robinson, October 4, 1893, WQG-LC; Voorhees to Cleveland, October 16, 1893, GC-LC.

22. Gresham to Butler, November 6, 1893, NCB-IHSL; Williams, *Years of Decision*, 77, 83-85.

23. Festus P. Summers, *William L. Wilson and Tariff Reform* (New Brunswick, N.J., 1953), 164-86.

24. Gresham to A.S. Willis, February 3, 1894, ASW-FC; Summers, *Wilson*, 187-193.

25. Gresham to Bayard, March 18, 1894, TFB-LC; J.W. Doane to Gresham, January 7, 1894, WQG-LC; Gresham to Mrs. Potter Palmer, March 26, 1894, Gresham Papers, Chicago Historical Society; Nevins, *Cleveland*, 569-72; Morgan, *From Hayes to McKinley*, 458-59; Richardson, *Messages and Papers*, 9:483-89.

26. Gresham to Mrs. Potter Palmer, March 26, 1894, Gresham Papers, Chicago Historical Society; Williams, *Years of Decision*, 86-87.

27. Henry Vincent to Gresham, February 22, 1893, Gresham to C.E. Dyer, May 2, 1894, WQG-LC; Gerald G. Eggert, *Richard Olney: Evolution of a Statesman* (University Park, Pa., 1974), 118-19; Carlos A. Schwantes, *Coxey's Army: An American Odyssey* (Lincoln, 1985), 166-84.

28. Gresham to Dyer, May 2, 1894, WQG-LC; Summers, *Wilson*, 193; Gresham to Bayard, June 7, 1894, TFB-LC.

29. Eggert, *Olney*, 133-47; Moore, Diary Memoranda, July 1894, JBM-LC.

30. Moore, Diary Memoranda, July 1894, JBM-LC; Eggert, *Olney*, 140-42.

31. Richardson, *Messages and Papers*, 9:500-501; Moore, Diary Memoranda, July 1894, JBM-LC; Gresham to E.M. Phelps, July 12, 1894, to John S. Cooper, July 26, 1894, WQG-LC; Eggert, *Olney*, 148-49.

32. Williams, *Years of Decision*, 92-96; Gresham to Henry Watterson, August 21, 1894, HW-LC.

33. Gresham to Bayard, July 22, 1894, WQG-LC; Gresham to Mrs. Potter Palmer, March 26, 1894, Gresham Papers, Chicago Historical Society.

34. Unknown to Joseph Pulitzer, June 6, 1893, GC-LC; Nevins, *Cleveland*, 511; Charles S. Hamlin, Index-Digest to Diaries, 1:229, Charles S. Hamlin Papers, LC; Gresham to Morris Ross, July 6, 1894, WQG-LC; H.L. Bryan to Bayard, March 19, May 9, 1895, TFB-LC; K.M. Landis to Moore, August 14, 1895, Borchard, "Moore's Memoirs," 125-26, JBM-LC.

35. Gresham to [J. Russell] Jones, undated draft, [1893], Gresham to Bayard, October 29, 1893, December 24, 1894, WQG-LC; Richard Megaree, "The Diplomacy of John Bassett Moore: Realism in American Foreign Policy" (Ph.D. dissertation, Northwestern University, 1963), 54-55.

36. Borchard, "Moore's Memoirs," 125-26, JBM-LC; Frederic Emory to Bayard, January 22, 1895, TFB-LC; Henry Cabot Lodge, "Our Blundering Foreign Policy," *Forum* 19 (March, 1895): 8-17.

37. Gresham to Bayard, January 21, 1894, WQG-LC. There are two drafts of this letter in WQG-LC. In one of them "demagoguism" is in place of "jingoism."

38. Gresham to Bayard, October 29, 1893, January 21, May 2, December 24, 1894, Isidor Raynor to Gresham, January 1, 1894, Gresham to R.Q. Mills, January 23, 1895, G.G. Vest to Gresham, January 28, 1895, WQG-LC; Gresham to Bayard, March 18, June 7, 1894, February 22, 1894 [1895], TFB-LC; Gresham to Moore, December 29, 1893, JBM-LC; Gresham to John M. Palmer, January 29, 1893 [1894], John M. Palmer Papers, ISHL; Gresham to Butler, January 11, 1895, NCB-IHSL.

39. Schuyler, "Gresham," 269; Peck, *Twenty Years of the Republic*, 308; Leopold, *The Growth of American Foreign Policy,* 109; William L. Wilson, diary entry for February 11, 1894, in Festus P. Summers, ed., *The Cabinet Diary of William L. Wilson, 1896-1897*, (Chapel Hill, 1957), 25.

40. See, for example, Dorwart, *Pigtail War,* and "Gresham and East Asia"; Goll, "Diplomacy of Gresham;" Paulsen, "Gresham-Yang Treaty," and "Secretary Gresham, Senator Lodge, and American Good Offices in China".

41. LaFeber, *New Empire,* 197-229; Williams, *Roots of the Modern American Empire,* 38, 365-66, 371-72.

42. Gresham to Morris Ross, August 1, 1892, to Dyer, May 2, 1894, to Wayne MacVeagh, May 7, 1894, WQG-LC.

43. Gresham to John Overmyer, July 25, 1894, WQG-LC; Memorandum of Conversation between Gresham and Prince Cantacuzene, March 16, 1893, Miscellaneous Memoranda of Conversations of the Secretary of State, 1893-1898, RG59-NA; Moore, Diary Memoranda, 1894, Moore to Charles C. Tansill, September 16, 1940, JBM-LC; *Northwestern University Law School Circular of Information for 1891-92* (Chicago, 1891), 6, 15; *Chicago Legal News,* September 24, 1892; Gresham, *Gresham,* 2:688.

44. Gresham to Schurz, July 11, 1893, to Overmyer, July 25, 1894, to William G. Shearman, March 5, 1895, WQG-LC.

45. Memorandum of Conversation between Gresham and Prince Cantacuzene, March 16, 1893, Miscellaneous Memoranda, RG59-NA; Moore, Diary Memoranda, 1894, JBM-LC; Gresham to Overmyer, July 25, 1894, WQG-LC.

46. *FRUS*, 1893, 38-39; *FRUS*, 1894, 577-89; Richardson, *Messages and Papers*, 9:529-30; Edwin F. Uhl to John Flagg, February 12, 1895, Gresham to Flagg, March 25, 1895, Uhl to E.E. Perry, March 12, 1895, Gresham to Davis & Lawrence Co. Limited, April 18, 1895, Domestic Letters of the Department of State, RG59-NA.

47. Gresham to Bayard, June 7, 1893, Instructions—Great Britain, to R. R. Fogel & Co., February 18, 1895, Uhl to Frederick Wesson, April 29, 1895, Gresham to J.T. Morgan, January 16, 1895, Domestic Letters, RG59-NA.

48. Uhl to Joseph Scranton, December 20, 1894, to the Marlin Arms Company, February 5, 1895, to James W. Marshall, February 6, March 1, 1895, Gresham to William F. Sheehan, August 25, 1894, to E.C. Potter, August 31, 1894, Domestic Letters, RG59-NA.

49. Robert Adams, Jr., "Faults in Our Consular Service," *North American Review* 156 (April 1893), 462; Richardson, *Messages and Papers*, 9:552; *Annual Report of the Secretary of the Treasury, 1894*, lxxii; *Annual Report of the Secretary of Agriculture, 1894*, 5; Gresham to Dyer, May 2, 1894, WQG-LC.

50. Gresham note on Bayard to Gresham, September 19, 1893, Dispatches—Great Britain, RG59-NA; *Annual Report of the Bureau of the American Republics, 1893*, 20; Cushman K. Davis, "Two Years of Democratic Diplomacy," *North American Review* 160 (March 1895): 272.

51. *FRUS*, 1894, 289-90, 333-34, 618-35; Salvador de Mendonca to Gresham, August 25, September 24, 1894, Notes from Brazilian Legation, Gresham to Mendonca, August 29, October 26, 1894, Notes to Brazilian Legation, Uhl to Flint and Company, September [?], 1894, Gresham to R.D. Carver, November 11, 1894, Domestic Letters, RG59-NA.

52. Richardson, *Messages and Papers*, 9:626; *Baltimore Sun*, May 27, 1895; Lodge, "Our Blundering Foreign Policy," 12.

53. J. Lawrence Laughlin and H. Parker Willis, *Reciprocity* (New York, 1903), 262-65; *FRUS*, 1894, 234-39; *Senate Executive Document 126*, 53d Cong., 2d sess., 2.

54. Richard Olney to Grover Cleveland, October 24, 27, 1894, GC-LC.

55. "Memorandum Concerning the Protest of the German Ambassador," [filed November 1894], GC-LC.

56. *FRUS*, 1894, 50-52, 205-6, 230-33; *FRUS*, 1895, 25-37, 210-11, 402-11, 497- 501; Gresham to Theodore Runyon, October 31, 1894 (telegram), Instructions—Germany, RG59-NA; *New York Times*, November 18, 1894; *Congressional Record*, 53d Cong., 3d sess., 92-93, 2206; Gresham to the secretary of agriculture, April 1, 1895, Domestic Letters, RG59-NA.

57. Davis, "Two Years of Democratic Diplomacy," 270-73; Lodge, "Our Blundering Foreign Policy," 12-13.

58. Henry White, "Consular Reforms," *North American Review* 159 (December 1894): 713; Thomas G. Paterson, "American Businessmen and Consular Service Reform, 1890's to 1906," *Business History Review* 40 (1966): 78, n. 1; Gresham to T.E. Benedict, February 6, 1895 (telegram), Alvey A. Adee to manager, American Press Association, April 28, 1893, Adee to A.N. Kellogg, April 28, 1893, Domestic Letters, RG59-NA.

59. Adams, "Faults in Our Consular Service," 461-66; Albert H. Washburn, "Some Evils of Our Consular Service," *Atlantic Monthly* 74 (August 1894): 241-52; William Slade, "Attractions and Abuses of Our Consular Service," *Forum* 15 (April 1893): 163-71; *New York Times*, March 13, August 2, 1893; *Nation*, September 26, 1895.

60. White, "Consular Reforms," 712; Gresham to the secretary of the treasury, February 1, November 20, 1894, March 21, 1895, Domestic Letters, Uhl to Morgan, May 12, 1894, Reports to the President and Congress, RG59-NA.

61. Wilbur J. Carr, "The American Consular Service," *American Journal of International Law* 1 (1907): 903; "Who's Who—And Why," *Saturday Evening Post*, January 27, 1923, p.

62; *Congressional Record*, 53d Cong., 2d sess., 3410, 4104, 3d sess., 1815, 1955, 1983-87; *Senate Report 886*, 53d Cong., 3d sess.; Richardson, *Messages and Papers*, 9:442; Warren Frederick Ilchman, *Professional Diplomacy in the United States, 1779-1939: A Study in Administrative History* (Chicago, 1961), 65-67; Paterson, "American Businessmen and Consular Reform," 88-94.

62. James C. Olson, *J. Sterling Morton* (Lincoln, 1942; rpt. 1972), 363-64; *Annual Report of the Secretary of Agriculture, 1893*, 48; Uhl to secretary of agriculture, January 16, February 15, April 23, May 14, 1894, January 10, 1895, to Charles W. Dabney, January 25, 1895, Gresham to secretary of agriculture, March 21, 1895, Domestic Letters, RG59-NA.

63. James F. Vivian, "The Commercial Bureau of American Republics, 1894-1902: The Advertising Policy, the State Department, and the Governance of the International Union," *Proceedings of the American Philosophical Society* 118 (1974): 555; *Annual Report of the Bureau of the American Republics, 1893*, 16-17, 20.

64. Vivian, "Commercial Bureau of American Republics," 555-58; *Annual Report of the Bureau of the American Republics, 1893*, 14; *New York Times*, September 21, 1894; Gresham to R. Wayne Wilson, September 20, 1894 (telegram), to Clinton Furbish, September 22, 1894, Domestic Letters, RG59-NA; *House Executive Document 116*, 53d Cong., 3d sess.

65. Lodge, "Our Blundering Foreign Policy," 8; *Baltimore Sun*, May 27, 1895.

Chapter 8. HAWAII

1. *FRUS*, 1894, Appendix 2, 197-98, 200-5, 219-22, 567-605; Michael J. Divine, "John W. Foster and the Struggle for the Annexation of Hawaii," *PHR* 46 (1977): 31-32.

2. *New York Times*, February 24-26, 1893; John W. Foster to Gresham, February 16, 1893, WQG-LC; Foster, *Diplomatic Memoirs*, 2:168, 273; Grover Cleveland to Daniel S. Lamont, February 23, 1893, in Nevins, ed., *Letters of Cleveland*, 319; *FRUS*, 1894, Appendix 2, 867-68; *New York Herald*, February 27, 28, 1893; *Journal of the Executive Proceedings of the Senate*, 52d Cong., 2d sess., 402. An undated memorandum by Gresham's son, Otto, in WQG-LC states that Cleveland, Gresham, and Carlisle decided at Lakewood to send a commissioner to Hawaii.

3. Richardson, *Messages and Papers*, 9:393; *FRUS*, 1894, Appendix 2, 1185-87; *DAB*, 2:388-89.

4. Foster, *Memoirs*, 2:168; "Memorandum for Mr. Parker," LTM-LC; *Public Opinion*, March 18, 1893; Benjamin Harrison to E.W. Halford, March 12, 1893, BH-LC; Lorrin A. Thurston, *Memoirs of the Hawaiian Revolution*, edited by Andrew Farrell (Honolulu, 1936), 560-61; Memorandum of Conversation among Gresham, Thurston, and W.R. Castle, March 10, 1893, Miscellaneous Memoranda of Conversations of the Secretary of State, 1893-1898, RG59-NA; J. Mott Smith to Sanford B. Dole, April 6, 1893, THA-UM; Cleveland to Carl Schurz, March 19, 1893, in Frederic Bancroft, ed., *Speeches, Correspondence, and Political Papers of Carl Schurz*, 6 vols., (New York, 1913), 5:133-34.

5. *FRUS*, 1894, Appendix 2, 1185-87.

6. *Senate Report 227*, 53d Cong., 2d sess., 386, 389, 397, 401-2, 406-7, 409, 411-14 (hereafter *Morgan Report*); *FRUS*, 1894, Appendix 2, 420-21, 470-74.

7. Thurston, *Memoirs*, 291-95, 296-301; Memoranda of Conversations between Gresham and Thurston, June 14, 16, August 14, 1893, Miscellaneous Memoranda, Thurston to Gresham, June 19, 1893, Notes from Hawaiian Legation, RG59-NA.

8. *FRUS*, 1894, Appendix 2, 567-605; Gresham to Schurz, September 14, November 21, 1893, CS-LC; *Morgan Report*, 395; *New York Times*, August 23, 1893.

9. Richard Olney to Gresham, October 9, 1893, WQG-LC. There is no direct evidence that Gresham at this time proposed the executive use of military force to restore the queen, but Olney's addressing himself particularly to that point suggests that Gresham was contemplating such a procedure.

10. *FRUS*, 1894, Appendix 2, 421; Wayne MacVeagh to Cleveland, June 12, 1893, J. Proctor Knott to Gresham, June 19, 1893, GC-LC; John Bassett Moore, Diary Memoranda, 1894, JBM-LC; *DAB*, 2:587-88, 20:304-5.

11. Gresham to Albert S. Willis, September 19, 1893 (telegram), Instructions—Hawaii, Willis to Gresham, September 19, 1893, Dispatches—Hawaii, RG59-NA; *FRUS*, 1894, Appendix 2, 432-33, 463-64, 1271.

12. *FRUS*, 1894, Appendix 2, 459-63. Gresham's wife and later historians erroneously concluded that this October 18 report constituted Gresham's "recommendation" to Cleveland about Hawaii. Gresham had presented his recommendation long before and had already adapted Olney's suggestions to his restoration plan. The previous day, October 17, Gresham's secretary requested Willis to be at the State Department at 10 A.M., October 18, the day he received his instructions, thereby indicating that a policy had already been arrived at. Gresham's report was a public relations device designed to put the best face on the restoration policy, which was bound to draw partisan criticism. See Gresham, *Gresham*, 2:746-52; Henry James, *Richard Olney and His Public Services* (Boston, 1923), 89; Eggert, *Olney*; 185; William Adam Russ, Jr., *The Hawaiian Revolution (1893-94)* (Selinsgrove, Pa., 1959), 228-29; Gresham to Schurz, September 14, 1893, CS-LC; K.M. Landis to Willis, October 17, 1893, ASW-FC.

13. *FRUS*, 1894, Appendix 2, 430-33, 1241-43; Willis to Gresham, December 9, 1893, GC-LC.

14. Gresham to Olney, November 18, 1893, RO-LC.

15. Thurston, *Memoirs*, 310-312; *New York Herald*, November 8, 9, 10, 1893; *Washington Post*, November 11, 1893; Russ, *Hawaiian Revolution*, 245.

16. Memorandum of Conversation between Gresham and Thurston, November 14, 1893, Miscellaneous Memoranda, RG59-NA; Thurston, *Memoirs*, 323-335.

17. *Public Opinion*, November 16, 23, 30, 1893; *Literary Digest*, November 18, 25, December 2, 1893; Harrison to Halford, November 20, 1893, BH-LC; Gresham to N.C. Butler, November 23, 1893, NCB-IHSL; Thurston, *Memoirs*, 335-40; *FRUS*, 1894, Appendix 2, 1246-57.

18. *FRUS*, 1894, Appendix 2, 442, 463, 464; Willis to Gresham, December 9, 1893, Charles Nordhoff to Gresham, December 9, 1893, GC-LC.

19. *FRUS*, 1894, Appendix 2, 437, 1262-82.

20. *FRUS*, 1894, Appendix 2, 1283-84; Gresham to Willis, January 12, 1894, ASW-FC; Moore, Diary Memoranda, 1894, JBM-LC.

21. *Congressional Record*, 53d Cong., 2d sess., 19, 61-73, 82, 194-99, 220-21; *House Miscellaneous Document 42*, 53d Cong., 2d sess.

22. Gresham to Moore, November 24 (telegram), December 29, 1893, Gresham-Moore draft, November, 1893, JBM-LC; Olney draft, December, 1893, RO-LC; Olney to Cleveland, December 16, 1893, GC-LC; *FRUS*, 1894, Appendix 2, 445-58.

23. Gresham to Willis, February 3, 1894, ASW-FC; *Congressional Record*, 53d Cong., 2d sess., 127-31, 189-90, 196-98, 204-6, 1300, 1594, 1813-22, 1825-51, 1879-89, 1942-72, 2000-2008, 2281-91, 3138-39; Gresham to Mrs. Bertha Honore Palmer, January 15, 1894, World's Columbian Exposition—Palmer Collection, Chicago Historical Society.

24. Gresham to John M. Palmer, January 29, 1893 [1894], John M. Palmer Papers, ISHL; Gresham to Thomas F. Bayard, December 17, 1893, Gray's remarks in Gresham to Bayard, January 21, 1894, WQG-LC; Thurston, *Memoirs*, 473-74.

25. *Morgan Report*, 1-30.

26. For debate in the Senate, see *Congressional Record*, 53d Cong., 2d sess., January-May 1894, passim; texts of various resolutions introduced appear on pages 523, 1220, 1308, 1313, 1446-47, 5127, 5195, 5246, 5369, 5434, 5499; Gresham to Willis, June 2, 1894, Instructions—Hawaii, RG59-NA.

27. Gresham to Schurz, October 6, 1893, to Bayard, December 17, 1893, January 21, 1894, to John Overmyer, July 25, 1894, to William G. Shearman, March 5, 1895, WQG-LC; Gresham to Butler, November 23, 1893, NCB-IHSL.

28. Thurston, *Memoirs*, 552; Gresham to Willis, January 12, February 3, March 14, 1894, ASW-FC; Gresham to Willis, February 9, 1894, Instructions—Hawaii, RG59-NA.

29. Gresham to John S. Cooper, February 5, 1894, WQG-LC; Gresham to Willis, January 12, February 3, March 14, 1894, ASW-FC.

30. *FRUS*, 1894, Appendix 2, 1313-14, 1343-50; Willis to Gresham, May 14, 1894, GC-LC; Willis to Gresham, July 9, 1894, WQG-LC; Gresham to Willis, August 7, 1894, Instructions—Hawaii, RG59-NA; Gresham's disapproval of the qualified recognition was in a private letter, Gresham to Willis, July 27, 1894, ASW-FC. In his official dispatch he termed it "clearly proper" (Gresham to Willis, August 8, 1894, Instructions—Hawaii, RG59-NA).

31. *Senate Executive Document 16*, 53d Cong., 3d sess.; Willis to Gresham, June 23, September 29, 1894, John G. Walker to Willis, June 12, 1894 (two letters), WQG-LC; Gresham to Willis, May 12, July 22, 27, August 31, 1894, ASW-FC; Gresham to Moore, December 22, 1894, JBM-LC; *FRUS*, 1894, Appendix 2, 1341-42, 1376-78.

32. Memoranda of Conversations between Gresham and H.A. Widemann, August 2, 4, 1894, and between Gresham and Samuel Parker, August 5, 1894, Miscellaneous Memoranda, RG59-NA; Cleveland's statement to royalists in memorandum, "Interview given out January 6/95 Papers of January 7/95," filed in GC-LC under date of August 11, 1894.

33. William Adam Russ, Jr., *The Hawaiian Republic (1894-98)* (Selinsgrove, Pa., 1961), 51-53; Willis to Gresham, September 29, 1894, WQG-LC; Willis to Gresham, [November 10, 1894] (telegram), January 5, 1895, Dispatches—Hawaii, Memorandum of Conversation between Gresham and Frank P. Hastings, November 19, 1894, Miscellaneous Memoranda, RG59-NA; *FRUS*, 1894, Appendix 2, 1392-93; Gresham to Olney, November 17, 18, 1894, RO-LC; Gresham to Willis, November 19, 1894, ASW-FC.

34. *Congressional Record*, 53d Cong., 3d sess., 17, 427, 555, 622-30, 693-94, 712-18; *Senate Executive Document 16*, 53d Cong., 3d sess.; Gresham to Moore, December 22, 1894, JBM-LC.

35. Willis to Gresham, December 14, 1894, January 11, 1895 (telegram), Dispatches—Hawaii, RG59-NA; *FRUS*, 1894, Appendix 2, 1393-94; *FRUS*, 1895, 818-20; *New York Times*, January 21, 1895.

36. Gresham to Roger Q. Mills, January 23, 1895, WQG-LC; *Congressional Record*, 53d Cong., 3d sess., 1133-39, 1167, 1170-74, 1200, 1205-13, 1277-83, 1329-36, 1408-12, 1460.

37. *FRUS*, 1894, Appendix 2, 1396-97; *FRUS*, 1895, 818-20, 834, 835, 843; Willis to Gresham, January 30, 1895, WQG-LC; Gresham to Willis, February 20, 1895, ASW-FC; Willis to Gresham, April 30, 1895, JBM-LC; Russ, *Hawaiian Republic*, 84-94.

38. *FRUS*, 1895, 842-43; Gresham to Bayard, February 22, 1894 [1895], TFB-LC; Moore, Diary Memoranda, 1895, JBM-LC.

39. *Congressional Record*, 53d Cong., 3d sess., 1969-70; Gresham to Shearman, March 5, 1895, WQG-LC; Gresham to Willis, February 20, 1895, ASW-FC; Moore, Diary Memoranda, 1895, JBM-LC.

40. Thurston, *Memoirs*, 526-27, 556-57; *FRUS*, 1895, 867-73; Memorandum of Con-

versation between Gresham and Thurston, February 16, 1895, Miscellaneous Memoranda, RG59-NA.

41. *New York Herald*, February 13, 1895; Thurston, *Memoirs*, 537-38, 557-59; *FRUS*, 1895, 876-79.

42. Richardson, *Messages and Papers*, 8:500, 783; Moore, Diary Memoranda, 1894, JBM-LC.

43. Gresham, *Gresham*, 2:776, n. 1; Gresham to Shearman, March 5, 1895, WQG-LC.

44. D.S. Alexander to Harrison, December 4, 1893, BH-LC.

Chapter 9. SAMOA

1. *FRUS*, 1894, Appendix 1, 508.

2. Paul M. Kennedy, *The Samoan Tangle: A Study in Anglo-German-American Relations, 1878-1900* (New York, 1974), chaps. 1-2; George H. Ryden, *The Foreign Policy of the United States in Relation to Samoa* (New Haven, 1933), 523-25; *FRUS*, 1894, Appendix 1, 510-11.

3. Kennedy, *Samoan Tangle*, 99-104; Gresham to Carl Schurz, July 11, 1893, CS-LC; Gresham to Thomas F. Bayard, July 14, 1893, Instructions—Great Britain, to William Blacklock, July 24 (telegram), September 7 (telegram), 1893, Register of Consular Communications Sent, RG59-NA; *FRUS*, 1894, Appendix 1, 511-12, 590, 594, 596-97, 679-85, 738-39; *Senate Executive Document 97*, 53d Cong., 3d sess., 270, 277, 301-7.

4. *FRUS*, 1894, Appendix 1, 590, 591, 685, 693-95, 698-702, 704-5; Julian Pauncefote to Gresham, June 21, 1893, WQG-LC; Bayard to Gresham, June 21, 27 (telegram), 28, 1893, Dispatches—Great Britain, Alvey A. Adee note dated December 1, 1893, attached to Blacklock to Josiah Quincy, November 7, 1893, Consular Dispatches—Apia, RG59-NA; Gresham to Schurz, July 11, 1893, CS-LC; Charles C. Tansill, *The Foreign Policy of Thomas F. Bayard, 1885-1897* (New York, 1940), 62-63.

5. John Bassett Moore, Diary Memoranda, 1894, JBM-LC; Richardson, *Messages and Papers*, 8:805, 9:439.

6. Moore to Gresham, April 2, 1894, Moore, Diary Memoranda, 1894, JBM-LC.

7. William L. Chambers to D.S. Lamont, January 3, 1894, GC-LC; *Senate Executive Document 97*, 53d Cong., 3d sess., 328-35.

8. *Congressional Record*, 53d Cong., 2d sess., 3493, 4537; Gresham to Schurz, May 26, 1894, CS-LC; Moore to Gresham, April 2, 1894, Moore, Diary Memoranda, 1894, JBM-LC; *Senate Eecutive Document 97*, 53d Cong., 3d sess., 336-38; *FRUS*, 1894, Appendix 1, 619.

9. This and the following five paragraphs are from *FRUS,1894*, Appendix 1, 504-13.

10. *Springfield Republican*, n.d., and *Chicago Inter-Ocean*, n.d., quoted in *Literary Digest*, May 26, 1894; *New York Mail and Express*, n.d., quoted in *Public Opinion*, May 17, 1894.

11. *Senate Executive Document 132*, 53d Cong., 2d sess.; *Journal of the Executive Proceedings of the Senate*, 53d Cong., 2d sess., 771-72.

12. *FRUS*, 1894, Appendix 1, 729-31; *Senate Executive Document 97*, 53d Cong., 3d sess., 376-78, 381-86; James H. Mulligan to Gresham, September 11, 1894, Consular Dispatches—Apia, RG59-NA; Richardson, *Messages and Papers*, 9:531-32.

13. Gresham to Bayard, February 22, 1894 [1895], TFB-LC; Edwin F. Uhl to John T. Morgan, December 7, 1894, Gresham to Morgan, December 8, 1894, Reports of the Secretary of State to the President and Congress, RG59–NA; Gresham to John Overmyer, July 25, 1894, WQG-LC.

14. *FRUS*, 1895, 1134-37; Uhl to Mullgan, June 16, 1895, Records of the United States Consulate in Samoa, Records of the Foreign Service Posts of the United States, Record Group 84, NA.

15. Gresham to Moore, December 28, 1894, JBM-LC; *Congressional Record*, 53d Cong., 2d sess., 1333-34.

16. Lodge, "Our Blundering Foreign Policy," 10.

17. *FRUS*, 1894, Appendix 1, 504-13; Gresham to Overmyer, July 25, 1894, WQG-LC; Moore, Diary Memoranda, 1894, JBM-LC.

Chapter 10. THE ORIENT AND THE LEVANT

1. *FRUS*, 1894, Appendix 1, 508.

2. For treatments of the Sino-Japanese War, see John W. Foster, *American Diplomacy in the Orient* (Boston, 1903), 332-43; Tyler Dennett, *Americans in Eastern Asia* (New York, 1941), 482-502; Dorwart, *Pigtail War.*

3. Dennett, *Americans in Eastern Asia*, 495; Charles I. Bevans, comp., *Treaties and Other International Agreements of the United States of America, 1776-1949*, 12 vols., (Washington, D.C., 1971), 9:471; *FRUS*, 1894, Appendix 1, 22, 37.

4. Richardson, *Messages and Papers*, 9:525; Memorandum of Conversation between Gresham and Japanese Minister Gozo Tateno, July 7, 1894, Notes from Japanese Legation, Gresham to Edwin Dun, July 7, 1894 (telegram), Instructions—Japan, Dun to Gresham, July 10, 1894 (telegram), Dispatches—Japan, Gresham to Thomas F. Bayard, July 20, 1894, Instructions—Great Britain, RG59-NA; Dorwart, *Pigtail War*, 23-24.

5. Memoranda of Conversations between Gresham and Julian Pauncefote, July [8], 9, 1894, and between Gresham and the Chinese minister, July 13, 1894, Miscellaneous Memoranda of Conversations of the Secretary of State, 1893-1898, RG59-NA; *FRUS*, 1894, Appendix 1, 36-37; *Washington Post*, July 19, 1894; *Public Opinion*, July 26, 1894; *Literary Digest*, July 28, 1894.

6. Gresham to Albert S. Willis, September 28, 1894, ASW-FC; Gresham to Grover Cleveland, October 2, 1894, GC-LC; *FRUS*, 1894, Appendix 1, 70-71, 78-79, 81-82; Gresham to Cleveland, October 12, 1894 (telegram), Cleveland to Gresham, October 12, 1894 (telegram), WQG-LC.

7. *FRUS*, 1894, Appendix 1, 73-77, 81-82; Charles Denby, Jr., to Gresham, October 27, 1894 (telegram), Charles Denby to Gresham, November 3, 1894 (telegram), Dispatches—China, Memoranda of Conversations between Gresham and the Russian Minister, November 15, 1894, and between Gresham and the French Ambassador, November 8, 1894, Miscellaneous Memoranda, RG59-NA.

8. *FRUS*, 1894, Appendix 1, 77-81; Gresham to Dun, March 26, 1895, Instructions—Japan, Dun to Gresham, November 17, 1894 (telegram), Dispatches—Japan, Gresham to Denby, December 2, 1894 (telegram), February 7 (telegram), 18 (telegram), 1895, April 12, 1894 [1895] (telegram), Instructions—China, Denby to Gresham, November 30 (telegram), December 20, 1894, February 26, 1895, Dispatches—China, Memorandum of Conversation between Gresham and the Chinese Minister, December 2, 1894, Miscellaneous Memoranda, RG59-NA.

9. Denby to Gresham, December 26, 1894, March 5, May 10 (personal), 12 (telegram), 16 (telegram), 1895, Dispatches-China, Gresham to Denby, April 12, 1895 (two telegrams), Edwin F. Uhl to Denby, May 14, 1895 (telegram), Richard Olney to Denby, June 22, 1895, Instructions—China, RG59-NA; Gresham to Denby, April 12, 1895, WQG-LC. After Gresham's death Acting Secretary Edwin F. Uhl instructed Denby to try to ensure that the United States received the same commercial advantages as other treaty powers resulting from the peace treaty between China and Japan (Uhl to Denby, June 8, 1895, Instructions—China, RG59-NA).

10. *FRUS*, 1895, 199-203; Philip Joseph, *Foreign Diplomacy in China, 1894-1900* (Lon-

don, 1928), 124-32; Marilyn Blatt Young, *The Rhetoric of Empire: American China Policy, 1895-1901* (Cambridge, Mass., 1968), 33.

11. Denby to Gresham, December 26, 1894, March 5, 1895, Dispatches—China, RG59-NA; *Literary Digest*, November 24, December 1, 1894.

12. *Senate Executive Document 36*, 53d Cong., 3d sess.; *FRUS*, 1894, 95-127; Tsungli Yamen to Yang Yu, August 18, 1894 (telegram), Yang to Gresham, August 22, 1894, Notes from Chinese Legation, Gresham to Yang, August 21, 25, 29, 1894, Notes to Chinese Legation, Gresham to Shinichiro Kurino, August 29, 1894, Notes to Japanese Legation, RG59-NA.

13. *FRUS*, 1894, 108-10, 119-22; *Senate Executive Document 36*, 53d Cong., 3d sess., 29-33; Gresham to John Bassett Moore, October 12, 19, 1894, Moore to Gresham, October 13, 1894, JBM-LC.

14. *Senate Executive Document 36*, 53d Cong., 3d sess., 37; Memorandum of Conversation between Gresham and the Chinese Minister, November 15, 1894, Miscellaneous Memoranda, RG59-NA; Gresham to Moore, November 30, December 22, 1894, Moore draft of Note to Chinese Minister, JBM-LC; *FRUS*, 1894, 124-27.

15. *Harper's Weekly*, December 1, 1894; *New York Times*, November 28, 29, 1894; *Literary Digest*, December 8, 1894; *New York Post*, December 3, 1894; Gresham to Moore, November 30, December 6, 1894, JBM-LC; Theodore Roosevelt to Henry Cabot Lodge, December 1, 1894, in Henry Cabot Lodge, ed., *Selections from the Correspondence of Theodore Roosevelt and Henry Cabot Lodge, 1884-1918*, 2 vols. (New York, 1925), 1:140; Richardson, *Messages and Papers*, 9:525.

16. Roosevelt to Lodge, December 1, 1894, in Lodge, ed., *Selections*, 1:140; *Congressional Record*, 53d Cong., 3d sess., 12, 39-41, 578, 967; Gresham to John T. Morgan, December 6, 1894, Gresham to John Sherman, December 6, 1894, Gresham to Denby, December 26, 1894, WQG-LC; Gresham to Moore, December 6, 1894, JBM-LC; Gresham to Noble C. Butler, January 11, 1895, NCB-IHSL; *Public Opinion*, January 24, 1895; Davis, "Two Years of Democratic Diplomacy," 270-84.

17. Paulsen, "Gresham-Yang Treaty," 281-91; 27 *U.S. Statutes at Large*, 25-26; *FRUS*, 1893, 234-35, 245-51, 253-58, 263-64; Gresham to Denby, April 24, 1893 (telegram), Instructions—China, RG59-NA; Morgan to Gresham, October 23, 25, 1893, WQG-LC; *Congressional Record*, 53d Cong., 1st sess., 1361, 2132, 2420-25, 2435-58, 2482, 2500, 2513-31, 2551-67, 2601, 2929, 3040-55, 3079-92. 3126, Appendix, 226-36; *House Report 70*, 53d Cong., 1st sess.; 28 *U.S. Statutes at Large*, 7-8.

18. Yang to Gresham, December 6, 9, 1893, WQG-LC; Yang to Gresham, December 26, 1893, January 8, 11, 24, 31, 1894, Notes from Chinese Legation, Gresham to Yang, January 5, 29, February 8, 1894, Notes to Chinese Legation, RG59-NA; *FRUS*, 1888, 398-400.

19. Yang to Gresham, February 19, 22, 1894, Notes from Chinese Legation, Gresham to Yang, February 20, 1894, Notes to Chinese Legation, RG59-NA; *FRUS*, 1894, 177-79.

20. *Public Opinion*, March 29, 1894; *Literary Digest*, April 7, September 1, 1894; Morgan to Cleveland, April 16, 1894, GC-LC; Morgan to Gresham, April 16 (two letters), May 26, July 9, 1894, Gresham to Morgan, July 10, 1894, WQG-LC; Moore, Diary Memoranda, 1894, JBM-LC; *Journal of the Executive Proceedings of the Senate*, 53d Cong., 2d sess., 773-75; *Congressional Record*, 53d Cong., 2d sess., 8499; Gresham to Denby, Jr., April 14, 1894, Instructions—China, Yang to Gresham, February 28, December 11, 28, 1894, Notes from Chinese Legation, Uhl to Yang, March 2, 1894, Gresham to Yang, December 26, 1894, Notes to Chinese Legation, Gresham to Stephen M. White, December 24, 1894, Domestic Letters, Gresham to the chairman of the Committee on Foreign Relations, December 24, 1894, Gresham to the chairman of the Committee on Foreign Affairs, December 24, 1894, Reports of the Secretary of State to the President and Congress, RG59-NA.

21. Gresham to Denby, December 1 (telegram), 4 (telegram), 1894, Instructions—China, Memoranda of Conversations between Gresham and the Chinese Minister, December 1, 10, 1894, Miscellaneous Memoranda, RG59-NA. The treaty remained in force until 1904, when China refused to renew it for another ten years (Paulsen, "Gresham-Yang Treaty," 297).

22. Dun to Gresham, February 21, April 21 (telegram), 30, September 8, 1894, Dispatches—Japan, Tateno to Gresham, March 14, May 28, July 19, 1894, Mutsu to Tateno, June 7, 1894, Memorandum of Conversation between Gresham and Tateno, July 7, 1894, Notes from Japanese Legation, Gresham to Dun, June 11, 1894, Instructions—Japan, Gresham to Bayard, July 23, 1894 (telegram), Instructions—Great Britain, Bayard to Gresham, July 25, 1894, Dispatches—Great Britain, RG59-NA; Tateno to Gresham, March 12, April 23, 1894, to K.M. Landis, March 29, 1894, WQG-LC; Payson J. Treat, *Diplomatic Relations between the United States and Japan, 1853-1895*, 2 vols. (Stanford, 1932), 2:418-427.

23. Tateno to Gresham, July 19, 1894, Kurino to Gresham, October 20, November 18, 1894, Notes from Japanese Legation, Gresham to Kurino, November 5, 22, 1894, Notes to Japanese Legation, RG59-NA; Kurino to Gresham, November 21, 22, 1894, WQG-LC; Bevans, comp., *Treaties*, 9:387-96.

24. Gresham to Morgan, January 10, 1895, WQG-LC; *Journal of the Executive Proceedings of the Senate*, 53d Cong., 3d sess., 845, 891, 906, 911-12, 917; *Public Opinion*, February 7, 1895; Gresham to Kurino, March 2, 27, 1895, Notes to Japanese Legation, RG59-NA.

25. Young, *Rhetoric of Empire*, 242, n. 72.

26. Bevans, comp., *Treaties*, 10:619-27; Richardson, Messages and Papers , 7:277-81; "Marsovan Incident," March 18, 1893, Reports of the Diplomatic Bureau, Gresham to Judson Smith, June 2, 1893, Domestic Letters of the Department of State, and Domestic Letters, passim, RG59-NA.

27. *FRUS*, 1893, 624-26, 656-57; *FRUS*, 1894, 702, 740; *FRUS*, 1895, 1236; Gresham to A.W. Terrell, March 20, 28, 1895, Instructions—Turkey, RG59-NA.

28. *FRUS*, 1893, 693, 699, 703, 715-16; *FRUS*, 1894, 693, 738-39, 752-56.

29. Uhl to Terrell, March 27, 1894, Instructions—Turkey, Terrell to Gresham, September 28, November 23, 1894, Dispatches—Turkey, RG59-NA. On one of these dispatches Gresham's private secretary, Kenesaw Mountain Landis, noted: "Not to go to Congress or in Foreign Relations. KML."

30. *New York Times*, November 17, 18, 1894; *FRUS*, 1894, 718-23; *Congressional Record*, 53d Cong., 3d sess., 12; Bayard to Gresham, December 10, 1894, TFB- LC; Gresham to Bayard, December 24, 1894, WQG-LC; Gresham to Terrell, December 19 (telegram), 26 (telegram), 1894, January 10, 1895, Instructions—Turkey, Terrell to Gresham, December 20 (telegram), 25 (telegram), 1894, Dispatches—Turkey, RG59-NA.

31. Gresham to Terrell, January 30, February 14, 1895, Instructions—Turkey, Terrell to Gresham, December 10, 1894 (with Gresham note), Dispatches—Turkey, RG59-NA; Lodge, "Our Blundering Foreign Policy," 11; *FRUS*, 1894, 744-45, 753-54, 767.

32. Gresham to Terrell, March 2, 1895, WQG-LC; Gresham to Terrell, March 6, 1895, Instructions—Turkey, Gresham to Judson Smith, February 11, 1895, to James L. Barton, March 26, 1895, Domestic Letters, RG59-NA.

33. Uhl to Terrell, April 8, 1895, Instructions—Turkey, to Secretary of the Navy, April 4, 1895, Domestic Letters, RG59-NA; *FRUS*, 1895, 1242-50; H.L. Bryan to Bayard, April 5, 1895, TFB-LC. Bryan, a State Department official, thought Gresham had gone "a little far in his disapproval [of Terrell], or rather in his desire to have it made public."

34. *FRUS*, 1895, 1238; Terrell to Gresham, April 21, 1895, Dispatches—Turkey, Uhl to Judson Smith, May 11, 1895, Domestic Letters, RG59-NA.

Chapter 11. THE WESTERN HEMISPHERE

1. John B. Henderson, *American Diplomatic Questions* (New York, 1901), 10-13.

2. Ibid., 12-14; *Senate Executive Document 67*, 53d Cong., 3d sess., 32-34; Tansill, *Bayard*, 456.

3. Henderson, *Diplomatic Questions*, 10, 14-31; Tansill, *Bayard*, 453-503; Robert Craig Brown, *Canada's National Policy, 1883-1900: A Study in Canadian-American Relations* (Princeton, 1964), 51-53.

4. Bevans, comp., *Treaties*, 12:220-25.

5. "Statement for Mr. Otto Gresham prepared by Henry W. Elliott," April 6, 1913, WQG-LC.

6. At Foster's suggestion, after the completion of oral arguments Halford was relieved and Foster assumed his responsibilities as disbursing officer. *New York Times*, March 31, April 1, 2, 3, 1893; Gresham to E.J. Phelps and James E. Carter, April 2, 1893, to John W. Foster, May 25, 1893, to E.W. Halford, May 26, 1893, Instructions—Special Missions, RG59-NA; Gresham to John M. Harlan, April 4, 1893, Foster to Gresham, April 4, 17, 1893, WQG-LC; Halford to Benjamin Harrison, April 8, 1893, Foster to Harrison, April 16, 1893, Harrison to Foster, May 1, 1893, unidentified newspaper clipping, April 15, 1893, BH-LC; Gresham to Foster, April 11, 1893, JWF-LC.

7. Gresham to Foster, March 21 (telegram), August 5, 1893, Instructions—Special Missions, RG59-NA; Gresham to Foster, July 14, 1893, JWF-LC; *Senate Executive Document 67*, 53d Cong., 3d sess., 23-26; Foster to Gresham, September 22, 1893 (copy), BH-LC.

8. *FRUS*, 1894, Appendix 1, 109-17.

9. Foster to Gresham, September 22, 1893 (copy), BH-LC; *Senate Executive Document 67*, 53d Cong., 3d sess., 23-26; Gresham to Bayard, September 13, 1893, to Foster, October 9, 1893, WQG-LC.

10. Brown, *Canada's National Policy*, 42-54, 91-124.

11. Gresham to Foster, September 11, October 9, 1893, to Bayard, October 29, 1893, January 21, 1894, Bayard to Gresham, November 25, December 28, 1893, February 6, 1894, WQG-LC; Gresham to Bayard, September 13, December 5, 1893, Instructions—Great Britain, to Phelps, October 27, 1893, Instructions—Special Missions, to Sir Julian Pauncefote, October 13, 1893, Notes to British Embassy, Bayard to Gresham, November 23, 1893, Dispatches—Great Britain, RG59-NA; H.L. Bryan to Bayard, December 1, 1893, January 30, 1894, TFB-LC; *FRUS*, 1894, Appendix 1, 118, 119, 120, 133, 136; Gresham to Oscar Straus, December 14, 1893, OS-LC; Bayard to Grover Cleveland, December 6, 1893, GC-LC; Gresham to John Bassett Moore, February 19, 1894, JBM-LC.

12. *FRUS*, 1894, Appendix 1, 140-42; Bayard to Gresham, November 23, 1893, Dispatches—Great Britain, Gresham to Bayard, December 5, 1893, Instructions—Great Britain, RG59-NA; Gresham to Bayard, December 17, 1893, to Foster, September 11, 1893, WQG-LC.

13. Gresham to Bayard, January 21, 1894, Moore to Gresham, January 22, 1894, John T. Morgan to Gresham, February 21, 1894, Gresham to Morgan, February 23, 1894, WQG-LC; Gresham to Morgan, February 19, 1894, JTM-LC; Bryan to Bayard, January 30, 1894, TFB-LC; *FRUS*, 1894, Appendix 1, 142-50, 156; Gresham to Bayard, March 20, 1894, Instructions—Great Britain, Memoranda of Conversations between Gresham and Pauncefote, March 7, 8, 23, 24, 1894, Notes from British Embassy, RG59-NA.

14. Memoranda of Conversations between Gresham and Pauncefote, March 23, 24, 1894, Notes from British Embassy, Memorandum Handed by the Secretary of State to the British Ambassador, April 7, 1894, Notes to British Embassy, RG59-NA; *FRUS*, 1894, Appendix 1, 165-66, 168-73, 178-81; Gresham to Morgan, February 23, 1894, Bayard to

Gresham, April 11, 1894, WQG-LC; *Congressional Record*, 53d Cong., 2d sess., 3385-89, 3400, 3413-15, 3457, 3471-73, 3611.

15. Bevans, comp., *Treaties*, 12:220-25; *FRUS*, 1894, Appendix 1, 121-22, 133, 135-38, 141, 153, 156-59, 161-63, 176, 185, 190-91, 201, 213-14, 216, 217-24; Gresham to Bayard, October 27, 1893, Instructions—Great Britain, to Edwin Dun, November 11, 1893 (telegram), Instructions—Japan, Dun to Gresham, November 21, 1893 (telegram), Dispatches—Japan, Japanese foreign minister to Japanese minister at Washington, November 26, 1893 (telegram), Notes from Japanese Legation, RG59-NA; Gozo Tateno to Gresham, November 21, 1893, Gresham to Prince Cantacuzene, March 24, 1894, to Morgan, May 12, 1894, WQG-LC; Moore, Diary Memoranda, 1894, JBM-LC; 28 *U.S. Statutes at Large*, 85, 1202-4.

16. *FRUS*, 1894, Appendix 1, 204-11; *House Executive Documents 132* and *310*, 53d Cong., 3d sess.; Pauncefote to Gresham, February 19, August 15, 1894, "Mr. Gresham's Counter Draft as Amended," August 14, 1894, Notes from British Embassy, Gresham to Pauncefote, August 8, 1894, Notes to British Embassy, Bayard to Gresham, March 9, 1894, Dispatches—Great Britain, RG59-NA; Gresham to Richard Olney, July 21, 1894, Pauncefote to Gresham, July 23, August 11, 1894, James E. Carter to Gresham, July 31, 1894, Gresham to Carter, August 3, 1894, to W.C.P. Breckenridge, February 20, 1895, Bayard to Gresham, March 9, 1895, WQG-LC; Gresham to Bayard, February 22, 1894 [1895], TFB-LC; *Congressional Record*, 53d Cong., 3d sess., 2961, 3040, 3139-41; Tansill, *Bayard*, 522-24.

17. *Senate Executive Document 67*, 53d Cong., 3d sess., 23-26; *FRUS*, 1894, Appendix 1, 226-28; *House Executive Documents 243* and *306*, 53d Cong., 3d sess.; *FRUS*, 1895, 593-608, 610-15.

18. Gresham to Moore, December 28, 1894, January 5, 1895 (telegram), draft of resolution, JBM-LC; *Congressional Record*, 53d Cong., 3d sess., 217, 926, 1258-59, 2361, 3010-13, 3139-41; Gresham to Carter, February 2, 1895, "Statement for Mr. Otto Gresham prepared by Henry W. Elliott," April 6, 1913, WQG-LC; *FRUS*, 1894, Appendix 1, 226-29.

19. *FRUS*, 1895, 615-23; Richardson, *Messages and Papers*, 9:630; Thomas A. Bailey, "The North Pacific Sealing Convention of 1911," *PHR*, 4 (1935): 1-14.

20. *Congressional Record*, 53d Cong., 3d sess., 3011-12; *FRUS*, 1894, Appendix 1, 228-29; Gresham to Bayard, March 20, 1894, Instructions—Great Britain, RG59-NA.

21. Gresham to Morgan, March 29, 1894, JTM-LC; Foster to Gresham, September 22, 1893 (copy), BH-LC; Gresham to Moore, January 29, 1895, Moore to Gresham, January 31, 1895, JBM-LC; Eggert, *Olney*, 250-53; John Bassett Moore, *History and Digest of International Arbitrations to Which the United States Has Been a Party*, 6 vols., (Washington, D.C., 1898), 1:962-89.

22. Salvador de Mendonca to Gresham, August 25, September 24, 1894, Notes from Brazilian Legation, Gresham to Mendonca, August 29, October 26, 1894, Notes to Brazilian Legation, RG59-NA.

23. João Pandía Calogeras, *A History of Brazil*, trans. and ed. Percy Alvin Martin (Chapel Hill, 1939), 276-95; E. Bradford Burns, *A History of Brazil* (New York, 1970), 209-14; June E. Hahner, *Civilian-Military Relations in Brazil, 1889-1898* (Columbia, S.C., 1969), 47-69; Thomas L. Thompson to Gresham, September 6 (telegram), 7, 1893, Dispatches—Brazil, RG59-NA; Salvador de Mendonca, "Latest Aspects of the Brazilian Rebellion," *North American Review* 158 (1894): 168.

24. Thompson to Gresham, September 8 (telegram), 28 (telegram), October 2 (telegram), 9 (telegram), 13 (telegram), 1893, Dispatches—Brazil, Edward H. Strobel to Thompson, September 28, 1893 (telegram), Instructions—Brazil, RG59-NA; *Report of the Secretary of the Navy, 1894*, 23; Henry F. Picking to Hilary A. Herbert, October 7, 14, 1893, Area 4 File, RG45-NA; *Rio News*, October 11, 1893.

25. Thompson to Gresham, October 12 (telegram), 21 (telegram), November 8 (telegram), 9 (telegram), 10, December 5, 1893, January 12, 1894, Dispatches—Brazil, Gresham to Thompson, January 10, 1894, Instructions—Brazil, RG59-NA; Herbert to Picking, October 9, 1893 (telegram), January 6, 1894 (telegram), Cipher Dispatches Sent, Picking to Herbert, October 20, November 15, 17, December 15, 1893, January 4, 10, 1894, Oscar F. Stanton to Herbert, October 22, 1893, Area 4 File, Picking to Herbert, January 5, 1894 (two telegrams), Cipher Dispatches Received, RG45-NA.

26. Gresham to Thompson, October 11, 1893 (telegram), Instructions—Brazil, Thompson to Gresham, October 12 (telegram), 13 (two letters), 1893, Dispatches—Brazil, RG59-NA.

27. Picking to Herbert, November 4, 17, 1893, Area 4 File, Picking to Herbert, November 13, 1893 (telegram), Cipher Dispatches Received, RG45-NA; Thompson to Gresham, October 30 (telegram), November 14, 1893, Dispatches—Brazil, Gresham to Thompson, November 1, 1893 (telegram), Instructions—Brazil, Gresham to Messrs. Lauman and Kemp, November 2, 1893, Domestic Letters of the Department of State, RG59-NA.

28. Thompson to Gresham, October 24 (telegram), November 10, 1893, Dispatches—Brazil, RG59-NA; Hahner, *Civilian-Military Relations in Brazil*, 67.

29. Henry Wheaton, *Elements of International Law*, notes ed. Richard Henry Dana, Jr. (Boston, 1866), 34-37; Memorandum of Conversation between Gresham and British Ambassador Sir Julian Pauncefote, February 5, 1894, Notes from British Embassy, Gresham to Thompson, October 25, 1893 (telegram), January 6 (telegram), February 5 (telegram), 1894, Instructions—Brazil, Thompson to Gresham, December 26, (telegram), 31, 1893, February 3 (telegram), 6, 1894, Dispatches—Brazil, RG59-NA.

30. Gresham to Thompson, October 25, 1893 (telegram), Instructions—Brazil, Minister of Foreign Affairs to Mendonca, October 23 (telegram), 24 (telegram), 1893, Notes from Brazilian Legation, RG59-NA; Herbert to Stanton, October 23 (telegram), 25 (telegram), 1893, Cipher Dispatches Sent, Stanton to Herbert, October 25, 1893 (telegram), Cipher Dispatches Received, Picking to Herbert, October 20, November 4, 17, 1893, Stanton to Herbert, October 22, 25, December 6, 7, 1893, Herbert to Stanton, December 7, 1893, Area 4 File, RG45-NA; *New York Times*, October 27, 1893; Gresham to Bayard, October 29, 1893, WQG-LC.

31. Thompson to Gresham, November 10, 1893 (telegram, letter), Dispatches—Brazil, Gresham to Thompson, December 20, 1893, Instructions—Brazil, Mendonca to Gresham, October 26, 1893, Notes from Brazilian Legation, Gresham to Mendonca, November 23, 1893, Notes to Brazilian Legation, RG59-NA.

32. Minister of Foreign Affairs to Mendonca, October 23 (telegram), 24 (telegram), 1893, Notes from Brazilian Legation, Thompson to Gresham, November 10 (two letters), 14, 1893, Dispatches—Brazil, RG59-NA; Herbert to Stanton, October 23 (telegram), 25 (telegram), 1893, Cipher Dispatches Sent, Stanton to Herbert, December 7, 1893, Picking to Herbert, November 4, 1893, January 15, 1894, Area 4 File, RG45-NA.

33. Picking to Herbert, December 10 (telegram), 13 (telegram), 16 (telegram), 1893, Cipher Dispatches Received, Picking to Herbert, December 15, 28, 1893, January 8, 1894, Area 4 File, RG45-NA; Thompson to Gresham, March 10, 1894, Dispatches—Brazil, RG59-NA.

34. Thompson to Gresham, December 17 (telegram), 21 (telegram), 1893, Dispatches—Brazil, William Townes to Gresham, December 22, 1893 (telegram), Consular Dispatches—Rio de Janeiro, "Bailey, Chairman" to Gresham, December 19, 1893 (telegram) enclosed in Gresham to Herbert, December 20, 1893, Domestic Letters, RG59-NA; Herbert to Picking, December 20, 1893 (telegram), Cipher Dispatches Sent, Picking to Herbert, December 23, 1893 (telegram), Cipher Dispatches Received, RG45-NA.

35. Thompson to Gresham, December 21, 1893 (telegram), Dispatches—Brazil, RG59-NA. Administration officials gave the press the substance of the complaint from the eight shipmasters. The *New York Times* Washington correspondent wrote: "Secretary Herbert has decided that he has no authority to instruct Capt. Picking in the premises, and that attempts to land cargoes from American ships by means of lighters or otherwise must be made at the risk of the commanders" (*New York Times*, December 22, 1893).

36. Uhl to Charles Morton Stewart and Company, December 28, 1893, Domestic Letters, RG59-NA.

37. Gresham to Thompson, November 20 (telegram), December 25 (telegram), 1893, January 4, 1894 (telegram), Instructions—Brazil, RG59-NA; Picking to Herbert, December 24, 1894 (telegram), Cipher Dispatches Received, RG45-NA.

38. Thompson to Gresham, October 3, 9 (telegram), 22 (telegram), December 9 (telegram), 13 (telegram), 14 (telegram), 1893, January 2 1894 (telegram), Dispatches—Brazil, Gresham to Bayard, December 18, 1893, Instructions—Great Britain, Bayard to Gresham, December 30, 1893, Dispatches—Great Britain, Gresham to W.H. Crossman and Brother, January 6, 1894, Domestic Letters, RG59-NA; Bayard to Gresham, December 28, 1893, Gresham to Bayard, January 21, 1894, WQG-LC.

39. Gresham to Isidor Straus, January 6, 1894, WQG-LC; William Rockefeller to Gresham, January 4, 1894, Area 4 File, RG45-NA; Gresham to Crossman, January 6, 1894, Uhl to Rockefeller, January 10, 1894, Uhl to Herbert, January 10, 1894, Domestic Letters, Gresham to Thompson, June 2, 1894, Instructions—Brazil, RG59-NA.

40. Picking to Herbert, January 5 (telegram), 8 (telegram), 13 (telegram), 1894, Cipher Dispatches Received, Herbert to Picking, January 6 (telegram), 9 (telegram), 1894, Cipher Dispatches Sent, RG45-NA; Gresham to Thompson, January 9, 1894 (telegram), Instructions—Brazil, Thompson to Gresham, January 12, 1894, Dispatches—Brazil, RG59-NA.

41. Gresham to Thompson, January 10, 1894, Instructions—Brazil, RG59-NA.

42. For a contrary view, see LaFeber, *New Empire*, 215-16; Williams, *Roots of the Modern American Empire*, 366, 515, n. 81; Hugh B. Hammett, *Hilary Abner Herbert: A Southerner Returns to the Union* (Philadelphia, 1976), 201. These writers imply that Gresham's instruction was somehow linked to the armed action by American Admiral A.E.K. Benham in Rio harbor on January 29. But the note was still in transit at that time, and Thompson did not acknowledge its receipt until February 11 (Thompson to Gresham, February 11, 1894, Dispatches—Brazil, RG59-NA).

43. John Bassett Moore, *A Digest of International Law*, 8 vols., (Washington, D.C., 1906), 2:1118; Alvey A. Adee to Moore, July 16, 1901, quoted in Moore, "Brazil—Revolution—1894," undated memorandum, JBM-LC; Gresham to Herbert, January 11, 1894, Domestic Letters, RG59-NA.

44. Stanton to Herbert, December 6, 7, 1893, Herbert to Stanton, December 7, 1893, Luiz Phillipe de Saldanha da Gama to G.B. Magnaghi, December 14, 1893, enclosed in Picking to Herbert, December 15 [sic], 1893, Area 4 File, Herbert to Benham, December 15, 1893 (telegram), Herbert to Picking, January 5, 1894 (telegram), Cipher Dispatches Sent, RG45-NA; *Report of the Secretary of the Navy, 1894*, 23; Thompson to Gresham, December 13 (telegram), 14 (telegram), 1893, Dispatches—Brazil, RG59-NA.

45. Benham to "Masters of Merchant Vessels," January 26, 1894, Benham to "Gentlemen," January 26, 1894, Picking to Herbert, January 12 [sic], 1894, Henry Kiehne to Benham, January 23, 1894, Benham to da Gama, January 24, 25, 1894, da Gama to Benham , January 25, 1894, Area 4 File, RG45-NA; Thompson to Gresham, January 26, 1894, Dispatches—Brazil, RG59-NA.

46. A. Robertson to Benham, January 26, 1894, Benham to da Gama, January 27, 28, 30, 1894, Benham to "Senior Commanding Officers," January 28, 1894, W.H. Brownson to Benham, January 30, 1894, da Gama to Benham, January 30, 1894, Benham to Herbert,

January 31, 1894, Picking to Herbert, January 12 [sic], 1894, Area 4 File, Benham to Herbert, January 28 (telegram), 29 (telegram), 1894, Cipher Dispatches Received, RG45-NA.

47. Gresham to Thompson, January 30 (telegram), February 1 (telegram), 1894, Instructions—Brazil, Thompson to Gresham, January 31 (telegram), February 1 (telegram), 1894, Dispatches—Brazil, RG59-NA; Herbert to Benham, January 30 (telegram), 31 (telegram), February 1 (telegram), 1894, Cipher Dispatches Sent, Benham to Herbert, February 1, 1894 (telegram), Cipher Dispatches Received, RG45-NA.

48. *Public Opinion*, February 8, 1894; *Literary Digest*, February 8, 1894; *Congressional Record*, 53d Cong., 2d sess., 1825, 2037; *Report of the Secretary of the Navy, 1894*, 23. After the passage of two weeks had demonstrated that the insurgents would not challenge Behnam and nearly two months after Thompson's controversy with Picking over what constituted a line of fire, Gresham told the minister, in response to his report of that controversy: "You appear to have comprehended what was necessary for the protection of American ships in the harbor." The reasons for this belated, grudging approval, which seemed to contradict Gresham's attitude in December, are obscure, but political considerations may have had an influence because the telegram was made public in a slightly altered form. As the architect of the abortive Hawaii policy, Gresham was extremely sensitive to criticism, and perhaps he took to heart comments on the Brazilian policy like that of the *Enquirer*. See Gresham to Thompson, February 14, 1894 (telegram), Instructions—Brazil, RG59-NA; Bryan to Bayard, May 31, 1895, TFB-LC.

49. The American press was nearly unanimous in seeing the agency of the United States in the insurgents' defeat (*Literary Digest*, March 22, 1894; *Public Opinion*, March 22, 1894). For similar historical judgments, see LaFeber, *New Empire*, 216-17; Williams, *Roots of the Modern American Empire*, 366; Hammett, *Herbert*, 201; Michael B. McCloskey, "The United States and the Brazilian Naval Revolt, 1893-1894," *Americas* 2 (1946): 321.

50. Picking to Herbert, January 12 [sic], 1894, Area 4 File, RG45-NA. For reports of continued fighting in the harbor, see Thompson's dispatches from February 1 to mid-March 1894, RG59-NA.

51. Thompson to Gresham, March 10 (telegram), 11 (telegram), 13 (telegram), 14 (telegram), 16 (telegram, letter), 19, April 18, 19, 1894, Dispatches—Brazil, Mendonca to Gresham, April 19, 1894, Notes from Brazilian Legation, RG59-NA; Calogeras, *Brazil*, 294-95.

52. Richardson, *Messages and Papers*, 9:524; Memorandum of Conversation between Gresham and Pauncefote, February 5, 1894, Notes from British Embassy, RG59-NA. Pauncefote remarked that he thought "Benham was justified in his action," and Gresham replied that the admiral had been "under instructions to maintain perfect neutrality between Brazil and the insurgents, to help neither party, but to protect American ships in the harbor in discharging or receiving cargoes *when not interfering with the reasonable and legitimate military operations of the insurgents*" (emphasis added).

53. Bevans, comp., *Treaties*, 12:105-8; Moore, *Digest of International Law*, 3:224-41.

54. *FRUS*, 1894, Appendix 1, 236, 243, 246-47, 266-67, 287-90; Lewis Baker to Gresham, May 2, 1894, Dispatches—Nicaragua, RG59-NA; Rising Lake Morrow, "A Conflict between the Commercial Interests of the United States and Its Foreign Policy," *Hispanic American Historical Review* 10 (1930): 3-4.

55. "Mosquito Territory—Course of Events, 1894," Memorandum, April 27, 1894, Reports of the Diplomatic Bureau, RG59-NA; *FRUS*, 1894, Appendix 1, 238-41, 256-64, 270; *Senate Executive Document 20*, 53d Cong., 3d sess., 52-56.

56. *FRUS*, 1894, Appendix 1, 239, 250-51; Baker to Gresham, March 15, 1894 (telegram), Dispatches—Nicaragua, RG59-NA; *Congressional Record*, 53d Cong., 2d sess., 2664-65; *Senate Executive Document 64*, 53d Cong., 2d sess.

57. *FRUS*, 1894, Appendix 1, 243-48, 252-53, 256-58.

58. Ibid., 258, 271; Gresham to Bayard, April 30, 1894, Instructions—Great Britain, RG59-NA.

59. *FRUS*, 1888, 759-67; *FRUS*, 1893, 313-18; Gresham to Bayard, June 7, 1894, TFB-LC.

60. *Senate Executive Document 20*, 53d Cong., 3d sess., 52-67; Gresham to Bayard, April 30, 1894, Instructions—Great Britain, RG59-NA.

61. Bayard to Gresham, May 22 (telegram), 28, 1894, Dispatches—Great Britain, RG59-NA; *FRUS*, 1894, Appendix 1, 311-12.

62. Memorandum of Conversation between Gresham and Pauncefote, May 31, 1894, Notes from British Embassy, RG59-NA. LaFeber (*New Empire*, 228-29) contends that Gresham aimed to replace British control with "a *de facto* American protectorate" and offers as evidence his reply to Pauncefote's assertion that Britain was bound to see that Nicaragua did not oppress the Indians: "We will see that she does not." LaFeber's citation for this quotation is Wilfred Hardy Callcott, *The Caribbean Policy of the United States, 1890-1920* (Baltimore, 1942), 77-78, which cites Gresham, *Gresham*, 2:782, a source of dubious reliability. There is no confirmation of this alleged statement in the contemporary correspondence or memoranda of conversations. Nor does it fit with the Gresham's argument to Pauncefote regarding the inviolability of Nicaragua's sovereignty from whatever source.

63. Baker to Gresham, May 2, 10, 30, 1894, Dispatches—Nicaragua, RG59-NA; *FRUS*, 1894, Appendix 1, 290, 296; Gresham to Bayard, May 2, 1894, TFB-LC.

64. *FRUS*, 1894, 465-77; Baker to Gresham, May 2, 4, 22 (telegram), June 11, 16 (telegram), 27, August 30, 1894, Dispatches—Nicaragua, Edwin F. Uhl to Baker, May 23, 1894, Instructions—Nicaragua, Horatio Guzman to Gresham, April 23, June 4, 1894, Notes from Nicaraguan Legation, RG59-NA; William McAdoo to Watson, May 14, 1894 (telegram), Cipher Dispatches Sent, RG45-NA.

65. August C. Radke, "Senator Morgan and the Nicaraguan Canal," *Alabama Review* 12 (1959): 12-13; *Congressional Record*, 53d Cong., 2d sess., 2664-65, 3265; Gresham to Bayard, May 2, December 24, 1894, Morgan to Gresham, March 29, 1894, Bayard to Gresham, April 11, May 29, 1894, WQG-LC; Gresham to Bayard, June 7, 1894, TFB-LC; Morgan to Gresham, January 16, 1894, GC-LC; Moore, Diary Memoranda, 1894, JBM-LC.

66. Baker to Gresham, January 11, 18, April 11, May 4, 25, June 9, August 14, 1894, Dispatches—Nicaragua, Uhl to Baker, February 27, 1894, Gresham to Baker, April 25 (telegram), May 1, June 2 (telegram), July 13, 1894, Alvey Adee to Baker, July 3, 1894, Instructions—Nicaragua, Gresham to Hiram Hitchcock, January 18, 1894, Domestic Letters, RG59-NA; Gresham to Bayard, May 2, 1894, Gresham to Hitchcock, May 9, 1894, WQG-LC; *FRUS*, 1894, 460-65, Appendix 1, 296-300.

67. Gresham had earlier written some "stuff" to the Nicaraguan minister about the canal's being built "under American auspices." Asked by Cleveland to make this statement, he soon regretted it. See Moore, Diary Memoranda, 1894, JBM-LC; Gresham to Bayard, June 7, 1894, TFB-LC; Memorandum of Conversation between Gresham and Pauncefote, May 31, 1894, Notes from British Embassy, RG59-NA.

68. *Senate Executive Document 20*, 53d Cong., 3d sess., 136-47; *FRUS*, 1894, Appendix 1, 302-6, 312-13.

69. Memorandum of Conversation between Gresham and Pauncefote, July 26, 1894, Notes from British Embassy, RG59-NA; *FRUS*, 1894, Appendix 1, 313, 322-23.

70. *New York Times*, August 17, 1894; Gresham note filed with Bayard to Gresham, August 10, 1894, Bayard to Gresham, November 24, December 22, 1894, Dispatches—Great Britain, Gresham to Bayard, December 3, 1894, Instructions—Great Britain, RG59-

NA; Bayard to Gresham, November 30, 1894, quoted in Tansill, *Bayard*, 685; Gresham to Bayard, December 24, 1894, WQG-LC; *FRUS*, 1894, Appendix 1, 360-62.

71. *FRUS*, 1894, Appendix 1, 329-34, 336-43, 346-53; Gresham to Baker, August 31, 1894 (telegram), Uhl to Baker, September 9, 1894 (telegram), Instructions—Nicaragua, Baker to Gresham, September 2 (telegram), 5 (telegram), 16 (telegram), 27 (telegram), October 6 (telegram), 26 (telegram), November 6, 1894, Dispatches—Nicaragua, RG59-NA; Gresham to Moore, March 12, 1895, JBM-LC; Bevans, comp., *Treaties*, 10:337-46.

72. Gresham to Moore, March 12, 1895, JBM-LC; Bayard to Gresham, November 24, 27, 1894, February 27, 1895, Dispatches—Great Britain, Baker to Gresham, April 15, 1895, Dispatches—Nicaragua, Memorandum of Conversation between Gresham and Guzman, April 18, 1895, Notes from Nicaraguan Legation, RG59-NA; Gresham to Bayard, December 24, 1894, WQG-LC; *FRUS*, 1895, 1025-29, 1031; Gresham to Bayard, March 31, April 23, 1895, TFB-LC.

73. Gresham to Bayard, March 31, April 23, 1895, TFB-LC; Gresham note filed with Baker to Gresham, April 13, 1895 (telegram), Dispatches—Nicaragua, RG59-NA; Gresham to Moore, March 12, 1895, Moore, Diary Memoranda, 1895, JBM-LC.

74. *FRUS*, 1895, 696-97, 1030, 1032-33; Bayard to Gresham, April 26, 1895, Dispatches—Great Britain, RG59-NA.

75. *Boston Journal*, n.d., quoted in *Literary Digest*, May 4, 1895; *New York Post*, May 4, 1895; John A.S. Grenville and George Berkeley Young, *Politics, Strategy, and American Diplomacy: Studies in Foreign Policy, 1873-1917* (New Haven, 1966), 146-47; Gresham, *Gresham*, 2:795.

76. Richardson, *Messages and Papers*, 9:528; Gresham to N.C. Butler, January 11, 1895, NCB-IHSL.

Chapter 12. LAST CRISIS

1. E.L. Godkin, "Diplomacy and the Newspaper," *North American Review*, 160 (May 1895): 571, 576; Lodge, "Our Blundering Foreign Policy," 8-17; Davis, "Two Years of Democratic Diplomacy," 270-84; Nelson M. Blake, "Background of Cleveland's Venezuelan Policy," *American Historical Review* 47 (1942): 264.

2. John Bassett Moore, Diary Memoranda, 1895, JBM-LC; George Gray, "Two Years of American Diplomacy," *North American Review* 160 (April 1895): 409-24.

3. *FRUS*, 1895, 1177; *New York Sun*, n.d., quoted in *Literary Digest*, March 23, 1895; *Public Opinion*, March 21, 1895.

4. *FRUS*, 1895, 1178-85, 1187-94; Gresham to attorney general, April 1, 5, 1895, Gresham to Charles O. Fink, April 27, 1895, Domestic Letters of the Department of State, RG59-NA.

5. *Correspondence in Relation to the Boundary Controversy between Great Britain and Venezuela* (Washington, D.C., 1896); Eggert, *Olney*, 200-201; *FRUS*, 1894, 803-5; Richardson, *Messages and Papers*, 9:441.

6. *FRUS*, 1894, 250-52, 810-40.

7. *Correspondence in Relation to the Boundary Controversy*, 204-5; Tansill, *Bayard*, 662-63; *FRUS*, 1894, 252.

8. Grenville and Young, *Politics, Strategy, and American Diplomacy*, 120-21, 133-40; E. Rojas to William L. Scruggs, June 18, 1894, Scruggs to Rojas, June 30, August 28, October 20, 1894, WLS-LC; William L. Scruggs, *British Aggressions in Venezuela, or the Monroe Doctrine on Trial*, 2d ed. (Atlanta, 1895), 23-24, 28-30.

9. *FRUS*, 1894, 252; Richardson, *Messages and Papers*, 9:526; Gresham to Bayard,

January 3, 1895, Instructions—Great Britain, Bayard to Gresham, March 9, April 5, 1895, Dispatches—Great Britain, RG59-NA.

10. *Congressional Record*, 53d Cong., 3d sess., 837, 1652, 1832-34, 1884, 2113, 2297, 2642; Scruggs, Memoranda, January, February 1895, WLS-LC; Gresham to H.D. Money [January 30, 1895], Reports to the President and Congress, Gresham to Bayard, April 9, 1895, Instructions—Great Britain, RG59-NA; Grenville and Young, *Politics, Strategy, and American Diplomacy*, 141-45.

11. Scruggs, Memoranda, February, March 1895, WLS-LC; Grenville and Young, *Politics, Strategy, and American Diplomacy*, 132-33, 146.

12. Gresham to Bayard, March 31, 1895, TFB-LC; Gresham to Moore, April 4, 1895, Moore, Diary Memoranda, 1895, JBM-LC.

13. Gresham to Moore, April 4, 1895, JBM-LC; Gresham to Bayard, April 9, 1895, Instructions—Great Britain, RG59-NA; *FRUS*, 1895, 558.

14. Moore to Cleveland, May 20, 1895, GC-LC; Gresham to Moore, April 11, 18, 1895, Moore to George Gray, November 17, 1895, JBM-LC; Gresham to Bayard, April 23, 1895, TFB-LC.

15. Cleveland to Gresham, May 4, 1895, WQG-LC; *FRUS*, 1895, 1485-86; Uhl to Bayard, June 5, 1895, Instructions—Great Britain, RG59-NA.

16. Henry Cabot Lodge, "England, Venezuela, and the Monroe Doctrine," *North American Review* 160 (June 1895): 651-58; Grover Cleveland, *Presidential Problems* (New York, 1904), 252-56; Cleveland to Olney, July 7, 1895, GC-LC; Moore to Gray, November 17, 1895, JBM-LC.

17. *FRUS*, 1895, 542-76; Eggert, *Olney*, 219-50.

18. *Baltimore Sun*, May 28-31, 1895; K.M. Landis to Moore, June 24, August 14, 1895, JBM-LC; Matilda Gresham to Bayard, July 5, 1895, TFB-LC; Gresham, *Gresham*, 2:791-92.

19. Matilda Gresham to Moore, June 28, 1895, JBM-LC; *Indianapolis Star*, September 7, 1930.

20. Cleveland to E. C. Benedict, June 9, 1895, in Nevins, ed., *Letters of Cleveland*, 397; Bayard to Cleveland, May 28, 1895, GC-LC.

21. *Literary Digest*, June 8, 1895; Henry L. Bryan to Bayard, May 31, 1895, TFB-LC.

22. Moore, Diary Memoranda, 1894, JBM-LC.

23. Katherine Crane, *Mr. Carr of State: Forty-seven Years in the Department of State* (New York, 1960), 13; *Philadelphia Telegraph*, n.d., quoted in *Public Opinion*, June 6, 1895; *Nation*, May 30, 1895.

24. Moore to Charles C. Tansill, September 16, 1940, JBM-LC; Gresham to John Overmyer, July 25, 1894, WQG-LC; Lodge, "Our Blundering Foreign Policy," 17.

BIBLIOGRAPHICAL ESSAY

Readers who desire a comprehensive accounting of the sources upon which this study rests should consult the chapter notes. The essay that follows is a suggestive overview of the more important sources that shed light on Walter Q. Gresham's life.

PRIMARY MATERIAL

The chief primary source for Gresham's career is the collection of his papers in the Manuscripts Division of the Library of Congress. The fifty-one volumes of this collection contain primarily correspondence, especially letters received, with some autograph letters and draft letters by Gresham interspersed. Fortunately, Gresham's letters to his wife during the Civil War and to his friend Thomas C. Slaughter in the 1860s and 1870s are included in these volumes and provide invaluable information and insight about the early phases of Gresham's career. The collection also includes letterpress copy books for the years he served in the cabinet, which are useful, and also a small amount of printed matter. Although this body of papers provides the nucleus of source material on Gresham, it is heavily weighted in the period he served as postmaster general and is thin in some other periods and, hence, must be supplemented by other sources.

Smaller Gresham collections are housed at the Chicago Historical Society, the Indiana Historical Society Library, the Indiana Division of the Indiana State Library, and the Rutherford B. Hayes Library.

Several collections of manuscripts of Gresham's close friends and associates contain letters from him. As one would expect, the closer the relationship he had with an individual, the more revealing are his letters. Among the most important of these collections is that of Noble C. Butler, Gresham's longtime friend and court clerk, in the Indiana Historical Society Library. Nearly as useful are the papers of David Davis (Illinois State Historical Library), Charles W. Fairbanks (Lilly Library, Indiana University), Benjamin Bristow, Grover Cleveland, John W. Foster (all in the Library of Congress), and John Marshall Harlan (Library of Congress and University of Louisville Law School Library). No study of Gresham's political career could be complete without an examination of the papers of his chief antagonists, especially Benjamin Harrison and Louis T. Michener (both in the Library of Congress) and Oliver P. Morton (a small collection in the Indiana Division, Indiana State Library). As the notes to the text indicate, scores of other manuscript collections contain material relevant to Gresham's career.

Letters in the Gresham Papers in the Library of Congress from Gresham to his wife during the Civil War are supplemented by official correspondence published in *The War of the Rebellion: A Compilation of the Official Records of the Union and Confederate Armies*, 128 vols. (Washington, D.C., 1880-1901), and unpublished correspondence in the General Records of the Office of the Adjutant General (Record Group 94) in the National Archives and in the Fifty-third Indiana Infantry Regimental Correspondence in the Archives Division of the Indiana State Library.

For Gresham's judicial career, the best sources are his published opinions in the *Federal Reporter* and Bissell's *Reports* for the years he was on the bench, 1869-83 and 1885-93, and, to a lesser degree, the *Chicago Legal News*. More than half the volumes of his papers in the Library of Congress cover the year and a half he headed the Post Office Department; much of this material pertains to patronage and to the presidential nomination campaign of 1884. For this period, one should also consult the General Records of the Post Office Department Record Group 28) in the National Archives.

For Gresham's two-year tenure in the State Department, the starting point is the published *Papers Relating to the Foreign Relations of the United States*. Because correspondence for these annual editions was selectively compiled, it must be used cautiously and should be supplemented by the unpublished official correspondence pertinent to foreign relations in the National Archives, principally the General Records of the Department of State (Record Group 59) and the General Records of the Navy Department (Record Group 45). In addition, the Gresham Papers (volumes 39-43 and 48 in the Library of Congress) contain much revealing private correspondence from the State Department years, as do the papers of Thomas F. Bayard, John Bassett Moore, John T. Morgan, and Carl Schurz (all in the Library of Congress).

As Gresham's career progressed and he gained prominence through the years, he received notice in the local, then state, and finally national periodical press. Most useful are the *New Albany Commercial, New Albany Ledger, New Albany Tribune, Indianapolis Journal, Indianapolis News, Indianapolis Sentinel, Chicago Tribune, New York Times, New York Tribune*, and *Washington Post*. Also useful are the summaries of editorial comment included in *Literary Digest* and *Public Opinion*. The chief sources of Mugwump opinion were *Harper's Weekly* and the *Nation*.

SECONDARY MATERIAL

Before the present work, the only full-length biography of Gresham was the *Life of Walter Quintin Gresham, 1832-1895*, 2 vols. (Chicago, 1919). Although this work appeared under the name of Gresham's wife Matilda, their son, Otto, actually wrote it, and Mrs. Gresham was a reluctant participant in the project. Otto used his father's papers and some public documents and newspapers, and he also collected reminiscences from many of Gresham's associates. The result is an uneven book, written in a rambling style that often loses focus. It contains errors of fact and suffers from the distortions frequently found in family memoirs: the late departed could do no wrong. The *Life* is not without value, however. Gresham's mother (who outlived her son by twelve years) and other acquaintances provided Otto with information on Gresham's background and early life otherwise inaccessible to the modern researcher. The *Life*'s appearance in nearly every bibliography on the Gilded Age testifies to its broad coverage and the importance of its subject, if not the value of its treatment.

In 1933 the *Indiana Magazine of History* (29: 297-338) printed an article-length biography by Martha A. Tyner, who was no more critical of her subject than the Greshams had been. *Their Infinite Variety: Essays on Indiana Politicians* (Indianapolis, 1981) includes a biographical essay by Charles W. Calhoun ("Republican Jeremiah: Walter Q. Gresham and the Third American Party System," pp. 223-63), which focuses on Gresham's disenchantment with Gilded Age political culture in general and with the Republican party in particular. A third short biography (Montgomery Schuyler, "Walter Quintin Gresham," in Samuel Flagg Bemis, ed., *The American Secretaries of State and Their Diplomacy*, 10 vols. [New York, 1927-29], 8:227-69), is a dated and generally unsatisfactory overview of Gresham's foreign policy.

Historians have treated Gresham's career in bits and pieces. Political histories of the Gilded Age (the best of which remains H. Wayne Morgan, *From Hayes to McKinley: National Party Politics, 1877-1896* [Syracuse, 1969]) mention Gresham as one of the men in the running for the 1888 Republican presidential nomination, briefly recount his various offices, but generally say little more. Indiana histories (see especially James H. Madison, *The Indiana Way: A State History* [Bloomington, 1986]; Emma Lou Thornbrough, *Indiana in the Civil War Era, 1850-1880* [Indianapolis, 1965]; and Clifton J. Phillips, *Indiana in Transition: The Emergence of an Industrial Commonwealth, 1880-1920* [Indianapolis, 1968]), note, more or less in passing, that he did not get along well with better-known Hoosier figures Oliver P. Morton and Benjamin Harrison. Morton needs a modern scholarly biography, and Harry J. Sievers's study of Harrison (*Hoosier Warrior* [Chicago, 1952]; *Hoosier Statesman* [New York, 1959]; *Hoosier President* [Indianapolis, 1968]) gives some attention to the Gresham-Harrison antagonism but is generally weak in analysis and does not fill the need for a substantial biography of Harrison. A detailed examination of Gresham's service in the 1861 Indiana legislature is found in Charles W. Calhoun, " 'Incessant Noise and Tumult': Walter Q. Gresham and the Indiana Legislature during the Secession Crisis," *IMH* 74 (1978): 223-51. Dorothy Canfield Fowler (*The Cabinet Politician: The Postmasters General, 1829-1909* [New York, 1943]) briefly describes Gresham's political activities as postmaster general but gives short shrift to his accomplishments as an administrator and his efforts to implement the Pendleton Civil Service Act.

Most modern scholars have focused on either of two aspects of Gresham's career: his attitude toward labor strikes while a federal judge or his service as secretary of state. Donald L. McMurry ("The Legal Ancestry of the Pullman Strike Injunction," *Industrial and Labor Relations Review* 14 [1961]: 235-56) and Gerald G. Eggert (*Railroad Labor Disputes: The Beginnings of Federal Strike Policy* [Ann Arbor, 1967]) recognize Gresham's contribution to the development of the labor injunction during the great railroad strike of 1877, but they and other historians fail to note the mellowing in his thinking in the 1880s and 1890s, culminating in his fervent opposition to Richard Olney's suppression of the Pullman strike in 1894.

The Introduction and Chapter 7 above contain discussions of the historiography regarding Gresham's term as secretary of state, which should be supplemented by an examination of the notes to Chapters 7 through 12. No previous published scholarly study has examined the entirety of Gresham's foreign policy. The biography published under his wife's name devoted seven of forty-nine chapters to the two years he headed the State Department, but the treatment betrays little or no analysis of the pertinent documentary evidence. The essay by Montgomery Schuyler in Samuel Flagg Bemis's *American Secretaries of State* series is perfunctory and of little value. The same is true of James R. Mock, "The Diplomacy of Walter Q. Gresham," *IMH* 31 (1935): 213-21, which appears to be based solely on the Gresham family biography and the Gresham Papers in the Library of Congress.

As noted in the text, Gresham is cast in a prominent role in the economic expansionist thesis expounded by Walter LaFeber, *The New Empire: An Interpretation of American Expansion, 1860-1898* (Ithaca, 1963), and William Appleman Williams, *The Roots of the Modern American Empire* (New York, 1969). Eugene W. Goll's doctoral dissertation, "The Diplomacy of Walter Q. Gresham, Secretary of State, 1893-1895" (Pennsylvania State University, 1974), takes issue with the "new empire" school, as does Thomas J. Osborne, *"Empire Can Wait": American Opposition to Hawaiian Annexation, 1893-1898* (Kent, Ohio, 1981).

Other works that focus on aspects of Gresham's foreign policy include Nelson M. Blake, "Background of Cleveland's Venezuelan Policy," *American Historical Review* 47 (1942): 259-77; Charles W. Calhoun, "American Policy toward the Brazilian Naval Revolt of 1893-94: A Reexamination," *Diplomatic History* 4 (1980): 39-56; Calhoun, "Morality and Spite: Walter Q. Gresham and U.S. Relations with Hawaii," *PHR* 52 (1983): 292-311; Calhoun, "Rehearsal for Anti-Imperialism: The Second Cleveland Administration's Attempt to Withdraw from Samoa, 1893-1895," *Historian* 48 (1986): 209-24; Jeffrey M. Dorwart, *The Pigtail War: American Involvement in the Sino-Japanese War of 1894-1895* (Amherst, 1975); Dorwart, "Walter Quintin Gresham and East Asia, 1894-1895: A Reappraisal," *Asian Forum* 5 (1973): 55-63; Michael B. McCloskey, "The United States and the Brazilian Naval Revolt, 1893-1894," *Americas* 2 (1946): 269-321; Rising Lake Morrow, "A Conflict between the Commercial Interests of the United States and Its Foreign Policy," *Hispanic American Historical Review* 10 (1930): 2-13; George E. Paulsen, "The Gresham-Yang Treaty," *PHR* 37 (1968): 281-97; Paulsen, "Secretary Gresham, Senator Lodge, and American Good

Offices in China, 1894," *PHR* 36 (1967): 123-42; William Adam Russ, Jr., *The Hawaiian Republic, 1894-1898* (Selinsgrove, Pa., 1961); Russ, *The Hawaiian Revolution, 1893-1894* (Selinsgrove, Pa., 1959); Charles C. Tansill, *The Foreign Policy of Thomas F. Bayard, 1885-1897* (New York, 1940); and Merze Tate, *The United States and the Hawaiian Kingdom: A Political History* (New Haven, 1965).

INDEX

Abdul Hamid II, Sultan, 181
abolitionism, 12, 13, 16, 27
Adams, Henry, 1
Adams, Robert, Jr., 138
Adee, Alvey A., 133, 200-201, 214
Agriculture, Department of, 140, 142
Alabama, 33
Alaska, 186-87
Alaska Commercial Company, 186
Alger, Russell, 97
Allen, William J., 107, 118-19
Allen County, Indiana, 62
Allianca, 214
Allison, William B., 88, 97
American, 96
American Board of Commissioners of
    Foreign Missions, 182, 185
American Federation of Labor, 128
American Law Review, 90
American party. *See* Know Nothings
Andrade, José, 215, 217-19
Apia, Samoa, 162, 169
Argentina, 139
Arlington Hotel, 125, 126, 220
Arlington National Cemetery, 221
Armenian question, 182-85
Army of the Tennessee, 33, 34
Army of the Tennessee, Society of the,
    57-59, 60, 64, 112-14
Arthur, Chester A., 2, 65; relations with
    Gresham, 3, 67, 80; appoints Gresham
    postmaster general, 66, 73; unpopular
    in Republican party, 72-73, 74; 1884
    candidacy, 74-81; appoints Gresham
    secretary of the treasury, 82; appoints
    McCulloch secretary of the treasury,
    83-84; appoints Gresham circuit judge,
    84; funeral of, 88
Arthur, P.M., 94-95
Associated Press, 98, 112
Atkins v. *Wabash, St. L. & P. Ry. Co.* See
    Wabash case
Atlanta, Georgia, 34
Australia, 164
Austria-Hungary, 136

Babcock, Orville, 44, 48
Baker, Conrad, 38
Baker, Lewis, 205, 207-10
Baltimore Sun, 139
Barker, Wharton, 96, 97
Bartlett, William A., 66
Bayard, Thomas F., 123, 124, 125; favors
    American role in Samoa, 163-64; and
    fur seal controversy, 187, 189, 191; and
    Brazilian naval revolt, 199; and
    Mosquito Reserve, 205, 206, 210; and
    Nicaraguan deportation of British
    consul, 212; and Venezuela-British
    Guiana boundary, 215-20; evaluation of
    Gresham's foreign policy, 221
Bayard-Chang convention, 178, 179
Beard, Charles, 1
Beard, Mary, 1
Beardslee, L.A., 158-59
Belgium, 102, 118, 136
Belknap, William W., 34
Benham, A.E.K., 201-04, 259 n. 42,
    260 nn. 48, 52
Bering Sea. *See* fur seal controversy
Berlin, General Act of. *See* General Act of
    Berlin
Beveridge, Albert J., 124
Bingham, Gordon, 44
Bingham, John, 44
Billings, Edward, 72
"Billion Dollar" Congress, 109
Blacklock, William, 165
Blaine, James G., 60, 63, 70, 75, 106; 1876
    presidential candidacy, 47-49; Gresham
    gives press information about railroad
    deals of, 48-49, 233 n.22; 1884
    presidential candidacy, 77-84; and 1888
    presidential nomination, 91-93, 96, 97,
    100-101; and opposition to Harrison,
    112, 114, 115; foreign policy, 135, 138,
    187, 192; mentioned, 72, 117, 155, 169
Blaine, Walker, 101
Blair, Francis P., 34
Bland-Allison Act, 55
Blatchford, Samuel, 128